Religion, Conflict, and Democracy in Modern Africa

Princeton Theological Monograph Series

K. C. Hanson, Charles M. Collier, D. Christopher Spinks,
and Robin Parry, Series Editors

Recent volumes in the series:

Sammy Alfaro
Divino Compañero: Toward a Hispanic Pentecostal Christology

David L. Balch
Finding A Woman's Place: Essays in Honor of Carolyn Osiek

Paul W. Chilcote
*Making Disciples in a World Parish:
Global Perspectives on Mission & Evangelism*

Eric G. Flett
*Persons, Powers, and Pluralities:
Toward a Trinitarian Theology of Culture*

Vladimir Kharlamov
Theosis: Deification in Christian Theology, Volume Two

Mitzi J. Smith
*The Literary Construction of the Other in the Acts of the Apostles:
Charismatics, the Jews, and Women*

Jon Paul Sydnor
*Ramanuja and Schleiermacher:
Toward a Constructive Comparative Theology*

Philip D. Wingeier-Rayo
*Where Are the Poor?: A Comparison of the Ecclesial Base Communities
and Pentecostalism—A Case Study in Cuernavaca, Mexico*

Religion, Conflict, and Democracy in Modern Africa
The Role of Civil Society in Political Engagement

Edited by
SAMUEL K. ELOLIA

Foreword by Afe Adogame

◥PICKWICK *Publications* • Eugene, Oregon

RELIGION, CONFLICT, AND DEMOCRACY IN MODERN AFRICA
The Role of Civil Society in Political Engagement

Princeton Theological Monograph Series 167

Copyright © 2012 Wipf and Stock Publishers. All rights reserved. Except for brief quotations in critical publications or reviews, no part of this book may be reproduced in any manner without prior written permission from the publisher. Write: Permissions, Wipf and Stock Publishers, 199 W. 8th Ave., Suite 3, Eugene, OR 97401.

Pickwick Publications
An Imprint of Wipf and Stock Publishers
199 W. 8th Ave., Suite 3
Eugene, OR 97401

www.wipfandstock.com

ISBN 13: 978-1-60899-856-2

Cataloging-in-Publication data:

Religion, conflict, and democracy in modern Africa : the role of civil society in political engagement / edited by Samuel K. Elolia ; foreword by Afe Adogame.

xiv + 372 pp. ; 23 cm. — Includes bibliographical references.

Princeton Theological Monograph Series 167

ISBN 13: 978-1-60899-856-2

1. Religion and politics — Africa. 2. Christianity and politics — Africa. 3. Democracy — Africa. 4. Church and state — Africa. I. Elolia, Samuel K. II. Adogame, Afe. III. Title. IV. Series.

BR115.P7 .R24 2012

Manufactured in the U.S.A.

*This book is dedicated to Nelson Mandela,
a great leader of exceptional courage
and a role model by excellence.*

Contents

Contributors / ix

Foreword—Afe Adogame / *xiii*

Introduction—Samuel K. Elolia / 1

PART ONE: The Theoretical Perspectives of Religion in Africa

1. Violence and Social Imagination: Rethinking Religion and Politics in Africa—*Emmanuel M. Katongole* / 21

2. The African Renaissance and Religion —*Elias K. Bongmba* / 51

3. Religion, Violence, and Conflict: Ujaama-therapy as a Dynamic Response to Ethnic Particularities in Africa —*Cyril Orji* / 78

PART TWO: Religion, Democracy, and Conflict Resolution in East Africa

4. Religion and the Road to Democracy in Kenya —*Samuel K. Elolia* / 101

5. Forgiveness: The Divine Gift of Peace, Reconciliation, and Healing—*Adam K. arap Chepkwony* / 131

6. Church and State Conflicts in Uganda: President Idi Amin Kills the Anglican Archbishop —*Emmanuel Kalenzi Twesigye* / 148

PART THREE: Religion and State Formation in the Shadow of Apartheid in South Africa

7. From Apartheid's Christian Hegemony to Religious Pluralism—*Samuel Paul* / 197

8 Instruments of Inhibitors of Civil Society?: The Role of Christians in the Formation of Public Policy
—*James R. Cochrane* / 230

9 Bahia and Zion: The Eruption of New Religions of the Poor, Political Implications of Afro-Brazilian and South African Independent Churches—*Iain S. Maclean* / 253

PART FOUR: Religious Pluralism and Social Change in West Africa

10 Religion and Social Change in Multi-Ethnic Nigerian Society—*Ukachukwu Chris Manus* and *Bolaji Olukemi Bateye* / 277

11 Shari'a, Democracy, and Civil Society: The Case of Northern Nigeria—*Umar Habila Dadem Danfulani* / 302

12 Nigerian Civil Government and the Application of Islamic Law: Can Conflict Lead to Accommodation?
—*Yushau Sodiq* / 342

Contributors

ELIAS K. BONGMBA is Professor of Religious Studies at Rice University, Houston, Texas. He holds a PhD from the University of Denver and the Iliff School of Theology. He is the author of *African Witchcraft and Otherness* (2001) and *The Dialectics of Transformation in Africa* (2006).

ADAM K. ARAP CHEPKWONY is Professor of Religion at Moi University, Eldoret, Kenya. He holds a DPhil in Religion from Moi University. He teaches in the areas of comparative religion, liberation theologies, new religious movements, African religion and theology. He has published chapters in a couple of books as well as in *Africa Ecclesial Review*. He is currently working on a book, tentatively titled: *African Traditional Counseling*.

JAMES R. COCHRANE is Professor of Religious Studies at the University of Cape Town, Cape Town, South Africa. He is also Co-Principal of the African Religious Health Assets Programme and Director of the Research Institute on Christianity in Southern Africa. He has written several books including: *In Word and Deed* (1990), *The Three-Fold Cord* (1991), and *Circles of Dignity* (1999).

SAMUEL K. ELOLIA is Professor of Christian Doctrine and World Christianity at Emmanuel School of Religion, Johnson City, Tennessee. He holds a PhD from St. Michael's, University of Toronto. He has contributed to several published works which include *The Church and Multiculturalism in Contemporary America*, *Missionary Education in Africa During the Colonial Period*, and *African Expressions of Christianity*. His recent work entitled *Ethnic and Religious Identity in Africa* is forthcoming with Pickwick Publications.

UMAR HABILA DADEM DANFULANI served as Dean of Students and Directorate of Student Affairs at the University of Jos, Nigeria from August 1999 to 2005. He holds a PhD from Uppsala, Sweden. His published works include: *Pebbles and Deities* (1995), *The Kadung of the Jos Plateau* (1999) and *Understanding Nyam* (2003).

EMMANUEL M. KATONGOLE is Associate Research Professor of Theology and World Christianity and is co-director of the Center of Reconciliation at Duke University Divinity School, Durham, North Carolina. He holds a PhD from Catholic University, Louvain. He is the author of several works, which include: *Beyond Universal Reason* (2000), *African Theology Today* (2002), and *A Future for Africa* (2005).

CYRIL ORJI is an Associate Professor at the University of Dayton, OH. He specializes in systematic and fundamental theology with emphasis on the work of Bernard Lonergan. He collaborates in inter-religious dialogue and engages in the intersection of religion and culture, inculturation, post-colonial studies and Black and African theologies. He has several journal articles. He also has a book *Ethnic and Religious Conflict in Africa: an Analysis of bias, decline, and conversion based on the works of Bernard Lonergan* (Milwaukee, WI: Marquette University Press, 2008). He also has another forthcoming book *Lonergan and Catholic Intellectual Tradition* (Minnesota: Anselm Press, 2013).

SAMUEL PAUL is the Director of Finance and Administration at the University of Southern California Center for Religion and Civic Culture. He holds a PhD from Fuller Theological Seminary. He recently published the book, *The Ubuntu God* (Pickwick, forthcoming).

IAIN S. MACLEAN is Associate Professor of Western Religious Thought at James Madison University. He is a graduate of the University of Cape Town, Rhodes, South Africa, Princeton and Harvard. He is the co-editor of two books: *Liberation Theologians and the Struggle for Democracy in Brazil*, and *Reconciliation*.

UKACHUKWU CHRIS MANUS is Professor of New Testament and African Christian Theology in the Department of Religious Studies at Obafemi Awolowo University, lle-lfe, Nigeria. He holds a PhD from Catholic University of Louvain. He is the author of *Christ, the African King* (1993) and *Intercultural Hermeneutics* (2003).

YUSHAU SODIQ is Associate Professor of Religion and Islamic studies at Texas Christian University. He holds a PhD from Temple University, Philadelphia, Pennsylvania. He has published articles on Islamic law, Islamic studies and Islam in America.

EMMANUEL KALENZI TWESIGYE is a Professor in the Religion Department at Ohio Wesleyan University. He holds a PhD from Vanderbilt University. He has written several books which include: *Religion & Ethics for a New Age* (2001), *African Religion, Philosophy, and Christianity in Logos-Christ* (1996).

BOLAJI BATEYE lectures in the Department of Religious Studies, Obafemi Awolowo University, Ile-Ife, Nigeria. She is a Resource Person at the OAU Centre for Gender and Social Policy Studies and also co-editor of the journal *Gender and Behaviour*. She served as a Leventis Scholar at the School of Oriental and African Studies (SOAS), University of London. Dr. Bateye has carried out fieldwork on health, healing, and African immigrant religiosity in the UK and in the United States of America.

Foreword

Religion, Conflict, and Democracy in Modern Africa: The Role of Civil Society in Political Engagement is a bold, refreshing contribution to the field. Its interdisciplinary nature, explores the crucial role and place of civil society in political engagement, and or disengagement, situating it within the wider discourse on the inter-mix of religion, conflict, and democracy in contemporary Africa. Obviously, religion plays an ambivalent role in fostering or combating conflict and intolerance on the one hand, but also peaceful coexistence and social cohesion. Religious values and beliefs could serve as a benchmark for imbibing, maintaining, and promoting democratic principles and praxis, but could also turn out as a subversive tool and roadblock for engendering sustainable political (dis)engagement. Political entrepreneurs and religious entrepreneurs could exist as strange bedfellows, and may thus have a tendency to be mutually manipulative, exploitative, domineering for selfish, ulterior ends. In other respects, they could both engage in meaningful, progressive dialogue that target social, economic, and political transformation and rebirth of their respective nation-states and constituencies. The instrumentalization of religion, politics, and democratic governance looms large in brokering peace or paving the way for conflict. This book thus make a significant contribution to deconstructing the myth of "rendering unto Caesar what is Caesar's, and unto God what is God's," which has hitherto rendered asunder any intricate interconnectedness of religion, governance, and democratic politics in pre-colonial, colonial, and post-independent Africa.

The quest for good governance, democratization, political change, and social transformation in Africa can perhaps best be interpreted as a revamp and re-sharpening of political voices by stakeholders, such as the civil society, an outcry necessitated by an overwhelming public disenchantment and disillusionment with previous political experiments, which often ended in total fiascos. These recent clamors for sustainable political and socio-economic changes parallel similar contestations during the era of imperial regimes in colonial Africa.

Any historiography of popular religion, politics, and democratic governance must grapple with contemporary states-of-affairs, but also undertake historical excursion to decipher the chemistry of religious politics, vexed politics of good governance, and democratization processes in sub-Saharan Africa.

Limited publications on similar subjects exist but are relatively dated. Besides, their geographical reach is also limited. Elolia's book will expand upon these earlier works and provide a predominantly "insider's perspective and interpretation" that complements but also critiques "outsider's purview and analysis" of the phenomena. Thus, one major contribution pertains to the "African voices" that characterize the book. The African multiple experiences (local, regional purview) will primarily comprise this voice. Since the discourse on the role of civil society in political engagement is one that embraces religion, religious pluralism, public life, civic role, governance, democracy, ethics, and (intra)national conflict and resolution, Elolia's sensitivity to the complexities of religion, conflict, and democracy in both traditional and contemporary Africa enable him to nuance the meaning and interpretation of religious and political phenomena enunciated in this book.

Afe Adogame
Lecturer in World Christianity, University of Edinburgh
and author of *Prophetic-Charismatic Movement*.

Introduction

Religion, Conflict and Democracy
The Role of Civil Society in Political Engagement

SAMUEL K. ELOLIA

THE ESSAYS IN THIS VOLUME REPRESENT VARIOUS GEO-POLITICAL REgions of Sub-Sahara Africa. The contributing scholars are quite diverse in their racial, ethnic, and gender composition and engage a broader sector of the populations. The scholars recognize the fact that the new world order that came into existence following the end of the Cold War and the fall of the Soviet Union has created a unique political climate in various African contexts marked by intense political engagement. Depending upon the political variables therein, these engagements have often culminated in multi-party elections, which have either failed or partially succeeded. What seems apparent in most cases is the fact that the transition has frequently been marked by violence, election fraud, and limited military interventions. It is quite evident from the observation drawn from the essays that the lack of political will has contributed to the abuse of justice—despite the experimentation of Western liberal democracy.

The struggle for democracy is not new in Africa. It has always existed as long as Africa's religious, social, and political rights were threatened. Throughout the period of Colonial domination of Africa, small-scale revolts against the colonial policies were apparent nearly everywhere. Some were quickly suppressed while others lasted much longer depending on the people's resistance. The African National Congress (ANC), one of the oldest political organizations, was founded in South Africa in 1912 with the objective to further the struggle for justice and democracy through constitutional and peaceful methods.

Nelson Mandela, one of its chief spokesmen in later years, stated, "If democracy would be best expressed by a one party system, I would examine the proposition very carefully. But if democracy could be expressed by a multi-party system then I would examine that carefully. In this country, for example, we have a multi-party system at present, but so far as the non-Europeans are concerned this is the most vicious despotism you can think of."[1]

In West Africa, the Igbo of Nigeria resisted the British until 1919. Samori Ture, the founder of a Mandingo empire, waged an eight-year campaign of remarkable tenacity against a colonial army. In Kenya the Kalenjin fought ferociously to protect their land and their leaders and were either jailed or exiled. In later years following independence, the MAUMAU movement put immense pressure to the British colonial rule.

After the Second World War, Africans who had been exposed to the world through travel returned home with high expectations and were determined to fight against European domination and abuse of human rights. They demanded a participatory role in matters that vitally affected African lives. Many believed that they had earned the right to demand some share in the government of their own countries. They were encouraged by the Atlantic Charter to demand their political rights.[2] Some of those leaders include Obafemi Owalowo, Kwame Nkurumah, Jomo Kenyatta, Julius Nyerere, Milton Obote, Patrice Lumumba, Seko Toure, Kamusu Banda, and Kenneth Kaunda, who led their respective countries to political independence. Given the rising expectations and challenges of ruling new nations, the leaders borrowed heavily from the West and progressively became dictators and amassed incredible wealth for themselves, relatives, and friends. By the end of the 1960s, the same leaders had become as repressive as the colonial leaders they had replaced. Corruption at every level entrenched the economies, and gradually many of the governments were overthrown and replaced by military regimes that were as ruthless and oppressive as the previous civilian governments. Some of those leaders

1. Mandela, *Nelson Mandela Speaks*, 12.

2. The Second World War shifted power away form Europe and its colonial powers. The United States and Soviet Union competed to fill the vacuum. The only common belief they shared was their anti-colonial sentiments. This led to the Atlantic Charter in 1941; Winston Churchill and Franklin Roosevelt were keen that postwar objectives should include self-determination for all colonized people.

tended to take their offices with seemingly good intentions but, once they tasted power, matters often took different turns. Laurenti Magesa's cynical observation seems to reflect that reality when he states: "They develop an allergy to freedom (and) become fearful of losing power because here in Africa, political power is about the only way which gives access to wealth, prestige and privilege."[3] Usually after taking power, authoritarian leaders often do whatever they can to thwart the voices of those who challenge their power. In such a setting, essential building blocks for democracy such as freedom of expression and voting rights were frustrated. It is no wonder it has sparked of coup d'etats in some of the countries.

At the height of the Cold War era, Africa increasingly became a battle field of contesting ideologies between the United States and USSR. Dictators who took power either through military or single party status took advantage of these geopolitics to entrench themselves in power. With unconditional financial and military support from the superpowers, many of the leaders became allergic to any dissenting voices. Opponents were dealt with ruthlessly in order to send terror to others.

While these events were taking place, some of the religious leaders who had earlier supported the nationalists felt obliged to render their support because most of the emerging political leaders claimed to be Christians. When the clergy were generally hesitant in making any opposing comments, the governments interpreted the hesitation as compliance. A few voices who dared to challenge the government were quickly silenced. The church leaders might have hesitated to criticize the government's corrupt policies out of fear of losing its considerable properties and influence.

The decade of the 1970s witnessed a tremendous social consciousness through the works of several African writers such as Ngugi Wa Thiongo(Kenya), Peter Abrams (South Africa), Sembene Ousmane (Senegal), Ayi Kwei Armah (Ghana), Okot P'Bitek (Uganda), Taban Lo Lyong (Sudan), Chinua Achebe, Wole Soyinka, and Emecheta Buchi (Nigeria). Their analysis captures the deteriorating state of affairs arising out of African leaders. Obviously, their concern was to sensitize a broader sector of the society towards reform and social consciousness. For that reason, most of them have become targets of corrupt totalitar-

---

3. Magesa, *Democracy and Reconciliation*, 12.

ian leaders and have often landed in detention. Those who escaped detention either went underground or into exile. It is often during such oppressive measures that the church has stepped up its efforts and called for reform.

Following the disintegration of the communist block in 1989 and the fall of their leaders like Ceausescu of Romania, many African countries came to the rude awakening, however short lived, that political and social change was inevitable, in spite of heavy government handedness and threats. It also became evident to some that no political system that refused to permit freedom of political expression and alternative systems of governance could continue to be sustained. Democracy on the other hand, is cherished when individuals are able to enjoy their freedom and realize their potential to pursue happiness without restrictions. Unfortunately, these human values are often stifled or ignored by many African leaders, who often in their fear of criticism constantly resort to violent means. Yet in the absence of constructive criticism there can be no genuine civil liberty. Moreover, where there are no liberties one can hardly talk of political or civil rights, which are essential components of democracy.

It is under such an undemocratic climate of repression that religious institutions collaborated with other civil society institutions on common political actions and called for change. In several countries for example, the church and its institutions became the primary channel for political opposition and a surrogate to other similar voices in civil society. Indeed, the church provided the institutional arena for political dissent and a base for direct opposition to the authoritarian regimes.[4] As political space opened up due to pressure, other actors that had previously suffered suspension found their voices and an arena to participate in the political life of their respective nations. The church also was able to represent social interests with relative effectiveness because of the stature and resources at its disposal, which included broad membership that spanned ethnic, regional, and socioeconomic boundaries as well as means of communication such us sermons, pastoral letters, and church media, not to mention a traditional social presence in schools and hospitals.[5]

---

4. Huntinton, *Third Wave*, 79.

5. In some countries, the church became the only organization with the ability to independently articulate opposition to the authoritarian regimes without being

It is the purposes of this book is to discuss how religion shapes political issues and to what extent religious forces influence the civil society. By civil society we mean an element in society that occupies the space outside the state and distinct from political groups associated with the state. It is made up of autonomous members of the broader society such as religious organizations, women's groups, lawyers, journalists, and trade unions. The goal for these agencies is to create a meaningful space that advances discourse that will eventually bring about a lasting and positive change. As one representative of civil society, the church engages the state to provide political space and resources otherwise controlled by authoritative regimes.

Evidently, the essays recognize the resilience that comes out of Africa even when the socio-political situation seems unbearable. African people are always hopeful and aware that the move towards democracy is categorically risky and requires enormous courage from those willing to pay the price. The essays that follow represent the struggle of how religious institutions engage the public domain. Our general perception recognizes the role of culture as a factor in understanding the value of any democracy.

Chapter Outline

There are four parts in the book organized according to the geo-political regions of Sub-Saharan Africa. The first three chapters provide the theoretical background for the book. Chapter 2 by Elias K. Bongmba argues that religious groups in Africa can be seen as civil society groups since they play roles played by civil society groups. As civil society groups, they have an obligation to embrace and promote the idea of the African Renaissance articulated by Thabo Mbeki. He reviews Mbeki's call and argues that religious groups and their leaders can contribute to a renaissance by promoting justice, championing cultural revival and transformation, promoting a humanistic agenda, and revitalizing education, especially the study of religion.

---

shut down. Because the church's presence was so pervasive through sheer numbers, as well as control of important resources, the regimes could not, or chose not, to apply harsher sanctions to religious entities. While the church became the only independent source of opposition to the authoritarian regimes, other social groups faced increased repression. The church used this position to lead the push for change

In chapter 1, Emmanuel Katongole discusses the greatest challenge facing Christians in Africa, which is essentially a cultivation of new social imaginations that can both resist and provide alternatives to the ever-increasing phenomenon of violence. For this to happen, Christian social ethics in Africa must rethink the relation between theology and politics, and thus assume new methodologies and directions. This argument is spelled out more explicitly in the fourth and last sections of the essay. The reason for this is that the reality of violence in Africa does not occur in isolation nor does it arise spontaneously out of some incomprehensible contradictions within "African culture." Violence, at least the sort of violence experienced in Africa, is the result of political formation, which is connected to stories that sustain nation-state politics in Africa. That is why it is important to attend to the story of Africa's politics, and the underlying stories and imaginations that sustain it. Once attention has been drawn to the story of nation-state politics in Africa, and the imagination and pattern of violence it forms, it becomes evident that Christian social ethics cannot proceed as usual by offering recommendations to help nation-state politics. Rather, it will have to reposition itself as a form of politics that is based on distinct stories, that is capable of forming alternative imaginations and patterns of social existence (as suggested in chapter 2 by Elias Bongmba).

Chapter 3 by Cyril Orji, "Religion, Violence, and Conflict: Ujamaa therapy as a Dynamic Response to Ethnic Particularities in Africa," discusses innovative ways of recovering authentic African ways of being human. The penchant for assimilating foreign conceptual modes of thought seems to have impaired the African existential reality, effecting a shift from authentic African core values to "modern" ones and leaving Black Africa in a crisis of identity. Orji sees ethnicity and religion as holding a terribly ambivalent position in African culture. While they serve as unifying forces and instruments of cohesion and advancement, they also have been used as instruments of hatred, destruction of lives and property. Conflict in Africa takes many forms. It is social, political, economic, and especially religious. The most pernicious of all these is ethnic and religious conflict. Although some of the reasons for these conflicts go back to the historical foundations of the many countries of sub-Saharan Africa, i.e., the colonial period, more troubling is the on-going exploitation of religious and ethnic differences by greedy politicians who use these to foster their selfish ends. The chapter also examines efforts by political and religious leaders to bring an end to these ravenous conflicts and suggests that the solution might lie, not just in the developing of a new ethic, but in retrieving the social and political virtues of our foremothers and forefathers. In this old African virtue, no one would kill or aim at another for ethnic or religious reasons, and, moreover, the ability to endure pain and injustice was a laudable virtue. Hence the chapter advocates Ujamaa-therapy as a way of retrieving these virtues of inclusive solidarity and transformation of injustice.

Part two is on the East African region and is represented by three chapters. The chapter by Samuel K. Elolia focuses on the role of religion in the democratization process in Kenya. He explores how the church has become the only cohesive institution to speak against the social injustices in Kenya and weather the consequences. Before, the institutions of higher learning were the ones who provided opposition to the government's corruption and misuse of power. When those voices were silenced, the churches spoke out.

The participation of the church intensified following the end of the Cold War in calling for fairness in political action. The clergy channeled their efforts through the National Council of Churches of Kenya and the Association of Catholic Bishops. Apparently, politics had been dominated by a one-party system for three decades. Consequently, that structure was slowly dying, giving way for a new political order with its own challenges.

This chapter also analyzes the current democratic practices and the impact on the masses on whose behalf these political forces claim to be working. Finally, the author considers the future prospects for democracy in Kenya. Obviously, these political changes are viewed in the light of Western liberal democracy, which might lead one to wonder whether Western democracy serves the interests of societies where ethnicity is still a part of the social structure.

The fifth chapter by Adam Arap Chepkwony entitled "Forgiveness: the Divine Gift of Peace, Reconciliation, and Healing" examines the role of Kalenjin women in peacemaking practices. He shows how the entire community depended on the wisdom and good will of their women to maintain peace and to control conflicts. He laments the lack of any discussions concerning the religious basis for peace and reconciliation from the perspective of religion. Worse still is the neglect of the role of women in peace initiatives in such traditions. Yet these are wealthy sources of information on this subject. Instead, more often than not, indigenous traditions are blamed for all the misery people encounter in modern society. A quick look at the recent literature in the African market on peace issues indicates that most women and men writers on peace ignore the role of women as peacemakers. It is common on the other hand to find articles and books that blame men, Christianity, African cultures, and Islam for men's plight.

In particular, Chepkwony points out that every society has a variety of culturally legitimated paths dedicated to resolution of conflicts, the settlement of disputes, and the allocation of responsibility among the members of that community. Similarly, there are rules that protect personal rights, communal interests, and public morality. These simple and local institutions serve as mediators, arbitrators, and adjudicators of individual and communal behaviors in the society. It is these often-neglected institutions that he sees as the undisputed contribution of African women in conflict resolution. He argues further that these roles are more significant among the indigenous people than the formal state-run legal institution. The importance of the local, unwritten legal codes in a community cannot be underestimated.

It is from this perspective that Chepkwony presents the role of Kalenjin women in peacemaking practices. He disagrees with William G. Blum and others who argue that African women were dependent upon men for overall protection, including that of their personal rights. Blum writes, "When wronged, women could do little by themselves to seek redress for their grievances: they had to look to a man or men: such as, a husband . . ." On the contrary, he shall argue here that members of the family and community at large sought mediatorship of women in times of conflicts for peaceful resolutions.

Chapter 6 by Emmanuel K. Twesigye explores the problems of church and state conflicts in Uganda that have resulted in the killing of millions of people, including church leaders such as the Anglican Archbishop Janani Luwum, murdered by Idi Amin in 1977. These tragic conflicts between church and state can be traced back to the British Anglican missionary strategies and ideals in the founding of colonial Christianity in Uganda. This process took place in the last quarter of the nineteenth century. The Christian establishment in

Uganda and the hostile rivalry of the Anglicans and Catholics led to confusion among the Ugandans, including the kings of Buganda.

As a result, there was a state persecution of Christianity led by King Mwanga of Buganda in 1885–1888. This Christian persecution led to the religious wars of 1888–1892, which led to the establishment of an Anglican hegemony in Buganda, and subsequently the rest of the kingdoms in Uganda. In these religious wars, the African traditionalists being supported by the nationalistic King Mwanga decided to get rid of all the "imported" foreign religions, namely, Islam, Catholicism, and Protestantism. Faced with extinction, the "three foreign religions" declared a truce and formed a religious military coalition that definitively defeated the African Traditionalist Party (the Pagans). Following this victory, the religious coalition between the Christians and Muslims broke down. The Muslims who had traditionally resented the intrusion of the Christians in their territory decided to get rid of the Christians and their European missionary teachers. The Muslims staged a coup against the Christians and installed Prince Kalema as a Muslim king and declared Buganda a Muslim country.

The deposed king Mwanga and the leading Christians fled into exile in Karagwe, northern Tanzania, and others fled to Buddu and Ankole in Southern and Western Uganda. At this time Catholics and Anglicans formed a new military coalition while in exile. Being helped by missionaries, they acquired guns and ammunitions, and were empowered to return to Buganda and overthrow the Islamic monarchy, reestablishing King Mwanga to the throne of Buganda. In the aftermath, Christian generals retained much of the power in the now officially new Christian country. However, the hostility between the Catholics and Anglicans soon reemerged, fanned by the European traditional rivalry and mutual intolerance for each other. As a result, the military coalition between Catholics, who called themselves "Bafransa" (the French) for being the followers of the French Catholic missionaries, and the Anglicans, who called themselves "Bangereza" (the English) for being the followers of the English missionaries, disgracefully brokedown.

Subsequently, the Ugandan Anglicans and the Catholics fought a serious war in which the local Anglicans and their British allies emerged as military victors. Since that time, the Anglican elites have ruled Uganda and excluded the Catholics, Muslims, and African traditionalists from power, except as political tokens or pawns in the Ugandan political game. All the kings of the Ugandan kingdoms became Anglican along with most of their major chiefs. The Anglican Church informally became the Established Church of Uganda. The Traditionalists (Bakafiri) or "Pagans" and "Muslims" (Basalamu) became completely disgraced. The religious and political hierarchy of privilege and power evolved with the Anglican elites at the top of the pyramid. The Anglicans as the ruling elites came first followed by the more numerical Catholics who were regarded as second-class citizens, followed by the Muslims as third-class citizens and the Traditionalists (Bakafiri) as fourth-class or the under-class of the disenfranchised and oppressed masses.

It is within this complex religious and political background and context that President Idi Amin, a Muslim, became the new Ugandan president through a military coup. He then decided to demolish the traditional hierarchical structure through the brutal and bloody strategy of extermination of the Anglicans. He decided to establish an Islamic hegemony in Uganda. He officially declared Uganda to be a Muslim country. Subsequently, Uganda joined the League of Arab Muslim Nations. As such, the assassination of the most reverend Janani Luwum, the Anglican Archbishop of Uganda in 1977, was a strategically planned move toward consolidation of Islamic power and state promotion of the Islamization process in Uganda.

This military and violent strategy failed to accomplish the results for which Idi Amin had hoped. However, thousands of Ugandan Christians were killed as part of Idi Amin's strategy for the statewide Islamization of Uganda by force. This included the persecution of Christians, terrorism or harassment, and mass arrests and murders of non-Muslims. As a result, almost one million Christians were killed in Uganda during President Idi Amin's "reign of terror" in 1971–1979. Most of these victims were Anglican Christian political elites, religious leaders, members of the civil service and the military. Some Roman Catholics who resisted Idi Amin's repressive regime also were killed. Benedicto Kiwanuka, the Chief Justice, and former Prime Minister of Uganda, Francis Xavier Tibayungwa, the Chief Administrator of the Kingdom of Ankole and Fr. Kiggundu, the editor of Munno, are outstanding examples of these Catholic victims.

Chapter 7 includes topics from Apartheid's Christian hegemony to religious pluralism in South Africa. In this chapter, Samuel Paul has shown that Christianity has been a dominant influence even though South Africa is a religiously plural country. The Afrikaner used his religion to separate, prevent inclusion, and suppress pluralism. The exclusion of otherness and other religious voices was clearly visible through Christian National Education. This was used as a political tool to procure hegemonic domination. The author has shown why religious pluralists would be suspicious with the traditional elitist salvific view to which most evangelical Christians hold. It is not difficult to see why exclusivist and elitist teachings like this could lead to the Afrikaners' discriminatory and non-egalitarian methods to control because they believed like Israel, that they were the chosen race.

South Africa's new constitution drew lessons from its past, an unjust, painful past, and therefore the right to equality, freedom of expression, religious freedom, and freedom of association were prioritized in the new constitution. It was set in place to promote affirmative tolerance with a celebration of religious pluralism, inclusivity, diversity, and community for healing, nation building, and national reconciliation, and for *ubuntu* to weave its presence into the fabric of this once-demoralized, segregated society, in order to now, in the present South Africa, embrace all of humanity as persons interrelated together into one common society. Therefore, it is not a separation of church and state, because South Africa fervently seeks to uphold religious practices in conformity with the egalitarian foundations of its new constitution. It is not a secular state either, because *ubuntu* is necessary for this community's survival, growth, and maturity. It was once a broken nation and now is on its way toward healing, reconciliation, repentance, forgiveness, and embraces democracy with egalitarian values. *Ubuntu* is the cement that holds this community together.

Chapter 8 by James Cochrane addresses the role of Christians in the formation of public policy in South Africa that recognizes the significance of civil society as increasingly crucial in the debates over the nature, the problems, and the potentialities of contemporary democratic, pluralistic societies. In this context, the role of religion is increasingly fore-grounded; a variety of public actors are realizing that the question of cultural and religious wellsprings for the generation of appropriate values cannot be sidestepped.[6]

This debate has obvious relevance in South Africa today. Christian churches, with their huge demographic base (more than 70 percent of the populace claim Christian allegiance), face the challenge of playing a role in constructing a new basis for civil society. But most often churches do not understand the implications of their demographic base and institutional reach for the construction and maintenance of civil society. Equally, secular organizations and the government fail to grasp the significance religion might have in building civil society. In both cases, a restricted, if not unhelpful view of religion dominates. This problem is not peculiar to South Africa.

Another feature of importance presented by Professor Cochrane is the extent of the forms of popular religion. In the context of South Africa, the demographic weight of Christianity lies with the African-initiated churches, a broad collection of thousands of small organizations. Here, popular religion and a mix of (contested) traditions hold sway. A key question is how such communications may be drawn into the essentially modernist project of constructing civil society. The answer includes a need to accept a different, more nuanced and positive understanding of the role of religion in the lives of ordinary people and of their wisdom and interpretive activity—despite limits—for sourcing values and practices which would contribute to the strengthening of civil society.

This chapter explores some of these problems in relation to work in progress in the field of public policy in South Africa. It argues for a hermeneutic approach to understanding public policy (as constructed in public discourse with various competing interpretive interests), thus inviting consideration of the significance of the production of appropriate values in supporting policy initiatives. In particular, the notion of democracy, as that which depends upon the interaction of a value-impregnated set of committed, publicly intelligible discourses, work with an assumption that marginalized discourses provide us with the perspectives on society which most readily expose the deficiencies of policy making and the (potential or actual) rupture of civil society.

---

6. Evidently, cultural education helps to shape people's attitudes, beliefs, practices, values and ways of behavior. Some of the most insightful cultural critics and advocates of freedoms are the African artists, including novelists. Most of them were lecturers at universities where they promoted the ideals of democracy and human rights.

The African-initiated churches exemplify the experience of marginalized discourse, and thus become a test case for the construction of civil society. Given the mix of tradition, modernism, and post-colonial elements to this discourse, the issue becomes one of how it is possible to find a role in the formation of public policy from the margins. The chapter attempts to suggest directions in which one might go in developing fitting processes to allow religion, specifically marginalized religion, to play a meaningful role in civil society and in the formation of public policy, which shapes this society.

In chapter 9, Ian MacLean presents a comparative study of the political implications and influences of African religions often assumed to be apolitical in South Africa and Brazil. Ironically, the Afro-Brazilian religions of Northeast Brazil and the African Indigenous Churches (AIC) of Southern Africa were earlier suspected by authorities of harboring nationalistic sentiments. Most twentieth-century scholarship has viewed them either as religions of resistance or as "havens for the masses." In either case, they are understood as religious expressions of suppressed political aspirations. Further, religious scholars often regarded them as "syncretic" and thus not worthy of study or valuable only for their preservation of authentic African traditions. This approach has sundered them from their (often conflictual) religious field, their interaction with other religions, and their impact upon dominant or historical religions.

Both South Africa and Brazil have recently democratized and have accepted constitutions, which guarantee freedom of political association and of religion. Surprisingly, the religious traditions took the forefront in the political democratization struggle (for example, "progressive Catholics" in Brazil, and the mainline mission churches in South Africa) are experiencing membership decline. The reasons for these are dependent upon internal as well as external factors, conditioned in both cases by the specifics of a conflictual religious field. While the impact of both AICs and Afro-Brazilian religions is not clear on the national political levels, they are functioning to create forms of civil society, to preserve and or to foster Black identity.

In chapter 10, Ukachukwu Chris Manus and Bolaji Olukemi Bateye discuss religion and social change in a multi-ethnic society, Nigeria. The paper focuses on Nigeria, the most populous nation in black Africa whose inhabitants are composed of diverse ethnic and cultural backgrounds. As a study done from a collegiate environment, it explores the primary role of religion in spite of the abhorrent manipulation of the three major religions in Nigeria—African Traditional Religion, Islam, and Christianity—by political demagogues. The phenomenological method is adopted in its critical, descriptive, and analytical forms. The purpose is to understand and to inform readers that in a multi-cultural polity as Nigeria, religion is a motive force. The dysfunctional role of religion in current political engineering in Nigeria is exposed. The study involved fieldwork observations and the interpretation of historical, sociological, and psychological data inherent in the Nigerian culturally and religiously pluralistic society. Serious efforts are made to address the head and only obliquely the heart with reference to religion as an agent of social change in the context of Nigeria's cultural pluralism, religious pluralism, and the politicization of religion. The paper concludes *inter alia* that since Nigerian cultures have both religious epistemology and ontology, religion's role as an agent in social change and development can only be felt through the corporate activism of institutions like CAN as a pressure group of civil society. The chapter concludes that this has become imperative if Nigeria is to survive as a viable nation.

Chapter 11 by Umar Habila Dadem Danfulani discusses Shari'a, democracy and civil society in northern Nigeria. Danfulani examines four areas of religion and politics in northern Nigeria. First, it concerns itself with democracy and the expansion of Shari'a in northern Nigeria. With the successful return of Nigeria to multi-party democracy in 1999, there have been two national elections (in 1999 and in 2003), with both witnessing mass irregularities. With a high youth bulge, high level of unemployment and unemployables, youth restiveness, violence and vigilantism, voting processes in the north witnessed cross-state and cross-border voting (with an influx of youths from Chad and Niger Republics), mass rigging, intimidation of party opponents and women, and the open operation of money bags, among others. Added to this was the entry of political Shari'a into Nigeria's body politics from 1999, which was not by accident, but is viewed by northern Muslims as a return to the pre-1960 status quo and the reclamation of the traditional heritage of Muslims. Thus from 1999 to 2002, twelve Muslim governors in northern Nigeria passed bills that introduced the Shari'a penal codes into their State Houses of Assemblies and signed the bill into law as a result of direct electioneering campaign promises. This work examines the politics of the expansion of Shari'a law from 1999 in northern Nigeria.

Secondly, the chapter provides an analysis of political Shari'a and human rights with particular focus on the rights of women, Hausa-Fulani Christians and other Christians in the north, and the rights of persons living on the fringes of Hausa-Fulani Muslim society, such as some Maguzawa who actively participate in mediumistic spirit possession (*wasan bori*), commercial sex workers (*karuwai*) and homosexuals (*yan daudu*). The chapter opines that from its expansion in 1999, Shari'a has had a tremendous negative impact on Christians living in the Shari'a-compliant states, contrary to the claim of political Shari'arists that Shari'a will not affect Christians.

Thirdly, the paper provides an analysis of political Shari'arists as emancipators of the masses (*talakawa*). It questions the validity of the emancipatory slogan of Shari'a propagandists by asking whether indeed the *talakawa* are yearning for Shari'a or for something else. For instance, has the living conditions of the *talakawa* improved with the expansion of Shari'a law according to the belief that it will usher into being a utopian world in northern Nigeria? What are the social-economic, industrial, educational, literacy, and health conditions in northern Nigeria today? Finally, what are the implications of politicians presiding over Shari'a expansion in northern Nigeria instead of the *ulama*? As already indicated by the Hijra or Taliban group of Kamanana of Yobe State, can extremists ever have enough of Shari'a, or, put differently, to what extent can Shari'a law be expanded to the satisfaction of anti-establishment Muslim extremist groups (such as El-Zakzaki of Kwarbai ward of Zaria and his Ikhwan, the Brothers)?

In chapter 12, Yushau Sodiq discusses "Nigerian Civil Government and the Application of Islamic Law": Sodiq's attempt in this chapter is to discuss the controversy about the constitutionality of the application of Sharia law in Northern Nigeria. Does the application of Sharia amount to Islam becoming the religion of the state? Does applying severe punishment on Muslims through Islamic laws discriminate against them? The author will bring forth the evidences for and against Sharia and analyze the causes of tension between the advocates of Sharia and its protagonists. While the supporters for and opponents of Sharia law hardly agree on what is to be done to solve the problem of Sharia, both parties can amicably work together and resolve this issue through a genuine dialogue and commitment to tolerance toward one another for the sake of peace. It is morally wrong for Muslims to impose their laws on those who do not adhere to their religious beliefs. Also, under democratic rule, citizens should be free to choose their legal systems even if these systems are informed by religious beliefs. Therefore, if Muslims opt to be ruled by Islamic laws, the Constitution should protect their interest and enable them to achieve their goals.

Bibliography

Huntington, Samuel P. *The Third Wave: Democratization in the Late Twentieth Century*. Tulsa: University of Oklohoma Press, 1991.

Magesa, Laurenti. *Democracy and Reconciliation: A challenge for African Christianity*. Nairobi: Acton, 1999.

Mandela, Nelson. *Nelson Mandela Speaks*. New York: Pathfinder, 1993.

PART ONE

The Theoretical Perspectives of Religion in Africa

1

Violence and Social Imagination

Rethinking Religion and Politics in Africa[1]

EMMANUEL M. KATONGOLE

The missionaries had come to the Congo eager to evangelize, to fight polygamy, and to impart to Africans a Victorian sense of sin. Before long however, the rubber terror meant that missionaries had trouble finding bodies to clothe or souls to save. Frightened villagers would disappear into the jungle for weeks when they saw the smoke of an approaching steamboat on the horizon. One British missionary was asked repeatedly by Africans, "Has the Savior you tell us of any power to save us from rubber trouble?"[2]

On 13 July the four bishops comprising the investigating committee published their report. In this they listed all the reasons advanced for or against removing the bishop, and tried to arrange them in some sort of order. This report seemed to support the bishop, but its recommendations seemed to acknowledge the basic justice in the rebel's cause. The first of these recommended that the diocese be split into three new dioceses, and the second that Bawoze remain as a diocesan bishop if requested to do so by any of the three new dioceses, or take early retirement within one year of the acceptance of

---

1. Originally given as a public lecture at Cambridge (UK), March 12, 2001, as part of the Lecture Series of "Mission and Theology" organized by *Currents in World Christianity Project*. In grateful memory of Msgr. William Mpuuga (R.I.P.), a priest of exceptional intellectual clarity, spiritual diligence and pastoral dedication. We are all much richer because of his friendship and the gifts of his ministry and scholarship. A slightly modified version of the essay was published as "Mission and Social Formation," in *African Theology Today*, 121–46.

2. Hochschild, *King Leopold's Ghost*, 172.

the report. This report however, solved nothing, because when Archbishop Okoth on 10 August visited the diocese to communicate the recommendations of the committee, the anti-Bamwoze faction refused to meet him in a hotel and assembled at the cathedral instead. The archbishop refused to speak to the crowd assembled inside on the technicality that he could not enter a cathedral in his province without the consent of the local bishop, and offered to address the crowd outside the cathedral. The "mammoth gathering which had now turned into a mob" insisted that he address them inside the cathedral, and began dragging him there. It was only with considerable difficulty that the archbishop reached his car, and managed to drive off, the "rear window smashed by stones thrown by the wild crowd." On 27 August [bishop] Bamwoze himself was subjected to similar physical violence at Batambogwe.[3]

Introduction: Religion and Social Formation in Africa

Facing "King Leopold's Ghost"

SOMETIME AGO IN THE SUMMER, I GOT A CHANCE TO READ ADAM Hochschild's *King Leopold's Ghost*—a very moving, but extremely disturbing book. It recounts the crazy and unstoppable ambitions of King Leopold II of Belgium and his domination and brutal plundering of the Congo Free State. It is the story of untold death, wanton destruction, and civilizing barbarism as Leopold used his mercenary army of *Force Publique* to drive the Congolese natives into mines and rubber plantations, to burn villages and mete out sadistic punishments, including the severing of hands and other forms of dismemberment. In numerous descriptions and personal narratives of survivors, one catches horrifying glimpses of how the natives viewed, endured, and suffered the throngs of what was later to be mythologized as the "wonderful benefits of cilivization." This is how, for instance, one Tswambe remembers the state official Léon Fiévez:

> All blacks saw this man as the devil of the Equator... From all the bodies killed in the field, you had to cut off the hands. He wanted to see the number of hands cut off by each soldier, who had to bring them in baskets... A village which refused to provide rubber would be completely swept clean. As a young

3. Gifford, *African Christianity*, 126–27.

man, I saw [Fievez's] soldier Molili, then guarding the village of Boyeka, take a net, put ten arrested natives in it, attach big stones to the net, and make it tumble into the river . . . Rubber causes these torments; that's why we no longer want to hear it's name spoken. Soldiers made young men kill or rape their own mothers and sisters.[4]

In one story after another, the tales of senseless violence are recounted. What perhaps is even more disheartening than these particular accounts is the realization that these were not isolated instances of a particular form of terror (rubber, and limited to King Leopold's Congo). Rather, as extreme and bizarre as these stories are, they reflect the sort of memories that will forever remain ingrained about the colonial presence in Africa. As Hochschild remarks: "What happened in the Congo could reasonably be called the most murderous part of the European scramble for Africa."[5] But is it just that—"the most murderous part." For the sad truth is that the men who carried it out for Leopold were no more murderous than the many Europeans then at work or at war elsewhere in Africa. Conrad said it best: "All Europe contributed to the making of Kurtz."[6]

Our intention in drawing attention to Hoschild's book in a discussion of mission and social formation is not to rehearse the somehow familiar and tired argument of mission as but just a form of colonial domination. Our goal rather is to explore what, if any resources mission can offer in the face of such violence and disposition. In this connection, I was particularly struck by a paragraph in Hochschild's account. Getting away from the accounts of torture, plundering and violence, Hochschild remarks:

> The missionaries had come to the Congo eager to evangelize, to fight polygamy, and to impart to Africans a Victorian sense of sin. Before long however, the rubber terror meant that missionaries had trouble finding bodies to clothe or souls to save. Frightened villagers would disappear into the jungle for weeks when they saw the smoke of an approaching steamboat on the horizon. One British missionary was asked repeatedly by

---

4. Hochschild, *King Leopold's Ghost*, 166.
5. Ibid., 280.
6. Ibid., 283.

Africans, "Has the Savior you tell us of any power to save us from rubber trouble?"[7]

That, I think is a significant question, for us today as well, even though we seem to be living in a completely different set of circumstances. For, in the Congo itself much has changed since the 1890s of King Leopold. For instance, the Belgian government would soon take over the administration of the Congo Free State, renaming the territory the Belgian Congo; King Leopold died in 1909, Congo became independent (and Congo Kinshasa) in 1960; became Zaire under Mobutu; and has since been re-named (by Kabila) the République Démocratique du Congo (RDC). The most significant development of all: over 60 percent of Congo's 50.5 million people are now Christians. A lot has changed.

Yet, from another point of view, a very disappointing point of view, one must admit not much has changed. Even though Congo remains one of the richest countries in the world in terms of natural, mineral and cultural resources, the Congolese people, whether under Mobutu's Zaire, or under the RDC of the Kabilas, have continued to live under the grip of massive poverty, military violence, and regimes as dis-empowering as King Leopold's rubber terror. This is not just true of the Congo, but of a great many of African countries. Nigeria, Liberia, Sierra Leone, Rwanda, Angola, to name but a few, all tell the same story of dictatorship, state-inspired corruption, the breakdown of social services, etc. Even within the more "promising" African countries by World Bank and IMF statistics, Uganda and Ghana, for instance, their much celebrated recovery or "economic turn around" has still to trickle down to the majority of citizens in terms of a better way of life and of stable structures of peace and progress.

If the name of King Leopold evokes a history of violence and dispossession in the Congo, then there is indeed something like a King Leopold's ghost hanging over a great part of Africa. Accordingly, I will use the metaphor of King Leopold's ghost to refer to the economy of violence, dispossession, and exploitation which greatly characterizes politics on the African continent. Neither Africa's independence nor what has been dubbed the "second revolution" of the 1980s has brought any significant gains for the majority of African peoples, but increasing marginalization and dispossession. Like the frightened vil-

7. Ibid., 172.

lagers in King Leopold's Congo, many in Africa today are wondering whether Christianity has any power to save them from this nightmare?

This question (whether Christianity can save Africa) lies at the heart of Christian social ethics in Africa and, in fact, of any discussion on mission and social formation. For, as I understand it, the topic of mission and social formation tries to underscore the role of the church in creating conditions for social life in all its forms. I do not think that the assumption, that mission creates, or at least ought to create, conditions for human social life in its richest and fullest sense, needs any justification. After all, mission, as Bediako notes following Sanneh, is *Missio Dei*, the same God who in Jesus Christ comes so that "they may have life, and have it to the full" (John 10:10).[8] What is at stake here is the fact that if such mission has to be relevant for Africa, then the question of whether Christianity can indeed save Africans from King Leopold's ghost is a relevant one. For the way the church will be able to provide resources to rightly name, confront, and conceive alternatives to this ghostly nightmare will be the litmus test of the church's mission in the twenty-first century. But this is a challenge not just for the African church, but for all Christian churches. For the way Africans meet, or fail to meet this challenge will reflect on the sort of resources available to us within Christianity, and on the sort of people we have become, or at least ought to become, if we are to embody the mission of the Church truthfully.

The question is not only significant and relevant for Africa, it is urgent for at least two related reasons. Within the context of Africa, it is urgent for at least two related reasons. First, given the fact that for some inexplicable reason the same continent that seems to be haunted by King Leopold's ghost is a massively Christian continent and secondly, given the growing skepticism concerning Christianity's ability to "save" Africa. I will briefly tease out the implications of each of these factors.

The Two Faces of Africa: Probing the Connections

The poverty, violence and distressing social and political conditions in Africa must be seen against the background of Africa as a Christian continent. Recently, Tinyiko Maluleke has drawn our attention to

---

8. Bediako, *Christianity in Africa*, 121.

the two valid but often perceived to be disconnected faces of Africa.⁹ On the one hand, there is the picture of a distressed and distressing Africa: widespread poverty, political instability, the civic unrest, and ethnic tensions/clashes in many countries. Add to these the tremendous health and infra-structure problems, recently complicated by the HIV-AIDS epidemic (and Ebola), then one sees how dire the situation is. In a slightly earlier article which assesses Africa's situation in the global economic situation, Maluleke had depicted Africa as a modern day Job sitting on the global rubbish dump.¹⁰ A very distressed and distressing picture of Africa which, perhaps not surprisingly, tends to generate an increasing mood of "Afro-pessimism."

There is, however, another face of Africa, of a massively Christian continent, and still growing. A look at recent statistics confirms this picture¹¹ which is not just due to the projected, but often misleading, accounts of population growth, but to a "momentous outpouring of Christian conversion throughout the continent." In fact, as a number of theologians have noted, in Africa, the church is one of the most widely spread and "most sustainable social institutions, especially in the rural areas."¹² Such indications of a massive Christian presence on the continent seem to ground a certain optimism not only from the fact that "the Christian way of life is here to stay,"¹³ but also from the sense that the future of the church might perhaps be in Africa.¹⁴

But how are these two faces—of a distressed and distressing Africa on the one hand, and, on the other, of a massively Christian continent—to be accounted for?¹⁵ Are these two faces of Africa just

9. T. S. Maluleke, "Letter to Job from Africa," 5.

10. Ibid.

11. On the statistical strength of Christianity in sub-Saharan Africa, see e.g., Gifford, *Christian Churches and the Democratization of Africa*, where a quick sample indicates that Christians make up 78 percent of Uganda's population; 60 percent of Ghana's; 65 percent of Cameroon's, and 75 percent of Zambia's (61, 119, 183, 251 respectively). The overall statistics for the continent indicate that over 41 percent of Africa's 550 million people were Christians; see Gibelleni, *Paths in African Theology*.

12. Mugambi, *From Liberation to Reconstruction*, 225; Cochrane, *Circles of Dignity*, 90.

13. Bediako, *Christianity in Africa*, 229

14. Catholics especially note this optimism through such questions as whether the next pope will be from Africa. For my more extended reflections on this optimism, see Katongole, "Prospects of Ecclesia."

15. M. J. Maluleke, *Ximakwa Xo Ka' Meno*, 332.

accidental or somehow also logically connected to one another? If so, how? Is Africa a distressed continent in spite of its being Christian, or perhaps because of it? What is the relevance of African religiosity for Africa's problems? "Is this religiosity authentic, or is it superstition arising from despair?"[16] These are indeed tough questions, which invite (and this is Maluleke's point) an honest and hard introspection as a first step toward a constructive way forward in African theology.

One lesson I have personally drawn from Maluleke's probing questions is the sobering realization that our theological investigations cannot proceed as "usual" by simply suggesting strategies to shoulder, repair or to make less distressing the distressed Africa, as if we ourselves (the church, Christianity) are external to (outside) the distressed Africa. For as Maluleke notes, Africa's troubles and problems are not just "events, processes and ideologies that take shape outside of the church and of Christianity."[17] Accordingly, our constructive suggestions for a way forward will involve a critical look at the history of the continent which Christianity has either simply assumed or/and unwittingly underwritten, thereby limiting her own resources for naming, let alone confronting and providing an alternative to, the story of violence and dispossession on the continent.

A Growing Skepticism: Can African Christianity Be "Saved"?

Any discussion of the mission and social formation in Africa must also take place against the backdrop of what seems to be an increasing skepticism, overt or implicit, regarding Christianity's potential role in the positive transformation of Africa. In a not too recent issue, *The Economist* (May 13, 2000) painted a very bleak picture of Africa as a continent slipping further into chaos and despair. The front cover of the issue said it all. Set within a map of Africa against a dark background was the picture of a young man carrying a heavy rocket propelled grenade on his right shoulder and wearing a murderous grin on his face. And above it, the title in big and clear yellow letters: "The Hopeless Continent."[18] Both the level of analysis (shallow) as well as the progno-

16. Ibid., 330.

17. Ibid., 325.

18. *The Economist* (Feb 24–March 2, 2001) paints a similar picture of gloom with its cover story of "Africa's Elusive Hope."

sis of Africa's problems left much to be desired, but I guess one should not expect much of either from this particular publication.[19] What, however, was striking was the eloquent absence of Christianity from the picture. The Christian churches received no mention at all, either as part of the landscape of the "Hopeless Continent" or, as I hoped would be the case, as part of the hope. How could the "most sustainable social institution in Africa" be simply and easily written out of the picture, even by a publication like *The Economist*? Was this another confirmation, if one ever needed one, of defective and misleading social analysis on Africa typical of many publications in the West? Or could this be a pointer to a very disturbing realization that, in spite of Christianity's massive presence in Africa, few are willing to take it seriously as a formidable social force.[20] It is not clear how widespread such skepticism is within Africa itself, but given the ambiguous role Christianity has had in Africa, and in more recent cases like Rwanda,[21] skepticism regarding the future role of Christianity in Africa may as well be on the rise. Maluleke himself, in the article referred to above, seems to harbor such doubts regarding the assumption that African Christianity can be shaped into a formidable weapon in the hands of distressed Africans. He notes:

> A question which is not entirely irrelevant for the purposes of our essay is whether the objective of shaping the Christian faith into a formidable weapon in the hands of the oppressed is either feasible or attainable. Can Christianity become a "for-

---

19. I for instance find both inadequate and misleading the *Economist's* attempt to blame Africa's current problems on its bad leaders, its traditions and culture, its environment, colonialism—on everything else, except the current institutions, national, and multinational.

20. Even Kwame Bediako, his positive, and almost triumphalistic assessment of African Christianity notwithstanding, seems, even though reluctantly and only hypothetically, to allow this possibility. Bediako, *Christianity in Africa*, 263.

21. The chilling story of the sixteen-year-old Josephine Uwamahoro (a name which literary means the "peaceful one") is as instructive as it is unnerving. Josephine lost all her family and all her friends in the massacre in the church at Nyamata, the same church in which she and her family had celebrated the Eucharist every Sunday together with some of the would-be murderous militias. That she herself survived was a miracle. She was left for dead in a heap of festering bodies of her family and friends after her neck and legs were hacked. After the war was over, she tearfully whispered to one of the missionaries: "We will never come back to this church. The angels have left us." See Hugh McCullum, *Angels Have Left Us*, xix.

midable" weapon? Has it become a formidable weapon? If so, why and how? And again, if not, why and how not?[22]

Coming from one of Africa's leading theologians, such doubts and hesitations need to be taken seriously, especially as they reflect a sense in which the question about Christianity's potential role in the social transformation of Africa is, in a great measure, also a question about Christianity's future in Africa. But we should also be careful not to allow the current shortcomings of the church in Africa to dull our imagination and blind us to the resources which Christianity can provide for social reconstruction. I personally remain a stubborn and hopeless optimist (the result of being both a Christian and an African?) regarding the church's potential for social transformation in Africa. Even then, I realize that for such potential to be realized, we must be willing to move beyond the present conceptions of church as well as present formulations of her social role. In other words, the first and primary challenge before any such potential can become available, is one of social imagination.

Constructively, the task of social imagination will require nothing less than a recovery of the church or, which is the same thing, as a willingness to engage a conversation of what it means for us Christians to be socially formed, thereby offering alternatives to the current narratives and social formations in Africa (I will come back to this in the last section of the paper). What must be noted now is that for such constructive social imagination to become a possibility, it must involve, and in fact begin with, a critical and thorough-going evaluation of some of the assumptions which have greatly shaped the church's social mission generally, and in Africa in particular. One such key assumption is the conception of the "social" and "religious" as two distinct spheres. When left unexamined, the distinction works to invest the presumably "neutral" state with the power to define, manage, and determine the particular form the social sphere takes. That this has

---

22. Malulek, "Christianity in a Distressed Africa," 330. To be sure, this is an issue that has bothered Maluleke for a while, but one to which he has not provided a definite answer even though on at least one occasion he has tentatively suggested that it might perhaps be time "to drink from our own wells"—thereby encouraging Black and African theologies to take more seriously African culture and African traditional religions, not just as "preparations for the Christian gospel," but in their own right as offering resources and "alternative strategies for survival" (Maluleke "Letter to Job from Africa").

certainly been the case for Christian social ethics in Africa is obvious from the way the different paradigms of conceiving the church's social role have not questioned the story of the nation-state.

Mission and Social Formation: The Current Paradigms

As a distinct and coherent discipline, Christian social ethics is relatively undeveloped in Africa. This however does not mean that contributions within African theology have shown little or no concern for social issues. On the contrary, given the often distressing social-political conditions in Africa, theological contributions have generally felt the need to be relevant to the demands of the times. At the risk of oversimplification, there seem to be three dominant paradigms from which the social concerns affecting Africa have been approached within African theology: a spiritual, a pastoral and a more explicitly political paradigm. Since these paradigms are not mutually exclusive, the scheme here may just reflect an emphasis adopted in response to a particular need, or just different faces within the mission of the church, generally understood.

(a) *A Spiritual Paradigm*. Theologians working from this paradigm exhibit the least engagement with social concerns, a trend often associated with evangelical theology but also with the dominant theologies of inculturation. According to this paradigm, the goal of mission is the formation of Christian *spiritual* identity. Among theologians, it is perhaps Kwame Bediako who provides the most articulate expression of this paradigm. Bediako understands his theological task in the "quest and demonstration of the true character of African Christian identity."[23] It is an identity, however, which Bediako understands or characterizes in primarily spiritual terms as the "history of *religious* consciousness" (emphasis added)[24] and as the process through which "Jesus Christ . . . has become a reality in the universe of their [African's] *religious* ideas, forces, powers and *spiritual* agency."[25] Of course it is not the case that Bediako thinks that there is no relationship between this spiritual process and the social/material conditions of the Africans in the world.

---

23. Bediako, *Theology and Identity*.
24. Bediako, "Roots of African Theology," 49.
25. Bediako, *Christianity in Africa*, 85 (emphasis added).

This spiritual process can have, and in fact has had, far reaching consequences. One such effect, Bediako notes following Sanneh, has been the way in which it has "imbued local culture with eternal significance and endowed African languages with a transcendental range."[26] Also, Bediako notes how this "spiritual" process can have significant consequences for African politics where a key problem, which has its roots in the ancestral world, is a tendency to sacralize power and authority. In contrast to this view of authority, one is confronted within Christian theology with Jesus Christ, who de-sacralizes all earthly powers and politics, thereby checking its inherent tendency to absolutize itself. Accordingly, "the recognition that power truly belongs to God, which is rooted in the Christian theology of power as non-dominating, liberates politicians and rulers to be humans among fellow humans, and ennobles politics . . ."[27] These, however, are not benefits which can be directly pursued by Christians. Rather, they are benefits that kind of "flow over" from the primary challenge of the formation of a true spiritual vocation or identity.[28]

(b) A Pastoral Paradigm: A more recent statement of the commitment to this paradigm can be found in Pope John Paul II's post-synodal extortion, *Ecclesia in Africa*. Coinciding with the 1994 Rwanda genocide, the synodal meeting of bishops expressed great concern about this event, and about the worsening social, economic and political conditions of Africa in general. "What has become of Africa?" the Pope and bishops wondered.[29] The synodal bishops were nevertheless convinced that the church can still make a difference and indeed be "Good News" "in a continent of bad news?" What sort of difference?

> For many synodal fathers contemporary Africa can be compared to the man who went down from Jerusalem to Jericho. . . . Africa is a continent where countless human beings . . . are lying as it were, on the edge of the road, sick, injured, disabled, marginalized and abandoned. They are in dire need of Good Samaritans who will come to their aid. For my part, I express

---

26. Ibid., 120.

27. Ibid., 247.

28. There might in fact be something like a Weberian scenario here where the less explicitly socially active forms of Christianity might, ironically, provide the far more enduring social benefits. Weber, *Protestant Ethic*.

29. John Paul II, *Post-Synodal Exhortation "Ecclesia in Africa,"* #39–40.

the hope that the Church will continue patiently to tirelessly do its work as a Good Samaritan.³⁰

To be sure, Catholic social ethics in Africa has been far more complex than this statement from the post-synodal exhortation seems to suggest.³¹ The statement is, however, consistent with the church's historical role in the provision of education, health and, more lately, development services generally. Such "outreach" has been sustained not just by a humanitarian concern but by the conviction that the Gospel is a liberating social force which can help the poor to "rediscover their humanity" and regain a sense of dignity. What is particularly noteworthy is the way in which this paradigm is often couched in terms of "intervention"—a response to a crisis (poverty, suffering, instability etc.)—situations which are either the direct result of government policies, or the cumulative effect of the breakdown of government services. Given the dismal failure of the nation-states in Africa, it is not surprising that the church in Africa has increasingly found herself engaged in programs and services meant to assist marginalized Africans to "recoup their energies so as to put them at the service of the common good."³² It is in fact against this background that the Christian churches in Africa have increasingly come to understand themselves as "partners in development"—partners, that is, with the state.

(c) A Political Paradigm: This paradigm reflects a call for the church to play a more explicit role of challenging oppressive political structures and urging political reform. The urgency as well as increasing prominence of this paradigm in Africa can be gleaned from a statement by José Chipenda, the then-general secretary of the AACC. Responding to the 1994 Rwanda tragedy, Chipenda noted:

---

30. Ibid., #41.
31. Katongole, "Prospects of Ecclesia."
32. John Paul II, *Post-Synodal Exhortation "Ecclesia in Africa,"* #41. Mugambi's suggestion for a theology of "reconstruction" also seems to boil down to this: The Gospel, Mugambi notes, ought to be Good News—which "rehabilitates individuals and groups that are marginalized by various natural and social circumstances. In contemporary Africa the Good News is understtood in this way, ought to rehabilitate the afflicted individuals in every region, country and locality. The Gospel ought to help Africans regain their confidence and hope . . ." (Mugambi, *From Liberation to Reconstruction*, 176).

> The concern for justice must permeate every action by churches; and justice involves looking at the murky political issues which cause massacres and refugee exoduses and denouncing injustice without taking partisan positions. It seems in the case of Rwanda that de-politicized emergency aid is easier than long-range initiatives for justice, peace and reconciliation.[33]

In the recent past such "initiatives for justice, peace and reconciliation" have been many, and have taken various forms. The 1993 Leeds Conference on "The Christian Churches and Africa's Democratization" took account of many of these initiatives especially in connection with Africa's second revolution.[34] They (initiatives) range from pastoral letters issued by bishops and religious leaders (individually and collegially) to denounce injustice, dictatorship and violence to bishops taking a more explicit involvement in the public affairs of society, say by chairing a national conference, or commissions of inquiry and/or reconciliation, as the case of the TRC in South Africa clearly indicates. The results of many of these initiatives have been significant, even granting the ambiguous political role of some of the churches.[35] What perhaps we need to note here is how theological discussions within this paradigm often appeal to "justice," "democracy," and "human rights" in a manner that assumes that these notions name (or at least are intrinsic to) the social order which is at once human and Christian. We thus get such calls for the churches to be "midwives of a democratic transition and reconstruction" and to provide an ethos for a culture of justice and human rights.[36] In what he has called a "theology of reconstruction," Villa Vicencio has in fact argued that the church not only has a stake in "responsible nation-building," but that at a deeper level, the task of nation-building, democracy, constitutionalism, the promotion and defense of human rights, on the one hand, and Christian theology on the other, converge. Both are about the "affirmation of a God who calls people ever forward to a new, better and transformed society."[37]

Even though the three paradigms seem to be markedly different in their theological self understanding, and provide different strate-

---

33. McCullum, *Angels Have Left Us*, 44.

34. Gifford, *Christian Churches and the Democratization of Africa*; Gifford, *African Christianity*.

35. Gifford, *Christian Churches and the Democratization of Africa*, 5

36. De Gruchy, *Christianity and Democracy*.

37. Villa-Vicencio, *A Theology of Reconstruction*.

gies for engaging the social order, they are sustained by the common assumption of the nation-state as the primary social/political actor. While the focus on a spiritual identity assumes a clear separation of church and state, the pastoral paradigm responds to the crises arising out of the nation-state's failure or breakdown by positioning the church as a "partner in development." The political paradigm seeks to make the nation-state more just or, which is assumed will have the same effect, more democratic. None of the paradigms, in other words, have been able to challenge, let alone provide an alternative to, the basic story embodied within the nation-state in Africa. In fact, even within more recent studies which underscore the role of the Christian churches in developing forms of civil society, the need for democracy (and by extension) the nation-state seems to be fore-grounded.[38] Not even within black theology in South Africa, radical as it was (is?),[39] was the nation-state ideology called into question. The moral and political legitimacy of an apartheid state was challenged, but not, it seems to me, the nation-state project *qua* nation-state. This inability to question the nation-state is perhaps not surprising given the dominant tradition which has shaped Christian social ethics since the Enlightenment. The tradition—a version of what Milbank has characterized as the liberal protestant metanarrative[40]—has tended to move in a Weberian fashion, by assuming that the "social" and "religious" constitute two distinct fields each with its own relative autonomy.[41] The effect of this distinction is to underwrite a specific conception of state–church relationship, in which the state becomes the primary social actor, with power to define, manage, and control the social realm, even as it is acknowledged that the "religious" field (managed by the church) can have far reaching "social implications."[42]

38. Gifford, *African Christianity*, and Nelson, *Civil Society and Democracy in Africa*.

39. The future of Black theology following the end of apartheid has been a matter of debate. Whereas many have been quick to write eulogies of Black Theology, Maluleke still sees a future for it. Maluleke, "Black Theology Lives!"

40. Milbank, *Theology and Social Theory*, 92.

41 For a more extended treatment of this assumption see my *Beyond Universal Reason*, especially, 180–212.

42. Troeltsch's *Social Teaching of the Christian Churches* has been the classical text on understanding the social role of the church. This tradition has been particularly dominant in America in the Social Gospel Movement of Raushenbuch, and following him the Niebuhr brothers. See Raushenbusch, *Theology for the Social Gospel*.

Once such an assumption has been accepted, however, it means that the church's social mission will always be externally driven, that is, conceived as an "extra" or a contribution to a neutral space which is already "given" (self-defining or defined by some other agency). As long as this is the case, then the need for a critical introspection which may reveal the church's *telos* to be an essentially social *telos* will never arise. Instead the church's relevance or significance, as well as her primary challenge, becomes one of devising "adequate" strategies or drawing relevant implications from its otherwise "religious" message to make both the state and the social sphere as a whole more nearly just.

But suppose the way in which the nation-state defines, narrates and frames the social sphere is itself the problem. Then the church is left with very little resources to challenge that narrative let alone provide an alternate definition, naming or conception of what it means to be socially located. This seems to be the case in Africa where the Christian churches find themselves caught up in an irony of importance and impotence: their massive presence notwithstanding, they have not become a formidable social force. The reason they have not, I suggest, has to do with their inability or failure to both challenge and provide an alternative to the story of the "social" realm which the nation-state in Africa embodies. The latter is a false story based on all sorts of lies and contradictions, particularly the violent suppression and exploitation of local aspirations and differences. It is in this connection that I see the African nation-states as an embodiment, and a tragic perpetuation, of the same story of dispossession, violence, and greed as the one depicted in Adam Hochschild's *King Leopold's Ghost*.

This is a very serious indictment of the nation-state which needs to be substantiated. I therefore need to look closely at the story embodied within the nation-state in Africa with a view of showing how and in what sense this story is false, and how, given its many contradictions, it has tended to inscribe the social order in Africa within an economy of ongoing violence and powerlessness. I do so by drawing attention to Davidson's work on the nation-state in Africa.[43]

---

43. Davidson, *Black Man's Burden*.

The Nation-State in Africa: On the Politics of Dispossession

The central thrust of Davidson's argument in *The Black Man's Burden* can easily be stated: Africa's crises of society derives from many upsets and conflicts. But the root problem seems to arise from "the social and political institutions within which decolonized Africans have lived and tried to survive. Primarily, this is a crisis of institutions."[44] More specifically, the crisis relates to the nation-state—"Europe's last gift to Africa"[45] whose introduction to Africa would be shrouded in myriads of ironic contradictions, none perhaps as frustrating to Africa's efforts towards peace and stability as the victory of the "national" struggle over the "social" struggle.[46]

One way in which Davidson develops this argument is by assembling, at various places in the text, helpful stories and discussions which provide a very interesting comparison of the process of nation-state formation in Europe with the African version of the same. One clear difference between the two is the role which local history—understood as the history of local struggles and aspirations—plays in each process. For example, Davidson recounts how the rise of nation-states in fifteenth- to sixteenth-century Europe would emerge out of the competing struggle of interests and ambitions, set within a shared history of customs, loyalties, and traditions. The "middle strata," as Davidson calls them,[47] would play a key role in this process, particularly in aligning their interests with the needs of the "laboring poor" and their hopes for a "better life" and fueling these into a sense of "nationalism" or "national consciousness" that would eventually find embodiment within the nation-state. As Davidson says,

> the rise of nationalism in its nineteenth-century context was the outcome of a combination of effort between the rising "middle classes" . . . and the multitudinous masses of the "lower orders" . . . Indispensable to nation-states success in all the

---

44. Ibid., 10.
45. Ibid., 188.
46. Ibid., 138.
47. Ibid., 135–38.

many upheavals of the nineteenth century . . . were the agitations and uprisings of peasants and urban workers.[48]

Whatever else one can say about the complexity and particular directions these agitations would take in the various European contexts—and Davidson provides helpful asides in this direction—the role of the *social* struggle is fore-grounded in the process that would eventually result in the nation-state as some kind of "supreme problem-solving formula"[49] within the European history of social existence. In any case, European nation-states are inconceivable except in terms of a *process* of transformation and adjustments within a local history, in which the social struggles would become the crucial factor, exerting, from below as it were, a force (nationalism) that would eventually shape and give legitimacy to the nation-state ideology.

It is precisely this bottom-top process—the valorization of local history and the social struggles it embodies as a force for nation-state formation—which is completely missing and which has been, from the very start, subverted within the story of the nation-state in Africa. One notices in the first place that whereas nation-state formation in Europe was a *process*, in Africa it became a *project* which both the departing colonialists and their nationalist-bourgeois successors would come to assume as inevitable for Africa's modernization and/or independence. But what is even more noteworthy is the fact that within this "peculiar chemistry of nation-state formation" as Davidson calls it, "the dynamic element which so decisively transformed the social struggle of the masses into the national struggle" was, on the whole, smuggled out of hearing.[50] In fact, the social struggle was not just smuggled out of hearing, but intentionally suppressed under the colonial lie of an "Africa without history"[51]—without, that is, any experience in social existence, customs, or traditions which could serve as a helping starting point in what was seen as an inevitable project of modernizing nation-statism.[52] Already under the colonial dispensation, and within the political and social anthropology that sustained it, but one that

48. Ibid., 134.
49. Ibid., 137.
50. Ibid., 159.
51. Ibid., 21–51.
52. Much of Davidson's work has been to show what a lie this is. See also Davidson, *Search for Africa*.

would remain greatly unchallenged much into the present time, all such local history would be de-valued into "folklore" while the rich wealth of cultures, traditions and social struggles would come to be branded as "tribalism," and "as such retrogressive."[53] As Davidson notes: "The diversity, it seemed, had to be just another hangover from an unregenerate past"[54] which would have to be superseded, and overcome, by the modernizing project of the nation-state.

Even though one may disagree with some of the assumptions that sustain Davidson's work,[55] his analysis of the factors that came into play in nation-state formation in Africa is highly instructive for locating the contradictions as well a source of many of the problems that would become endemic to African nation-states, thus frustrating Africa's social existence and stability. Five key ones stand out.

First, the fact that the nation-state was accepted as the "only available escape from colonial domination" helps somehow to explain the superficial character of African nation-states. Not founded on any enduring sense of historical adjustments within the local aspirations and struggles, the nation-state as well as other institutions of Africa's "independence" would evolve out of a void. They were, accordingly, bound to become "shell states,"[56] having juridical statehood, but not empirical statehood. This greatly explains why even today, as Gifford notes, "not a few countries in Africa are countries in a cartological sense only."

Secondly, Davidson's analysis also helps to show how a peculiar feature of Africa's politics is the way in which the national struggle remains alienated from the social struggle of the masses. Davidson traces

---

53. Chapter 4 is particularly telling on the invention of "tribalism" and the decisive role this invented notion would play in the purported and highly misleading debate between the "Modernizers" and the "Traditionalists" (or "tribalists").

54. Ibid., 99.

55. For instance, there seems to be an underlying positivism in Davidson's work, which seems to assume class structure, capitalism, the nation-state as the natural flow and final destiny of all social formations. His argument seems to suppose that left within their history, African forms of social existence would eventually have turned into nation-states similar to the ones in Europe (the case of Asante: which is "not peculiar" but only drawn on given its "dramatic clarity" [52–73]). Another problematic assumption by Davidson is the way in which he projects Enlightenment sociological views of religion upon African colonial history (religion as a sacred canopy to provide coercive force to independently originating social norms [81ff.]).

56. Ibid., 12.

this alienation back to the inherited colonial attitude towards Africa's pre-colonial past. By accepting the story which viewed Africa's pre-colonial history in terms of "tribalism" and stagnation, and committing themselves to "modernization and civilization, the 'new nationalists' who would become Africa's future leaders, accepted their own self-alienation as a necessary process of liberation."[57] But this would also mean that the "national" power which they sought and over which they would come to preside would stand in constant tension with the local history and social struggle of the masses, from which they had not only become alienated, but set out to overcome in the name of modernity and civilization. In other words (and the comparison with the European case is obvious), it would not be the struggle for the social improvement of the masses—Africa's "laboring poor"—which would be at the center of, or which would come to characterize, nationalist politics. On the contrary, "the competing interests of the 'elites' as they began to be called by sociologists and others, took primacy over the combined interests of the 'masses.' The 'social conflict' . . . was subordinated to the 'national conflict.'"[58]

Thirdly, and what would become a significant aspect of African politics, is the new exploitative relationship that would develop between nationalist politics, on the one hand, and the masses and their social struggles, on the other. For, as Davidson shows, lacking any social struggle in which it would be grounded, the nationalist rhetoric began to sound vacuous and self-serving. Once the nationalists realized this, they "discovered" that they needed the masses, and they took steps to recruit them:

> Having formed their parties of national liberation, the educated elite had to chase their [masses'] votes. And so they did, penetrating places never before seen, crossing rivers never before encountered, confronting languages never before learned, and all this with the help of local enthusiasts *somehow recruited*. They thus made contact with these "masses" quite often with only the assistance of aged Land Rovers able, with their four-wheeled drive, to go where no other vehicles had ever been, but only just able, and not seldom abandoned by the way.[59]

---

57. Ibid., 50.
58. Ibid., 112.
59. Ibid., 108. Emphasis added.

We need to dwell a little longer on the phrase "somehow recruited" for its significance for African politics even today. For, instead of being a force which shapes and determines the national debates, the masses and their aspirations are only belatedly "discovered" and only "somehow" recruited within the nationalist politics in an occasional, token, and exploitative manner. It could be, as it were, that the various "tribalisms" (in the sense of all local and particular social struggles)—once rejected and dismissed—would now be "discovered" to be potent political capital, to be exploited by the nationalists seeking political power. This factor alone explains the ambiguous role "tribalism" plays within African politics. Leaders openly declare "tribalism" to be the key enemy to national unity, and therefore vow to fight it. Ironically, however, without appealing to some kind of "tribal" loyalty, they would lack even the slight support they have. The "recruitment" also greatly explains how what develops out of this "discovery" of the masses is really not "the politics of tribalism, but something different and more divisive. This was the politics of clientelism."[60] However, except on these occasional "contact with the masses" in search of votes, the aspirations and social struggle of the masses are simply smuggled out of hearing, or censored out of sight. As Davidson notes in relation to the pre-independence nationalists: "Having won their national struggle as they thought, they completely forgot about all the social struggle."[61]

Fourthly, the "somehow recruited" is important from another angle as well, a lesson that Africa would learn soon after independence, when the "competing interests" of the nationalist elites would increasingly take a violent turn. This outcome should perhaps not be surprising since a political order founded on violence—in this case the denial, suppression and exploitation of local aspirations—would increasingly appeal to violence to affirm its legitimacy. In this sense, the colonial dispensation itself was sustained largely by its coercive sophistication. What, however, would become a distinct feature of the post-independence violence of military coups, civil and/or ethnic clashes was the fact that these were struggles between competing interests of the nationalist elites, in which once again the masses would get "somehow

---

60. Ibid., 206. Gifford, *African Christianity*, 1–20 too has noted this aspect of Africa's politics in reference to the authoritative work of Bayart (1993).

61. Ibid., 145.

recruited." Once again, the various "tribalisms" would become "useful" for providing the stronghold or bases of the violent schemes of the competing nationalist politicians. Again what develops here is really not a politics of tribalism, but an exploitation and recruitment of local differences at the service of the nationalists' struggles, turned violent. This is not to suggest that there was no violence in pre-colonial Africa, but one needs to see that the form of "pathological violence" prevalent in Africa today is incomprehensible without the particular history we have outlined above. Any attempt to abstract it from this particular story makes violence a bizarre cultural trait of Africans or, as it is often put: "one of the many things we don't understand about Africans."

The result of this endless cycle of violence in terms of destruction of life and property as well as the psychological impact and frustrations of local ideals cannot be overstated. A far more serious and long-term consequence, however, lies in the gradual naturalization of violence within the social order and within individual lives. For as the social order gets increasingly mired in violence, violence becomes so ingrained that the only way to deal with difference or to advance one's ideals is through violence. With the naturalization of violence, the menacing grip of King Leopold's ghost has come full circle, with the line between the ghost and its victims becoming increasingly blurred, and eventually lost.

The fifth and final point. The combined effect of this top-bottom trajectory within Africa's politics is to make obvious the sense in which the story embodied within the nation-state underwrites a sense of helplessness, disempowerment, de-valuation, indeed frustration of the everyday local struggles of the masses. I think it is quite true that the most damaging impact of colonialism in Africa was psychological: the freezing of Africa's history, and the erosion of her self-confidence. But to the extent that this same story is embodied and perpetuated within the nation-state, the latter has indeed become a burden—"the black man's burden" and even an "enemy"[62]—whose constraining grip and violence the "masses" would constantly have to survive in an attempt to advance their social struggles. In the final analysis, the critical issue arising out of this discussion is really not about the failures of the nation-state in Africa. The question is not so much one of what the nation-state has failed to do *for* Africans, but what it is doing *to*

62. Ibid., 9.

Africans—how it is narrating, defining and structuring their lives in terms of helplessness, dis-empowerment and violence.

In terms of *telos*, this means that everyday practices cease to have any meaningful *telos* to energize them into forms of commitment, precisely because they are defined or narrated by the overriding story in such a way that denies them of being capable of any *telos*. This is indeed dis-empowering and points to the need for alternative narratives which can radically challenge and even provide an alternative definition of everyday social struggles in view of energizing those activities within a hopeful *telos*. Without any such alternative, the majority of Africans will feel condemned to a wobbly existence where "survival" becomes their chief and perhaps only project.[63]

If this has been a long discussion, it has been worthwhile. For the story of the nation-state is rarely told, least of all from a theological point of view. As I noted earlier, Christian social ethics in Africa has simply accepted the nation-state, without ever looking at the story which informs the nation-state. The result has been that her greatest engagement with the social order has been limited to a challenge of offering suggestions aimed at making the nation-state more just or democratic. What these standard approaches may not realize is that by assuming the story of the nation-state, they unwittingly allow the church's own *telos* to be narrated and defined by this story. In this way, the church herself gets reduced to the space of the social—the "merely" social—to become part of the local/everyday history, which history, as per the nation-state story, does not really matter or has no *telos*. Perhaps this "placement" explains the irony of importance and impotence in which the church is caught up in Africa. For even as the "most influential and most sustainable social institution," the church has not become a "formidable weapon" of social transformation. It *cannot*, given the story above. For now reduced to the social space, the church, just like all the other "tribalisms" that make up this space, is regarded by the dominant story at once as "temporary nuisance" to be tolerated and as potential capital, to be "somehow recruited" into its ever expanding web of clientele politics. Accordingly, within this politics, the church is awarded all sorts of favors from the "right to

---

63. As William Sissane remarks in relation to Guinea, a remark that could be made in reference to much of post-independence politics. "Sekoure Toure's revolution has created there types of mutants: the flatters, the floaters, and the deflated" (Manthia, *In Search of Africa*, 50).

worship," tax exemptions, and all sorts of "facilitations" to ensure their "non-partisanship" publicly, and their support privately. The most unfortunate consequence of this "placement," however, is that once it has assumed the dominant story, the church's own existence and practices come to be increasingly marked by the same economy of hopelessness, despair and violence as other struggles within the everyday space. Nowhere is this disturbing reality more dramatically portrayed than in the story of bishop Bamwoze referenced in the second epigram at the start of this essay.[64]

Towards a Constructive Social Imagination

We need to return to the question which started off this inquiry in the first place. Can Christianity save Africans from King Leopold's ghost, that is, from the politics of dispossession, violence and powerlessness? If our analysis concerning the sort of practices and characters which the African nation-state engenders is correct, then any hope for salvation cannot assume the nation-state. Rather, it must come in terms of an alternative story capable of engendering new practices set within a *telos* of hopeful peace. No doubt, to many the claim of Christianity providing an "alternative" will sound like a dangerous form of theocracy—an attempt to establish some kind of Imperial Christendom of the European Middle ages. To view it in this way, however, is to still suppose something like a neutral social sphere out there (as a "given") to which either the state or the church can externally *impose* its narrative agenda or frames or reference.[65] The effect of our analysis has been to call into question this assumption of the social realm as a "given," and to show how it is constantly being narrated, framed and constructed in a particular way by the politics of the nation-state. While

---

64 The story is set in 1993 in the Anglican diocese of Busoga (Uganda) where the diocesan bishop Bamwoze was the center of controversy and leadership struggle. Gifford, *Christian Churches and the Democratization of Africa*, 126–27. If one thought that the church had more (or better) resources to conceive and deal with power and differences, that belief is shattered by the way in which Bamwoze's church based power struggle perfectly mirrors the same story of violence and intrigue as any nationalist power struggle. The biggest irony of course is that the onus would fall on the nation-state agencies, the police in particular to "pacify" the competing church-struggles!

65. For my more extended discussion on the category of "story" within politics and theology as an "alternative" story of "in the beginning," see Katongole, *Beyond Universal Reason*, 214–51.

this conclusion allows us to see the limitations and effects of the story embodied by the nation-state in Africa, an even more determinate effect is to challenge the church to re-think her own *telos* and the place of social formation within that *telos*. For once the social is not a "given" but rather in great part dependent on how different politics narrate or define it, then the most determinate task and challenge of theology becomes one of social imagination, i.e., one of imagining new and better ways of conceiving those everyday struggles and aspirations which lie at the basis of a people's social existence. In the remaining part of the essay, I will outline—a full fleshing out of this outline would be the task for another occasion—the direction which the theological task of social imagination needs to take.

Church as Social Mission

The first and primary task of social imagination must be to rethink the church's own *telos* in such a way that social formation is seen to be an integral, in fact, the core of that *telos*. Those familiar with the work of Stanley Hauerwas will, I am sure, recognize how much the above claim draws on his sustained argument to the effect that a social ethic lies at the heart of the church's existence and mission in the world.[66] To put it in this way might in fact still be misleading. For Hauerwas does not simply suggest that the church ought to contribute to social formation or transformation, but rather, that the church itself is social formation. This is to say, the church is not simply called upon to develop a relevant and effective social ethic; but to be a social ethic, which in effect provides an *alternative* to the story embodied within nation-state politics. As Hauerwas notes:

> The church does not exist to provide an ethos for democracy or any other form of social organization, but stands as a political alternative to every nation, witnessing to the kind of social life possible for those that have been formed by the story of Christ.[67]

---

66. This has been the central thrust of Hauerwas's constructive re-visioning of Christian social ethics. It is therefore difficult to give it a localized reference. Whereas his later work assumes this argument, it is in his earlier work that Hauerwas more explicitly states or argues this thesis. See particularly Hauerwas, *Community of Character*; *Peaceable Kingdom*.

67. Hauerwas, *Community of Character*, 12.

Whereas such a claim might sound extreme and even dangerous, it represents an attempt to shift the locus of the church's social mission from being the state or the world (outside there) to the church herself. This shift is made possible by a recognition that the church's own story involves—or rather is—a politics (a distinctive way of naming, narrating and framing what it means to be socially formed). In other words, the call to discipleship is not just a call to "believe" certain things about God, Christ, and the World, which beliefs might have social implications. It is a call for Christians to be socially formed in a distinctive way. But this formation is not an "extra" to what it means to be Christians. It is at the core of the call to discipleship. For without being so socially formed, Christians would not even know what it means to have the convictions they have, let alone to claim those convictions as true. In any event, once one has accepted that the Christian story is a politics, then the call for imagination is a call for the church to see that the story of the nation-state is not "inevitable." Instead, the church can (ought to) embody a different (better) narrative of social existence than the one embodied by the nation-state in Africa. Another way to underscore this alternative is to point to the embodied nature of social imagination.

Embodied Imagination

While the recommendation for an alternative *narrative* or *definition* may easily suggest an intellectual exercise, what actually is at stake is not just the framing of new doctrines or formulations, but the availability of an alternative set of practices. This is not to suggest a misleading dichotomy between doctrine and practice, but to insist on the embodied existence of the church as itself being the narrative. In other words, the alternative "story" the church provides cannot be separated from the social existence concretely and historically embodied by the church. Social imagination, as Hauerwas notes, is "not something we have in our minds. Rather, the imagination is a pattern of possibilities fostered within a community by the stories and correlative commitments that make it what it is."[68] The church is, or at least ought to be, such a community. This is what makes the question of mission and

---

68. Hauerwas, *Dispatches from the Front*, 179; Hauerwas, *Against the Nations*, 51–60.

social formation essentially an ecclesiological question—an inquiry into what it means to be the church, i.e., a people formed by the story of Christ's life, ministry, death and resurrection as contained in the scriptures and witnessed within various historical communities across time. It would, in this connection, be interesting to survey this ecclesiological dimension in relation to the classical claim of *extra ecclesiam nulla salus."* For our purposes here it simply means that for people living under the story of the nation-state in Africa there is no way for them to even know that there is another (hopeful) way of narrating their social struggles apart from the existence of communities who live by a different story of what it means to be socially formed. Accordingly, the most urgent task for the church in Africa is the building or realization of such local communities of hope, precisely because they have come to locate their social struggles and aspirations within a hopeful *telos*.[69]

Valorization of the Everyday

But what does this Christian *telos* concretely look like? At the risk of underwriting a misleading spiritual–material dichotomy, the embodiment referred to above sits very uneasily with the highly spiritualized or pietistic accounts of salvation characteristic of a great deal of African Christianity today. Instead, the social imagination envisioned will have to draw on those biblical narratives and early church tradition which portray salvation in terms of concrete and material expectations. Different from the banal sense in which the gospel serves to secure material rewards, the biblical narratives portray Jesus' life, cross and resurrection as the inauguration of the Kingdom of God—as a Kingdom of hope, peacefulness and forgiveness. In any event, it is a Kingdom whose site is "on this mountain," i.e., within the space of everyday social struggles and aspirations (Luke 4:16–21).

Accordingly, what the discussion in the previous chapter showed as lacking in Africa, and what the task of social imagination seeks to recover is a valorization of the daily struggles and the ability to re-energize these everyday struggles within the hopeful *telos* of the

---

69. It is in this respect that one can say that "the church does not have a social strategy; the church is a social strategy" (Hauerwas, *Dispatches From the Front*, 43).

Christian story. For, as J. M. Ela notes in a critical essay aimed at overly spiritualized accounts of salvation within African Catholicism:

> We must rediscover the gospel as a decisive force in history's march to the fore . . . the Kingdom of God (manifests itself) wherever the new universe is under construction—not a new world in the sense of a world-beyond, but in the sense of a different world right here, a world being gestated in the deeds of the everyday.[70]

If we must take this call seriously, especially in Africa where, as our analysis in Part III shows, the everyday is increasingly marked by an economy of hopelessness and violence, then the task of social imagination cannot be separated from a concern for the material production within those communities. There can be no blueprints for the form which such local communities can and will eventually take. But the call to social imagination seeks to realize communities in which the daily tasks of ploughing, harvesting, or pasturing—in which the cultivation of vegetables and the digging of wells, the immunization against malaria and the construction of pit latrines—is as much a matter of Christian salvation as the celebration of baptism, the Eucharist and the reading of the scriptures.

If this sounds like a utopian vision, it is because Christian imagination is always a call to realize and embody an utopian dream of the Kingdom of God. At any rate, the church is not without resources from which it can realize this imagination. Certainly not for Africa where "the church is one of the most sustainable social institutions, especially in the rural areas."[71] Unfortunately, it is here in the rural areas that the worst effects in terms of exploitation, dispossession and violence of the nation-state's story are felt. For the church so located, the realization of such local communities of energized social existence is at once an urgent but viable necessity. Whereas such communities cannot be a panacea to all Africa's problems, which are connected to many other global processes as well, they will at least provide African Christians not just with resources to name the violence and despair that is part of their daily lives, but also an alternative way to conceive and narrate their lives and ordinary struggles in a purposive manner. What an exciting possibility this will be. Not just for Africa, but for

70. Ela, *African Cry*, 53.
71. Mugambi, *From Liberation to Reconstruction*, 225.

the church as a whole, such communities will be an instructive experiment towards a novel understanding and exemplification of mission and social formation.

Bibliography

"Africa's Elusive Hope." *The Economist*, Feb 24–March 2, 2000.
Bayart, J. F. *The State of Africa: The Politics of the Belly*. London: Longman, 1993.
Bediako, Kwame. *Christianity in Africa: The Renewal of a Non-Western Religion*. Maryknoll, NY: Orbis, 1996.
———. "The Roots of African Theology." *International Bulletin of Missionary Research* 13 (1989) 58–65
———. *Theology and Identity: The Impact of Culture upon Christian Thought in the Second Century and in Modern Africa*. Oxford: Regnum, 1992.
Cochrane, J. R. *Circles of Dignity. Community Wisdom and Theological Reflection* Minneapolis: Fortress, 1995.
Davidson, Basil. *The Black Man's Burden: Africa and the Curse of the Nation-State*. Oxford: James Currey, 1992.
———. *The Search for Africa: A History in the Making*. Oxford: James Currey, 1994.
De Gruchy, John. *Christianity and Democracy*. Cambridge: Cambridge University Press, 1995.
Diawara, Manthia. *In Search of Africa*. Cambridge: Harvard University Press, 1998.
Ela, Jean Marc. *African Cry*. Maryknoll, NY: Orbis, 1986.
Gibellini, Rosino, editor. *Paths of African Theology*. Maryknoll, NY: Orbis, 1994.
Gifford, Paul. *African Christianity: Its Public Role*. Bloomington: Indiana University Press, 1998.
———. *The Christian Churches and the Democratization of Africa*. Leiden: Brill, 1995.
Hauerwas, Stanley. *Against the Nations. War and Survival in a Liberal State*. Notre Dame: University of Notre Dame Press, 1992.
———. *A Community of Character: Toward a Constructive Christian Social Ethic*. Notre Dame: Notre Dame University Press, 1981.
———. *Dispatches from the Front. Theological Engagements with the Secular*. Durham, NC: Duke University Press, 1994.
———. *The Peaceable Kingdom: A Primer in Christian Ethics*. Notre Dame: University of Notre Dame Press, 1983.
Hochschild, Adam. *King Leopold's Ghost*. New York: Mariner, 1998.
"The Hopeless Continent." *The Economist*, May 13–19, 2000.
John Paul II. Post-Synodal Exhortation *"Ecclesia in Africa."* Vatican City, 1995.
Kasfir, Nelson, editor. *Civil Society and Democracy in Africa: Critical Perspectives*. London: Frank Cass, 1998.
Katongole, Emmanuel. *Beyond Universal Reason: Questioning the Relation Between Ethics and Religion in the Work of Stanley Hauerwas*. Notre Dame: University of Notre Dame Press, 2000.
———. "Prospects of Ecclesia in Africa in the 21st Century." *Logos* 4 (2001) 179–96.
Maluleke, Tinyiko S. "Black and African Theologies in the New World Order: A Time to Drink From our Own Wells." *Journal of Theology for Southern Africa* 96 (1995) 3–19.
———. "Black Theology Lives! On a Permanent Crisis." *Journal of Theology for Southern Africa* 9 (1995) 1–30.

———. "Christianity in a Distressed Africa: A Time to Own and Own Up." *Missionalia* 26:3 (1995) 324–40.
———. "A Letter to Job from Africa." *Tam Tam* (September/October 1997) 5.
Maluleke, M. J. *Ximakwa Xo Ka' Meno*. Pretoria: J. L. van Schaik, 1998.
McCullum, Hugh. *The Angels Have Left Us: The Rwanda Tragedy and the Churches*. Geneva: WCC, 1995.
Milbank, John. *Theology and Social Theory: Beyond Secular Reason*. New York: Blackwell, 1990.
Mugambi, Jesse K. N. *From Liberation to Reconstruction: African Christian Theology After the Cold War*. Nairobi: East African Education, 1995.
Raushenbusch, Walter. *A Theology for the Social Gospel*. Nashville: Abingdon, 1945.
Troeltsch, Ernst. *The Social Teaching of the Christian Churches*. New York: Macmillan, 1931.
Villa Vicencio, Charles. *A Theology of Reconstruction: Nation-Building and Human Rights*. Cambridge: Cambridge University Press, 1992.
Weber, Max. *The Protestant Ethic and the Spirit of Capitalism*. London: Routledge, 1992.

2

The African Renaissance and Religion[1]

Elias K. Bongmba

ONE GREAT IDEA THAT HAS RECEIVED ATTENTION IN POSTNEOCOLOnial Africa is the African renaissance that has been championed by former South African President Thabo Mbeki.[2] The idea of a renaissance is more than a decade old now, but it still holds promise because African states have not made a complete recovery from the economic and political challenges they faced in the decades after independence. In this essay, I argue that civil society groups could strengthen the adoption and implementation of a renaissance in a more effective way because of their connection to the grassroots. In order to do this, I adopt a broad definition of civil society, which includes religious groups who will be the focus of this essay. I have argued elsewhere that civil society refers "to groups that have evolved in history as separate associations that are recognized by the state as spheres and articulations of privileges, freedoms and rights of individuals who also compete with other groups who share similar interests; all of which carry out their goals in dialogue or contestation with a constituted government."[3] Historically, those groups have defended private spaces

---

1. This essay draws from previous versions published in *The Journal of Southern African Studies* 30.2 (June 2004) 289–314, and also in *The Dialectics of Transformation in Africa* (New York: Palgrave McMillan, 2006).

2. The discussion of the African Renaissance here draws from and refers to some of my previous studies on the African Renaissance and gender studies. See Bongmba, "Reflections on Thabo Mbeki's African Renaissance," 289–314; *Dialectics of Transformation in Africa*.

3. Bongmba, *Dialectics of Transformation in Africa*, 95. This definition is adapted from Salvador Giner's definition in "Civil Society, and its Future," 304.

as important locations for members of the political community to act in promoting markets, private, as well as public issues which could promote the well being of the community. Civil society groups pursue their goals through negotiation and confrontation with the state and these strategies have often taken different forms in political communities as political and legal systems have grown and expanded.[4] In such negotiations and confrontations, civil society groups have attempted to curtail the totalization of human existence by an almighty state.[5] One must also note that civil society groups also establish relations of interdependence with groups that have similar interests, and when necessary collaborate with the state where such constructive engagements, rather than confrontation, might yield better results.[6]

I contend that civil society groups in Africa could play a key role in furthering and consolidating a renaissance. For the sake of this essay, I include religious communities and Faith Based Organizations (FBOs) as part of civil society. The discussion of the African renaissance that follows will be limited because I will focus mainly on religious groups and their leaders. This move does not jettison groups that are often considered civil society in the Hegelian sense such as trade unions, professional groups, but simply recognizes that in some African communities, religious communities have performed roles which under Hegelian formulation, were played by civil society groups; hence it is reasonable to expand the notion of civil society to include religious groups. I am aware that even such an inclusive grouping of civil society groups is not without its problems because some religious groups' have a history of uncivil actions that have led to catastrophic consequences for their societies. But possibilities exist for religious groups to play a more constructive role in reform agendas across the continent, and it is this possibility that makes it reasonable to consider religious groups part of civil society. I should also point out that in the African context, civil society also includes local ethnic development associations, old boys and old girls associations formed

---

4. Seligman, *Idea of Civil Society*; See Gellner, *Conditions of Liberty*; Hall, *Civil Society*; Cohen and Arato, *Civil Society and Political Theory*; Keane, *Democracy and Civil Society*; Przeworski, *Capitalism and Social Democracy*.

5. Markovitz, *Studies of Power and Class in Africa*, 10.

6. Sitoe has argued that regardless of how one looks at it, Africa's weak states still influence civil society and make room for it. See Sitoe, "State and Civil Society in Africa," 203–4.

to promote the interests of their former schools, FBOs, non governmental organizations (NGOs), and private voluntary organizations (PVOs). These groups play roles that are similar to what civil society groups are known to have played in Europe. Such a reclassification of civil society groups is necessary in the context of Africa. Jean and John Comaroff have argued: "until we leave behind stereotypic, idealized Euro-concepts, we foreclose the possibility of looking critically at either African or European civil society."[7] Furthermore, advocates of civil society in Africa cannot ignore its relationship to democracy and economic liberalization because a functioning civil society provides a social climate for democratic aspirations, freedoms, and the recognition of human rights.

The groups in this inclusive definition of civil society have a stake in promoting changes that are necessary to achieve recovery. The idea of a renaissance offers a long-term project for civil society groups to work on. It is therefore necessary that religious communities and their leaders reflect on the African renaissance in its current incarnation for two reasons. First, the idea of renaissance itself is pregnant with multiple meanings which, if explored, have linkages to religious metaphors. Secondly, Mbeki's call for a renaissance is expansive because it involves a reconfiguration of the socio political culture of the postneocolonial state. Changes in these areas would also require changes or a renaissance in religious life and its institutions.

The idea of a renaissance in Africa has etymological connections to religion and religious life. The English term, "renaissance" derives from the Italian term, *rinascere* that means "rebirth." Rebirth is also what Christians call "born again," and refers to a change of priorities and commitments in one's life. The Christian perspective on rebirth is based on the narrative in the Gospel According to John, chapter three, where Jesus tells a visitor that he must be born again in order to enter into the reign of God. Members of the Christian tradition argue that one can only establish a relationship with the divine through a connection with Jesus. The connection is often described as a new birth, or a born again experience. The idea of a new birth symbolizes the death of one's previous faith commitments and points to a new religious experience that is accompanied by an alignment with and adoption

---

7. John and Jean Comaroff. *Civil Society and the Political Imagination in Africa*, 23.

of the values of a new community. The full implication of the term being born again refers to taking new and Christian values, although in the past proselytizers have used the born again experience as a way of distancing new converts from their cultures. In the fullest expression of the term, to be born again is to be converted to a new way of life and becoming part of a faith community. I will not focus on this idea of rebirth or conversion, but discuss rebirth and renaissance as part of a broad change of priorities and obligations by political communities in Africa.

The idea of rebirth, or if we stay with the word renaissance, implies that something which existed is being transformed. The old may not necessarily be destroyed, but is reconstituted with new principles, priorities, and praxis. In the case of a political community, the institutions and structures of society may not change but its priorities ought to change for a rebirth to occur. In cases where the structures and the institutions have become ineffective, a rebirth might actually require the dismantling of old institutions and the creation of new institutions that would reflect new values. In both cases, rebirth occurs when previous priorities and in some cases institutions have died. If we stretch the metaphors a little bit here, rebirth could be seen as a violent act that displaces ideas and institutional frameworks that are outmoded. A renaissance then is a revolution that affects all sectors of society and marks the beginning of a new vision for a political community and its members. The religious life and institutions of a political community cannot ignore such a revolution. Religious establishments and institutions must be part of such a change and religious leaders have an obligation to work with other sectors of society in a critical dialogue to facilitate such a social rebirth.

The question at this point is how can religion facilitate or promote an African renaissance in the post afro-pessimism era? There are no easy or simple answers for this question. In order to highlight areas where religion could play an important role in the rebirth of the continent, it is necessary to examine the idea and the scope of the African Renaissance that Mbeki and others in South Africa have promoted. The idea of a renaissance appeared on the political landscape of Africa when Nelson Mandela referred to a change in a speech at the Organization of African Unity meeting in Tripoli.[8] It was Mbeki who

---

8. Several scholars have discussed the African Renaissance and some of them have presented the history of this debate in Africa. For discussion of the African renais-

as Deputy President provided the intellectual structure for the recent conception of an African Renaissance and made it part of his governing philosophy and a condition for the possibility of socio economic and political recovery in Africa. Mbeki made several speeches in which he announced and promoted the African renaissance. First, on May 18, 1995, Mbeki presented an inaugural address as Chancellor of the University of Transkei in Umtata in which he called on the university community to embrace the task of "safeguarding an accelerated as well as sustainable social, economic and cultural renaissance."[9] A year later, Mbeki projected the renaissance in his famous "I am an African" speech to the Constitutional Assembly of South Africa. On a visit to the United States in 1997, Mbeki spoke to the Corporate Council on Africa in Chantilly, Virginia, and argued that a renaissance was taking place in Africa. The evidence that a rebirth was taking place was the enormous transition that was going on in the new South Africa at that time, and a number of conflict resolution campaigns in Angola and The Democratic Republic of the Congo. Mbeki argued: "Those who have eyes to see, let them see. The African Renaissance is upon us. As we peer through the looking glass darkly, this may not be obvious. But it is upon us."[10] Besides these two examples, what else was taking place in Africa, which convinced Mbeki that a rebirth was occurring?

Mbeki further outlined aspects of the African Renaissance in different speeches. He pointed out that democratic transitions were taking place in Africa because Africans had finally rejected regimes that had a disappointing record on governance. He argued that Africans who have lived under tyranny now reject poor governance practices. Africans are rethinking their relationship to the rest of the world because they will not continue to live on charity because of political misrule. Africans have worked for liberation that included the emancipation of women and freedom from underdevelopment in order to end historical dependence on other nations. He expressed the hope

---

sance see, Bongmba, "Reflections on Thabo Mbeki's African Renaissance," 290–316.; Bongmba, *Dialectics of Transformation,* 106–22; van Kessel "In Search of An African Renaissance," 43; Maloka, "South African 'African Renaissance' Debate." See also Vale and Maseko "South Africa and The African Renaissance," 271–87; van Hensbroek, "Philosophies of African Renaissance," 129; Hollis, *Edward Wilmot Blyden*; Hollis, *Selected Letters of Edward Wilmot Blyden*; Mudimbe, *Invention of Africa.*

9. Mbeki, *Africa The Time has Come*, 38.

10. See Mbeki, "Africa's Time Has Come," 200–204.

that as this rebirth continues, many of the Africans in the diaspora would return home and contribute to the building of a new society. Mbeki called on the global community to contribute to these changes by investing in Africa to support economic reforms that would ensure stability, development, and economic growth in which African businesses would provide a stronghold for the economy, a role which was played in the past by foreign companies whose interest was merely to exploit the resources of the continent and take away their profits.[11]

I have argued elsewhere that Mbeki's call for a rebirth on the continent to counter negative growth and to do away with the indignities of the human condition in Africa was correct.[12] However, the conflicts he referred to did not end. While I endorse the renaissance project, it is clear that Mbeki painted a rosier picture because the conflicts in Eastern Congo did not end. Genocide was started and has continued in the Darfur region of Sudan; recently, conflicts erupted in Somalia, although the long struggle in Sierra Leone has finally ended. The democratic movements that Mbeki touted suffered a setback, and in many countries, even though multiparty elections were instituted, it is now clear that the new democratic transitions were still born. Zimbabwe has continued its political and economic decline, and even Mbeki himself has not been able to do anything about it, a situation that has made several of his critics suspicious of his renaissance agenda. Above all, a lack of political will and aggressive planning has turned Africa into the epicenter of the HIV/AIDS epidemic with Mbeki himself under attack for his controversial remarks and policies on fighting the disease. However, Mbeki and his supporters in South Africa continued to push the idea of rebirth and the African National Council (ANC) launched the African Renaissance Institute in 1999. The ANC also made the African Renaissance part of the governing philosophy.[13]

Mbeki's idea of an African Renaissance has received mixed reviews. Two African theologians have offered different assessments of Mbeki's renaissance project. First, Emmanuel Katongole has criticized the easy link between a renaissance and development, which as an

---

11. Mbeki, "African Renaissance." Mbeki also referred to the Cape Town Olympic bid, asking other African countries to support that bid, but the African delegates did not do so.

12. Bongmba, "Reflections on Thabo Mbeki's African Renaissance."

13. Maloka, "South African 'African Renaissance' Debate."

economic agenda, has had serious problems in Africa.[14] The heart of his criticism is that Mbeki's renaissance project was another way of imposing World Bank and International Monetary Fund neo liberal economic principles on Africa. He described these solutions as the type of solutions crafted in New York, Cape Town, and Kampala, which often ignore the needs of Africa, and for that reason these calls for a renaissance are "overpowering and totalizing" narratives."[15] Katongole has appealed to the narratives of the gospel where a rich individual, Zaccheus, who was accused of defrauding the people turned to Jesus and changed his fraudulent activities. Katongole uses this story to call on African theologians to raise their critical voices against corruption and neglect of the poor by African political elites, and engage in a critical social analysis of the situation on the continent. This appeal for a critical theology that searches for justice on the continent is right, but it is not a valid reason to reject the call for a renaissance. One should not exaggerate the differences here because it is clear that both President Mbeki and Katongole desire a just and humane society. Katongole has been instrumental in establishing a Center for Reconciliation at Duke University Divinity School, where Katongole teaches courses that address issues like the Rwandan Genocide, violence and theology, politics, and HIV/AIDS.[16] The purpose is to carry out the Apostle Paul's message that God is reconciling the world through Christ, and its focus on training new leaders who will carry out the message of reconciliation in a global climate is admirable and hopeful. A vision like this has opened the door for people around the world to address the kinds of problems that have led to the decline of the postneocolonial state and therefore it is very much in keeping with the spirit of an African, or we might call it a global renaissance. I can only note that the limitation of the project might be its Christocentric and church centeredness. Nevertheless, it is still an invaluable voice in a world of violence. However, such a constructive vision and voice does not warrant a rejection of the broad call for a rebirth and renewal in Africa where political corruption and injustice have caused untold sufferings. Nearly ten years after Mbeki called for a renaissance, I am

---

14. Katongole, "African Renaissance and the Challenge of Narrative Theology in Africa," 30.

15. Ibid., 32.

16. Online: http://www.divinity.duke.edu/reconciliation/pages/aboutus/index.html.

convinced that his broad agenda is still crucial for recovery in Africa today. I do not think one should dismiss it simply as the imposition of World Bank and IMF neoliberal policies on Africa.

The other African theologian who has responded to the call for a renaissance in Africa is John de Gruchy who has described Mbeki's call as: "visionary yet expressed in more sober terms than those which characterized the rhetoric of many leaders of African liberation."[17] De Gruchy has argued that the African church should respond to the renaissance in two ways. First, the Christian church should continue to play a priestly role through which it could provide support for "the moral, cultural and spiritual transformation of the continent, as well as the healing of its past memories and the reconciliation of communities and nations divided by ethnicities and war." Second, the Christian church also has a prophetic role to play. Its prophetic task if to check "[Mbeki's] vision of African renaissance, and especially its implementation, against the more radical vision of the reign of God with its insistence on justice, compassion and the humanization of life."[18] I share de Gruchy's sentiments on the African Renaissance because a rebirth is needed in many areas of public life in the African context to facilitate a recovery of our common humanity.

Besides theological perspectives, scholars in other fields have reflected on the African renaissance. Some have argued that the project is merely promoting South Africa as a giant in the region to which all of Africa has to turn. For example, Graham Evans has argued that Mbeki was elected on the basis of domestic policies, but he has also turned his attention to international issues and is promoting the renaissance to define ANC's policies and relationship with the rest of the continent.[19] Evans and other scholars have pointed out the controversies about South Africa's relationship with the rest of Africa because some people in South Africa think that the country would be better served if she cultivates a better relationship with the richer countries of the North than those of Sub-Saharan Africa. Other voices who have supported Mbeki's foreign policy goals have called for an emphasis on ethics as South Africa develops solidarity with the rest of Africa.[20]

17. de Gruchy, "Christian Witness at a Time of African Renaissance," 477.
18. Ibid.
19. Evans, "South Africa's Foreign Policy After Mandela," 621.
20. Ibid., 623.

The debate on the African Renaissance in South Africa is not surprising. It is also not surprising that others see it as an ideological project that is aimed at enhancing South Africa's standing in the region. Other critics have pointed out correctly that Mbeki needed to work hard to bring the Congress of South African Trade Unions (COSATU) on board the renaissance agenda. That is certain in articulating the need for an African Renaissance, Mbeki wants South Africa and the rest of Africa to be part of the global economy. In this regard, Mbeki has sent a strong signal that South Africa and the rest of the continent can grow and must work together to achieve sustainable economic growth.[21]

Mbeki's call for a renaissance is reasonable and religious communities can contribute to the actualization of a renaissance agenda. It is an opportunity for the African community to move beyond the blame game and take responsibility for what is happening now. I do not want to imply that ending the blame game erases historical memory of global events like colonization, the slave trade, or current imbalances in trade or global economic policies that have indebted Africans. Africans need to keep such historical memory alive, yet take responsibility for their own actions that have exacerbated hardships on the continent. Mbeki has called on Africans to avoid the pattern of letting outsiders poison their souls and detract them from their duty and responsibility to build the African state. In light of this, Mbeki has argued that forces within the African continent (meaning Africans themselves) have caused most of the problems that Africans face. Since most of the problems are home grown, Africans also could deploy homegrown solutions, drawing on the material, intellectual, cultural, and spiritual resources of the continent.

The question now is what can religious communities do to further the vision of a renaissance in Africa today? First, religious communities can contribute to a genuine renaissance by establishing a broad agenda for justice. A resolve by religious communities to work for justice promotes the Renaissance because central to Mbeki's ideals is the fact that a negative political culture has taken over political leaders and institutions in Africa and rendered the African states ineffec-

---

21. I have stated elsewhere that Evans has overstated his case, but I believe he is also correct in stating: "It is not, therefore, fanciful to interpret the African Renaissance idea as representing Thabo Mbeki's grand design to re-invent South Africa as a global trading state with strong regional and continental interests." Ibid., 627. See Bongmba, *Dialectics of Transformation*, 117.

tive. Such a condition has resulted in gross injustice against the people. Therefore, calling for a Renaissance was an invitation for Africans to envision and promote a new political culture that would indicate that politics involves more than establishing institutions and is an activity that seeks to address the conditions under which Africans live. Such a political culture is a liberative activity which works for new and concrete freedoms for women who are trapped under patriarchy, pays attention to the youths of the continent who have been abandoned in the wake of the collapse of the postneocolonial state, and establishes an open society. Mbeki's idea of an open society is a political community where people participate in the governing process. In addition, Mbeki called for the cultivation of many of the ideas that have been considered as part of a genuine recovery in Africa, such as the promotion of good governance, strengthening of the private economic sector, the development of social policies which would promote growth such as good education policies, paying attention to the health care system, housing, sanitation, clean water, etc. Accordingly, Mbeki called on Africans to reject corruption, inefficiency, and ineffective leaders whose only goal for serving in a public office was self-enrichment.[22] Mbeki stated, "I am certain that none of us present here will dispute the fact that the cancer of self-enrichment by corrupt means constitutes one of the factors which accounts for the underdevelopment and violent conflicts from which we seek to escape."[23] The restructuring of the political process and the establishments of operations that are devoid of theft, graft, and inefficiency, are all important ingredients in the rebirth of society.

These issues are important and deserve the attention of religious groups because African states cannot deliver social and economic justice in a society where corruption reigns. The African Renaissance agenda calls on all Africans to work for a concrete rebirth of ideas and values because such a change could facilitate the practice of justice. All religious communities in Africa would serve their communities and the rest of the continent well if they established a dialogue through which their leaders and people could address issues that have led to the breakdown of the economy, encouraged a political culture that

22. Mbeki, "On the African Renaissance," 5–10.
23. Ibid., 6.

is devoid of respect, and established a political economy that is controlled by a few elites.

In order to promote justice, it is important for religious leaders to promote African aspirations for a democratic society. Religious leaders in Africa have a long history of involvement in the question for justice that goes back to the colonial period when indigenous religious leaders like Kinjikitile, Islamic reformers like Sheikh Uthman Dan Fodio, and Christian leaders like John Chilembwe fought for justice. In different parts of Africa, Islamic movements like the *Mourides,* founded by Ahmadou Bamba, in 1927, the *Mahdist* Sudan, reform Islamic leaders in Morocco, all worked in different ways for a just society. Religious communities and their leaders actively fought against racial discrimination and the Unilateral Declaration of Independence (UDI) in former Southern Rhodesia, now Zimbabwe. Religious communities and theologians fought against apartheid in South Africa, to the extent that one could argue that South African theology in the past millennium was a quest for justice in an apartheid society. Religious leaders played a crucial role to encourage dialogue and national reconciliation during the period of the democracy movement that emerged in response to the collapse of the postneocolonial state.[24] Although Pierre Titi Nwel of Cameroon has pointed out that some of the members of the clergy were not prepared for this new role, it is evident that where they were involved, they helped establish dialogue and pave the way for political competition.[25] Religious leaders in Mozambique promoted talks that led to conversations between Renamo rebels and President Joachim Chissano's government and the establishment of a Peace and Reconciliation Commission chaired by the Reverend Lebombo Dinis Sengulane, the Anglican Bishop of Maputu.[26]

In addition to facilitating this constructive dialogue as part of a quest for justice, religious communities have given room for members of the public to engage in critical dialogue with the state. Alice Lakwena's Holy Spirit Movement in Uganda started as a critical voice

24 For this section, I have taken some of the materials from Bongmba, *Dialectics of Transformation*, chapter 7. For a discussion of the role of Religious leaders, especially Catholic clergy, see Eboussi-Boulaga, *Christianity Without Fetishes*; See also his article in *Jeane Afrique,* June 26–July 10, 1991, 16–25.

25. Nwel, "Churches and Democratic Upheaval," 171, 178.

26. Paul Gifford edited a book on the contribution of churches to democracy in Africa. See Vines and Wilson, "Churches and the Peace Process in Mozambique," 138.

for the Ugandan state. The movement unfortunately decided to carry out a brutal war, but it offered a space for protest.[27] South African theologian Charles Villa-Vicencio in a rhetorical question about why protesters turn to religious symbols has asked: "Could it have something to do with the depth of the sense of marginalization and alienation experienced by the historic poor? Historic and enduring, impacting on the body, limb and soul, with implications for social identity, human meaning and what is left of hope, the cry is from and to the very ground of being itself. It is a cry to the most essential sources of life—the ancestors, the spirits, the soil, tradition and the gods."[28] The space created by religious communities for people to raise their voices against tyranny is crucial and also could be used for dialogue on rebirth of social and political life in Africa. It is unfortunate that rather than talk openly about power abuse, some religious groups have undermined critical dialogue in the spaces which religious communities provide by endorsing politicians who have dominated their people and compromised their freedoms. A glaring example was the tacit support and blessing given to the regime of Daniel Arap Moi by the Redeemed Gospel Church, whose leaders described President Moi as a "God-fearing man."[29] By doing this, these leaders limited the space available in their religious community for protest against Moi's regime that was accused of committing human rights violations and promoting ethnic violence. In order to keep open spaces for dialogue and promote rebirth, religious communities might need a renaissance within their own communities to get rid of violence, which in many contexts have actually contributed to the destabilization of the postneocolonial state. The dispute on the sharia has taken many lives in Nigeria and Sudan. The negative and deadly role played by some religious leaders during the Rwandan genocide has been well documented.[30] Despite the fact that people have used religion to foment conflicts and cause undue sufferings to others, I am still convinced that religious communities and their leaders could work to end violence and use their space to cultivate peace, and organize peacebuilding activities.[31]

27. See Behrend, *Alice Lakwena and the Holy Spirits War in Northern Uganda*.

28. Quoted in Bongmba, "Reflections on Thabo Mbeki's African Renaissance," 173.

29. Gifford, *Christian Churches and the Democratisation of Africa*, 4.

30. See Longman "Christianity and Crisis in Rwanda."

31. Bayart, "La Function Politique des Eglise au Cameroon," 514–36.

What I am suggesting is that the fight for justice by religious communities could call attention to management errors; it could also be a struggle to introduce a new spirit, new priorities and a new way of conducting state and public business. I know that one cannot always be under the illusion that religious communities would always do this. As I indicated earlier, some religious communities also have contributed to the problems in Africa. Some people have employed religious ideas and institutions to promote their own ambitions and in so doing create chaos. This is not an activity that is unique to Africa, but Africans must ask themselves if they want to imitate any wrong thing that takes place in other parts of the world. Describing the conflicts that have taken place between Christians and Muslims in Nigeria, Bishop Matthew H. Kukah, has argued: "the religious question . . . is now the single greatest threat to the existence of the Nigerian state."[32] The situation he decries has come about because religion and religious leaders have failed to promote a change and rebirth on the continent. Other religious leaders have courted the support of politicians and for that reason, lost the moral will to criticize those politicians. Some religious leaders have followed the examples of politicians by using their offices for self-aggrandizement and embourgiousiement. I interviewed a school teacher in Cameroon who stated that some church leaders and leaders of church schools also take bribes and do the same illegal things politicians do.[33]

In places where there is a revival of indigenous religious beliefs, like the Mungiki in Kenya, scholars have pointed to a non-progressive agenda that could have dire consequences for justice and attainment of a renaissance. This particular movement has tried to revive traditional culture and act as a cultural police that encourages and enforces practices like female genital cutting, the singing of traditional music, and wearing of dread locks. Some of their members have attacked women for wearing trousers, although they claimed that they were out to fight

---

32. See Kukah, "Religion, Ethnicity and the Politics of Constitutionalism in Africa." I am indebted to Rosalind Hackett for this quotation. Quotation taken from Rosalind I. J. Hackett, "Prophets, "False prophets," and the African State," 151–78, 152.

33. This conversation took place at Bamenda, Northwest Province of Cameroon. See also Bayart, "La Function Politique des Eglise au Cameroon"; Gifford, *Christian Churches and the Democratisation of Africa*, especially see his discussion of the Catholic church and development in Uganda; Mbembe, *Afriques Indociles*, 96; Hayness, *Religion and Politics in Africa*, See especially chapters 5, 6, and 7

against the regime of Moi which abets poverty, insecurity, killings and social instability."³⁴ My point here is that it is going to take serious thought and purposeful action on the part of religious communities to think in a constructive manner and promote a renaissance because of their participation in conflicts. I have focused on the search for justice because socio-political and economic neglect reflects a policy of selfishness and corruption that can only be eliminated by the introduction of new thinking and new actions. Maintaining an active struggle for justice then is one way of promoting new values and rebirth.

Outside the religious community, it is ironic that rather than enhance growth and development, economic resources in many parts of Africa have been used to fuel conflict. For example, the rich deposits of diamonds and oil that brought about $5 billion in annual revenues supported the civil war in Angola that displaced an estimated 1.5 million people and caused an estimated 330,000 people to leave the country.³⁵ There is enormous literature now on blood diamonds, and the use of a country's resources to fund violence has been well documented in the literature on civil strife on the continent. I agree that conflicts pose a threat to the renaissance agenda but it would be a mistake to reject Mbeki's call for a renaissance.

While the renaissance implies big ideas such political and economic liberalization, it is also an invitation for leaders to develop values that would cultivate the common good. Mbeki has argued that, "an enormous challenge faces all of us to do everything we can to contribute to the recovery of African pride, the confidence in ourselves that we can succeed as well as any other in building a humane and prosperous society."³⁶ According to Mbeki, centuries of denial and abuse of black humanity has taken its toll on Africa. Africans must use all resources including the arts to get rid of this subservience. In this process, intellectuals have a key role to ensure that they articulate the issues well because the African renaissance involves, "the education organization, and energization of new African patriots who, because

---

34. "Exposed, Terror Gang of Kayole"; Mwai, "What Makes Mungiki Tick?"

35. Anstee, *Orphan of the Cold War*; see also Reno, *Warlord Politics and African States*; Chabal and Daloz, *African Works*.

36. Ibid., 10.

to them yesterday is a foreign country, join in the struggle to bring about an African Renaissance in all its elements."[37]

Second, religious communities could champion the African renaissance by promoting cultural revival and transformation. African communities have a rich cultural heritage that has survived the assault of colonial encounters, religious attacks, and globalization. In the context of a renaissance as articulated by Mbeki, one could start working on cultural revival and transformation by examining his notion of an African. Mbeki's idea of an African is stated in light of the complex identities that are found on the continent today. In his "I am an African" speech, Mbeki highlights a plural identity for Africa. I have argued elsewhere that this search for an African identity cannot simply be taken to mean a black identity or that the South African was promoting a new version of black nationalism, although many Africans have to come to terms with the idea of blackness if a renaissance is going to succeed.[38] Mbeki, like other African thinkers, has called for a revival of African identity which one could say was instrumental in building the African civilization. Africans also have demonstrated a sense of identity through movements like Pan-Africanism, the Garvey Movement, Négritude, Black Power, and Black is Beautiful.[39] These identities have been shaped by the many cultures and cultural values on the continent. Promoting rebirth calls for a cultural retrieval and a respect for the rich cultures of Africa. It must promote a diversity of values and goals. To talk of individual identity that is rooted in culture requires, for example, taking seriously cultures like the Wimbum culture, Yoruba culture, Zulu culture, Akamba culture, Semitic cultures, and White cultures because many of these people call Africa home. Here religious communities can play a crucial role. For example, members of different religious communities need to study in a new way what it means to be Wimbum, or Gikuyu and Christian. African religious leaders need to work out carefully what it means to Yoruba and Muslim or Zulu and Jewish. These are not easy issues to resolve, but they call for a dialogue and in such a conversation one would hope that religious communities would continue to be sensitive to the cultural values of the

---

37. Ibid.

38. Bongmba, *Dialectics of Transformation*.

39. Vale and Maseko rightly point out that Mbeki links reconstruction in *Africa with African Identity*, 278.

people on the continent. One would assume that this is obvious, but in some communities, religious leaders have asked members of their communities to stop participating in their traditional dances which involves masquerading. For example, I have attended funerals in the Wimbum area where religious leaders have prohibited mourners from singing non Christian songs. They also have prohibited masks from closed association such as *nwarong,* society, a regulatory institution found in many Wimbum villages and most of the Northwest Province of Cameroon, from performing on grounds that these things are pagan activities. Many of the new Pentecostal churches in Africa and in the African diaspora, now constantly criticize and reject aspects of African culture which they refer to in a derogative manner as "ancestral curses." I do not think that promoting a renaissance would succeed if Africans do not celebrate their cultures.

Perhaps one area where cultural practices often come into conflict with human dignity is in the area of gender roles. Gender disparities exist in many African communities and very often, some people defend these disparities as "African culture." What some people refer to as African culture simply means something that many people in different communities have carried on a particular practice for a long time. Sometimes people call certain things cultural because there are no prohibitions against it, or it is allowed in that culture. A good example of this is the practice of polygyny, also called polygamy. The practice of polygyny is a highly contested practice and religious communities, especially Christian communities, have not had a very good record of dealing with it.

Gender division of labor exists, and many women do not have the economic power they need. In the postneocolonial state, women have not had the same access to power and resources that men have had. There are signs of hope now that the number of women being elected to parliament is growing. One also hopes that with the election of Ellen Johnson-Sirleaf as the first female president in Liberia, a new partnership in politics will begin. Religious communities face a daunting task here because some religious groups do not support the ordination of women or accept women to be leaders in the church. Those communities have endorsed a social and religious conservative culture that has limited the role of women to the domestic sphere. A rebirth in society and the entire political community can only take place if women are free as human beings to participate in all aspects of life in the community. One of the religious groups in Africa that pays attention to these disparities is The Circle of Concerned African Women Theologians. Members of the Circle in numerous publications have highlighted gender disparities in the home, local communities and in political life across the continent.[40] The Circle's journal *AMKA* (a Swahili word that means arise) is a call for women to arise and assume and take responsibility. The Circle has employed cultural hermeneutics to probe religious texts and religious traditions in the context of women's lives in a local, as well as global context.[41] Members of the Circle have been engaged in a renaissance because they speak out frequently on culture, rituals, and religious issues from the perspective of women in Africa.[42] They promote a rebirth of thinking about women that is crucial for any reform or renaissance.[43]

It is important to point out here that it would be unwise to declare war against African culture because that could undercut attempts at reforms. However, aspects of culture call for serious thinking in light of present exigencies. It is no doubt now that some initiation rituals which are vital to life cycle transitions in different communities, have been called into question for a very long time because of the risk present to participants. Many people consider female genital cutting a highly problematic cultural ritual because of the dangers it presents to the young females. The fight against this practice in Kenya might have gotten a wrong start because Christian missionaries did not hold the type of dialogue necessary to end the practice. Today the struggle to end female genital cutting is being mounted on a number of fronts including an active critique of the ritual by African women, international organizations, and legal instruments around the world. Prior to his death, the distinguished Senegalese novelist and filmmaker,

---

40. Oduyoye and Kanyoro, *Will to Arise*.

41. Oduyoye, "Spirituality of Resistance and Reconstruction," 169.

42. For a bibliography of publications by members of the Circle, see Pemberton, *Circle Thinking*.

43. Hodgson and McCurdy, *'Wicked' Women and the Refiguration of Gender in Africa*; Ifi Amadiume, *Male Daughters, Female Husbands*; Chukwuma, *Accents in the African Novel*; Davies, "Introduction," in *Ngambika: Studies of Women in African Literature*; Nnaemeka, *Sisterhood, Feminism, and Power*; Olu Obafemi, *Towards Feminist Aesthetics in Nigeria*; Ogundipe-Leslie, *Re-Creating Ourselves*.

Ousmane Sembene, turned his attention to the struggle to end female genital cutting and made the film *moolade*.

The other cultural practice that has also been called into question by many women groups and religious leaders is widowhood rites. These rites have been the subject of several studies because many of the things done to a widow are inhumane, and have no bearing to culture. Leading these studies was a theological study by a Roman Catholic Missionary in East Africa, Michael Kirwen, titled *African Widows*.[44] Other works that followed include *Widows in African Societies*, edited by Betty Potash in 1986.[45] More than 10 years ago, Kenda Beatrice Mutongi carried out doctoral research on the subject titled, "Generations of Grief and Grievances: A History of Widows and Widowhood in Maragoli, Western Kenya, 1900 to Present."[46] Kirwen's study was a theological critique of the failure of the Catholic Church to take local culture seriously and as a result, he endorsed widow inheritance which has also become very controversial, especially in a world where HIV/AIDS has become the leading cause of death. The other books, as well as recent discussions of the status of a widow in some African communities, call attention to serious problems with the practice.

African women are critical of the fact that widows are often suspected to have used witchcraft to cause the death of their spouses. Women also are critical of rituals which make them stay at home, and go to extremes to mourn for their husbands. In many cases the time spent in extended mourning, which also includes prohibition from engaging in any productive work or attending a market, causes economic hardship on the woman who in some cases, also must provide the resources needed for the various celebrations of her husband's death. Perhaps the most egregious practice is the belief and practice that permits members of the deceased husband's family to take away everything the late husband owned including houses, land, and bank account. This renders the widow poor and compromises her ability to survive and raise the family with whom she is left. In such circum-

---

44. Kirwen, *African Widows*.

45. Potash, *Widows in African Societies*.

46. Mutongi, "Generations of Grief and Grievances"; see also Mutongi, *Worries of the Heart*.

stances, the set-back is experienced not by the widow alone, but by the children who must now struggle to support themselves.

Kirwen's study is critical of Roman Catholic missionaries for condemning levirate marriage. At the death of a husband in the Lou community, the woman can enter a levirate union with a relative of the husband or return to her relatives. If she chooses the second option, then her parents must return the bride wealth to the husband's family.[47] African church leaders who support levirate marriages argue that such a marriage ensures that some will care for the widow and she will continue to have children. However, they stress that the widow's sexual needs are not the primary concern.[48] Kirwen points out that at the heart of the leviratic system is the notion that the woman is still married to her deceased husband who still influences her life.[49] Among the Kwaya, if the widow and the levirate husband love each other, he can take care of her as his own wife. The implication here is that such a loving relationship may not be common practice. Inheritance has not always solved the problems of widows because in many cases, the relatives who inherited the widow do not always provide for her needs and the needs of the children. Besides the question of support, decisions about inheritance, in many cases, are made without consulting the widow, who is often considered property of the family because her bride wealth was paid.

These and other practices which set women back in the African community ought to be studied by religious groups as they search for ways of revitalizing the community. A genuine rebirth of culture and humane values, which strengthens Africans and their community today, requires that those cultural practices which pose a challenge to the realization of one's humanity should be changed. In the case of Christian churches in Africa, it is good to point out the recent developments in biblical interpretation favors looking for ideas and meanings in the texts that would empower and transform the widows, rather than continue to encourage them to go through rituals that have no meaning for their lives today.[50]

---

47. Ibid., 30.
48. Ibid., 11.
49. Ibid., 35–36.
50. See Dube, *Other Ways of Reading*; Dube, *Postcolonial Feminist Interpretation of the Bible*; Sugirtharajah, *Asian Biblical Hermeneutics and Postcolonialism*, 22–23.

Thirdly, religious communities can contribute to the African Renaissance by supporting a humanistic agenda. Supporters of Mbeki's call in South Africa have argued that The African Renaissance calls for the expression of ubuntu values.[51] Scholars and cultural leaders who have conceptualized ubuntu in South Africa have pointed out that it reflects African values such as community, humanity, or a humane way of living and relating to other people. These values are important to religious communities and their leaders especially when some religious traditions claim that humanity is created in the image of God.[52] Ubuntu is helpful because in raising our awareness of the community, the idea also points to the importance of the individual and his or her responsibility in the community. Political leaders in South Africa have incorporated the idea of ubuntu into the social and professional lives of people. "The Principle of caring for each other's well-being ... and a spirit of mutual support... Each individual's humanity is ideally expressed through his or her relationship with others and theirs in turn through recognition of the individual's humanity. Ubuntu means that people are people through other people. It also acknowledges both the rights and the responsibilities of every citizen in promoting individual and societal well-being."[53] Encouraging ubuntu values certainly is one of the ways to counter what Mbeki in his speeches has called the negative psychology which Africans have inherited from the colonial rhetoric which emphasized that Africans were not capable of governing themselves or doing anything to help themselves. Ironically, French President Nicolas Sarkozy has never abandoned this view of Africans, if one considers his recent address to students and faculty at the university in Dakar, Senegal. One of the great ironies of Mbeki's thought is that after that speech which was condemned by Africans, Mbeki wrote a very conciliatory letter to the French President, calling him a friend of Africa. It might be Mbeki took that action because Sarkozy also called for a change of values, and Mbeki identifies with such a call for change. However, observers did not see anything humane in Sarkozy's speech.

---

51. The literature on ubuntu is growing. The journal *Quest* XV.1–2 (2001) has a bibliography of works on the African renaissance and the concept "ubuntu" 145–53.

52. I have discussed the notion of the image of God (*imago dei*) in a recent publication of HIV/AIDS. See Bongmba, *Facing a Pandemic*. See particularly chapter 2.

53. See online: http://www.gov.za/whitepaper/index.html.

While it would be false to claim that religious community has a monopoly on what it means to be created in the image of God, or live according to humane principles, it is crucial that religious communities that have great influence on people in Africa today promote this concept to recapture a human spirit that has been destroyed by the negative political praxis of the postneocolonial state. Beyond the individual level, religious communities could work with other organizations and leaders of their political communities to apply an ubuntu ethic on the continent to help stem the tide of violence. Where violence exists already, a humanistic approach requires that the resources of the community be used to find peace and encourage a peaceful coexistence.

One way in which religious communities could promote the values of ubuntu in the quest for a rebirth of the African community is for religious communities to call for a new way of understanding and providing health care in Africa. Health and physical wellbeing have always been a concern for religious communities in Africa. The concern for good health was one of the contributing factors to the rise in African Initiated Churches (AIC). African therapeutic and medical systems existed and provided health care to people, although these systems were disparaged by Colonial and missionary medical practice. Missionary organizations that sent workers to Africa also sent out medical missionaries who catered for the health of the missionaries and the communities they served.[54] In Africa, Baptists established medial work in the Congo, The Universities Christian Missions established medical work in 1885, the CMS sent Hartord-Battersby as a missionary doctor to Nigeria; The London Missionary Society (LMS) established medical work in South Africa; and the North American Baptist General Conference started missionary work in Cameroon in 1938.[55] Although the term medical missionary is obsolete today, many of the institutions that were established remain today and in many African countries remain the only places where good biomedical care is available. A recent study by James Cochrane and an international team of researchers, titled *Religious Health Assets*, has demonstrated

---

54. Moorshead, *Heal the Sick*, 28.

55. Lewis, "Medicine at Molepolole." See also Etherington, "Missionary Doctors and African Healers," 77–92; Tih, *History of the Cameroon Baptist Convention Health Board*.

that religious communities in Africa have available to them a huge amount of health assets that are sometimes underutilized.[56] It is important to point out that not every community in Africa has a religious health care institution. However, the ones that do, have an opportunity to use those facilities to provide healthcare and also begin a national conversation on significant ways to rebuild our common humanity at a time when the image of God has been compromised by infectious diseases like HIV/AIDS. The late Steve de Gruchy of the University of Kwa Zulu Natal called on religious communities to be involved in public health and take an active part in addressing the pain and suffering brought about the HIV/AIDS and other infectious diseases. He argued that in doing so, religious communities would be learning to speak its mother tongue, meaning returning to some of its core values.[57]

This is particularly important for religious communities in Africa today because HIV/AIDS involves all aspects of life and continues to spread. The spread of the virus is facilitated by numerous social, political and economic forces such as poverty, marginalization and domination of women, abuse of young girls, discrimination and stigmatization, a holier than thou attitude from some religious communities, neglect and lack of political leadership, and the lack of resources and drugs to combat the disease. In some cases the fight against the disease has been hampered by political and scientific debates which have drawn on leaders like President Mbeki, the champion of the African Renaissance. While he might indeed be one of the few politicians in Africa who committed resources to addressing the pandemic, he also sent many wrong signals by questioning the link between HIV and clinical AIDS. President Mbeki's debates about the toxicity of antiretroviral drugs delayed treatment for many people. With millions infected, it seems to me that there is no more humane agenda for religious communities in Africa today than to engage in the fight against HIV/AIDS.

Finally, religious communities also can contribute to the African Renaissance by revitalizing scholarship, especially religious scholarship on the African continent. In his discussion of the African Renaissance, South African philosopher Anto van Nierkerk has pointed out that the European Renaissance which placed emphasis on the

---

56. African Religious Health Assets Programme, *Appreciating Assets*.
57. de Gruchy, "Relearning our Mother Tongue?"

worth of the human being also promoted the studies of the humanities.[58] Religious communities, especially communities which have an educational program on the continent, would do well to promote not only the humanities, but also to consider seriously the study of the sciences in Africa today. There was a time when many people felt that religious organizations had no business in education, and some governments like the military regime of General Murtala Mohammad of Nigeria, actually nationalized education. If we have learned anything from the decline of the state in the postneocolonial state, it is the fact that no state in Africa is self-sufficient to the extent that it can provide the educational needs of all its citizens. There is room for religious communities to contribute to the education of the citizenry and the training of future citizens and leaders. Such education ought to be open to all members of the political community regardless of religious affiliation. The educational institutions run by religious communities should not be a venue for proselytization or a place where undue religious expectations are placed on students. These religious institutions should foster the humanities in the hope that students will continue to be fascinated by disciplines that give them an opportunity to explore human values and human institutions. However, it is important that a rigorous scientific education should continue to receive emphasis in these institutions. In South Africa, concerned scientists have called for a rigorous scientific inquiry, pointing out that Africa cannot afford to sacrifice scientific research.[59] Unfortunately, scientific studies have been compromised in many African countries because of the lack of resources. We face a situation in Africa today where most of the continent's scientists have moved to other countries, not merely because of money, but because the regimes have failed to establish a humane environment for them to live and do their work. It seems to me that today the most pressing question in education in Africa is how do African communities restore the desire for and drive for basic research in a robust liberal arts education where the arts and sciences are promoted with equal rigor? The answer to this question would depend on how much resources religious communities today are willing to put

---

58. van Niekerk, "The African Renaissance."

59. See the essay by Alexander, "African Renaissance or Descent into Anarchy?" 423–26.

into the revitalization of education in order to encourage the rebirth of the continent.

In closing, I do not imply that the study of religion is unimportant. The modern study of African religions was launched at the University of Ibadan in Nigeria with Geoffrey Parinder as professor. Religious studies continue to thrive in South Africa, Botswana, and Ghana. However, many scholars are working against all odds to keep religious studies alive in Kenyan, Nigerian, Ethiopian, and Cameroonian universities, to mention only a few places. Religious communities have a responsibility to open up dialogue with government leaders and private donors, and to cultivate a new interest in religious studies. This could go a long way in promoting change on the continent. Such scholarship should build on current curriculum, but expand it to study indigenous religious life in all parts of the continent, as well as study Christian and Islamic traditions throughout the continent. Some of the most untapped resources for religious studies on the continent might still be hidden in the ancient manuscript of Timbuktu. In addition, many in Africa have very little knowledge of Egyptian and Ethiopian Christianities that have left enormous documentation. A new renaissance in religious studies requires that African communities seek ways of accessing the knowledge and intellectual values that were developed by the religious communities, especially Timbuktu and Ethiopia.

Bibliography

African Religious Health Assets Programme, *Appreciating Assets: The Contribution of Religion to Universal Access in Africa*. Cape Town: ARHAP, commissioned by the World Health Organization, 2006.

Alexander, W. J. R. "African Renaissance or Descent into Anarchy?" *South African Journal of Science* 95:10 (1999) 423–26.

Amadiume, Ifi. *Male Daughters, Female Husbands: Gender and Sex in an African Society*. 7th ed. London: Zed, 1997.

Amba Oduyoye, Mercy, and Musimbi R. A. Kanyoro, editors. "Spirituality of Resistance and Reconstruction." In *Women Resisting Violence: Spirituality for Life*, edited by M. J. Mananzan, M. A. Oduyoye et al. Maryknoll, NY: Orbis.

———. *The Will to Arise: Women, Tradition and the Church in Africa*. Maryknoll, NY: Orbis, 1992.

Anstee, M. J. *Orphan of the Cold War: The Inside Story of the Collapse of the Angolan Peace Process, 1992–93*. Basingstoke: Macmillan, 1996.

Bayart, Jean François. *The State in Africa: The Politics of the Belly*. London: Longman, 1993.

———. "La Function Politique des Eglise au Cameroon." *Revue Française de Science Politique* 3 (1973) 514–36.

Behrend, Heike. *Alice Lakwena and the Holy Spirits War in Northern Uganda 1985–97*. Translated by Mitch Cohen. Oxford: James Currey, 1999.

Bongmba, Elias K. *The Dialectics of Transformation in Africa*. New York: Palgrave Macmillan, 2006.

———. *Facing a Pandemic: The African Church and Crisis of Aids*. Waco, TX: Baylor University Press, 2007.

———. "Reflections on Thabo Mbeki's African Renaissance." *Journal of Southern African Studies* 30:2 (2005) 289–314.

Chabal, Patrick, and Jean-Pascal Daloz. *African Works: Disorder as Political Instrument*. Oxford: James Currey, 1999.

Chukwuma, Helen. *Accents in Nigerian Novel*, Enuga, Nigeria: New Generation, 1991.

Davies, Carole Boyce. "Introduction: Feminist consciousness and African Literary Criticism." In *Ngambika: Studies of Women in African Literature*, edited by C. B. Davies and Anne Adams Graves, 6–22. Trenton, NJ: Africa World, 1986.

Cohen, Jean L., and Andrew Arato. *Civil Society and Political Theory*, Cambridge, MA: MIT Press, 1992.

Comaroff, John and Jean. *Civil Society and the Political Imagination in Africa: Critical Perspectives*. Chicago: University of Chicago Press, 1999.

de Gruchy, John W. "Christian Witness at a Time of African Renaissance." *The Ecumenical Review* 49 (1997) 476–82.

de Gruchy, Steve. "Relearning our Mother Tongue? Theology in Dialogue with Public Health." In *Religion and Theology*, special issue on Religion and Public Health, edited by Elias Bongmba and James Cochrane, forthcoming.

Dube, Musa. *Other Ways of Reading: African Women and the Bible*. Atlanta: Society for Biblical Literature, 2001.

———. *Postcolonial Feminist Interpretation of the Bible*. St. Louis: Chalice, 2000.

Eboussi-Boulaga, Fabien. *Christianity Without Fetishes*. Maryknoll, NY: Orbis, 1984.

Etherington, Norman. "Missionary Doctors and African Healers in Mid-Victorian South Africa." *South African Historical Journal* XIX (1987) 77–92.

Evans, Grapham. "South Africa's Foreign Policy After Mandela: Mbeki and His Concept of An African Renaissance." *The Round Table* 352 (1999) 621–28.

"Exposed, Terror Gang of Kayole." *The Daily Nation* (Nairobi), October 25, 2000.

Gellner, Ernest. *Conditions of Liberty: Civil Society and Its Rivals.* London: Hamish Hamilton, 1994.

Gifford, Paul, editor. *The Christian Churches and the Democratisation of Africa.* Leiden: Brill, 1995.

———. *Exporting the American Gospel: Global Christian Fundamentalism.* London: Routledge, 1996.

Hall, John A., editor. *Civil Society: Theory, History, Comparison.* Cambridge: Polity, 1995.

Hackett, Rosalind I. J. "Prophets, 'False Prophets,' and the African State: Emergent Issues of Religious Freedom and Conflict." In *New Religious Movements in the 21st Century: Legal, Political, and Social Challenges in Global Perspective*, edited by Phillip Charles Lucas and Thomas Robbins, 151–78. New York: Routledge, 2004.

Hassan Kukah, Matthew. "Religion, Ethnicity and the Politics of Constitutionalism in Africa." Lecture delivered at Ohio University, Athens, Ohio, November 13, 2000.

Hayness, Jeff. *Religion and Politics in Africa.* London: Zed, 1996.

Hodgson, Dorthy, and Sheryl McCurdy, editors. *'Wicked' Women and the Refiguration of Gender in Africa.* Oxford: James Currey, 2001.

Hollis, Lynch. *Edward Wilmot Blyden: Pan Negro Patriot, 1832–1912.* London: Oxford University Press, 1967.

———. *Selected Letters of Edward Wilmot Blyden.* Milwood, NY: 1978.

Katongole, Emmanuel. "African Renaissance and the Challenge of Narrative Theology in Africa." *Journal of Theology for Southern Africa* 102 (1998) 29–39.

Keane, John. *Democracy and Civil Society.* London: Verso, 1988.

Kirwen, Michael. *African Widows: An Empirical Study of the Problems of Adapting Western Christian Teachings on Marriage to the Leviratic Custom for the Care of Widows in Four Rural African Societies.* Maryknoll, NY: Orbis, 1979.

Lewis, R. H. "Medicine at Molepolole." *Chronicles of the London Missionary Society* XV (1906).

Longman Timothy P. "Christianity and Crisis in Rwanda: Religion, Civil Society, Democratization and Decline." PhD diss., University of Wisconsin-Madison, 1995.

Maloka, Eddy T. "The South African 'African Renaissance' Debate: A Critique." *Polis RCSP CRSP* 8 Numéro Special (2001) 291–316.

Markovitz I. L., editor. *Studies of Power and Class in Africa.* New York: Oxford University Press, 1987.

Mbeki, Moletsi. "The African Renaissance: Myth or Reality?" Address to the SAIIA, Jan Smuts House, Johannesburg, October 21, 1997.

Mbeki, Thabo. *Africa The Time has Come: Selected Speeches.* Johannesburg: Mafuba, 1998.

———. "On the African Renaissance." *African Philosophy* 12 (1999) 5–10.

Mbembe, Achille. *Afriques Indociles: Christianisme, Pouvoir et Etat en Societé Postcoloniale,* Paris: Karthala, 1988.

Molara, Ogundipe-Leslie. *Re-Creating Ourselves: African Women and Critical Transformations*. Trenton, NJ: Africa World, 1994.

Moorshead, R. Fletcher. *Heal the Sick: The Story of the Medical Mission Auxiliary of the Baptist Missionary Society*. London: Carey, 1929.

Mudimbe, V. Y. *The Invention of Africa: Gnosis, Philosophy and the Order of Knowledge*. Bloomington: Indiana University Press, 1988.

Mutongi, Kenda Beatrice. "Generations of Grief and Grievances: A History of Widows and Widowhood in Maragoli, Western Kenya, 1900 to Present." PhD diss., University of Virginia, 1996.

———. *Worries of the Heart: Widows, Family, and Community in Kenya*. Chicago: University of Chicago Press, 2007.

Mwai, Mathui. "What Makes Mungiki Tick? *Daily Nation* (Nairobi), October 23, 2000.

Nwel, Pierre Titi. "The Churches and Democratic Upheaval in Cameroon 1982–1993." In *The Christian Churches and the Democratisation of Africa*, edited by Paul Gifford, 168–87. Leiden: Brill, 1995.

Nnaemeka, Obioma. *Sisterhood, Feminism and Power in Africa: From Africa to the Diaspora*. 1998.

Obafemi, Olu. "Towards Feminist Aesthetics in Nigerian Drama: The Plays of Tess Onwueme." In *Critical Theory and African Literature Today: A Review*, edited by Eldred D. Jones, 84–100. African Literature Today Series 19. Oxford: James Currey, 1994.

Pemberton, Carrie. *Circle Thinking: African Women Theologians in Dialogue with the West*. Leiden: Brill, 2003.

Potash, Betty. *Widows in African Societies: Choices and Constraints*. Stanford, CA: Stanford University Press, 1986.

Przeworski, Adam. *Capitalism and Social Democracy*, Cambridge: Cambridge University Press, 1985.

Seligman, A. *The Idea of Civil Society*, New York: Free, 1992.

Sitoe, Eduardo. "State and Civil Society in Africa: An Instance of Asymmetric Interdependence?" *Quest* XII (1998) 203–4.

Reno, William. *Warlord Politics and African States*. Boulder, CO: Lynne Rienner, 1998.

Sugirtharajah, R. S. *Asian Biblical Hermeneutics and Postcolonialism: Contesting the Interpretations*. Maryknoll, NY: Orbis, 1998.

Tih, Pius M. *A History of the Cameroon Baptist Convention Health Board 1936–1996*, Bamenda, Cameroon: Unique Printers, 1997.

Vale, Peter, and Sipho Maseko. "South Africa and The African Renaissance." *International Affairs* 74 (1998) 271–87.

van Hensbroek, Pieter Boele. "Philosophies of African Renaissance in African Intellectual History." *Quest* XV:1–2 (2001) 129.

van Kessel, Ineke. "In Search of An African Renaissance: An Agenda for Modernisation, Neo-traditionalism or Africanisation." *Quest,* XV:1–2 (2001) 43–52.

van Niekerk, Anton A. "The African Renaissance: Lessons from a Predecessor." *Critical Arts* (1999) 66–71.

Vines, Alex, and Ken Wilson, "Churches and the Peace Process in Mozambique." In *The Christian Churches and the Democratisation of Africa*, edited by Paul Gifford, 130–47. Leiden: Brill, 1995.

3

Religion, Violence, and Conflict

Ujamaa-therapy as a Dynamic Response to Ethnic Particularities in Africa

Cyril Orji

THIS ESSAY SEEKS INNOVATIVE WAYS OF RECOVERING AUTHENTIC African ways of being human. The penchant for assimilating foreign conceptual modes of thought seems to have impaired the African existential reality, effecting a shift from authentic African core values to "modern" ones and leaving Black Africa in a crisis of identity. In the traditional African ways of conceptualizing the human person, the wall of separation as found in some Western societies between the secular and the sacred was non-existent, and the living, the dead, and the yet to be born formed a *communio*. The scramble and the desire to be competitive, however, in a new global world order has called into question this sacred union, sometimes making ethnicity and religion, two intrinsically related and revered forces of cohesion and advancement in traditional Africa, ambivalent. Benezet Bujo has cautioned that contemporary political life conceived along the lines of the European-American model fragments the human person in such a way that the religious appears a completely separate sphere.[1]

There is also the fact of the competing influences of Islam and Christianity that have created in the African psyche a "clash of civilizations." While theologians and scholars of African history and religions have lauded the continued growth of Christianity (and Islam) in Africa, not much has been done to examine why the rise of these "for-

---

1. Bujo, *Foundations of an African Ethic*, 96.

eign" religions seem to be precipitating violence among communities of sisters and brothers.[2] African regional and national Episcopal conferences have analyzed the situation and made Declarations to bring an end to the carnage they experience as a reality in their countries and sub-regions. But their proffered "solution," although helpful, often represents only a partial (i.e., Christian) viewpoint, which members of other religions, particularly Islam, find unacceptable.

My goal in this essay is to attempt a deeper social analysis of the socio-political problems of Black Africa in a non-sectarian way and by so doing arrive at a "comprehensive viewpoint," i.e., that "higher viewpoint" that Lonergan speaks of as capable of overcoming "the perpetual temptation to adopt the easy, obvious, practical compromise."[3] In my analysis, I shall use Viktor Frankl's notion of "tragic triad" to depict how the loss of the traditional African sense of community leads to "pain," "guilt," and "death," which find expression in ethnic and religious violence. I shall explain ethnic and religious prejudice as forms of "bias" which, as Lonergan persuasively argues, distorts the dialectic of community and cumulatively deteriorates the social order.[4] I shall then explain the laudable attempts by African regional and Episcopal conferences at a solution as part of that quest Frankl sees as "tragic optimism" in the face of "tragic triad." For in their declarations, African bishops, in a way akin to Frankl's logotherapy, show how one might, in spite of the crumbling of traditions, transform despair into triumph. For Frankl, understanding that life holds a potential meaning, even under miserable conditions, leads to self-transcendence.[5] Frankl's idea of self-transcendence is similar to that of Lonergan for whom self-transcendence is realized in conversion from one's biases, particularly one's individual and group bias. Thus my analysis of conversion, like that of bias, shall follow that of Lonergan for whom conversion is intellectual, religious, and moral. When conceived along these lines, conversion becomes therapeutic and transformatory, particularly when it is seen as a way of coming to terms with one's hidden prejudices, propelling one to reconcile with one's community, *ujamaa*.

---

2. See Sanneh, *Whose Religion is Christianity?*; Uzukwu, *A Listening Church*; Okolo, *Liberating Role of the Church in Africa Today*; and Ela, *My Faith as an African*.

3. Lonergan, *Insight*, 259.

4. Ibid., 254.

5. Frankl, *Will to Meaning*, ix.

What I have termed *Ujamaa*-therapy is the ultimate realization of conversion, analogously taken as "friendship" and *communio* with all of one's brothers and sisters, and even with members of diverse ethnic and religious groups with whom one may or may not have any affiliations. For *ujamaa*-therapy seeks the best of the African because it is indigenous, inclusive, and also Christ-centered.

The Problem Reconfigured

In the traditional Africa that values life of harmony with nature and one's community in the interdependent networks of relationships, carnage, such as the Hutu-Tutsi conflict of the 1990s, would be inconceivable and genocide like that in Sudan that still trickles down to this day would be next to impossible. We speak of the African Traditional Religions (ATRs)[6] in the plural because of the recognition that these indigenous belief systems and practices objectified values in a way that connote plurality of expression of these values. But Black Africa has since departed from this inclusive way of engagement and is today caught in the spiral web of discord and rivalries that threaten its survival. The violence sweeping across the continent can be configured as a kind of blind rage; "blind" in the sense that the rage is neither planned nor organized.[7] Why the "rage?" I shall suggest four main reasons.

Foreign Incursion into African Territory

Foreign incursions into African territory came mainly in two forms: the Trans-Atlantic slave trade and its resultant offshoot, colonialism. The eighteenth and nineteenth century European exploration of the African hinterland led to colonialism, the context under which Christianity was reintroduced to Africa after the failed Portuguese attempt of the 15th century. While not attempting a rehash of these incursions, which many Africans resent as dark moments in African history, it is a well-known fact that foreign interventions disrupted the

---

6. I have invented ATRs as the proper designation for African Traditional Religions instead of the commonly used "ATR," which does not highlight the plurality of these religious expressions. "ATRs" is preferred to "ATRS."

7. Donovan, *Christianity Rediscovered*, 177.

existing social harmony, thereby disturbing the peace. Colonialism in particular, destroyed indigenous value systems and was in many ways destructive of African originality. Colonialism introduced alien forms of social organizations that induce conflict. It is in this sense that the Symposium of Episcopal Conferences of Africa and Madagascar's (SECAM) speak of conflicts in Africa as stemming from "structures put in place by powers external to Africa during colonialism and the Cold War."[8]

There is no gain saying that the colonial incursion severely impaired African symbol systems. The social identity, cohesion, and continuity of a society, as sociologists would attest, rest on the strength of its symbol systems, which contain and communicate a society's common meanings, values, perceptions, judgments, goals, and worldview, without which a society gradually falls apart.[9] In many ways colonialism proved to be a liability. It disharmonized political and ethnic boundaries with the creation of artificial boundaries that had no regard for the ethno-cultural realities of the existing African states. The 1994 African Synod of Bishops sees a correlation between the on-going violence and the existing artificial boundaries. In their well articulated view, the superficial coexistence of ethnic groups with different traditions, languages, and religions, create serious obstacles.[10] Supporting this line of reasoning, the eminent African historian, Adu Boahen, speaks of the newly created independent African states as "artificial construction" responsible for serious unsolved problems.[11] This feeds into the feeling, widespread in much of Black Africa, that political independence did not come with political self-determination, a sentiment that fosters the perception that Africa's political leadership is still in control of powers extraneous to Africa. This is why SECAM speaks of two kinds of war in Africa: those that are fought by Africans on their own account and "wars by Proxy," i.e., wars waged at the instigation of foreign powers, as in Angola and the Democratic Republic of Congo.[12]

---

8. SECAM, *Pastoral Letter*, 8.
9. Hillman, *Toward an African Christianity*, 9.
10. See "Message of the Synod" in Braown, *The African Synod*.
11. Boahen, *African Perspectives on Colonialism*, 95–96.
12. See SECAM, *Pastoral Letter*.

Western marauderization was not the only foreign incursion into African soil. There was also the seventh century Arab conquest of North Africa that expunged Christian religion from the Old Roman Empire, replacing it with Islam. North Africa came in contact with Islam through the merchants who controlled the trade and caravan routes. "At first it was the religion of small foreign communities who resided near political capitals to conduct trade and other business; but in time political rulers in the medieval West African states came into contact with the religion which they tolerated within their kingdoms."[13] Islam took root in African societies because of their ingenious method of conversion and the creative way they assimilated elements of African culture and traditions. In no time Islam found a congenial home, not only in North Africa, but also beyond the regions they designated the Maghrib. The attempt to re-introduce Christianity in the wake of the colonial experiment of the 18th and 19th centuries resulted in a confrontation between these two foreign religions (Islam and Christianity). Sanneh explains that from its very first encounter with West Africa, Christian missionaries fostered the idea that overtaking Islam was an overriding consideration. The myth, according to him, was perpetuated that Christianity is locked in a bitter rivalry with Islam, a myth, we must add, that trickles down to this day and is bolstered by disgruntled elements who feed on religion for personal gain. In Sanneh's view, Western colonialism bolstered this competitive myth and invested it with greater potency and Africa served as the arena and the prize.[14]

Impact of Globalization

Related to the idea of foreign incursion is the fact of globalization. In spite of its many advantages (like improvement in the quality of life and easy access to information), globalization destroys long held value systems, calls into question the autonomy of the human person, and dissolves the cohesion of societies.[15] In the assessment of the African Synod, globalization has created ideologies that are alien to African cultures and is at the root of the "fratricidal genocide" that now seem

---

13. Sanneh, *West African Christianity*, 212.
14. Ibid., 210.
15. Schmitz, *Fortschritt ohne Grenzen?* xi.

common place.[16] Drawing attention to what he sees as the ambivalence of globalization, Bujo suggests that it creates a monoculture, particularly in cultures that are non-Western. He observes that apart from the fact that cultures that are non-Western scarcely assert themselves and make their voices known in the competitive market of globalization, the mass media, as "protégés of the West," is used to disseminate and spread ideologies that destroy whatever is good in non-Western cultures. For Bujo, cultural traditions of the West, which are embodied in the mass media, do not promote non-Western cultural ideals. Democracy, for example, is transposed to Black Africa and promoted within a largely illiterate populace by means of mass media (e.g., television and radio) and in the guise of democracy modern technology promotes a new culture, destroying the world in which Africans have traditionally lived.[17] In the same vein, both the African synod and John Paul II's post-Synodal Apostolic Exhortation speak of the mass media as constituting a kind of culture or civilization in need of evangelization.[18]

Africans, like other ethnic and transnational groups, are not immune to the allure of science and technology and the new ways of life that science and technology brings. In a competitive market of ideas, Africans have adopted en masse foreign modes of thought and their by-products, Islam and Christianity in particular. The question has been raised as to whether the unprecedented Church growth in Africa is a consequence of the gospel of Jesus received and understood or a mere element in the colonial process of Westernization that promotes a foreign religion together with all the other exports from Europe: western clothing, schooling, music, languages, technologies, economies, ideologies, and weapons?[19]

Surprisingly though, while there have been no skirmishes associated with the mass "defection" of Africans to these "foreign religions," there have been violent animosities between converts of Christianity and Islam, lending weight to the argument that foreign incursion and globalization are essentially to blame for the rash of violence in the continent. Rivalry between warring Christian and Muslim groups, like

---

16. See Proposition no. 2 in *African Synod*.
17. Bujo, *Foundations of an African Ethic*, xii.
18. See *Ecclesia in Africa*, 71.
19. Hillman, *Toward an African Christianity*, 3.

ethnic stereotypes and prejudices, can be understood as instances of what Lonergan speaks of as "bias." For Lonergan, bias is an aberration of understanding, a scotosis with a resultant blind spot, scotoma. "Fundamentally, the scotosis is an unconscious process. It arises, not in conscious acts, but in the censorship that governs the emergence of psychic contents."[20] Such scotosis can also be deliberate, say due to pride, dread, horror, and the refusal to accept what is right. In this way, bias is a kind of egoism that deludes one into thinking more highly of oneself than one actually is. It is a scotoma that when established, stands in the way of proper development of one's affective attitudes. Lonergan suggests four variants of bias. There is the bias arising from the psychological depths, there is individual bias of egoism, there is the group bias with its class conflicts, and there is a general bias of common sense that tends to set common sense against reason. Like individual bias, group bias feeds on group feeling of superiority, invariably leading to the formation of "classes," which in turn create a deep feeling of frustration, resentment, bitterness, and hatred on the part of a group, setting them against another.[21]

Lack of Social Capital

There is also the lack of "social capital" in many sub-Saharan African countries that feeds individual and group frustrations. Robert Putnam has devised the argument that good democracies require a significant level of active civic participation by its citizens. He reasons that to effectively sustain a democracy, a high level of civic participation, which he calls "social capital," is required. A good social capital speaks to the strength of a society, i.e., its complex web of human relationships that include kinship groupings, voluntary association of varying purposes, labor unions and free political parties.[22] Many of the so-called democracies in Black Africa still lack social capital. At an Abuja (Nigeria) colloquium (August 2007), organized to assess the state of democracy in Nigeria, most of the participants, among whom were former members of cabinet and past political leaders, all agreed that the political leaders in Nigeria do not understand the meaning of constituted government,

---

20. *Insight*, 215.
21. Ibid., 249.
22. Hollenbach, *Global Face of Public Faith*, 220.

let alone putting it into practice. They concluded that the system of governance in Nigeria has constituted an impediment to rule of law and constitution. Like Nigeria, many African nations still labor under authoritarian and oppressive regimes that deny their citizens their personal freedom and fundamental human rights. The denial of freedom of association, political expression, and the right to self-determination by free and honest elections sometimes provoke "tensions that degenerate into armed conflicts and internal wars."[23] Perhaps this is the "cry of the African" that Jean-Marc Ela argued theology must be committed to address.[24]

Democracy, the African synod has observed, cannot succeed if the masses are not properly educated about the process. Lack of political self-determination and corrupt political process feed the "seeds of division and hate, which give rise to wars."[25]

Economic Crisis

Political independence, as can be gleaned from what we have said so far, did not bring economic self-reliance to Black Africa. A society without economic sustainability, according to Reinhold Niebuhr, creates instability and aggravates existing injustices from which its citizens already suffer.[26] Abdullahi An-Na'im, in an organized project on cultural transformation and human rights in Africa, underscored that economic and cultural rights are at a serious risk in sub-Saharan Africa because of their structural adjustment programs (SAP).[27] The SAP program is further compounded by inept government leaders who are adept at conniving with domestic and foreign private interests. They "divert national resources for their own profit and transfer public funds to private accounts in foreign banks."[28]

It is not possible to have a well-ordered, dignified, and fruitful life that is not founded on the recognition, the protection, and the

---

23. *Ecclesia in Africa*, 112.
24. See Ela, *My Faith as an African*.
25. Message of the Synod, no. 35, in *African Synod*.
26. Niebuhr, *Moral Man and Immoral Society*, 257.
27. See An-Naim, Madigan, and Minkley, "Cultural Transformations and Human Rights in Africa."
28. *Ecclesia in Africa*, 113.

promotion of the citizens' fundamental rights, especially right to economic self determination. In the field of human rights, the individual and community are interdependent. The rights of the individual are defined and preserved vis-à-vis the community, just as the rights of the community are defined and preserved vis-à-vis the individual. The state preserves its own identity by respecting the rights of the individual, just as the individual preserves their identity by respecting the rights of the state.[29] Some African theologians in the mold of Canana Banana, have connected the capitalist economy with the constant violation of individual rights in sub-Saharan Africa. Banana, a South African liberation theologian, connects racism and class struggle to structures of exploitation, which he argues, breed different kinds of injustices and violations of human rights.[30]

"Tragic Triad": Logotheraphy and Conversion

In a network of human relationships, openness to the other obliges one to see existence, to use Rahner's "pessimistic realism," as "dark and bitter and hard, and as an unfathomable and radical risk." According to Rahner, human existence radically and inescapably has to undergo suffering, and even death.[31] The Judeo-Christian tradition understands suffering as unavoidable, and in light of the *eschaton*, "it is obvious that the meaning of suffering eludes an attempt to understand it along the lines of purely analytic and dynamic interpretations."[32] Suffering, as the Auschwitz survivor Viktor Frankl well attests, is neither pathological nor pathogenic, but an understandable existential frustration that is part of everyday living. Frankl argues that suffering (or conflict) does not portend pathological phenomenon and is not a symptom of neurosis. Some amount of conflict, in his view, is normal and healthy. "Suffering may well be a human achievement, especially if the suffering grows out of existential frustration."[33] It is a dangerous misconception of mental hygiene to assume that one needs equilibrium or

---

29. Hollenbach, *Global Face of Public Faith*, 220.
30. See Banana, *Gospel according to the Ghetto*.
31. Rahner, *Foundations of Christian Faith:*, 403–4.
32. Frankl, *Will to Meaning*, 78.
33. Frankl, *Man's Search for Meaning*, 124–25.

"homeostasis," i.e., a tensionless state,[34] since a certain degree of tension is needed for mental health. Should we then assume that the tensions in Black Africa are good for the health of the state? Are the issues of globalization, colonialism, foreign incursion, economic crisis, and the lack of social capital that are everywhere evident in Black Africa indispensable parts of the process of attaining success? Are ethnic and religious tensions a by-product of "human achievement?" Even if one answers in the affirmative, how can these "existential frustrations" be made redemptive, not destructive? How can the African relish in their grandeur experience and vitality of human life, i.e., the suffering, transitoriness, and disappointments of life that in Rahner's term, opens one to the reality of life freely and unsystematically, as long as one does not absolutize either suffering or death?[35] If it is the function of culture to discover, express, validate, criticize, correct, develop and improve one's meaning and value, as Lonergan suggests, then the answer to these questions may well lie in an old African ethic that places the human person at the center of the universe, not in an egoistic manner, but in communion with God and union with other persons in the community. This traditional African ethic (of which I shall return later) is that ethic of value Lonergan speaks of as a person in his or her transcendence, as loving and being loved, as originator of values in him or herself and in his or her milieu, as an inspiration and invitation to others to do likewise.[36]

Frankl develops his logotherapy as a counterforce to the "tragic triad," suggesting that when one is circumscribed by pain, guilt, and death, this should be met with a "tragic optimism," i.e., the human optimism that at its best turns suffering into human achievement, helps one change oneself for the better, and enables one to derive from life's transitoriness an incentive to take responsible action. "Logotherapy teaches that pain must be avoided as long as it is possible to avoid it. But as soon as a painful fate cannot be changed, it not only must be accepted but may be transmuted into something meaningful, into an achievement."[37] Frankl speaks of the transmutation of a predicament into achievement, triumph, and heroism in terms of creative,

---

34. Ibid., 127.
35. Rahner, *Foundations of Christian Faith*, 405.
36. Lonergan, *Method in Theology*, 32.
37. Frankl, *Will to Meaning*, 72.

experiential, and attitudinal values that help one find meaning in life. "The first is what *he gives* to the world in terms of his creations, the second is what *he takes* from the world in terms of encounters and experiences; and the third is the stand *he takes* to his predicament in case he must face a fate which he cannot change."[38] Thus in Frankl's logotherapy, there are three main ways of deriving meaning in life: doing a deed, loving, experiencing or encountering someone, and rising above oneself when confronted by a fate one cannot change. In these value laden actions is found "the defiant power of the human spirit" that helps one understand "how to suffer" and creatively change the situation that gives rise to suffering.[39] In this way logotherapy creates hope, even where all seems forlorn.

The attitudinal value concept of logotherapy is tenable whether or not one espouses a religious philosophy. "The attitudinal value concept does not result from a moral or ethical prescription, but rather from an empirical and factual prescription of what goes on in man whenever he values his own or another's behavior."[40] It is therefore possible for a Christian, Moslem, Hindu, ATRs, and other faith traditions to espouse a common ethical value in a polity. The communiqués, press releases, admonitions, and exhortations of "hope and encouragement to [the] family of God in Africa"[41] by African regional and national Episcopal conferences such as the Symposium of Episcopal Conferences of Africa and Madagascar (SECAM), Association of Episcopal Conferences of Anglophone West Africa (AECAWA), Association of Member Episcopal Conferences in East Africa (AMECEA) and the 1994 African synod of bishops are sentiments that all ethnic and religious groups share. Their search for dialogue and conversion of mind and heart, are exercises in "tragic optimism," showing Africans how to creatively turn despair into a human achievement. This is captured in the synod's question: In a continent full of bad news, how is the Christian message Good News for Africans? In the midst of an all-pervading despair, where is the hope and optimism the Gospel brings? Is Africa a mere irrelevant appendix in a world controlled by the rich and powerful nations? The synod sees nothing but optimism and hope in the face of hatred and

---

38. Ibid., 70.
39. Frankl, *Man's Search for Meaning*, 161–73.
40. Frankl, *Will to Meaning*, 71.
41. *Ecclesia in Africa*, 13.

violence, conflicts and wars, proclaiming "hope of life rooted in the Paschal Mystery."[42]

The synod's optimism is not a mere symbolic optimism of African Catholics, but the hope of all women and men in the continent. The optimism that the triad of hatred, violence, and wars can be overcome through conversion and dialogue recalls Lonergan's helpful argument that the refusal of insight that belies individual and group bias, which is responsible for the destruction of nations and civilizations, can be overcome through a "higher viewpoint," or "cosmopolis."[43] "If the sins of dominant groups are bad enough, still the erection of their sinning into universal principles is indefinitely worse; it is the universalization of the sin by rationalization that cosmopolis has to ridicule, explode, destroy."[44] Cosmopolis is an acknowledgement and submission to a higher principle. In the way Lonergan explains it, cosmopolis makes operative the ideas that general bias of common sense make inoperative. It breaks the vicious circle of illusion that is at the root of general bias of common sense and its longer cycle of decline.

In *Method*, Lonergan conceives the "explosion" or "destruction" of "sin" as a resultant effect of self-transcendence, which leads to conversion. Conversion is a movement into a new horizon that involves an about-face. Conversion may be intellectual, religious or moral. "While each of the three is connected with the other two, still each is a different type of event and has to be considered in itself before being related to others."[45] Intellectual conversion liberates one from the blunder that knowing is like looking and helps one break long-ingrained habits of thought and speech. In the African context, intellectual conversion would help one overcome the blunder of a narrow conception of ethnicity, helping one come to the realization that God's children are found in all ethnic and tribal groups and that embracing people from other ethnic groups as one would embrace members of one's own tribe is to discover the self-transcendence proper to the human process of coming to know oneself. Religious conversion, which for Lonergan, is being grasped by ultimate concern, is the other-worldly falling in love, the total and permanent self-surrender without conditions, quali-

---

42. *Ecclesia in Africa*, 57.
43. *Insight*, 259.
44. Ibid., 264.
45. Lonergan, *Method in Theology*, 238.

fications and reservation.⁴⁶ In the African context, religious conversion would be envisioned as that love of God that floods the heart of a Christian, Muslim, or members of African traditional religions (ATRs), which transforms their living and feeling, words and deeds, and effecting in them the realization that the Christian, Muslim, ATRs, Hindu, Buddhist, and even atheists, are all God's children in need of one's love and kindness. Moral conversion, for Lonergan, changes the criterion of one's decisions and choices from satisfactions to values. It "consists in opting for the truly good, even for value against satisfaction when value and satisfaction conflict."⁴⁷ In the African context, moral conversion would be choosing and opting for that which leads to the common good, as against that which is beneficial only for oneself and one's tribe or ethnic group.

Transforming Clan Consciousness Using the "Family" Model

The political, economic, social, and religious problems that have beleaguered Black Africa are not isolated issues. Their roots are in the checkered history of the slave trade, colonialism, and neo-colonialism. Thus the current ethnic and religious violence is "a symptom of the mental confusion and personality disorientation which some conflicting but rootless ideologies have brought upon Africans."⁴⁸ Even the technological advancement that was introduced into modern Africa has been contemporaneous with a frightening degree of human disintegration, depersonalization and despiritualization.⁴⁹ But given that these problems are largely human problems, Africans bear more responsibility for them. Some of these problems would have been unthinkable in the African traditional society that places the human person at the center of the universe, and God as its creative and sustaining force. A person in traditional society is organically linked in a series of associations that include the community and the ancestors. There was no such thing as an individual achievement because it was the community that conferred on one identity and rights, which one exercised for the good

---

46. Ibid., 240.
47. Ibid.
48. Ehusani, *An Afro-Christian Vision*, 209.
49. Ibid., 203 and 208.

of the community. The point of reference for anything valuable was the community. In this way, unity was forged between one and one's community. Clan consciousness, which was an African version of "human rights," protected both communal and individual rights. In his well-researched work, Chris Mojekwu shows how the African concept of human rights is different from that of Western Europe. He suggests that communal rights are fundamental to a proper understanding of African culture, politics, and society. Mojekwu reasons that one "should not make the mistake of thinking that the colonial interlude washed away these fundamental cultures in society."[50]

The African sense of oneness, i.e., clan or community consciousness, can no longer afford to be ethnically particular and should be widened to include both civil and national communities in ways that go beyond ethnic particularities. A search for a true and balanced African values is necessary to halt any cultural confusion. At no time, as Bujo suggests, did African ethos, especially with its holistic way of conceiving the human person, put forward ethnocentrism as an ideal. Ethnicity may be used as a starting point of all relations, but such relations must go beyond ethnic particularities and reach out to other groups and communities. In the network of interrelationships of modern life, "hospitality, daily friendship, and dialogue with the members of other ethnic groups are vital laws from which no one is exempted"[51] As Paul VI clearly admonished in his 1969 address to the parliament of Uganda, African nations will truly be independent only to the extent that they are capable of collaborating freely with other states, including the entire international family of the world. The challenge of the moment is how to reject a way of living that does not correspond to the best of African traditions and the Christian faith.[52] In keeping with African tradition and the Christian attitude, "a Christian will expect modern politicians to fulfill their duties in ways that do not contradict the fullness of life promised by the proto-ancestor, Jesus Christ, and this expectation is completely in accord with African tradition, that the modern state be so organized that an unworthy politician will be

---

50. Mojekwu, "International Human Rights," 92; cited in Hollenbach, *Global Face of Public Faith*, 221.

51. Bujo, *Foundations of an African Ethic*, 5–6 and 104.

52. See *Ecclesia in Africa*, 48.

deposed by the people as a whole, both in the name of the ancestors and with an appeal to the proto-ancestor, Jesus Christ."[53]

From an African Christian perspective, the "family" model is a helpful way of conceptualizing the new network of relationships that should exist among ethnic groups, tribes, and communities in a given nation-state. The African synod speaks glowingly of this model because the "family" is, by its nature, open to other families and societies; meaning that in the new world order, any form of ethnocentrism, tribal groupings or associations (religious or civil) that are exclusive and closed to members of the wider community (i.e., state), are undesirable and unfit for the civil society. For the "family" has no place for any form of "ethnocentrism and excessive particularism." By its nature, it signifies solidarity, warmth in human relationships, acceptance, dialogue, respect for one another, and mutual trust.[54]

Ujamaa-Therapy

I have tried to show that the reality of colonialism and foreign incursions into African territory have resulted in the kind of situation Viktor Frankl characterized as an "existential frustration," a cumulative result of one's concern for the worthwhileness of life and despair that follows it when one does not seem to maximize one's life potentials. In Black Africa, "existential frustration" is made manifest in violence, particularly ethnic and religious conflicts. Existential frustration, in and of itself, as Frankl reminds us, is neither pathological nor pathogenic. It is part of the organum of being human. In Christian parlance, as Rahner well articulates it, the reality of the Cross of Christ suggests that to be human is to "recognize that life is threatened radically in order to grasp what God is and wants to be for us." The Christian life is the acceptance of human existence as radically threatened by suffering, as opposed to final protest against it.[55] Could ethnic and religious conflicts in Black Africa portend "protest" as against "acceptance" of the (African) human condition? In this respect, *Ujamaa*-therapy, conceived along the lines of Frankl's Logotherapy, becomes a creative way of dealing with, as well as transforming life's transitoriness and suffering.

53. Bujo, *Foundations of an African Ethic*, 105.
54. *Ecclesia in Africa*, 63.
55. Rahner, *Foundations of Christian Faith*, 403.

Ujamaa-therapy is derived from two sources: *Ujamaa* and Viktor Frank's logotherapy. *Ujamaa* is a Swahili word for the traditional African symbol system, customs, rituals, familyhood, sisterhood, and brotherhood. Inspired by the strong nationalistic feelings that swept through the whole of Black Africa in the early twentieth century, many African leaders turned to traditional customs and value systems for an authentic African identity. Kwame Nkrumah of Ghana developed the notion of "Consciencism."[56] Leopold Sedar Senghor of Senegal and Aime Cesar coined "Negritude" as a way of being Africa.[57] Kenneth Kaunda of Zambia came up with "Zambian Humanism,"[58] while Julius Nyerere of Tanzania built on traditional African sense of hospitality and friendship for a "Uhuru na Ujamaa."[59] One of the things these post-colonial ideologies have in common is their emphasis on unique personality of Africans and their family and kinship values, alongside their cosmology and historical evolution. They suggest that these be taken into consideration when designing a political system for new nations.[60] Common to them also is the idea that there is profound meaning in African symbols, customs and rituals, from which genuine African values can be rediscovered. Nyerere explains *Ujamaa* (which he sometimes calls "African socialism") as a vision of society in which all members have equal rights and opportunities, and in which everyone lives in peace with their neighbors without suffering and without imposing injustice.[61] *Ujamaa* must not be understood in the ordinary sense of a nuclear family. "In Kiswahili, one would speak of *jamaa*, a much more comprehensive expression covering all the relatives of the extended family, which itself includes the living, the dead, and those not yet born."[62]

The *Ujamaa* ethic understood suffering as an essential part of life and for this reason emphasized communion of the living, the dead, and the yet to be born. In the old African social organizations, suffering and the ability to endure pain and humiliation was considered a

---

56. See Nkrumah, *Consciencism*.
57. See Senghor, *Foundations of "Africanaite."*
58. See Kaunda, *A Humanist in Africa*.
59. See Nyerere, *Freedom and Socialism*.
60. Hilman, *Toward an African Christianity*, 83–84.
61. Nyerere, *Ujamaa, Essays on Socialism*, 340.
62. Bujo, *Foundations of an African Ethic*, 153.

virulent virtue. Suffering was accepted as part of everyday life because of the idea that the human person lives a life of confrontation with the physical universe. When one was aggrieved by other members of the community, such persons turned to the community for "inner strength." Although there were few instances of tribal skirmishes, there was no such thing as "wars of religion" as we have them today. Even when tribes went to war, it was only for honor and the good of the community.

Ujamaa is an attitude of the mind, not a rigid adherence to a political pattern, which ensures that people care for each other's welfare.[63] It is communitarian in the sense that no one was singled out for excessive adulation or recognition. There was no value attached to individual achievement. Even where excellence and personal accomplishment was glamorized, it was only in the context of community because there was the idea that all have to stand and fall together. In this way cut-throat competition and self-aggrandizement at the expense of other members of the community was discouraged and even severely punished. Julius Nyerere speaks of this traditional sense of oneness with the community as different from the capitalist tendency to build a society on the basis of individual achievement or exploitation. He also speaks of it as opposed to doctrinaire socialism that tries to build a happy society on a philosophy of inevitable conflict between persons in society. Thus, the extended family, the bedrock of *Ujamaa*, requires that all be cared for.[64]

Logotherapy aids *Ujamaa* in urging that good deeds be done across tribal lines; that one encounters someone in a non-sectarian way, and that one makes lasting connections that go beyond ethnic particularities. *Ujamaa*-therapy is a re-education of the African to the basic core values of the traditional society, a retrieval of "our former attitude of mind." Regaining this attitude of mind *ipso facto* rejects group or class conflict. Nyerere reminds us that the word "class" does not exist in any indigenous African language. What exists is a more inclusive word "family." Family or *ujamaa* is a way of being that extends beyond the tribe, community, and even nation to include anyone with an African orientation. It is that "community society" that stresses, according to Senghor, the group, rather than individual, solidarity,

---

63. See Nyerere, "Ujamaa," in Hord and J. S. Lee, *I am Because We Are*.
64. See Nyerere, *Freedom and Socialism*.

rather than the activity and needs of the individual, and communion of persons, rather than their autonomy.[65] The *Ujamaa* ethic therefore, although anthropocentric, does not exclude connections to the monotheistic God, for Africans, as Bujo reminds us, do not think in terms of "either/or" when thinking about the person and God, but in terms of "both/and" categories.[66]

Conclusion

In the wisdom of Lonergan, the drama of life forces one who is attentive and intelligent to "pause and with a smile or a forced grin ask what the drama" of life is. Lonergan observes that when one does this, one realizes that in "his culture is his capacity to ask, to reflect, to reach an answer that at once satisfies his intelligence and speaks to his heart."[67] It is only in the context of culture that one can meet the challenge set by major decline and its longer cycle and through that culture offset tendencies to aberration.[68] Using the African culture as a starting point, I have attempted to "create a theology that arises from and accountable to the African people."[69] Black Africa today is faced with the challenge of halting the downward spiral and decline brought about by years of ethnic and religious prejudice (bias). Retrieving from that which is good and worthwhile in (African) culture, particularly the African idea of community that includes the monotheistic God, deceased ancestors, and the yet to be born, an idea that embodies the respect and the dignity Africans accord the human person and the entire creation,[70] I have proposed a revitalization of the social and religious ethic that sustained our ancestors, a revitalization that can be done through *Ujamaa*-therapy.

Ujamaa-therapy envisions one African family or community that stands or falls together, even willing to "suffer," when such suffering is inevitable in affirming the dignity and solidarity with members of the larger community. *Ujamaa*-therapy is a creative attempt

---

65. Senghor, *On African Socialism*, 93–94.
66. Bujo, *Foundations of an African Ethic*, 1.
67. *Insight*, 261.
68. Ibid., 261–62.
69. Appiah-Kubi and Sergio, *African Theology en Route*, 193.
70. Bujo, *Foundations of an African Ethic*, 1–2.

to derive meaning from suffering and turn life's negative aspects into something positive. In the years following the independence of many African nations, ethnicity and religion, two of traditional Africa's most valuable assets, unfortunately have been turned into instruments of hardship. To reclaim the traditional African values that sustained our forebearers, ethnicity and religion must play a large role because both are fundamental to African society. The future of civilization and the future of religion, as Reinhold Niebuhr once observed, are inseparable because religion must be involved in the ethical reconstruction of modern society.[71] This is more true in Black Africa where traditionally religion and ethnicity have been inseparable and constitute the ethos of communal activity. *Ujamaa*-therapy seeks an orientation to African attitudes about life and community living, i.e., an inclusive clan-conscious, community conscious, and nation-state conscious ethic that is at the same time Christocentric. The Christian faith, although, may be qualitatively different, is not a quantitative addition to African anthropology. Both the Christian faith and African anthropology have the same objective and goal, the vocation of the human person with God.[72]

---

71. Niebuhr, *Does Civilization Need Religion?* 17.
72. Bujo, *Foundations of an African Ethic*, 102.

Bibliography

Ahmed An-Naim, Abdullahi, Amy Madigan, and Gary Minkley. "Cultural Transformations and Human Rights in Africa: A Preliminary Report." *Emory International Law Review* 11:1 (1997).

Appiah-Kubi, Koffi and Torres Sergio, editors. *African Theology en Route: Pan African Conference of Third World Theologians, December 17-23, 1977, Accra Ghana*. Maryknoll, NY: Orbis, 1979.

Banana, Canan *The Gospel according to the Ghetto*. Rev. ed. Gwelo: Mambo, 1981.

Bujo, Benezet. *Foundations of an African Ethic: Beyond the Universal Claims of Western Morality*. Translated by Brian McNeil. New York: Crossroad, 2001.

Boahen, A. Adu. *African Perspectives on Colonialism*. Baltimore: Johns Hopkins University Press, 1987.

Browne, Maura SND, editor. *The African Synod: Documents, Reflections, Perspectives*. Maryknoll, NY: Orbis, 1996.

Crowe, F., and R. Doran. *Insight*. Collected Works of Bernard Lonergan 3. Toronto: University of Toronto Press, 1997.

Donovan, Vincent. *Christianity Rediscovered*. Maryknoll, NY: Orbis, 1985.

George Ehusani. *An Afro-Christian Vision "Ozovehe:" Toward A More Humanized World*. Lanham, MD: University Press of America, 1991.

Ela, Jean Marc. *My Faith as an African*. Translated by John Brown and Susan Perry. Maryknoll, NY: Orbis, 1988.

Frankl, Victor. *Man's Search for Meaning*. revised and updated. New York: Washington Square, 1946.

———. *The Will to Meaning: Foundations and Applications of Logotherapy*. Expanded ed. New York: Penguin, 1988.

Hillman, Eugene. *Toward an African Christianity: Inculturation Applied* New York: Paulist, 1993.

Hollenbach, David *The Global Face of Public Faith: Politics, Human Rights, and Christian Ethics*. Washington, DC: Georgetown University Press, 2003.

Kaunda, Kenneth. *A Humanist in Africa*. London, 1966.

Lonergan, Bernard. *Method in Theology*. Toronto: University of Toronto Press, 1996.

Mojekwu, Chris. "International Human Rights: The African Perspective," in *International Human Rights: Contemporary Issues*, edited by Jack Nelson and Vera Green, 92. Stanfordville, NY: Human Rights Publishing Group, 1980.

Niebuhr, Reinhold. *Does Civilization Need Religion? A Study in the Social Resources and Limitations of Religion in Modern Life*. New York: Macmillan, 1928.

———. *Moral Man and Immoral Society: A Study in Ethics and Politics*. New York: Scribners, 1960.

Nkrumah, Kwame. *Consciencism: Philosophy and Ideology*. New York, 1970.

Nyerere, Julius. *Freedom and Socialism* (Uhuru na Ujamaa). New York: Oxford University Press, 1971.

———. *Ujamaa, Essays on Socialism*. Dar es Salam: Oxford University Press, 1968.

———. "Ujamaa: The Basis of African Socialism." In *I am Because We Are: Reading in Black Philosophy*, edited with an introduction by F. L. Hord and J. S. Lee. Amherst: University of Massachusetts Press, 1995.

Okolo, Chukwudum. *The Liberating Role of the Church in Africa Today.* Eldoret, Kenya: AMECEA Gaba, 1991.

Rahner, Karl. *Foundations of Christian Faith: An Introduction to the Idea of Christianity.* New York: Crossroad, 1997.

Sanneh, Lamin. *West African Christianity: The Religious Impact.* Maryknoll, NY: Orbis, 1983.

———. *Whose Religion is Christianity? The Gospel Beyond the West.* Grand Rapids: Eerdsman, 2003.

Schmitz, Phillip. *Fortschritt ohne Grenzen? Christliche Ethik und technische Allmacht.* Freiburg, 1997.

SECAM. *Pastoral Letter.* October 2001.

Senghor, Leopold. *The Foundations of "Africanaite."* Paris, 1971.

———. *On African Socialism.* Translated by Mercer Cook. New York: Praeger, 1964.

Uzukwu, Elochukwu. *A Listening Church: Autonomy and Communion in African Churches.* Maryknoll, NY: Orbis, 1996.

PART TWO

Religion, Democracy, and Conflict Resolution in East Africa

4

Religion and the Road to Democracy in Kenya

SAMUEL K. ELOLIA

History of Church and State Relations.

ALTHOUGH KENYA IS A SECULAR STATE, LIMITED RELIGIOUS PAR-TICIpation with the State has always existed since the Colonial era. Missionary leaders such as the Reverend Dr. Arthur of the Church of Scotland Mission and Archdeacon Beecher of the Church Missionary Society were both nominated to represent African interests on the legislative and executive Councils of the Colonial government. Furthermore, he management of education and health facilities came under the docket of the missionaries.

When Kenya attained independence in 1963, the same arrangements continued between the state and the church. In fact Kenyatta called upon the Church to assist in the efforts of nation building. Moreover, there was a consorted effort to nationalize the church leadership under the ecumenical National Christian Council of Kenya (NCCK) whose African staff were eager to render their support in building the new nation. The only time the church spoke strongly against the Kenyatta government was during the oath taking associated with the MAUMAU following the assassination of Tom Mboya in 1969. Apparently, the protest which had been endorsed by the churches succeeded in stopping the oath practice. The Church considered the oath-taking practices as repugnant and contrary to Christian theology. Apart from that, church–state relations remained cordial. That might be attributed partly to the fact that most of the nationalists were church members with a majority belonging to the Kikuyu ethnicity, as David Throup observed:

> ... the CPK, the Presbyterian Church of East Africa (PCEA) and the Roman Catholics after independence had all become increasingly dominated by Kikuyu churchmen and their congregations in Central province, whose lay members often led influential position in the government.[1]

Upon assuming leadership in 1963, Kenyatta realized the considerable resources of the churches and welcomed their participation in the immediate task of nation building. Apparently, the participation was limited to education and development. This notion was evident in the words of the nation's first Minister of Education, J. T. Otiende, who captured the sentiment of the time when he stated that "Public schools must be for all comers and the service of the church in the school must place no group under special disabilities. The Church must look upon its services as a public service, not as a service of church members."[2]

The church's involvement with education goes back to the colonial period when missionaries established schools. After independence, the mainline churches continued to support schools and mandated them to come under the noted NCCK. In fact, the NCCK made an effort to combine education and vocational training to support the government's efforts for nation building. Such an approach did not pose any political threat to Kenyatta's government, which was eager to finance the projects of the new government. In fact, when Kenyatta opened the AACC conference in 1966, he encouraged the churches to serve as the conscience of society. Kenyatta died in 1978 and was replaced by his long time Vice-President, Daniel Toroitich arap Moi.[3]

When Moi became president, he inherited a government that was built by Kenyatta with personalities from the Kikuyu ethnic group from Kiambu. They occupied strategic positions in the civil-service structure, all reporting to the office of the president. It was through this system of civil service that Kenyatta ruled and sustained power. The long-time powerful minister in the Office of the President in charge of the civil service was Kenyatta's brother-in-law, Mbiu Koinange. Other

---

1. Throup, "Render unto Caesar the Things that are Caesar's," 146.
2. Ibid.
3. Moi was elected into legislative council to represent the Rift Valley Province in 1958.

influential Kikuyu politicians from Kiambu included the Minister of Defense James Gichuru and Foreign Affairs Minister Njoroge Mungai who was once the President's personal physician.

At one point before Kenyatta's death, a debate of succession was casually staged by prominent Kikuyu politicians and plans to change the constitution were put forward to prevent the Vice President from automatic succession to the presidency. The goal was to keep power in the Kikuyu hands indefinitely. Apparently, that debate was put down on Kenyatta's orders with the help of Attorney General Charles Njonjo. When Kenyatta died, the secret to prevent Moi from succession failed and Moi took over as President and quickly succeeded in winning the confidence of the common people. At his inauguration, Moi promised to follow Kenyatta's footsteps (*Nyayo*) a term that was later to be symbolized with his rule. Later, Moi used the term *Nyayo* to articulate his philosophy of love, peace, and unity, in fact the term *Nyayo* or footsteps implied that Moi was to follow the footsteps of Kenyatta and Kenyans were supposed to follow Moi's footsteps. Moi's reforms at the early stages of his rule gave him an instant popularity with the Kenyan population. He traveled the country widely conducting fundraising drives (Harambee) for development projects that are apparent in the Nyayo maternity wards in almost every district and the scores of girls' high schools bearing his name throughout the country. Furthermore, those fundraisers became stages for competition between politicians who wanted to show off their wealth as well as vie for the President's inner circle of loyal friends.

Like other one-party systems of rule, the *Nyayo* philosophy is predicated on hierarchical leadership. On the civil administration, the President is at the top as a symbol of governmental authority. The power and services are distributed accordingly to the citizens through the provincial commissioner, district commissioners, district officers, chiefs, and assistant chiefs. The provincial commissioners were handpicked by the President on the basis of their political loyalty. The same applied to other senior positions in the government. On the political front, power concentrated on the district development committees; the latter became responsible for approving and coordinating all development initiatives. Basically, this body monitored political patronage on the district level. Loyal prominent politicians ran for party leadership on the district level where they asserted their influence, while at the same time showing their loyalty to the president who was also the party's national leader.

One-Party Autocracy

In the general elections of 1988, KANU introduced the infamous queuing system. The policy required the electors to physically stand behind their candidate of choice or the candidate's agent. The candidate's agent stood in front of the line holding the candidate's photograph. The candidate must be a Kenyan citizen, with an identity card, a voter's registration card, and a KANU life member. The candidate who obtained 70 percent of the total votes during the primary selection in his/her constituency would be declared the winner and would proceed to parliament unopposed. Those who did not make the 70 percent rule had to face elections. The returns of the 1988 general elections were not a surprise when a majority came into parliament under the 70 percent rule. There were no election petitions. The procedure made clear that critics of the government and the president were denied a chance to parliament. As noted by Waruhia, "Returning to parliament were members who had backing from the government, some had no chance of being returned to parliament unless the elections were rigged in their favor."[4]

The elections of 1988 gave the President a landslide victory and the resources he needed to build up the power of his office and the political party so that what he could not get through parliament, he could get through the ruling party. In doing so, he undermined parliamentary checks and balances. In reality, it was the decision of the party-elected officials that controlled parliament and the country.[5]

In the same manner, the office of the President was expanded to include the Ministry of Defense, Provincial Administration, and Security. Also, the government extended its influence to parastatal bodies and non-government organizations such as the National Cereals and Produce Board, Kenya Co-operative and Creameries, and Kenya Farmers Association. All these bodies were closely monitored by the state machinery, and the President had the powers to hire and fire any of their employees.

4. Waruhia, *From Autocracy to Democracy in Kenya*, 90.
5. Ibid., 103.

Moi's popularity continued until 1982, when his government was shaken by a military coup attempt. Right before the coup, Moi had signed a section of the constitution that formally rendered Kenya a one-party state and adopted the Kenya African National Union (KANU) as the official party of the state. The reason for the enactment was a reaction to suspected dissident voices from the university fraternity and from former detainees, including politicians who felt excluded from power. Key among them were veteran politicians George Anyona and Oginga Odinga, who had expressed intentions to form the Kenya Socialist Alliance. Unfortunately, that could not take place because Anyona was arrested and detained while Odinga was put under house arrest.

Two weeks after the enactment of the constitution, junior officers of the air-force attempted to overthrow the government but the attempt was quickly put down by the Army. Among those charged included Raila Odinga, the son of Jaramogi Odinga. Obviously, President Moi was terribly shaken by the attempted coup. Furthermore, Kenya's perceived image internationally as an island of peace in a sea of turmoil was shattered. The coup attempt made President Moi suspicious of some of the key leaders around him. Immediately, Charles Njonjo became one of the first victims of the president's suspicions. Njonjo was charged with treason for allegedly using his office as the Ministry of Constitutional Affairs to subvert the authority of the President.[6] Similarly, the universities which were suspected as hotbeds of anti-government activities were targeted for a major crackdown with some of the scholars detained or forced into exile.[7]

Following the coup attempt, Moi continued the process of weeding out disloyal elements in his government (from the previous regime) and replacing them with members from other ethnic groups, as well as some of the Kikuyu previously associated with MAUMAU who had been alienated earlier by Kenyatta. Moi's style was often crude and swift. The only way that one would learn that he had been dropped was that his name was not in the list announced on the radio. The radio announcements were usually made at lunch time when the old officer

---

6. Waruhia, *From Autocracy to Democracy in Kenya*, 81.
7. Abuom "Church Involvement in the Democratization Process in Kenya," 98.

would invariably be away working, only to be informed by those who listened to the radio that he was no longer in the service.[8]

The sole purpose for these actions was to establish a leadership that was loyal to the President and the party. In fact, it was common those days for the President to travel the nation endorsing those he deemed loyal to the government, asking voters (*Wananchi*) for their support. Any act that would go contrary to the President's plea met with drastic measures such as withdrawing allocation of minimal development funds to that particular region.

One of the first casualties within the new government ranks was Charles Njonjo, who was removed as Minister of Constitutional Affairs. The office was initially created for him by Moi when Njonjo shifted to politics from Attorney General—a post he held since independence. Njonjo was charged for allegedly subverting the powers of the President. Like his predecessor, who had suppressed his opponents, Moi began to do the same. However, unlike his predecessor, who maintained a strong central government that was supported by a loyal civil service personnel, Moi appealed to the populace for support and later shifted to the ruling party KANU. But first, he had to develop the party and increase its authority. In July 1985, KANU held its first national elections, and the party's disciplinary committee became the vehicle through which the party's doctrine was expressed.

> Since Kenya became a *de jure* [One-party State] the party has moved forward with unprecedented fervor, and has now become the undisputed center of political power where independent policies are formulated and implemented without necessarily having to seek legislative approval.[9]

Another action was the systematic destruction of institutions that would normally ensure democracy, for example, removing security of tenure for certain public servants such as judges of the high court, the members of public service commission, the Attorney General, the controller and auditor general. In introducing the amendment, the Attorney General termed the provisions that gave judges and other public officers security of tenure "a relic of colonialism."

After the 1982 failed coup attempt, the government resorted to centralizing its power. That entailed the control of expression enjoyed

---

8. Waruhia, *From Autocracy to Democracy in Kenya*, 82.
9. Quoted in ibid., 82.

by the media while limiting the autonomy of the judicial branch. Other measures included the move towards a one-party state and the limitation on the activities of professional ethics and religious organizations. Opposing voices who demanded change were labeled "tribalists" and "anti-unity" and their initiators branded traitors or dissidents. Political association was restricted from any gathering or access to the process of transforming information and ideas into action.[10]

As a consequence, a culture of defiance emerged, characterized by extensive violence, censorship, detentions without trial, deadly use of police and armed forces, and, furthermore, contacts among members of civil society were severely limited. The government monitored the activities of its opponents and on several occasions, attacked them publicly in the hope of alienating them from public support. That brought about a certain fear in the civil society.

Those in university were first targeted for their lack of support of the party and were branded as "ideological upstarts" influenced by foreign thoughts and ideologies.[11] Moi's government expected university students to evolve into intellectual home-guards against what he saw as intellectual terrorism, political agitation, and subversion.[12] Instead of the opposition, Moi expected those in the universities to take the intellectual lead in providing an academic atmosphere in which the students would orient themselves toward positive thinking, national consciousness, and a predilection for good work and social improvement.[13]

In addition to the civil liberties' abuses, there were widespread corruption and mismanagement of the countries resources which resulted in unemployment and insecurity. A reminder of the height of the corruption in those days is represented by the Goldenberg scandal that robbed the country of billions of shillings. These were the conditions that prompted the church to stand up to the KANU government. The church had endorsed Kenyatta and Moi's earlier policies. However, with time the mainline churches began to be critical of the government's abuses, especially when other civil society bodies were silenced. The churches became the only cohesive institution to speak

10. Friedmann, CJAR/RCEA 29:3, 433. See also Widner 1992, 162–65.
11. Moi, *Kenya African Nationalism*, 177.
12. Ibid., 130–31.
13. Ibid., 130.

against corruption, and the abuse of civil liberties and managed to weather any subsequent consequences.

In addition to its local and international support base, the church commands a sizeable material base as well as a tremendous organizational capacity that provides various services to the general society through broad networks, stretching to the grassroots level. Those structures and services enabled the church to serve the interests of the masses within the civil society, making it an enduring political competitor. Such an institutional power is acknowledged by many in the church, particularly the clergy. Although the outspoken clergy were mainly Protestants, they represented the growing sentiments of many who felt that the church was obliged to constantly remind the state of the standard of righteousness and justice which alone exalts a nation as well as the church's duty to lend moral and practical support to the state when it upholds the proper standards and to responsibly criticize those in authority when they depart from it.[14]

It was on these grounds that the Anglican clergy B. Njoroge Kariuki could state:

> The absence of other organizations of political nature . . . that can confront the excesses of the state means that the church is the only nation wide body which because of its institutional strength and its sense of obligation for public morals and social justice can speak and act in implicitly political ways. The social evils of out time are so great that Christians with any compassion cannot be indifferent of or complacent about human lives in Kenya.[15]

In a special issue of *Finance* the author acknowledged the role of the clergy as the true representative of the most cohesively structured and firmly unified institution in the country—the church.[16] Similarly, in his article on the church of the Province of Kenya, Sobar Friedman presents the rationale for the church leaders' response to society:

> The Church could not remain blind to social evils . . . many also crafted their role and that of their institutions not as rival

---

14. Gitari, *Let the Bishop Speak*, 86.
15. *Law*, 24 September, 1990, 29
16. *Finance*, February, 1999, 39.

claimants over state power, . . . but rather as complementary to politicians.[17]

It was on these grounds that the church saw itself as commanding a large constituency that reached beyond any political boundaries. The Rev. Timothy Njoya of the Presbyterian Church was aware of this leverage when on New Year's Day of 1990 delivered a scathing sermon at St. Andrew's Church argued that the undemocratic one-party systems in Africa was at the brink of collapse and should be replaced by multi-party systems. He drew comparisons with the crumbling dictatorships in Eastern Europe. Njoya's statement hit a nerve in the Kenyan political system and provoked a tremendous anger from the politicians, including President Moi.

In April 1990, Bishop Henry Okullu, an Anglican, followed suit and called for an amendment of the constitution to remove the clause that made Kenya "a de jure" one-party State. The Bishop's call started a national debate and was soon joined by lawyers and more clergy interested in the multi-party debate. Until this time, no one dared to challenge the government directly and managed to get away with it. Previous political critics, including J. M. Kariuki and Tom Mboya, were assassinated. Others like Ngugi Wa Thiong'o were detained and arrested while Oginga Odinga was constantly under house arrest.

Clergy, however, seemed to enjoy a certain leverage that the other members of civil society lacked. Former cabinet ministers Charles Rubia and Kenneth Matiba who had been expelled from KANU were drawn into the debate. In July 1990, Matiba and Rubia were arrested and detained without trial. Apparently, they had applied for a license to organize a public rally in Kamukunji for July 7th. The detention added fuel to the debate. Calls for a multi-party system and respect for individual human rights increased, resulting in the release of Matiba and Rubia. On another front, Oginga Odinga, who had been released from house arrest, announced that he was ready to launch a national Democratic party as an opposition to KANU. However, the registrar general could not register it, citing section 2A of the constitution as an excuse. In the course of the year, the National Council of Churches of Kenya (NCCK) and the Law Society of Kenya collaborated to launch a Justice and Peace Convention. The intention was to organize prayer meetings and symposia throughout the country to sensitize people

---

17. Sobar Friedman, 435.

by discussing political reforms and democracy. Those plans were frustrated when a planned procession from the railway station to All Saints Cathedral was undermined.

By June 1991, religious leaders attempted to forge alliances with other groups in civil society with the goal to create a forum for political debate that would benefit the country. The Anglican Bishop of Maseno, the most Rev. Henry Ogullu, and the leader of the Kenya Law Society, Paul Muite, agreed to organize a prayer meeting for peace and justice. The people were to pray for current problems of widespread poverty rooted in the mismanagement of the economy and unequal distribution of national wealth. On the same breadth, they advocated for a democratic space as part of the solution to the underlined problems.[18] When the government and the ruling party got wind of the planned prayer meeting, it moved swiftly and declared both the coalition and the intended prayer meeting illegal, and dangerous and the prayer meeting was called off.

In July, another attempt for a prayer meeting was made by the Anglican Archbishop, Manasseh Kuria, who extended an invitation to all the political leaders to attend a prayer meeting at All Saints Cathedral in the heart of the city. KANU politicians including President Moi saw this as a threat and warned against it and succeeded in stopping the meeting.[19] Meanwhile, Oginga Odinga and other politicians had managed to organize a political opposition forum which they named the Forum for the Restoration of Democracy (FORD). The increasing mobilization of opposition from both the churches and FORD continued to increase pressure on the government and forced KANU to repeal article 2A of the constitution to make way for multi-party politics.

In August 1991, Oginga Odinga with eight others succeeded in organizing a pressure group—the Forum for the Restoration of Democracy (FORD). The founding members took advantage of a constitutional clause that permitted the formation of pressure groups without government registration. The government responded by declaring FORD illegal on the grounds that it was not registered. To its defense, FORD organizers argued that it was a lobby group and not a political party.

---

18. *Weekly Review*, June 21 1991, 14.
19. *Weekly Review*, August 2, 1991, 3.

FORD expressed its belief that it was only genuine pluralist democracy that could ensure the observance and the safeguarding of human rights and democracy. . . . FORD therefore demanded the immediate convocation of a constitutional convention to be chaired by an independent chairman to . . . draft a constitution that was among other things to provide for (i) multi-party democracy; (ii) an independent electoral commission; (iii) abolition of detention without trial; (iv)restoration of independence of the judiciary; (v) legislative supremacy of parliament; and the limitation of the Presidential term to two terms of five years each.[20]

As the debate gained momentum, the advocates of pluralism pressed upon the government to repeal section 2A of the constitution. In June 1990, KANU finally responded to the pressure by appointing a review committee made up of KANU prominent members chaired by the Vice President George Saitoti. The committee's main task was to travel the nation and listen to and sense the masses' opinion with regard to the much-hated queue-voting, presidential tenure of office, and multi-party system.

At first response, many saw this move with suspicion. The majority, particularly those in opposition, thought that the review committee was established by the government to buy time and avoid a national conference or a referendum that had been proposed by church leaders.[21] Whatever the motivation, the committee traveled the country and people expressed their views openly. It was during one of those meetings in Eldoret that the Anglican Bishop Alexander Muge challenged the members of the committee to explain how they acquired their wealth. Some still think that it was that particular confrontation that led to the Bishop's mysterious death shortly thereafter.

The report which was presented to the KANU delegates on December 1990 proposed, among other recommendations, a limitation of the presidential tenure, a multi-party system, and a restoration of security of tenure for members of the judiciary and other public posts. Moreover, the committee found it easier to recommend the scrapping of the unpopular queuing system as well as the 70 percent rule and the discipline of party members. Those measures did not sat-

20. Waruhia, *From Autocracy to Democracy*, 97.
21. Ibid., 94.

isfy the public and the international bodies who were expecting more reforms.

During the same time, Western leaders meeting in Paris suspended aid to Kenya and gave President Moi and his government six months within which to institute meaningful political and economic reforms as a prerequisite to resuming aid. Some political activists led by the Presbyterian cleric Timothy Njoya had presented written submissions to the donor's meeting in Paris making a case for suspension for aid unless reforms were realized. Taking into consideration the mounting pressure from the churches, the mobilization of the opposition and the pressure exerted by foreign governments, Moi took an abrupt turn and urged KANU leaders to repeal article 2(A) of the constitution and allow the formation of multiple parties in the country. On December 6, 1991, the party approved the changes and several days later parliament voted the constitutional changes into law.

Although political pluralism had now been legalized, a few politicians who felt threatened sought to undermine the process by revisiting an earlier idea of regionalism (majimboism). The idea is rooted in the nation's early history when majimboism was debated and rejected. The regionalism advocated by the politicians during this time entailed confinement of all ethnic groups to their areas of origin. This marked the beginning of politically motivated ethnic clashes and the subsequent zoning of certain ethnographic areas for political advantages.[22] The churches played an important role during the period of ethnic violence as well as in the preparation for the general elections. Both the NCCK and the Conference of the Catholic Bishops united in monitoring and providing assistance to those affected by the violence. The Catholic Church was especially vocal in challenging the government for not doing enough to prevent the conflicts. In fact, as early as September 1991, the Catholic Bishops noted that the conflicts between the Kisii and Maasai communities appeared to be politically motivated and called on the government to intervene and settle the conflicts without bloodshed.[23] In their January 1992 statement, the Bishops noted that the government had done very little to stop the clashes that had escalated and resulted in the loss of both property and human life. The Bishop's statement of 1992 implicated Moi's government and re-

---

22. Abuom, "Church Involvement," 104.
23. *Pastoral Letter of the Bishops of Kenya*, 2.

jected the regime's explanation that the violence was a sign of failure of the multi-party system. The Bishops also condemned the government for failing to provide protection or relief to the victims of the clashes.

Similarly, the NCCK and its member churches, particularly the Presbyterian Church and the Anglican Church, issued harsh statements criticizing the government for its complicity and failure to provide security in the affected areas. With the help of some non-governmental organizations, NCCK spearheaded an investigation into the violence and contracted Major John Seii, a former army officer, to carry out the investigation in the affected areas of the Rift Valley. Major Seii stated in his final report: "We have clearly observed that certain influential personalities in the government are directly involved in fanning tribal sentiments that has led to acts of lawlessness, hooliganism, and violence."[24]

The harshest condemnation came from a non-partisan delegation representing both NCCK and the Catholic Conference of Bishops. In their bold statement directed at President Moi, they stated:

> Whether you like it or not the truth is that the people have no confidence in you and those close to you. . . . Every citizen has the right to live in peace and security. At present, you seem to be securing the interest of a small clique of rich and powerful men who are surviving at the cost of life, blood and misery of thousands of small people . . . We believe God wants you to think of Kenya and all its people.[25]

In the preceding months, the churches continued to condemn the regime's failure to promote a truly democratic politics in the country. They pointed to several issues including the lack of accountability and transparency, widespread corruption, intimidation of the opposition and politicization of union organizations such as the central organization of trade unions (COTU) and the Kenya National Union of Teachers (KNUT). The churches also condemned the practice of declaring certain areas of the country as KANU zones and the harassment of leaders of opposition parties. The churches supported the opposition in calling for the registration of all voters and fairness in the political process.[26]

---

24. APS, April 6, 1992, 3.
25. *Weekly Review*, May 8, 1992, 21.
26. Apparently, when registration of voters was announced, only a very limited

The Transition to Multi-Party Politics

In 1992, Moi finally succumbed to the increasing pressure and called for elections. After many years of one-party rule, many Kenyans had forgotten how to vote fairly in an election. The churches accepted the challenge to offer civil education alongside other civil society bodies. In preparation for the 1992 multi-party elections, the NCCK established the Education for Participatory Democracy (EPD) to foster voter education. EPD conducted seminars, workshops, and conferences at a local level where people were taught election procedures and distributed reading material in English and Kiswahili. Its main challenge was how to reach the illiterate sector of the population.[27]

A few months later NCCK collaborated with the Kenya Episcopal Conference of the Catholic Church Bishops to form the National Ecumenical Civil Education Program (NECEP) to educate voters and monitor elections alongside other international groups.[28] Other monitoring bodies included the International Republican Institute (IRI), the National Elections Monitoring Unit (NEMU), the International Commission of Jurists (ICS), the Federation of Women's Lawyers (FIDA), and the Bureau of Electoral Education, Research and Monitoring (BEERAM).

The programs were to ensure public awareness while at the same time calling upon the government to live up to its promises for multi-party politics. The founders, who included clergy, community leaders, and scholars, deliberated on the best means and ways possible to promote civic education among the marginalized in the society. After the consultation, long-term objectives were formulated as indicated by the following objectives:

1. Promotion of Public awareness and the facilitation of enlightened participation in the multiparty elections as a formal political contribution to the democratic process.

---

amount of time was allowed. Furthermore, the President withheld the election date thereby denying the opposition parties' time to prepare. Secondly, no arrangements had been made to issue identity cards required at voting time.

27. Hoffman, *The Church and Its Influence*, 368.
28. *Weekly Review*, (March, 1992) 21.

2. Encouragement of members of the Kenyan public to involve themselves directly in pluralist democracy as a means of protecting their fundamental human and civil rights.

3. Sensitization of the Kenyan people to the political reality of the public policy environment and education on the values and virtues intrinsic to peaceful development of a democratic culture consistent with their historical heritage and in affirmation of their aspirations.[29]

To support the long-term objectives, short-term feasible goals were stated and they included the empowering of the marginalized majority to realize their potential through fair electoral processes. They also drew attention to obstacles that could frustrate the fairness of elections. In accordance with these short-term goals, NECEP produced training and educational materials to train district coordinators who were in turn responsible in training community animators.[30] One of the NECEP founders, Agnes C. Abuom, recounts the effectiveness of this organization particularly in its vision to register remarkable accomplishments within a brief period of six months, as well as its visibility in the monitoring of the 1992 elections.[31] Civic Education endeavors helped restore the citizens' confidence in the ballot box after many years of one-party elections. The educational endeavors also sensitized the people to corruption in politicians seeking their votes.[32]

As the general elections approached, NECEP organized forums aimed at providing opportunities for dialogue among the political parties and other interested groups representing civil society. The mediators hoped to appeal to the government to stop its hostility towards the opposition. Unfortunately, the KANU government saw the churches' efforts as a front for the opposition and refused to attend the planned meetings. The government's observation was not far-fetched, for the churches ended up mobilizing the opposition parties together. Some of the outspoken clergy in NECEP, including Timothy Njoya, Henry Okullu and David Gitari, were opponents of the government and worked with the opposition parties to defeat the KANU government.

29. Abuom, "Church Involvement," 107.
30. Ibid., 108–9.
31. Ibid., 109.
32. Ibid., 111.

The Evangelical Fellowship of Kenya (EFK), representing the more conservative churches, sided with the government and enjoyed the patronage of the President. EFK leaders criticized the role of the NCCK and urged its member churches to preach obedience to the government. The largest of the EFK member churches, the Africa Inland Church, had earlier pulled out of the NCCK in support of President Moi. Similarly, another EFK church, including the African Independent Pentecostal Church of Africa (AIPCA), pledged its loyalty to the government and to KANU.

Despite the confidence with which the mainline Protestant clergy invigorated the opposition, their efforts to bring about the unity of opposition parties failed. The major opposition parties, FORD and the Democratic Party (DP), could not unite. Moreover, FORD split into several factions and could not forward one presidential nominee. Martin Shikuku and Kenneth Matiba broke away to form the FORD-Asili while Oginga Odinga formed FORD-Kenya. The three opposition parties presented their candidates against the incumbent president and Moi won with 36 percent of the vote. It was obvious that Moi had the advantage of the government machinery, and the disunity of the opposition proved advantageous. In 1997, the same scenario was repeated. Once again Moi took advantage of the government machinery and the division of the opposition to claim another victory.

The Triumph and Crisis of Multi-Party Politics

The general elections of 2002 were a bit different from previous elections in that Moi was absent from the ballots. He had completed his two terms as per the new constitution. However, to the surprise of many, he picked Uhuru Kenyatta to succeed him as the KANU candidate for the Presidency. Long-time prominent party members and senior cabinet ministers who had presidential ambitions such as Raila Odinga, George Saitoti, Nicholas Biwott, Kalonzo Musyoka, and William Ole Ntimama, had hoped that the nomination of the KANU presidential candidate would be carried out by the delegates in an open manner. Saitoti had served as Vice President for about thirteen years while the others had served as cabinet ministers for many years and were more experienced than Kenyatta who had been defeated in the 1997 elections and only had been nominated in October 2001.

It is against this background that the older and more experienced KANU politicians felt betrayed. Consequently, they teamed up with other opposition political parties such as the Democratic Party, FORD-Kenya, FORD-Asili, Social Democratic Party and twelve others to form the Rainbow Coalition and registered it under the name National Rainbow Coalition (NARC). The opposition had learned a lesson from the 1992 and 1997 elections when they lost to KANU. Raila Odinga used his charisma to unite the opposition and led the party to nominate Mwai Kibaki as their candidate. Kenyans turned out to the polls in great numbers on the election day of December 27, 2002, and NARC registered an impressive victory over KANU.

The formation of NARC as a broad, multi-ethnic coalition in 2002; the victory of the coalition and its presidential candidate, Mwai Kibaki, in the 2002 General Elections; the peaceful retirement of Daniel arap Moi after twenty-four years at the helm and the ousting of KANU, the ruling party, culminated in a moment of great public expectation and hope. NARC had stayed true to its alliance.[33]

At inauguration, Kibaki reiterated his campaign pledge to fight corruption and address the country's economic woes. Consistent with his pledge and commitment, Kibaki created a governance and ethics body and appointed John Githongo as Permanent Secretary. The Secretary was to advise the President and the government on the monitoring and strengthening of holistic policies and strategies meant to fight corruption and improve accountability and transparency in the conduct of national affairs. The department was mandated to work closely with the Ministry of Justice and Constitutional Affairs, the Anti Corruption Commission, the Director of Public Prosecutions, the Central Intelligence, and the Police. One of Githongo's priorities was to set up a commission to investigate the Goldenberg financial scandal of the 1990s that had swindled the treasury of billions of shillings in hard currency. While the investigation was going on, Kibaki was enjoying popular public support for his tough talk on corruption and the provision of free primary education. Unfortunately, that popularity was slowly undermined by various actions.

First, the cabinet voted unanimously to hike the salaries and benefits of its members. Second, after two years, the report on the Goldenberg scandal was released and the suspects were released

---

33. Lynch, "Ethnic Spokesmen and Ethnic Coalitions."

and set free from any further prosecution. They included prominent people in Kibaki's government such as George Saitoti, the former Vice President in the previous government, and the Minister of Education in Kibaki's government, Wilfred Koinange, Kamlesh Pattni, a prominent businessman, James Kanyotu, former Intelligence Chief, and Eric Kotut, the former Central Bank governor. The only winners were the commissioners and their assisting counsel who were paid a staggering Sh.350 million ($4.2 million).

The government began implementing some of the key reforms in various areas by introducing an effective and efficient administration of justice, safety, and security and the protection of property and the reconstruction of a dilapidated infrastructure. Within a short time, Kibaki's government saw the economic benefits of its efforts in an increase in revenues and improved tax collection. That was followed by investor confidence and the resumption of donor aid. With such confidence, Kibaki implemented his other pledge of free primary education. Unfortunately, this turned out to have been a matter of political expedience rather than a planned reform. Like his predecessors, Kibaki and his government did not carry out an analysis prior to the implementation of the free primary education. The consequences became apparent in the poor quality of education as a result of overcrowding, and a lack of teachers and learning materials.

After less than a year, Kibaki's cabinet voted again to increase its salaries and benefits. That trend continued almost every year, raising the salaries of Kenya's politicians to a record high in comparison to their counterparts in other developing countries. One wonders what criteria was used to arrive at such outrageous figures when the counties' GPA is only $450.

In February 2005, John Githongo resigned his post as Permanent Secretary for Governance and Ethics. This act dealt a blow to President Kibaki's election pledge to root out public corruption. Githongo's resignation was greeted with an outcry from the public and a host of civil society organizations. The resignation took place amidst deteriorating relations between Kenya and the United Kingdom (UK) due to allegations of massive corruption involving top officials in Kibaki's government. The UK government promised to offer whatever assistance necessary to support a return to the fight against corruption.[34]

34. "Kenya's Anti-Graft Czar resigns" BBC News February 7, 2005, World News 9 February, 2005, 2.

The British High Commissioner to Kenya, Sir Edward Clay, accused President Kibaki and his government of failing to take action against top government officials linked to shady multi-million dollar contracts. The High Commissioner was speaking at the annual Journalists of the Year Awards Dinner held at the Hotel Inter-Continental, Nairobi. To support his allegations, the envoy promised to hand over to the government a list of over twenty suspect procurement deals to the authorities for investigation. Sir Edward poked fun at the level to which members of the government have downplayed the impact of corrupt deals since the NARC government took power and demanded that those mentioned should quit their jobs to pave the way for independent investigations.

> Four of the deals on the list I have given to your authorities are larger than the infamous passports' scam run by Anglo leasing, which caused such a stink. So they must surely rate a commensurately bigger furor in demanding explanations.[35]

Other Western counties including Canada, the USA, Germany, Japan, Norway, and Sweden echoed the same concerns and called on Kibaki to conduct an immediate investigation of his governments' approach in dealing with corruption and to take action and restore credibility. It was at this time that the Finance Minister, David Mwiraria, a close friend of the President and a confidant, resigned to be followed by Muranguri, Murungi, and Muthengi. Others who were implicated, including Muthaura and Vice President Moody Awori, refused to resign. It is clear from these resignations that the younger group jostling for influence in Kibaki's government was crumbling, giving way for the old guards such as Karume and Michuki to entrench themselves as the principle power brokers around the President.

Like the previous government, the NARC government attempted to use intimidation whenever possible to silence any whistle blowers. But in an information age, such efforts are sometimes leaked to the press, and that is why on March 2006, armed police believed to be on government orders stormed the offices of the Standard Media group. The act was to obtain records that might implicate certain government officials with the Anglo-leasing scandal.[36]

35. *The Standard Sunday* (February 3, 2005) 3.

36. Some donors estimated that up to $1 billion had been lost to graft between 2002 and 2005.

Kibaki lost the public's confidence when it came to the fight against corruption. His hands-off style of leadership has been taken as license to loot by those who seemed to be close to him. The talk of investigation does not instill confidence in the public who have learned over the years that investigating the government really means the matter is being removed from the public eye and is being suppressed.

Kibaki's style of waiting for the ministers in question to be pricked by their conscience and resign did not work. As a result, their actions resulted in broad cynicism and apathy throughout the country. Despite great opportunity, in the level of political freedoms. Cronyism, nepotism, tribalism, and corruption have continued.

In the past, such acts were met with resistance from both civil society and the international community. So far, the international community, particularly, the United Kingdom, has spoken sharply. The churches that had previously championed the cause for a multiparty democracy in the 1990s have not come forth in the same force against Kibaki's government. The Catholic Bishops statement of early 2005 urged President Kibaki to take immediate action against corrupt civil servants.

> ... the country has become poorer while a few people in the government accumulated enormous wealth in a short time. . . . [T]he government's promise for zero tolerance against corruption had yielded nothing.[37]

The Catholic Archbishop, Ndingi Mwana A' Nzeki, who was a staunch critic of Moi's government, has occasionally spoken against abuses but not forceful enough to make any impact. Similarly, the Protestants who were noted for their courage in condemning the previous government are not as vocal today. Instead of condemning the corruption and the social ills that affect human relationships, they seem to be preoccupied with mundane things. A case in point is the fight in the Presbyterian Church over the stained glass windows at St. Andrews Church, which are alleged to resemble Masonic symbols. Timothy Nsoya, the leading critic of government abuses in Moi's government was on the forefront of the stained glass dispute but relatively quiet on the corruption in Kibaki's government. In fact, several

---

37. *The Standard*, February 12, 2005, 1.

Presbyterian clergy publicly endorsed their total support for President Kibaki for the Presidency in the 2007 general elections.[38]

One of the challenges facing Kenya is tribalism. In fact the tribal card shaped the general election of 2007. Incidentally, the presidential candidates had united in the last elections and defeated KANU. In 1995, the unity split over the constitution. The constitutional debate has a long history and any attempts in the past have proved to generate heated debates and disagreement. NARC government promised to deliver the constitution in 100 days but they disagreed over the powers of the executive, the checks and balances required to curb presidential powers. On November 21, 2005, a simple yes/no vote was held on the wako draft. Fruit metaphors were employed to sell the idea to the public. A symbol of a banana was used to indicate support for the draft and an orange its rejection. Ethnicity became a significant factor during the referendum campaign. In this case, Kikuyu stood behind Kibaki. The claims of corruptions associated with his inner circle politicians seemed to do little to dent his image among his Kikuyu supporters. The opposition, Raila Odinga, William Ruto, and Musyoka Kalonzo mobilized their respective bases to vote against the referendum. President Kibaki responded by dismissing from his cabinet all the ministers who opposed the memorandum. Without ministerial positions, Raila and Musyoka were joined by other opposition voices against Kibaki and registered their coalition as the Orange Democratic Movement. The movement posed the greatest challenge to President Kibaki's re-election bid. Later on, the coalition split over leadership struggles. Kalonzo Musyoka led the ODM-Kenya faction while Raila Odinga remained with the original ODM. Kibaki responded by mobilizing the remaining political parties under the newly formed Party of National Unity. They include his Democratic Party (DP), the Shirikisho Party and KANU. The flamboyant Raila Odinga succeeded by mobilizing both the Luhya and his own Luo base and used that base to hit hard at Kibaki on corruption and gained support in other ethnic communities in western Kenya and the Rift Valley. Also, Raila Odinga seemed to hold more promise among the youth who appeared to hold the deciding vote for the future of Kenyan politics.

---

38. Historically, the British Colonial government, for fear of tribal/ethnic strife, divided Kenya into missionary spheres of denominational influence. Today, most Presbyterians in Kenya belong to the Kikuyu ethnic group.

The following poem represents the cynical attitudes of most youth who communicate through blog media.

> Watu Wote na Kibaki
> Vijana na Kibaki (the Youth with Kibaki)
> Warembo na kibaki (The beautiful women with Kibaki)
> Wakanga na kibaki (The diviners with Kibaki)
> Wezi na Kibaki(thiefs with Kibaki-Angloleasing)
> Uhuru na Kibaki (Uhuru with Kibaki)
> Moi na Kibaki (Moi with Kibaki)
> Sasa watu wote na Kibaki (All people with Kibaki)
> Kibaki akibaki atamaliz mali yote iliyobakiswha na Anglo leasing (If Kibaki remains he will take whatever was left by Anglo leasing).[39]

Since no ethnic group constitutes a majority in Kenya, no one party is believed to be capable of winning an election on its own without a multi-ethnic coalition. Certainly, this factor was to determine the winner of the 2007 general elections. Unfortunately, the ugly tribal card was used and the results were devastating with 1,500 people dead and 250,000 more left homeless.

The 2007 general elections were truly a test for Kenya's democracy when both Presidential contenders claimed victory. What seemed to have been a successful election with a record voter turnout turned ugly when election irregularities were noted on the night of the election returns. The discrepancies ranged from delayed election results to suspicious tally sheets reportedly from the Mt. Kenya region, the home of the incumbent President Mwai Kibaki. On December 30th, the election chairman Stephen Kivuithi surprised the world when he made the announcement that Kibaki was the winner and within a few hours Kibaki was sworn in for his second term. Many Kenyans, including Western diplomats and observers, were surprised by the results and the rush with which Kibaki was sworn in.[40] Raila Odinga and his ODM followers rejected Kibaki's victory and accused Kibaki and the government of blatantly rigging the results. The international observ-

---

39. MMN June, 7, 1955.

40. It has been a Kenyan tradition to hold celebrations of national significance at Uhuru Park in front of Kenyans and diplomats. It involves days of preparation to allow people to travel from the countryside as well as representatives from the neighboring countries of Uganda and Tanzania that form the East African community. This was the case when Kibaki was elected president in 2002.

ers also expressed doubts about the poll and called for an independent inquiry. The Chief European representative, Alexander Lambsdorff, expressed his doubt with a statement that asserted that the results were terribly flawed and he wished for an investigation.

The opposition party which had won most of the seats to parliament vowed to inaugurate its leader as the people's President. Thousands of youth supporting Odinga burst out of the poor shantytown of Kibera, (Odinga's constituency) waving sticks, smashing windows and hurling stones, and marched towards the city center where Odinga had planned a mass rally. Similar protests took place in parts of the country that voted overwhelmingly for Odinga, particularly western Kenya and the Rift Valley. They unleashed their anger and frustrations on people of Kikuyu ethnicity whom they believed voted for Kibaki. The government responded swiftly by sending soldiers into the streets to stop the protests, mostly with excessive force.

As the riots spread, the government took further steps toward martial law and banned all live media broadcasts, thus making it difficult for observers to better assess the level of the protests. Meanwhile, the opposition urged Mwai Kibaki to step down until the votes were fairly tallied. Kibaki responded defiantly and asked Odinga to legally contest his claims in the court of law. Odinga dismissed such gestures knowing well how corrupt the courts were.

While Kibaki and Odinga were exchanging harsh words, ethnic violence engulfed much of the country. Kikuyu families who sided with Kibaki were targeted and driven out of their homes. Some boarded crowded buses headed towards their ancestral lands in the Central Province.[41] The majority could not do so and ended up in police stations, churches, or stadiums where they were given police protection. Within a week, over a thousand people had been reported dead and thousands more left homeless. The most troubling incident was the massacre of fifty people who had taken refuge in a church in a burnt forest near Eldoret town. The carnage in this incident was widely condemned not only because the people had taken refuge in a church but because the majority of those killed were defenseless women and children.

41. The Kikuyu has dominated business and politics in Kenya since independence in 1963. Some migrated after independence and settled in former settler farms in the Rift Valley, the ancestral land of the Maasai and the Kalenjin. The December 27 elections seemed to ignite old tensions.

After two weeks of protests, the Kenyan economy, which had dominated the region, was beginning to show signs of despair. Furthermore, shipment containers destined for the Sudan, Uganda, and Rwanda were piling to capacity in the port of Mombasa. There was no question that the ethnic conflict was threatening the decades of stability that had set Kenya apart from so many of its neighbors.

In mid-January 2008, the former United Nations Secretary General flew to Kenya to begin peace negotiations. He came after the failed peace attempts that had begun earlier by the Africa Union Chairman and Ghanaian President, John A. Kufour. He was initially invited by President Kibaki, but after listening to both sides he realized the complexity of the situation and recommended high powered brokers, which he impressed upon Kofi Annan. Annan arrived and urged the two contending leaders to appeal to their supporters to stop the violence in order for peace talks to start. Annan made a brief visit to the affected areas in the Rift Valley and had seen the loss of life, the destruction of property and the plight of thousands of people. He appealed to the government to increase security and investigate the perpetrators of the clashes. After several weeks of closed door meetings and negotiations with each group, Annan brought the two parties to the table for serious talks and finally, a road map towards a coalition government had been reached. The coalition would include the creation of a new position of Prime Minister to be filled by the opposition leader, Raila Odinga.

Several countries joined Kenyan citizens and called on President Kibaki and opposition leader Raila Odinga to put down their differences for the sake of the country. International countries that have a close relationship with Kenya, including Britain and the United States, as well as development partners such as the World Bank and the European Economic Union, pressured the Kenyan political leaders to adopt a coalition government with genuine power sharing in order to restore peace in the country. In fact, the United States Secretary of State, Dr. Condoleezza Rice, made a brief visit to Nairobi and warned that America would take action should the Kenya National Accord fail to be fully implemented.[42]

---

42. U.S. ambassador Michael Ranneberger elaborated Rice's comments that diplomatic ties between Washington and Nairobi were pegged on the implementation of the accord.

In February 2008, the Kenyan Parliament was convened to elect a Speaker of the House which was overwhelmingly won by an ODM candidate, Kenneth Marende. Shortly after that, Parliament passed a motion for the creation of a position of Prime Minister as well as two positions for Deputy Prime Ministers. They also proceeded to work towards filling ministerial positions for the coalition cabinet. It took over a month before reaching an agreement on a new power-sharing cabinet. The delay was caused by disagreements over the size of the ministerial positions and the allocation of significant cabinet posts. Apparently, Kibaki's party had appointed ministers for seventeen ministries, including the significant ministerial positions of Finance, Energy, and Foreign Affairs. Because of that earlier action, and the imminent need to share power, Kibaki was in no position to listen to those who were advocating for a smaller government. Apparently, he succeeded in winning ODM to his side and finally a deal had been hammered.

In the middle of April 2008, President Kibaki announced the new cabinet, thus ending the long running dead-log that was sparked by the controversial elections. He named opposition leader, Raila Odinga, as the new Prime Minister. The two deputy prime ministers are Uhuru Kenyatta of Kibaki's National Unity Party and Musalia Mudavadi of Odinga's Orange Democratic Movement. The forty ministerial posts created were split between the two parties as per the power sharing agreement. The only major concern with this action seemed to lie on the size of the government. Many observers wondered how the Kenyan struggling economy could possibly sustain such a bloated government. The civil society reacted to the 40-member cabinet with fury. They accused President Kibaki and his Prime Minister Raila Odinga of ignoring the peoples' wishes for a 24-member cabinet. According to the 2007/2008 budget estimates, the 40 member cabinet would cost Kenyan tax payers an average of Sh.350 billion ($7 billion) per annum. Furthermore, the elevation of some departments to full ministries was burdensome and would end up with duplication of roles.[43] The Kenya National Commission on Human Rights (KNCHR) issued a statement that the bloated Cabinet was an act of impunity by the political elite towards the impoverishment of the poor majority.[44]

43. *The Standard*, April 15, 2008, 1.
44. Cabinet ministers are paid a monthly salary of about U.S. $18,000 a month of

Although the government is too large, there was little resistance from the public. Kenyans had been exhausted by the post election conflict and were ready to accept any condition for peace. They found it easy to compromise so that the country could move forward and begin to heal from the crisis that was sparked by presidential elections. The challenge ahead is for the cabinet to frame a new constitution that will tackle the long-standing grievances over land and distribution of wealth and power. For now, it is hard to tell how a country with an average annual income of about $450 can manage such a huge and expensive government.

In the 1990s, a good number of prominent church leaders, including Rev. Timothy Njoya and Bishop David Gitari were on the forefront in opposing President Moi, a Kalenjin by ethnicity. It is easy to attribute the silence partly to the fact that the mainline churches with a large Kikuyu following aligned with Kibaki and his government against the opposition. This might be attributed to two possible reasons. Firstly, Kibaki is a Catholic and therefore received the support of the Catholic Archbishop Ndingi Mwana A' Nzeki. In addition, Kibaki received the endorsement of both the Anglican and Presbyterian churches whose presiding clergy belong to the President's ethnicity. It is unfortunate and quite disappointing that ethnicity determined Kenya's 2007 multi-party elections after the last successful elections that gave Kibaki the victory over KANU's forty-year domination. What happened this time should not have happened. It will definitely take a long time for Kenyans to trust their politicians and the election process.

When Kenyans united in the 2002 elections that gave Kibaki the victory, many thought that Kenya had overcome ethnic politics only to succumb to it in 2007. One of our concerns was to find out why the church, which was expected to champion unity and justice, seemed timid this time around. When the churches did little in condemning the election irregularities or the expansion of government, it became

---

which only $3,000 is taxable. Assistant ministers earn $15,000. The new prime minster and two new deputy Prime Ministers are paid more. Other expenses, including security, traveling allowances, house allowances, health insurances and club membership dues to a staggering figure of about $1.8 million a month for each of the 40 ministers. This makes them the highest paid legislators in the world. Kenyan presidents make more than American presidents, yet Kenyas economy does not come close to that of the United States. Kenya's GDP is about $35 billion compared to U.S.A. GDP of $13 trillion. See *Sydney Morning Herald*, http://www.smh.com.au/world/politicians-pay-rise-riles-kenyans-20100702-zu0g.html.

clear that it had opted to operate within tribal lines. Even though the churches became refuge centers for the thousands of people driven out of their homes, the posture of silence had left many unanswered questions. A politician in the Rift Valley made a sinister comment that when the churches helped the displaced, it was only because the people driven out of their homes were mostly Kikuyu. Unfortunately, the church cannot challenge such allegations given its timid response to the 2007 elections. In addressing the Kalenjin elders in June 2010, NCCK general secretary Rev. Peter Karanja referred to the book of Ecclesiastes that there is a time to talk and a time to be silent. This might explain the NCCK silence after the election violence. The burning question is how can the church be silent when the poor are denied their rights? What happened to the church's historic role of serving the underclass who have often been victimized by the systems of power, tribalism, and patronage?

Conclusion

In the past, the church in Kenya has demonstrated moral courage in pointing out the evils that have affected society. It is a courage worth remembering and cherishing. To echo the words of Bishop Muge, the church has been the voice of the voiceless when other voices have been silenced by government authorities. Because of its courage, the church has earned the wrath of politicians who often accuse the church leaders of meddling with politics. The irony is that the same politicians do not tell the church leaders to keep out of politics when it comes to soliciting votes but when churches resist their policies, the admonition is quick to come. The point is that the church will be left undisturbed as long as it agrees to support the government's policy. The moment the church becomes critical, it is dismissed as too political. The politicians, though, are well aware that once the churches raise the popular expectations of the masses, their power is gone. They would rather have a docile church that would sanctify the status quo.

It is important to note that the church has a mandate through its agencies such as the NCCK and the Catholic Episcopal Conference to be a witness of God in all areas of life, including social and political. This is because the church leaders see themselves as Christians and responsible citizens and therefore their participation in the state is a moral duty. They locate their prophetic mission in the tradition of the

Hebrew prophets whose mandate was to proclaim the message of liberation. Yahweh, the liberator of slaves, is concerned about social justice and the building of a communitarian society. As de Gruchy points out, this meant that social inequities were to be regularly redressed as prescribed, for example, in the teaching of the jubilee (Leviticus 17). This is a prophetic vision of a transformed society in which human beings live together in peace with their neighbors and in harmony with the whole of creation (shalom).[45] It is also in following the lessons of Jesus who identified with the prophetic tradition and proclaimed God's righteousness against the injustices of his day. Jesus identified his mission from the start as good news to the poor, release for prisoners, healing for the blind, freedom for those victimized by society as well as proclaiming the year of the jubilee in which the renewal of society and the environment is part in effect (Luke 4:16–20). Through interpersonal relations, Jesus turned social relations upside down and sought to establish an egalitarian society. In living within social borders, he challenged the authoritarian and patriarchal society of the day for misusing power.

As seen in Jesus' ministry of healing and driving away demonic powers, the concern was with the wholeness of individual people and the freedom from bondage of dehumanizing powers. Similarly, while addressing the ills in society, the church must be careful not to be identified with any party's ideology. It must retain its critical distance because its loyalty is not to any particular party but rather to a system that promotes the interest of all the citizens. While doing so, the church must not lose sight in championing the cause of the poor who are often oppressed in society.[46]

If a political system operates in such a way that puts human dignity is at risk, then the church ought to ponder the prophetic witness to the reign of God against injustice and discrimination. The church should not only be a conscience of the society but attempt to resist the evils that affect society and ensure that those in power are made accountable and the powerless empowered. Those who have no meaningful way of participating in the democratic process have no ability to protect what is justly theirs.[47] The church must stand with the masses to ensure a political system that will consider the basic human rights

---

45. de Gruchy, *Church Struggle in South Africa*, 44.

46. Ibid., 90.

47. Ibid., 255.

such as provision of clean water, adequate housing, health care, employment, and a decent education. Without these things, democracy will lose its legitimacy.

While freedom is a valuable virtue for social and political determination, it is doubtful that Western liberal democracy is suitable for Africa. First of all, the starting point for Western liberalism is individual rights rather than the society/community. For African societies, community rather than individualism forms the basis for understanding human identity. This does not negate the protection of human rights and freedom. It is in this vain that John de Gruchy argues that Western liberal democracy is historically and culturally determined and to suggest that all societies must accept its worldview as a form of cultural imperialism.[48] The pathos of modernity is to be discerned in both the failed experiments of modern totalitarian regimes and the insidious homogeneity of consumer culture.[49] Africa must find its own way that is rooted within its social, cultural, and religious values. Africa should not forget the mistakes it has made by uncritically adopting the colonial models of governments. The popular liberal democracy system might be necessary for now to modify and correct failed systems, but it should not be adopted blindly without checks. Similarly, African leaders who have come to think of leadership as a birthright and an inheritance to be kept indefinitely seriously ought to be challenged and forced out. Africa must dig deep into its heritage and come up with its own fashion of democracy that is grounded on communitarian values. This might be fitting with the democracy John Dewey had in mind when "the task of democracy is forever the creation of a freer and more human experience in which all share and to which all contribute."[50] However noble this sounds, it remains to be experienced in Africa.

In closing, I urge religious leaders to adhere to their moral task of instilling and serving as custodians of moral values in society. In other words, they must maintain their moral integrity at all times and guard themselves from succumbing to acts that might compromise their integrity to exhort and challenge. By virtue of their citizenship, they have the obligation to criticize the government when the government is in the wrong. At the same time, they have a responsibility to support and collaborate in areas of mutual concerns.

48. Gunton cited in de Gruchy, *Christianity and Democracy*, 29.
49. Ibid., 29.
50. Dewey, "Creative Democracy" in Fisch, *Classic American Philosophers*, 394.

Bibliography

Abuom, Agnes. "The Church Involvement in the Democratization Process in Kenya." In *Peacemaking and Democratization in Africa*, edited by Hiskias Assefa and George Wachira. Nairobi: East African Educational, 1993.

de Gruchy, John W. *The Church Struggle in South Africa*. Grand Rapids: Eerdmans, 1986.

Dewey, John. "Creative Democracy-The Task Before Us." In *Classic American Philosophers*, edited by Max Fisch. New York: Appleton-Century-Croft, 1951.

Gitari, David. *Let the Bishop Speak*. Nairobi, Kenya: Uzima, 1988.

Githure, Peter, and Diane B. Santon. Religion and Politics in Africa: Theological Reflections for the 21st Century. Nairobi: Paulist Africa, 2008

Haynes, Jeffrey. *Religion and Politics in Africa*. New Jersey: Zed, 1996

Hoffman, Thomas. *The Church and its Influence on Democratic Transitions: Brazil, the Philippines, and Kenya compared Vol.1 A Dissertation*. East Lansing: Michigan State University Press, 1995.

Lynch, Gabrielle. "Ehnic Spokesmen and Ethnic Coalitions: Multi-Party Politics in Kenya." Balliol College, Oxford University. Online: http://politics.ox.ac.uk/materials/state_and_ethnic_definition /Gabrielle_Lynch_paper.

Moi, D. T. *Kenya African Nationalism*. Nairobi: Macmillan, 1986.

Opoku, Kofi Asare. *Informal Conversations*. November 20, 2006.

Pastoral Letter of the Bishops of Kenya, Nairobi (1991).

Throup, David. "Render unto Caesar the Things that Are Caesar's: The politics of Church-State Conflict in Kenya 1978–1990." In *Religion and Politics in East Africa*, edited by Holger Bernt Hansen and Michael Twaddle. Athens: Ohio University Press, 1995.

Waruhia, S. N. *From Autocracy to Democracy in Kenya: Past Systems of Government and Reforms for the Future*. Nairobi: S. N. Waruhia, 1994.

5

Forgiveness

The Divine Gift of Peace, Reconciliation, and Healing

ADAM K. ARAP CHEPKWONY

Introduction

IN ANY DISCUSSIONS CONCERNING THE RELIGIOUS BASIS FOR PEACE and reconciliation, rarely are indigenous religious traditions considered. Worse still is the role of women in peace initiatives in such traditions. Yet these are wealthy sources of information in this subject. Instead, more often than not, indigenous traditions are blamed for all the misery people encounter in modern society. A quick look at the recent literature in the African market on peace issues indicates that most women and men writers on peace ignore the role of women as peacemakers. It is common on the other hand to find articles and books that blame men, Christianity, African cultures and Islam for women's plight. The editors of the recent book, *Conflicts in Africa: A Women Response* summarizes the theme of the book thus:

> This is the thread of thought that runs across all the articles: That African religion, Christianity and Islam ought to live up to that which they entail: recognition of humanity and the call to live in fullness, especially as relates to the concerns of women.[1]

In an earlier book, *Violence Against Women*, similar lamentations are evident. Here African culture gets a whipping and the authors re-

---

1. Getui and Ayanga, *Conflicts in Africa*, xi–xii.

joice at the fact that at least they have been liberated from a culture that silenced women. They write:

> If today African women are able to name the oppressive aspects of our cultures, it has not come easily. For centuries African women have gone so far along with cultural prescriptions that we came to believe that our lives were to be managed by the commands of culture. The fear of breaking taboos silenced us into a state where we act without questioning what we do.[2]

The contributors of both books mentioned above are women. Although I agree with them that women undergo a lot of discrimination in our present society, and that some of the reasons can be attributed to culture, I also note that modern scholars handily exploit the cultural elements that favoured and empowered women.

In particular, it is true that every society has a variety of culturally legitimated paths of behaviours dedicated to resolution of conflicts, the settlement of disputes, and the allocation of responsibility among the members of that community. Similarly, there are rules that protect personal rights, communal interest, and public morality. These simple and local institutions serve as mediators, arbitrators and adjudicators of individual and communal behaviours in the society. It is in these often-neglected institutions that I see the undisputed contribution of African women in conflict resolution. I shall argue here that these roles are significant among the indigenous people than the formal state-run legal institution. The importance of the local, unwritten legal codes in a community cannot be underestimated:

> For although they lack the formality of written legal codes administered by specialists and enforced by means of coercive powers to exact restitution or retribution, they are often the principal means by which disputes are settled, conflicts resolved, and the moral fabric of the community maintained and enforced.[3]

In *Subverting Hatred*, Daniel L. Smith-Christopher has demonstrated how the Native America Chief of the Southern Cheyenne nation serves as a model of indigenous traditions of peacemaking. In support of the fact that indigenous traditions have a wealth of teaching about peace, he suggests that

2. Wamue and Getui, *Violence Against Women*, back cover.
3. Avruch, *Conflict Resolution*, 107.

In contemporary indigenous societies around the world, the persistence of peacemaking traditions gives voice to the religious hope of "subverting hatred". In some small and localized groups, perceptions of holiness and religious values have let many people to stand against the practice of warfare within the traditions. In some cases, these values have led members of these traditions to carry their values of peacemaking into dialogue with wider societies.[4]

What follows is an explanation of the role of Kalenjin women in peacemaking practices. I shall show how the entire community depended on the wisdom and the good will of their women to maintain peace and to manage conflicts. I therefore disagree with William G. Blum and others who argue that African women were dependent upon men for overall protection, including that of their rights. He writes, "When wronged, women could do little by themselves to seek redress for their grievances: they had to look to a man or men: such as, a husband . . ."[5] On the contrary, I shall argue here that members of the family and community at large sought mediatorship of women in times of conflicts for peaceful resolutions.

The Kalenjin community of Kenya, which is made up of the Kipsigis, Nandi, Keiyo, Marakwet, Tugen, Sebei and Pokot, recognized the role of women leadership in conflict control management. I shall indeed show how the Kalenjin women assist the community to resolve conflict and to maintain peace. To do this I shall first assess the reasons why the Kalenjin community resorts to the services of women as peacemakers. Second I shall survey the role of women in conflict management within the family and community. Third I shall examine the place of women in conflict resolution between warring communities. Fourthly, the unique religious responsibility women undertake to avert conflict that arise between human being and the Supreme Being, often presented in violence through natural catastrophes is presented. I shall finally make some concluding remarks in the form of recommendations and suggestions.

---

4. Smith-Christopher, *Subverting Hatred*, 85–86.
5. Blum, *Forms of Marriage: Monogamy Reconsidered*, 120.

Women as Peacemakers

Although women feminists in Africa and elsewhere have tended to blame African culture as the vehicle which propagates women inferiority theory, history shows the contrary. Indeed, the great Western philosophers of history are partly responsible for perpetuating sexism. Plato, Aristotle and Steven Goldberg for example all agreed that women were inferior.[6] Similarly, the early Christian Philosophers, Augustine (354–430 AD); the father of modern philosophy René Descartes (1596–1650); the enlightenment philosophers Immanuel Kant, Jean-Jacquers Rousseau and Sigmund Freud reinforced female inferiority theory on the grounds that women were irrational, emotional and morally inferior to men. It was thus argued that women should submit to the authority of men. Rousseau, for example wrote:

> Woman was made especially to please man. . . . This is the law of nature. If woman is formed to please and to live in subjection, she must render herself agreeably to man instead of provoking his wrath: her strength lies in her charms.[7]

In his book, *Points of Discord*, Mokwugo Okoye has discussed at length the origin of women degradation. He has shown that Western culture and Christianity were responsible for the degradation of woman. He has also shown that although indigenous African communities perceived women negatively, in some communities women were regarded highly and were given respect. He notes for example that in Abyssinia, women held the same status as that of men. He writes:

> On the other hand, as far back as 1854, James Bruce reported that Abyssinian "married women ate, drank and smoked like men" as they still do to this day all over non-Moslem Africa . . .[8]

It was only at the turn of the century that scholars like the French philosopher Simone de Beauvoir (1908–1986) began to repudiate the theories that claimed that women were morally inferior to men. This period also marked the growth of women movement that defended the image against women as the weaker sex. The women's liberation

---

6. Boss, *Analyzing Moral Issues*, 624.
7. Ibid., 625.
8. Okeye, *Points of Discord*, 99.

movements have thus been at the forefront in calling for justice towards the female sex.

The inspiration of some of the contemporary women's movements and more so those which originated from the West do not augur well with African way of thinking. The teachings advocated by some radical feminist movements, for example, poses a threat to the right of women to be women as understood by an African women. This is the right to promote the ideals of family, marriage and motherhood. It is these ideals that form the basis for entrusting women with peacemaking initiatives in an African setting.

Without necessarily going into the debate of the merits and demerits of the feminist movements, I shall concern myself with the biological make-up and other natural qualities that make women the peacemakers among the Kalenjin. It is these female differences that we shall consider and argue that it should be preserved and studied closely. If the African past found values in a woman that assigned her the role of a peacemaker, it is most likely that a modern woman experience can contribute valuable insights that can transform the present conflict prone culture.

African communities recognize, first and foremost, the role of women as mothers. A woman is seen as a co-creator of life with God. The business of making human beings is paramount in an African mind. Hence women who devote their energies and talents in this job are appreciated and honored. For this is the most productive work. In the eye of an African, there is no work that can be compared to or better than mothering.

It is interesting to an African man or woman therefore to read comments that denounce the role of a woman as a mother. Some feminists, for example, have proposed that mothering is a hindrance to women's development and should be eliminated.

> According to feminist theory, mothering causes class thinking, and classes are the cause of all evil. The only way to save the world is to eliminate mothering.[9]

Contrary to these sentiments by radical feminist, Africans have a strong mother-child attachment that seems to last throughout one's lifetime.

---

9. O' Leary, *Gender Agenda*, 135.

King explains the reason behind this child-mother interconnectedness with early childhood experiences. She suggests that motherhood

> Carries a rich resonance due to its close association with early human experience of intimacy, comfort, nourishment, assurance and support patterned by relationships of tenderness care and love which all of us need to become and be fully human.[10]

Motherhood is greatly celebrated and even worshipped not only among Africans, but also among the majority of the peoples of the world. Motherhood is seen as a profound analogy of the creative power so often symbolized in religion in the form of the goddess.[11] As a co-creator with God, a woman is depicted as being motherly and constantly in her mothering duties with God. This same God is also depicted as a mother who tenderly cares for his children. Hebblethwaite depicts this powerful mother imagery of God and woman thus:

> A baby feeding at the breast, or sleeping on the breast full satisfied and loved, is a wonderful image of God's care for us; the breast unites food, warmth and intimacy with the giver of our life.

African people see the motherly qualities inherent in a woman as the ones that make her acceptable as a perfect peacemaker. These virtues include; honesty, patience, humility, faithfulness, kindness, trustworthiness, dutifulness and courage. But more importantly, like God, a woman has the gift of forgiveness. Forgiveness among the Kalenjin is an important concept associated with the Supreme Being and symbolized by women. It is thus argued that no one should ever refuse to accept an apology for it is only God who does not commit sins. The same God does recognize the weakness of human beings and thus has provided divine forgiveness for whoever asks for it. Like God, women have a big heart and are ready to forgive others regardless of the nature of the offence. This concern is portrayed in the Kalenjin saying, "it is only the mother who knows the pain of child birth." The Kalenjin believe that there is nothing that cannot be forgiven, therefore, it is an offence to refuse to accept an apology from anyone who has asked for forgiveness. Individuals are thus admonished to forgive anyone who asks for forgiveness regardless of the offence. Forgiveness

---

10. King, *Women and Spirituality*, 79.
11. Ibid., 75.

is thus regarded as the divine gift that enables the individual and the community to heal, reconcile and to create a peaceful environment.

Women as mediators within the family

Kalenjin women are generally allowed considerable control to create harmony between the members of her family. When a family seems to have a lot of internal conflicts, it is suspected that the woman or women in that home are not shrewd. This is due to the fact that a wise mother is known to create a peaceful atmosphere in the family. For in matters of peacemaking, the Kalenjin culture gives women respect, trust and affection.

The respect and trust accorded women is evident in the role they are given to control the family property. Although a man is the head of the family, the woman owns the grains, the cattle and in case of divorce, children. Indeed, a man's wife or wives and not sons inherited the land. This may explain why all-important decisions in the family are made in consultation with women in each home. These include decisions on issues relating to migration, marriage of children, who to go for or to seek help from and even when the man desired another marriage.

Whenever there is any conflict or misunderstanding between the members of the family, it is the mother, who is looked up to, to intervene. For example, when the man beats up his child(ren), he is expected to stop immediately if a woman pleads with him to do so. Likewise, when a woman herself is beaten by her husband or anybody, such a person stopped immediately upon the plea of a child. Women therefore trained children from a very young age on what to say or do in conflict situation.

In some cases, a son would beat up his wife due to a domestic misunderstanding. When the mother hears such commotions, she would go near the house and draw their attention by saying, "Children what is the matter?" To this the man is expected to answer and at the same time stop beating his wife immediately. In a case where the fight is too much and the wife decides to run away to her home, it is the mother, or another women, accompanied by a neighbor appointed for this purpose, who went to ask for forgiveness from the woman's parents and also went to bring her back. When she finally returns, she stayed with her mother-in-law sometimes to allow for the situation to normalize and also to give her instructions on how to maintain peace in her house. She would also separately instruct her son and whenever necessary, they were both brought together before the members of the family to be admonished.

Women as Mediators within the Community

A Kalenjin saying *"mami tum ne mami chepyosa"* warns, "there is no ceremony/ritual that is done in the absence of a woman." This depicts the unquestionable role women play in conflict resolution in the community. Women thus attend all gatherings including those meant for peace and conflict resolution. Generally, the community conflicts that arise include conflicts between individual members, among clans and those between ethnic groups. In any such disputes, women hold significant bargaining power in peacemaking efforts. The major reason is that, like God, women are honest and dislike evil deeds. To illustrate this point, no bride wealth negotiations are done in the absence of women. It is believed that if in the future a dispute arose as to how many animals and which ones were agreed upon, a woman played an important role of preventing conflicts by saying the truth.

Apart from that, women have the authority invested on them by the society to directly stop individual fights, and ethnic wars. This power was symbolized in the form of a waist belt (girdle) worn by women after birth known as *legetiet* in the past. It is said that if a woman found two people fighting, she would normally persuade them to stop fighting. However, should the two refuse and in the judgment of the woman the fight is likely to end up in serious injury or death, she would untie her *legetiet* and put it down. On seeing this, the two men were bound to stop immediately.

Similarly, if two men were fighting and one was hard up and he ran where a woman or women were, the opponent was forbidden to pursue him further. In the same way to date, runaway women and children are protected by women who take care of them for some time and finally take them back to their homes where they would plead for forgiveness on their behalf if they were wrong. If on the other hand the runaway is wronged, the women found a way through family negation to solve the dispute. In difficult conflict situations, the women advise the offended to seek redress from the court of elders for justice. No one dares, regardless of the nature of the offence, to punish an individual of whom forgiveness has been asked on their behalf. There is nothing so bad that cannot be forgiven. Nothing.

In the past the above procedure was also applicable in cases of clan or ethnic clashes. If two clans fought and the women felt that the clashes was uncalled for, or the war was most likely to cause much death, the women intervened. At the same time, when the fight was on and heavy casualties were reported on either side, the women stopped the fight by removing their *legetiosiek* and placed them on the boundary. In an interview with an eyewitness to such an occasion, Mr. James Chelanga of Moi University narrated the following story to me:

> I was still a young boy, sometime in the 1950's. There was a big land disputes between the Kapchesang and Kapnyekwel families. The incident took place at Issas village Tugen. The cause was boundary dispute between two families of Tala clan. The tension was so high that the warriors from both sides prepared for war. Efforts were made to reconcile the two groups in vain. Finally war was declared and the warriors were ready. It was then that the women hurriedly gathered and placed their *legetiosiek* along the boundary and the warriors were warned not to cross. They did not. This stoppage allowed for the tension to subside, as reconciliation meeting was organized.[12]

During ethnic wars, a phenomenon that is rare at present, women also played a dangerous mediator role between the warring groups. If a Kalenjin group felt that they were not ready for war or when, it was necessary to ask for amicable resolution instead of war, an elderly woman or a pregnant woman was sent to the opponent to request for a peaceful settlement. This was a dangerous errand since in some occasion the tension was so great that a woman on such an errand was killed before she reached the rulers to deliver the message. Yet women did so for the sake of the community, thus displaying courage and determination in order to see peace prevail.

On the other hand, when the Kalenjin community decides to end perpetual hostility with another community inter-marriage is encouraged. This is done to bind the two communities by creating relationship among them. It was a taboo to go to war with your own relatives

---

12. Interview with Mr. James Chelanga of Moi University.

since you might kill your own children. There were cases, therefore, when the Kalenjin community gave their daughters for marriage in order to create lasting relationships which in turn deterred conflicts.

One such case is preserved in the legendary story of the famous Luo leader, Lwanda Magere. Lwanda Magere was a strong and mysterious leader who defeated the Kipsigis in most of their battles. To discover the secret of his powers, the Kipsigis opted to give their best daughter for marriage to the ruler, Lwanda Magere. In the story below, the Kipsigis are referred to as Lango:

> Then after Magere had won countries battles against them, Lango elders assembled to discuss ways of ending the glorious career of this all-conquering her... They debated the problem at length, until they decided to give Magere a Lango girl. And so word went out that the most beautiful girl known among the Lango should be found and sent to the elders' assembly. A girl was found... no girl could match her for grace and beauty. They sent her to Magere and he fell in love with her at once.[13]

Although the above story ended in a sour note as it was a trick similar to that of Samson and Delilah in the Old Testament, it nevertheless demonstrates the important role woman played in controlling inter-tribal wars and the personal sacrifice for the sake of the community.

Women as Mediators between Human Beings and Asis

The Kalenjin believe in a Supreme Being known as *Asis*. *Asis* is the creator, the controller and sustainers of the skies, the earth the celestial bodies as well as all the invisible things. *Asis* was approached by individuals, family and the community at a shrine known as *Kapkoros*. The Kalenjin community believes that *Asis* is benefactor and the giver of all things, life, children, health, rain, cattle, food and everything else people and other creatures require. However, when people sin by failing to maintain the full standards of duty and respect to other fellow human beings, the ancestors, the spirits, other creatures and the environment, they faced retribution from Asis. The punishment was proportionate and inevitable to the individuals or the community following the commission of the transgression.

13. Onyango-Ogutu and Roscoe. *Keep My Words*, 143–48.

In his own wisdom, *Asis* punishes the community upon commission of sin by the individual or community through epidemics, drought, and other natural catastrophes. In such times, women undertake the unique religious responsibility to avert conflicts that arise between humans and God. It is believed that origin of the role of Kalenjin women as mediators between the people and *Asis* can be traced to a legend which explains how a young girl was to be sacrificed to the god of rain for propitiation after a long drought. The name of the girl was Chepto ne lel, which means, "the white, dazzling, pure or holy girl."

> A very long time ago when "people" (Kipsigis) were living in the same parts of the country, there came a severe period of drought. Everywhere was dry. There was no grass and therefore cattle and people died of starvation. Then people got together and reasoned among themselves about what to do to remedy the situation. They said that the god of rain was not happy because of one thing or another and that he wanted some propitiation before he could open the gates of rain.
>
> They decided to get a girl—the only child of any family and sacrifice her to the god of rain. News was sent out and a girl, having neither a sister nor a brother, was procured. She was decorated in pure white. The people assembled and performed a ritual ceremony and the girl was taken and placed on an island where she was to be taken away by the god of rain. The girl's sweet heart, a Maasai moran, heard of the conspiracy against his sweetheart. He took with him a sword, a spear and a panga- all were as sharp as the edge of a razor blade. When he arrived at the island he found his sweetheart singing thus: "Tule we Kimase, kagigonin chepto nemami karna ne matinye". This literally reads, "You Kimase, thunder violently, you have been given a girl of which there is no ornament she does not have".
>
> Before long the god of rain arrived. He went round the island and approached his victim. But the young man speared him and cut him into two. He rescued his sweetheart. He was allowed to marry her latter. Since it had began raining when the god of rain thundered it continued to rain.[14]

The legend above shows the important role taken by *Chepto ne lel* to save the people and other creatures from death due to drought. Today, the most popular attribute of God is *Asis Cheptalel* which means the "God of *Chepto ne lel.*" As an attribute of God, *Cheptalel* conveys

14. Chepkwony "African Religion in the study of Comparative Religion," 194–95.

two aspects of the nature of *Asis*. First, that *Asis* is accessible to people through prayer and that he cares for the well being of humanity by providing rain and all necessities of life. Second, that *Asis Cheptalel* is the life-giver, protector and helper of all creatures.

The quality that made the sacrificial girl acceptable to *Asis* was her purity or righteousness as suggested by her name. Since *Asis* is holy the Kalenjin believe that only the righteous can intercede for them before *Asis*. It is for this reason that women are generally seen as holy as opposed to men who are believed to cause the majority of serious evils that disrupt harmony and in particular destruction of human life. Robert J. Schreiter confirms the fact that men are the source of violence when he suggests that: "One of the central facts that must be faced in a ministry of reconciliation is that men are most frequently the source of violence that rends families and nation apart."[15]

It was because women had the acceptable character before God that in the past, they were allowed to perform purification rites to avert dreaded epidemics like small pox, malaria, measles and anthrax that attacked both humans and cattle. All types of epidemic were averted by the *piretab peek* (slucing of water) ceremony. The entire community attended the epoch but the main actors were women. The ceremony was done at sunrise in the river. On the day of the ceremony, each woman carried a *kerebet* (basket) full of finger millet.

In the river they planted the sacred sosiot plant (wild palm date) in the middle of the river and went around it four times. Then each woman picked a black stone from the bottom of the river and placed it on the basket. They then climbed out of the river facing East and never looked back. East was the direction of *Asis* and all prayers to him were made in that position. At the bank, they poured some of the finger millet into a skin garment spread for that purpose by an old woman. The grain collected here went towards the contribution of ceremonial beer used on that occasion.

Thereafter, the women dressed and went to the hut where the community and the ritual leaders waited. They then knelt around the ritual elder holding their baskets containing the remaining finger millet and the black stone. The ritual elder blessed each one of them as he recited the blessing.

---

15. Schreiter, *Ministry of Reconciliation*, 25–26.

After this each woman went to her house and posited the black stone in her water pot. The stone was believed to possess the power against all forms of impurities because of its contact with water for a long time. Keeping it in the pot of drinking water in each home was not only a reminder of the need to live an upright life but a symbol of continued purification of the family and the entire community. The finger millet in the basket was then mixed with ordinary water and a meal was prepared for the family. Through the meal, the entire community was involved in the process of purging themselves of evil and restored normal relationships with *Asis*.[16]

Another purification rite performed by women took place when there was drought. Drought poses a great threat to human life, animals and the environment as portrayed in the legend of Chepto ne lel. Like other crisis in the community, drought is presumed to be punishment upon the people by *Asis*. The women were thus entrusted with the responsibility of asking for forgiveness from *Asis* on behalf of the society. This is done through a ceremony known as *Sosimo*.

The women who normally prepared *Sosimo* ceremony are from the toyoi clan. On the agreed day, women gather at sunrise at a selected crossroads in each community. There an arch is constructed in such a way that everybody who passes that route went through it. Passing through the arch was considered a prayer of confession to *Asis* to deliver the community from the crisis. It also symbolized that *Asis* had accepted, cleansed and forgiven the participants on behalf of the entire community.

After this, the women went to the river where they bath and splash water into the air while facing east direction. At the same time, they plead with *Asis* to bring rain saying:

Tom Koropon	It has not rained
Kokekolse	We have planted
Ago tom kopista peek	And the grains has not spouted
Yamene Lagokyok	What shall our children eat
Ngetu buch segetian empty	This spoon (wooden) shall be

---

16. Chepkwony, "African Religion in the Study of Comparative Religion," 302.

Tun komami ametuogikab segetiani for the spoon	There will be no food
Eeh! Asis, gonech ropta	Oh! Asis give us rain
Sarun tamanosiek	Rescue the expectant woman
Sarun lagok	Rescue children
Sarun tuga	Rescue cattle

After the prayers, the woman walk home singing the *sosimo* song. Their prayer for rain is always answered. The most recent case of drought in which the *sosimo* ceremony was performed was January 1993. It was reported that for the two cases recorded at Kenegut and Ingilot in Kericho among the Kipsigis, it rained immediately after the ceremony.[17] A case recorded by Dinah Changwony among the Keiyo in Mutei Location in March 1993 produced similar results. She writes:

> One morning I saw the women gather at the crossroads to perform the ritual . . . I keenly observed and recorded all that pertained to the rite. Interestingly, it rained in the evening of the same day.[18]

These are some of the few examples that demonstrate the indispensable role that women played in conflict situations. One wonders why such scenarios cannot be reconstructed in our present society. And if it were, one is prompted to speculate the reaction of the women liberation movements. I suspect that some would see this as another way of relegating woman to the background, a position associated and attached to the traditional woman position in the kitchen. But is it? To me I see the role of peacekeeping as the highest and most respectable duty in the land. All traditions in the world talk and yearn for peace. In spite of these talks, human history shows that in every tradition there has been war. Today, the world is marred by violence, wars, intolerance, corruption, discrimination, conflicts and other numerous evils. In the present situation where even the United Nations has found it difficult to control the many conflicts in the world, it makes sense to re-visit the role of indigenous institutions. Although it is true that such institutions did not completely prevent all conflicts from arising, it had however sure mechanisms which averted and stopped conflicts.

---

17. Ibid., 305.
18. Changwony, "Role of Women in Keiyo Traditional Religious Rites, 70.

Concluding Remarks

After reading how the indigenous Kalenjin community went into pains to avert conflicts, one is disturbed by what is going on in the world today. Peace seems to evade humanity in the 21st century. The wars in Russia, Britain, Sierra Leone, Sudan, Ethiopia, Eritrea and Iraq among others are buffeted animosities that are part of history coupled with contemporary responses to oppressive attitude and inequities. No one seems to respect even the United Nation's effort in peace keeping as was evident in Ethiopia, Bosnia and more recently in Sierra Leone, Iraq and Democratic Republic of Congo where UN peacekeepers have been attacked and several killed.

Today one cannot point at an effective solution to conflicts. There is need therefore for further research on how to curb violence, aggression and dominance. This calls for solid, thoughtful and scholarly research from all disciplines that can possibly come up with realistic and long lasting solutions to conflict. Indigenous wisdom is one such area of study that requires attention.

The African religious experience has been ignored and it is time that scholars re-visited the wisdom of its traditions. The example of the role of women in conflict management discussed here is a perfect example. Fortunately, this phenomenon is not unique to Kalenjin women, rather, it is a widespread experience throughout Africa. For example, in his article, Chris Ukhun has quoted the experience of Iyede women of Southern Nigeria who averted conflicts by threatening to go nude.

> Iyede Women Council could also threaten to go nude before any person or persons they felt were responsible for ignoring their aspirations or anyone who precipitated a crisis which threatened the well being of the community.[19]

It is important to note here that not everything has been lost in this regard. The Kalenjin women discussed here are today still engaged in their roles as conflict managers especially in the family and to some extent, at the community level. It is not an exaggeration to say that the majority of families in Africa today are held together by the wisdom and the forgiving spirit of women.

There is no doubt then that women were and still are good conflict managers. There is need, therefore, to stress the value of women's

---

19. Deusdedit and Levis, *Developing A Culture of Peace and Human Rights*, 20.

natural qualities that can enable them procure leadership position. One recent example of women leadership and peacemaking is that of the Member of Parliament of Kenya, Mrs. Lina Kilimo. For many years, the Marakwet and Pokot communities were involved in bitter strife involving cattle raids and killings. The governments' efforts to bring peace among the two communities were in vain for the last ten years. In the 2002 elections, the Marakwet community elected a woman because they wanted peace which none of the men who lead them before provided. Indeed, Mrs. Kilimo was thus nicknamed *Legetiot* to signify her new expected role to bring peace. Since her election, there has been a drastic reduction in conflicts between the two communities as testified to by Oriang'. She writes thus, "Both the Pokot and the Marakwet respect the Leketio. With the election of *Leketio* Kilimo, the locals were literally laying the peace belt between them. It has held for more than a year now."[20]

As if to reaffirm their traditional role of peace making, the women of pastoralist communities in Kenya and Uganda met recently on April 2, 2004 to probe the root cause of cattle rustling among their people. In a strong statement, the head of the task force and also the East Africa Legislative Assembly M.P, Prof. Margaret Kamar, clearly indicated that women can intervene and bring peace among pastoralist communities. She was quoted thus saying:

> It is sad to see innocent women and children die while homesteads are destroyed during violent cattle raids. I am sure we are capable of telling our men to stop stock theft if we forge a common front.[21]

I see the women's liberation movement in Africa using these powerful and God given abilities as the starting point of their liberation theology. The organizing principle of such theology shall be based on the spirit embedded in motherhood. It is this spirit that challenges women to act fairly and to promote the gift of divine forgiveness that brings peace, reconciliation and healing.

---

20. Oriang, "We are the World," 30.
21. "Women Pastoralists Meet," 11.

Bibliography

Avruch, Kevin, et al. *Conflict Resolution: Cross-Cultural Perspective*. London: Greenword, 1991.

Blum, William G. *Forms of Marriage: Monogamy Reconsidered*. Eldoret Kenya: Gaba, 1989.

Boss, Judith A. *Analyzing Moral Issues*. London: Mayfield, 1999.

Changwony, Dinah Jerotich. "The Role of Women in Keiyo Traditional Religious Rites". MPhil diss., Moi University, 1996.

Chepkwony, Adam K. arap, "African Religion in the study of Comparative Religion: A Case Study of Kipsigis Religious practices." DPhil diss, Moi University 1997.

Deusdedit, Nkurunzia R. K., and Mugunya Levis, editors. *Developing A Culture of Peace and Human Rights*. Adenauer Stiftung, 2003.

Getui, Mary N., and Hazel Ayanga, eds. *Conflicts in Africa: A Woman Response*. Nairobi: Circle of Concerned African Women Theologies, 2002.

King, Ursula. *Women and Spirituality*. London: Macmillan, 1989.

Okeye, Mokwugo. *Points of Discord: Studies in Tension and Conflict*. London: Fredrick Muller, 1973.

O' Leary, Dale. *The Gender Agenda*. Lafayette, LA: Vital Issues, 1997.

Oriang, Lucy. "We Are the World." *Nation* (March 8, 2004) 30.

Onyango-Ogutu, B., and A. A. Roscoe. *Keep My Words: Luo Oral Literature*. Nairobi: East African, 1974.

Schreiter, Robert J. *The Ministry of Reconciliation*. Maryknoll, NY: Orbis, 2000.

Smith-Christopher, Daniel L, editor. *Subverting Hatred: The Challenge of Nonviolence in Religious Traditions*. Maryknoll, NY: Orbis, 1998.

Wamue, Grace, and Mary Getui, editors. *Violence against Women*. Nairobi: Acton, 1996.

"Women Pastoralists Meet." *East Africa Standard* (April 15, 2004) 11.

6

Church and State Conflicts in Uganda
President Idi Amin Kills the Anglican Archbishop

EMMANUEL KALENZI TWESIGYE

THE PROBLEMS OF CHURCH AND STATE CONFLICTS IN UGANDA[1] HAVE been more serious and destructive than in other countries of Africa, with the exceptions of Northern Nigeria and Sudan, where more than two million Christians have been killed by the Arab Muslims. These tragic religio-political conflicts in Uganda led to the rise of President Idi Amin. They also tragically resulted in the brutal murder of the Anglican Archbishop Janani Luwum of Uganda on the evening of February 16, 1977. In the case of Uganda, these tragic conflicts between Church and State can be traced back to the British Anglican missionary strategies and ideals in the founding of Christianity in Uganda.[2]

---

1. This chapter was originally written as a paper that was delivered at the annual professional meeting of the American Academy of Religion in November 2000, in Nashville, Tennessee, USA. This material is also a portion of a forthcoming book on *Religion and Politics in Uganda*.
    The funds for research in Uganda were provided by the Ohio Wesleyan University and awarded from the Thomas E. Wenslow (TEW) grants for outstanding academic and scholarly activities. I am very grateful to the Provost's Office and to Professor Richard Fusch, the former Associate Dean for Academic Affairs and the OWU's TEW Grant Committee, and the GLCA (Great Lakes Colleges Association) travel grants for the generous support for my research travels to East Africa, in 1999, 2002 and 2004. I am also grateful to Samuel Chesser and Matthew MacKenzie, my student editorial assistants, and to Beatrice Twesigye for proof-reading, and Kandi Akers for providing valuable secretarial support.

2. For instance, see Hansen, *Mission, Church and State in a Colonial Setting*. This is the most comprehensive presentation and analysis of the problem. Professors Semakula Kiwanuka's *History of Buganda from Foundation to 1900* and Samuel Karugire's *Political History of Uganda*, also contain good coverage of the problem.

This process took place in the last quarter of the nineteenth century. The Christian establishment in Uganda and the hostile rivalry of the Anglicans and Catholics led to confusion among the Ugandans, including the kings of Uganda, who were all Anglicans.[3] This oppressive Anglican hegemony is the root cause of political instability in Uganda, since the Roman Catholics and Muslims outnumber the Anglicans, and yet, political power has been traditionally monopolized by the Anglican political elites, kings and most chiefs.

General Introduction

There was a devastating state persecution of Christianity in the Kingdom of Buganda, from 1885–1888, which was decreed by King Mwanga. Mwanga was a newly enthroned nationalist and traditionalist young king who wanted to eliminate Christianity, as a new foreign and divisive religion. This systematic state Christian persecution, finally, led to the religious wars of 1888–1892 in Buganda. These religious wars led to the establishment of Anglican hegemony in Buganda, and subsequently, the rest of the kingdoms in Uganda. In these religious wars, the African traditionalists, being supported by the nationalistic King Mwanga, decided to get rid of all the "imported" foreign religions, especially Islam, Catholicism and Protestantism, from the country. Faced with extinction, the "three foreign religions" declared a truce and formed a religious military coalition that definitively defeated the African Traditionalist Party (the Pagans). Following this victory, the religious coalition between the Christians and Muslims broke down. The Muslims, who had traditionally resented the intrusion of the Christians in their territory, decided to get rid of the Christians and their European missionary teachers. The Muslims staged a coup against the Christians and installed Prince Kalema as a Muslim King and declared Buganda a Muslim country.[4]

The deposed King Mwanga, and the leading Christians fled into exile in Karagwe, northern Tanzania, and others fled to Buddu and Ankole in Southern and Western Uganda. The Catholics and Anglicans formed a new military coalition in exile, and were helped by the missionaries to acquire guns and ammunition, returned to Buganda and

3. Ibid.
4. Ibid.

overthrew the Islamic monarchy and reestablished King Mwanga on the throne of Buganda with the Christian generals retaining much of the power in the now officially new Christian country. However, the hostility between the Catholics and Anglicans soon reemerged, fanned by the European traditional rivalry and mutual intolerance for each other. As a result, the military coalition between Catholics, who called themselves "*Bafransa*" (the French), for being the followers of the French Catholic Missionaries, and the Anglicans, who called themselves "*Bangereza*" (the English), for being the followers of the English Missionaries, disgracefully broke-down.

Subsequently, the Ugandan Anglicans and the Catholics fought a serious war, in which, the local Anglicans and their British allies emerged as military victors. Since that time, the Anglican elites have ruled Uganda and excluded the Catholics, Muslims and African traditionalists from power, except as political tokens or pawns in the Ugandan political game. All the kings of the Ugandan kingdoms became Anglican, along with most of their major chiefs. The Anglican Church informally became the Established Church of Uganda. The Traditionalists (*Bakafiri*) or "Pagans" and "Muslims" (*Basalamu*) became completely disgraced. The religious and political hierarchy of privilege and power evolved with the Anglican elites at the top of the pyramid. The Anglicans as the ruling elites came first, followed by the more numerical Catholics, who were regarded as second class citizens, followed by the Muslims as third class citizens, and they were followed by Traditionalists (*Bakafiri/*"Pagans"), as fourth class citizens. The Traditionalists were considered as the underclass of the disenfranchised and oppressed African rural masses.[5]

It is within this complex religious and political background and context that President Idi Amin, a Muslim, became the new Ugandan president through a military coup. He then decided to demolish the traditional hierarchical structure through the brutal and bloody strategy of extermination of the Anglicans. President Idi Amin decided to establish an Islamic hegemony in Uganda. President Amin, as a Muslim extremist, and religious fundamentalist, officially declared Uganda, a predominantly Christian country, to become a Muslim country. Subsequently, Uganda joined the League of Arab Muslim Nations. As such, the assassination of the Most Reverend Janani Luwum, the

---

5. See Hansen, *Mission, Church and State in a Colonial Setting* 29–57.

Anglican Archbishop of Uganda in 1977, was a strategically planned political event, by President Amin, as a move toward his consolidation of Islamic power, and the state promotion of the Islamization process in Uganda.[6]

This military and violent strategy failed to work and accomplish the results for which President Idi Amin had hoped. However, thousands of Ugandan Christians were killed as part of Idi Amin's strategy for the state Islamization of Uganda by force. This included the persecution of Christians, terrorism or harassment and mass arrests of non-Muslims and mass murders. As a result, almost one million Christians were killed in Uganda during President Idi Amin's "reign of terror" from 1971–79. Most of these victims were Anglican Christian political elites, religious leaders, members of the civil service and the military. Some Roman Catholics who resisted Idi Amin's repressive regime also were killed. Benedicto Kiwanuka, the Chief Justice, and former Prime Minister of Uganda, Francis Xavier Tibayungwa,[7] the Chief Administrator of the Kingdom of Ankole, and Fr. Kiggundu, the editor of *Munno*, are outstanding examples of these Catholic victims.

Nevertheless, the Church and State conflicts in Uganda also go back to the time of Jesus Christ, and both his rejection and persecution by the Jewish religious establishment, and finally, his crucifixion, by the Roman governing authorities on the charge of treason. The Ugandan Evangelicals found Jesus' story of innocent suffering, persecution, arrest, trial, conviction, crucifixion and resurrection, a source of deep faith and necessary courage to stand firm against the evils of injustice and tyranny by the State.

---

6. See Hansen and Twaddle, *Religion & Politics in East Africa*, 1–30.

7. Mr. Tibayungwa was also the father of my wife. He is one of the major examples of Catholic high-ranking leaders and politicians, who were killed by Idi Amin, out of fear due to their political power. These selective assassinations and murders of major Catholic politicians, indicates that President Idi Amin may have primarily killed more Anglican politicians and later the Archbishop Luwum, the Anglican Archbishop of Uganda, Rwanda, Burundi and Boga-Zaire, in 1977, mainly because of their perceived political power and threat to his illegitimate political military regime. If Catholics had been the ones in political power, they would have been the main focus of his Christian persecution. Muslims who opposed President Idi Amin, like Prof. Ali Mazurui, of Makerere University, also were subjected to harassment and persecution. As a result, Prof. Mazurui was forced to flee into exile, in the USA.

Uganda's Church and State Conflicts in a Global Historical Context

Through the ages, Christians have had a strange relationship with the State and political power structures of their own time. This is partly because Christians worship a loving, good, omnipotent Creator-God, and yet, they are called to follow Jesus as the Christ and their own personal Lord-Saviour. Jesus was himself persecuted, arrested, and tried for treason against the State.

Subsequently, he was unfairly convicted, tortured and executed by being crucified on the cross by the State officials of his own day. For Christians, loyalty to God comes first. Loyalty to the State and earthly rulers, such as the emperors, kings and presidents, comes second. By virtue of the sacrament of holy baptism, Christians pledge to become the citizens of the Kingdom of God first, and secondly, to live as good citizens of the earthly kingdoms, or their respective countries in which they live.[8] As a result, the Jehovah's Witnesses prefer a life based on the citizenship in God's Kingdom alone. Subsequently, they refuse to engage in the political activities of their earthly nations, such as voting or holding a political office.

However, Jesus was a pacifist who never taught his faithful followers to fight against Roman imperialism or to revolt against the oppression of the state. Jesus taught the moral imperative and universal absoluteness of nonviolence and agape. As a result, he rebuked and prevented Peter from defending him from an unjustified arrest by the agents of the State. He declared that "those who live by the sword would also perish by the sword" (Matt 26:50–52). Jesus also had conservatively taught his followers to pay taxes "and give to Caesar what belongs to Caesar, and to God, what belongs to God" (cf. Luke 20:20–26). To complicate this scenario, Jesus also taught his followers, that there was a high cost for discipleship, or following him, and obeying both his religious and moral teachings. To this end, Jesus asked that the people, who wished to follow him had to deny themselves, and carry their own crosses (cf. Mark 8:34–38). The cross was a Roman imperial symbol of State power to arrest, torture and kill, by crucifying the enemies of the State. The political enemies were people who were Roman subjects that failed to obey the laws of Rome, as formulated

---

8. See the Episcopal Church (Anglican) *Book of Common Prayer*, 301–8, 858–59.

and instituted by Caesar (Emperor), or the Roman Senate. They assumed that the persecution of Christians was legal, good and just, and therefore, sanctioned by the Roman gods.

Jesus and his followers were acutely aware that they were men and women who belonged to two opposing kingdoms. That is, they belonged to the Kingdom of God and the kingdom of the earthly rulers or the State. Until 313 CE, when Emperor Constantine legalized Christianity, and later *Theodosius* established it as the state religion, Christianity was an illegal and persecuted minority religion within the Roman Empire. In this period, many Christians were arrested, tried, tortured and condemned to painful forms of death by the Roman officers operating in all the provinces of the Roman Empire.[9]

Constantine's conversion to Christianity and adoption of the formally persecuted Christianity into a privileged imperial established religion put Christianity into a new strange relationship of power in relationship to the state or the earthly kingdoms. At the beginning, the Emperor Constantine began to interfere in the moral, spiritual and doctrinal matters of the state. He dictated what the true doctrine should be, as in the case of the Nicene Creed and Christological controversies that had divided the Christians and his empire. Later, the Church became too powerful and subordinated the emperors and kings of Europe to it until the rebellion of King Henry VIII, in the sixteenth century.

The conflicts between the Church and State, or conflicts between religion and politics, are universal and common problems. In ancient times, the problem was dealt with in two main ways. In many cases, the conflict between the Church and State was resolved by the king or emperor claiming divine powers or taking over the position of the archbishop or archpriest of the nation, as in the case of Henry the VIII, or the leader of the Church could take the place of the Head of the State, as in the case of the Pope. This is the essence of theocracy, or God's Kingdom in the world.

In a theocracy, God indirectly rules the world through the king, emperor, chief, judge, or other political and military leaders. According to St. Paul, and the Roman culture, the Caesar (or Roman emperor) was considered as God's agent on earth. Therefore, the Caesar was both valued and worshiped as God's agent of law, order and peace. This is

9. See Gonzalez, *A History of Christian Thought*, 261–87.

the kind of context in which St. Paul claimed that all kings and rulers are appointed by God to rule the people in God's name and should be obeyed by Christians (Romans 13). But, when evil kings, emperors and rulers, such as Adolph Hitler of Nazi Germany, and Idi Amin of Uganda arose, to become these kinds of rulers, St. Peter said, "We will obey God, rather than men" (Acts 4:19). These kinds of evil rulers were the antichrists to be opposed as the representatives of the Devil rather than God.

Divine kingship as in the case of the African kings, such as the Egyptian pharaohs, Ethiopian emperors, and Ugandan kings, as well as the Roman, Japanese and Chinese Emperors, and the medieval European kings, were a universal theocentric principle and ideal practice in the absence of true democracy and theocracy. This theocratic principle has survived in the modern era in various forms, such as the papacy and some *Shari'a* based Islamic nations, like Saudi Arabia and Iran.

Like Mosaic Judaism, Islam also has provided a solution for the conflicts between Church (Religion) and State by adopting a theocracy. This is akin to that theocracy of Moses, the Pope, and the Da Lai Lama as the Ruler of Tibet. In this scenario, the senior clergy, such as the Ayatollah Khomeini serves as the pharaoh, pope or Vicar and HighPriests of God on the Earth by divine power, unites and rules over both the Church and the State. As a result, Islam imposes its will and God's moral or religious law over the State. This is the traditional position of Islam. Islam is the context in which the nation or state arises and the *Shari'a* (Islamic law) shapes the conscience of the individual Muslims and their collective religious and political consciousness as a nation. In this respect, a charismatic Muslim leader, such as the Ayatollah served as a pope for the nation and people, who were under his religious and political control.

In medieval Europe, the Pope could crown and depose the kings in Europe. They paid homage and tribute to him until Henry VIII, the King of England, rebelled against what he believed to be both religious and Roman political imperialism. He formed his own Anglican Church, with himself as its Head. This Anglican Church was later exported to the British colonies abroad, including Uganda. The Anglican missionaries tried to promote the establishment of a local Anglican Church at the expense of the other religions, including Islam, native religions and other Christian denominations, including Roman Catholicism. The Anglican missionaries also brought their own traditional religious prejudice and hostility against the Roman Catholic Church.

At the time the Anglicans came into Africa, in the nineteenth century, Islam and the African Traditional Religions, were already well established. Islam itself was intolerant of Christianity. Subsequently, many Muslim nations have persecuted Christians and other non-Muslims in the name of God (*Allah*). Sudan is a modern example. The destructive war between the Christian South and Muslim North has been fought in the name of God. About two million people have been killed in this holy war (*jihad*), most of them being those non-Muslims from the South. Some of their children have been sold into slavery to the Muslims in the North. Uganda to the South of Sudan also suffered a series of religious wars, and the most destructive was President Idi Amin's persecution of the Anglican Church of Uganda, which culminated in the assassination of the Most Reverend Janani Luwum, the Anglican Archbishop of Uganda, Rwanda, Burundi and Boga-Zaire, on the evening of February 16, 1977.

The serious problems of Church and State conflicts and tragedies in Uganda illustrate what happens when God and Caesar or Church and State come into serious conflict. In some non-democratic African nations, such as Uganda during President Idi Amin's "reign of terror," in 1971–1979, the Church, and its members were persecuted and murdered by the hostile State.

However, President Idi Amin was not the first head of state to assassinate an Archbishop or head of the Church. The assassination of the Archbishop Oscar Romero during Mass in 1978, in El Salvador may have been more dramatic than that of Janani Luwum, but both of them were equally gruesome. Archbishop Romero's assassination is almost similar to the twelfth century (Dec. 29, 1170) murder of the Archbishop Thomas Becket of Canterbury, in the cathedral, at the orders of King Henry II. This appears to sound like a precursor for the State directed murders of critical and prophetic archbishops, bishops and priests. It also mirrors or sets a model for later conflicts between Church and State. These archbishops refused to compromise with evil (the State) and became willing to die as martyrs for their religious faith and moral principles. The spiritual sword (Church) is often physically oppressed, or silenced and nearly destroyed by the physical sword (the

State) with its military power. Church censorship, persecution and oppression by State in the former Soviet Union and Communist China provide examples of this scenario.

In the above cases, the Church is oppressed and its members are killed by the State. But, the Church recovers to challenge the State, yet again. This has been true in Uganda since the time of King Mwanga, when in 1885 he killed Bishop James Hannington, and then, ordered a mass arrest, trial and execution of leading Christians at his court on charges of treason and insubordination to the king. President Idi Amin, almost duplicated this scenario nearly a century later. His Christian persecution and mass murders of Christians were more massive and national than those of King Mwanga. The same spirit of African nationalism and hostility directed against the Ugandan Christian leaders and the European Christian missionaries underlies both eras of Christian persecution in Uganda by the Ugandan State.

In these instances, it is the kings, emperors and rulers who use their power of the sword or gun to subdue the Church and assassinate the Church leaders, such as the bishops and archbishops. In this case, St. Augustine's militaristic analogy of the Church and the State as the possessors of God's mutually complimentary swords, namely, the spiritual sword in the case of the Church and the military sword in the case of the State is an interesting one. In the case of Uganda, the swords have come into conflict, and the military sword has beheaded the defenseless wielders of the powerless spiritual sword.

The Archbishop Janani Luwum's holy Bible and the Episcopal cross were effectively used as the holy weapons of Christian moral crusade and nonviolence, to challenge and fight against Christian persecution, and the abuses of President Idi Amin's crushing power of the gun and the military might. The Anglican Church's nonviolent moral crusade was brutally crushed by President Amin's military might, and thousands of Christians were killed. This tragedy confirmed the self-evident truth, that in this world, when God and Caesar come into conflict, it becomes the replay of Christ's arrest, trial and crucifixion by the state.

The Church, Politics and State Formation in Uganda

The State or kingdoms of Uganda predate Christianity or the Christian Church. In fact, it was King Mutesa I, as the king of Buganda that wrote a royal letter, in 1875, to Queen Victoria of England requesting her to send Christian missionaries, engineers, diplomats and traders to his African kingdom. In this respect, the Church or Christianity was viewed as a tool of the State to foster international relations, national development, education and trade.[10]

However, when the Anglican missionaries arrived in Buganda, they refused to engage in trade and military affairs of King Mutesa. As a result, Kings Mutesa I and Mwanga, his successor, rejected the unpractical Christian missionaries, and sought to expel them from Uganda. On seeing the mutual European religious intolerance, cantankerous quarrels, and degrading religious feuds between the Anglican and Catholic Christian missionaries, Mutesa was both disillusioned and distressed.

Subsequently, Prince Mwanga, his son and successor tried to expel them from the country, once he had become the new king of Buganda. This scenario illustrates that religion and the Church, were considered relative institutions that were subordinate to the king, and subject to obey the laws of the king or the State. Like Emperor Constantine, the kings of Uganda, especially Mutesa I, and later President Idi Amin, religion and the Church were economically and politically viewed and most valued as tools for State ends, such as nation-building, unity, defense and the economy.

Ultimately, the pre-colonial religious wars, Christian persecution, and state censorship and control of religion, education, politics, information, speech, and later, the colonial control of academic freedom, constituted the historical background and religious context which created violent religio-political monsters in the form of Kabaka Mwanga of Buganda and later President Idi Amin of Uganda. Idi Amin was a poorly educated and semi-illiterate Muslim from West Nile, who later became the military President of Uganda, through a military coup.

Furthermore, due to Uganda's unique history of religious intolerance, rivalry, violence and wars, Idi Amin's persecution of the Christians led to the tragic mass murders of the Anglican elite that had tradition-

---

10. See *A Century of Christianity in Uganda*, 2–4.

ally dominated the Ugandan political affairs. The Anglican Christian civilians were perceived as the real threat to President Idi Amin and the Muslims in their desperate military attempt to usurp power from the established Anglican political power structure, and the Anglican Church of Uganda, as its traditional and moral base.

At the beginning of Idi Amin's repressive rule, some people felt that these actions also were probably carried out of justice and the need to redistribute political power more evenly among the different religious groups. Muslims and the Catholics had been excluded from equal opportunities for uncensored access to equal sharing of political power in Uganda. This was the case ever since the combined ecumenical Christian defeat of the Muslim forces led by Kabaka Kalema of Buganda in 1890, and the subsequent definitive Anglican victory of 1892 over the Catholic military forces which were in alliance with Kabaka Mwanga. Following this Anglican political and religious military victory, there was an imposition of the Anglican religio-political establishment and dominion in Buganda and the rest of Uganda.

Subsequently, this Anglican Church establishment structure in the Buganda Kingdom became the normative paradigm for the other kingdoms and districts of Uganda. The Anglican hegemony was established over the rest of Uganda through the British colonial policy of indirect rule through the Baganda Anglican chiefs. The Anglican Baganda chiefs were considered to be the appropriate local agents of the British imperial and colonial government in Uganda. The Baganda Anglican converts also went out as Christian missionaries and educators. The combined team of Baganda Anglican missionaries and the Anglican Baganda chiefs deployed over Uganda as the agents of British colonial rule, effectively converted and transformed Uganda's traditional political structures and religion into those of national and local Anglican establishment, elitism and hegemony.

The Catholics were permanently relegated to second class citizenship and the Muslims became third class citizens, both in education and political power. The African Traditionalists were called "pagans" and "uncivilized."[11] These African Traditionalists were completely marginalized and never accounted for much in the new religious hierarchical power structure and politics of colonial

---

11. See: Twesigye, *African Religion, Philosophy, and Christianity*; Tuma, *A Century of Christianity*, 10–13.

Uganda. In order to disenfranchise these traditionalists and many illiterate Catholics, *Uganda Peoples' Congress* (UPC), which was predominantly Anglican and elitist, demanded that the electorate for national independence in 1962 be limited to those who could read and write! Reading and writing had been taught by the Anglicans as necessary universal prerequisites for adult baptism. This was a mere political strategy to exclude many Catholic illiterate Christians from voting for the *Democratic Party* (DP).

Education and Anglicanism became synonymous and intrinsically inseparable that the local people simply came to refer to Anglican Christians as "*Abasomi*" (Readers or the educated), and correlatively, the Anglican form of Sunday worship was referred to as "*Kusoma*" (to read or to be educated). In contrast, the Catholics who did not emphasize literary mass education (*kusoma*), referred to their sacramental worship as "attending the Mass" (*Missa*). This difference in missionary strategy and approach to education explains why the Anglicans had numerically fewer converts, but more influential, educated and powerful people in political and economic affairs of the kingdoms and the nation compared to the superior numbers of mainly poorly educated and illiterate masses of people, who had little political influence in Uganda's political and economic affairs.

Therefore, the Ugandan dilemma was self-evident. If true democracy is to be measured in terms of free elections, in which there is a policy of one person one vote, based on the reality of religiously based political parties of Uganda, then without a doubt, Catholics and their political party known as the DP (*Democratic Party*) would win!

However, in reality, the traditional Anglican power structure has not allowed for this kind of free democratic political process to occur. Elections have been constantly rigged. This has taken different forms, such as the falsification of poll results, drawing electoral boundaries or electoral districts along religious lines, or banning multiparty politics as President Obote did in 1969, leaving only the UPC. President Yoweri Museveni, another Anglican, like Obote, also managed to continue one party mass democratic process to avoid a DP victory in a free multiparty election. President Museveni's strategy was successful in that he engineered the 1995 constitutional ban of all multiparty politics and elections in Uganda until a national referendum could be conducted on the issue!

One can already predict the results of the referendum. They are likely to be the results that favor a continuing constitutional ban on multiparty politics and elections of the past, mainly because of the negative experience of hooliganism, vandalism, violence, corruption and rigging of elections that were closely associated with Uganda's past sectarian politics of divisiveness and violence. This was mainly due to the kind of mutually exclusive political hostility between the political parties as a result of being directly related to the traditional religious divisions, hostilities, and ethnic sectarian politics.

Apart from some parties forming along these mutually exclusive and traditional religious hostilities and sectarianism, some Ugandan political parties also were formed on the basis of exclusive local ethnic nationalism, such as *"Kabaka Yekka"* (The King of Buganda Alone) in the Kingdom of Buganda. *Kabaka Yekka* was founded in 1961 to protect the integrity of Buganda's Kingdom and independence in an independent Uganda. This Baganda exclusive ethnic nationalism later challenged the central government of Uganda's power, thereby provoking President Obote's political wrath and retaliation.

In order to effectively unify the ethnically pluralistic and politically diverse people of Uganda into one politically homogeneous nation, President Obote abolished the kingdoms in Uganda in 1969. This Baganda nationalism and separatism also led President Idi Amin, a Muslim, the self-imposed military Head of the State of Uganda, to intervene in the Anglican Church's internal affairs in 1971, when the Anglican Diocese of Namirembe and other Buganda dioceses voted to secede from the rest of the Anglican Province of the Church of Uganda. Both presidents Obote and Idi Amin censored Buganda Kingdom's political and religious affairs, for fear of Buganda's strong ethnic nationalism both in matters of Church (or religion) and State (or politics).[12]

Uganda's political dilemma, official persecution and martyrdom of many Christians under *"Kabaka"* (King) Mwanga of Buganda in the

---

12. President Idi Amin being a Muslim, yet showing real concern for Anglican Church unity for his own political reasons, such as to prevent the secessionist attempt of the Anglican Church of Buganda from the rest of the Anglican Church of Uganda, provides more evidence that the Church was valued by the State as a tool of national unity, economic and political stability. However, Bishop Festo Kivengere, called President Idi Amin's intervention God's redemptive work. See Festo Kivengere, *I Love Idi Amin.*

years of 1884–1887, and later, under the Muslim President Idi Amin in the years of 1971–1979, is largely due to the fusion, and confusion of Church and State affairs, or religion and politics in Uganda. Christians were persecuted because they were the most educated, and when ecumenically united together, presented the most important major challenge, and voice of opposition and criticism to the tyranny and abuse of power and human rights by the respective despot of the time.

In essence, the Christians in both eras were persecuted and killed by Kabaka Mwanga in Buganda, during the 1885–1887 royal purge of Christians, and later, by President Idi Amin in the years of 1971–1979. This persecution of Christians occurred because both heads of state were Muslims and dictators, who feared the combined force of the Christians as a potential threat to their political power and survival in office.

The brutal official persecution of Uganda's Christians was in both cases undertaken by non-Christian dictators in order to purge the country of Christianity. In both cases, the Christian persecution was carefully designed to purge the country of foreign religions and colonial influences, which were both implicitly and explicitly associated with the presence of the foreign Christian missionaries and their local Christian converts.

Conversion to Christianity was negatively regarded as conversion to foreign cultures and values, and becoming an indirect colonial agent, an econo-political remote-controlled tool for foreign imperial governments in Europe, and their colonial or neocolonial interests in Africa. Both Kabaka Mwanga and Idi Amin sought to expel foreign missionaries from the country and then to exterminate the local Christians, especially those with major local influence, such as the clergy, teachers, chiefs, and Christians in high-ranking offices in the military.

President Idi Amin's Reign of Terror and Christian Persecution

President General Idi Amin was a Muslim. He was a member of a traditionally marginalized religious group, and when he overthrew President Milton Obote, an Anglican, both Catholics and Muslims rejoiced. They erroneously believed and hoped that a new political era of democracy had dawned.

However, President Idi Amin's brutal persecution of Christianity, and mass murders of Christians, particularly the Anglican elite in Uganda, finally met with Christian resistance. The bishops were persuaded to respond, and protect the Christians, by denouncing President Idi Amin as a political dictator, and a mass murderer. To this end, the Christian resistance and political protest was led by the Anglican Bishops and the Anglican Church. Their formal and public protest letter of February 10, 1977, provoked President Idi Amin's wrath and deadly retaliation. In their Episcopal letter to President Idi Amin, the Anglican Bishops protested against Idi Amin's repressive government and reign of terror, and persecution of the Christian Church that had led to the mass murders of thousands of Christians, and other people suspected to be opponents of Idi Amin's Muslim military government in a predominantly African Christian country.[13]

These tragic and gruesome acts of Christian persecution were characterized by horrifying acts of brutality, including intimidation, censorship, arbitrary arrests of Christians, torture, and the mass murder of people, particularly the Christians and their sympathizers. These tragic acts were designed to censor, terrorize, demoralize, and exterminate the Ugandan Christians, and thereby, transform Uganda into a Muslim country.

The Church's bold formal protest and nonviolent Christian resistance against Idi Amin's Islamization program and Christian persecution provoked Idi Amin's outrage, brutality, and deadly retaliation against the Christian Church leaders, and was particularly directed against the Anglican Church leaders and all influential lay Christian leaders in the nation, including the remote rural area local Christian chiefs and community leaders. The retaliation led to the serious trumped-up charges of treason, and an attempt to overthrow President Idi Amin's Government by the Anglican Church leaders. This Christian religious coup against Idi Amin was supposedly to be accomplished through force of arms in order to restore the deposed and exiled former President Dr. Milton Obote, an Anglican, back to power.

Subsequent to the Anglican Church Bishops' formal protest, Idi Amin called a public meeting of religious leaders, ambassadors, and

---

13. See James Tumusiime, *Uganda 30 Years*, 43–54.

military officers. The staged public military trial of the Church leaders took place on the morning of February 16, 1977, at the Nile Mansion. This was the government-owned hotel, which Idi Amin and his military officers had transformed into their own headquarters and offices. At this meeting and public military trial, the Anglican Church leaders, particularly the bishops and other influential Anglicans, were publicly accused of being traitors and having committed the terrible crimes of treason and sedition, which were punishable by death. The Vice-President of Uganda presided over these public proceedings. Finally, he asked: "What should we do with these traitors?" The army shouted in a deafening angry roar as if they had been coached to chant: "Kill them! Kill them! Kill them! Kill them!" This act had serious implications and consequences for the Church and Christians in Uganda.[14]

This tragic event was planned by President Idi Amin and his Muslim advisors. It was nationally televised and broadcast live on Uganda Radio. It was Idi Amin's orchestrated public military trial of the Anglican Church and its leaders as criminals and traitors whose crimes deserved the death sentence which his officers were already carrying out in an extra judiciary manner. Symbolically, at this meeting or trial, Idi Amin wished to send an explicitly intimidating and ominous message to the nation, and the world that the Anglican Church of Uganda had been tried by the military, and found guilty of treason and sedition, which were crimes punishable by death!

According to this understanding, every Anglican had symbolically become guilty of resistance to Idi Amin's government, and guilty as accessories to the Church leaders' supposed sedition and treasonous plot to overthrow the government. Subsequent to this guilty verdict that was passed against the Anglican Church leaders by the soldiers, and having announced the death sentence to the Church leaders, there followed the arrest and subsequent gruesome murder of the Most Reverend Janani Luwum, the Anglican Archbishop of Uganda, on that fateful day of February 16, 1977. This assassination of the Anglican Archbishop horrified and shocked the nation and the Christian world. The martyrdom of the Anglican Archbishop of Uganda, along with the Lt. Col. Erinayo Oryema and Hon. Charles Oboth Ofumbi, two prominent Anglicans serving as Cabinet Ministers in Idi Amin's Government, made headlines all over the world.

14. Coomes, *Festo Kivengere*, 355–64.

Following the murder of the Archbishop, many members of the Anglican clergy, teachers, college professors, and influential Christians were put under surveillance. A great number of these Christians were arrested and killed by the State Research Bureau intelligence officers and those of the Public Safety Unit. Many Anglican bishops fled into exile. A year later, Bishop John Wasikye of Mbale was arrested and taken to the military barracks in Jinja where he was interrogated, tortured, and finally killed.

President Idi Amin's assassination of the Anglican Archbishop of Uganda along with some Anglican cabinet members in his own government, only makes sense when one places these horrendous political murders within the context of Ugandan history, politics, and the complex relationship between Church and State. Uganda's complex history of the religious sectarianism and the rivalry between Anglicans, Catholics, and Muslims created President Obote, Idi Amin, as well as the President Yoweri Kaguta Museveni.[15] These presidents had waged a "liberationist holy war" against each other and the mutually hostile, religiously based political parties in order to root out corruption, injustice, genocide, and both political and religious intolerance.

It is due to this political excuse of getting rid of corruption and political dictatorship that Gen. Idi Amin's military coup was originally staged, and subsequently, many tragic wars were fought in Uganda, including those against Idi Amin, Milton Obote and Yoweri Museveni. President Museveni's *National Resistance Army Movement* (NRM), came to power through war in 1986, and in 1987, Alice Lakwena's *Holy Spirit Mobile Forces* (HSMF), emerged to overthrow him in the name of God. When it failed, Joseph Kony, established the *Lord's Resistance Army* (LRA) to overthrow President Museveni's secular NRM Government, in order to establish God's theocracy, under the Pope, that would be based on the Ten Commandments of God.

These destructive revolutionary, murderous and military trends began with Gen. Idi Amin, as the president of Uganda. To this gruesome and tragic end, President Idi Amin would also later purge the military of most of its high-ranking Christian officers following his military coup on January 25, 1971, and the violent overthrow of Dr.

15. See Museveni, *Sowing the Mustard Seed*. President Museveni provides a good analysis of the political, economic and religious problems of Uganda, and discusses how he has tried to solve them, with the *National Resistance Movement* (NRM) as his invented political vehicle.

Milton Obote's UPC (*Uganda People's Congress*) Party which was predominantly Anglican (Protestant) in its foundation, leadership and composition. As a result of this religio-political establishment in both colonial and postcolonial Uganda, most of the high-ranking military officers and government leaders who were arrested and killed following the coup were predominantly Anglican.

Nevertheless, several hundred Roman Catholics who occupied positions of privilege or influence, such as Benedicto Kiwanuka (k. 1972), the Chief Justice of Uganda and former Prime Minister of Uganda; Francis Xavier Tibayungwa (k. 1972), the Administrative Secretary of Ankole Kingdom; Father Clement Kiggundu (k. 1972), the critical editor of *Munno*, the influential Luganda newspaper; Theresa Nanziri (k. 1976), the Warden of Africa Hall, Makerere University, and thousands of others, were killed. For instance, the Langi and Acholi people in the military were lined up, disarmed, and massacred *en masse* following General Idi Amin's military coup, just because they were President Obote's supporters and members of his Luo ethnic group.

The Catholic professional leaders and civil servants were murdered because they would not actively support Idi Amin's repressive regime and abuse of human rights, and just because they were Catholic Christians. For instance, Idi Amin had appointed Kiwanuka, a prominent Catholic DP leader and former Prime Minister of Uganda, and a leading Muganda politician in Uganda, to the position of Chief Justice of Uganda for obvious political reasons.

General Idi Amin as President and False Messiah

In 1971, the politically marginalized Catholics and Muslims, joined the politically oppressed Baganda to celebrate Gen. Idi Amin's military coup against President Milton Obote, their supposed nemesis and oppressor. They saw him as their deliverer, or political messiah to liberate them from their traditional state of political oppression and religious marginalization in the country. They wanted a positive political change that would catapult them into political power in the country, which they correctly believed they deserved.

The Catholics also wrongly believed that Idi Amin, who lacked a good education and political skills, would honor his pledge to hold a national election to elect a new president and members of the national parliament. The Catholics believed that since they had a numerical majority they would win a national election, by supporting fellow Catholics, who were members of the *Democratic Party*, which was predominantly Roman Catholic. In contrast the UPC was predominantly Anglican, or Protestant, both in membership, and church affiliation.

At the national level, Kiwanuka's appointment was calculated to appease Catholics and frustrate Protestants who may have wished to appeal against Idi Amin's illegal decrees to the Supreme Court. The appointment also was designed to project a false sense of alliance between President Idi Amin's Military Government and the Catholics, as the group which had been unfairly disenfranchised by the Anglicans and Protestants.

Therefore, Idi Amin hoped that he would be able to mobilize the disgruntled and oppressed Catholics to support him in his bid for power. This was based on the local, historical religio-political understanding that since like these disenfranchised Catholics, he was also a member of a religio-politically disenfranchised and aggrieved Muslim group, they would empathize with his cause. Idi Amin hoped that Catholics would be motivated by their political and economic self-interest to rally behind him. He hoped that at least, they would support him as a fellow member of the political minority who had been traditionally discriminated against, oppressed, and disenfranchised as a socio-religio-political group by the ruling Anglican religio-political establishment.

At the local level, Benedicto Kiwanuka's appointment to the esteemed position of Chief Justice of Uganda, by President Idi Amin, was hailed as a great triumph for Buganda and all the Catholics in Uganda. It politically catered well for Christian Catholic sectarianism, as well as for the Kingdom of Buganda's traditional ethnic nationalism and pride. The Baganda hoped that the next step was the restoration of Buganda's political Kingdom, especially after Idi Amin had, in April 1971, brought back the body of Kabaka Edward Mutesa II, from England, where he died in political exile, for full royal burial with full military honours. Idi Amin's political gesture of goodwill and support of the Baganda had brought him many praises from the Baganda ethnic nationalists, who deeply hated Obote and both his ethnic Langi dominated regime, and the military. In this political support for Idi Amin, Baganda Anglicans, Catholics, and Muslims were united through Buganda's ethnic nationalism which was the unifying common ground for these traditional rivals and "enemies."

Similarly, the Baganda students at Makerere University had formed an association called *"Bana Be Ngoma Ye Buganda"* (Children of the Kingdom of Buganda) in defiance of the abolition of the Kingdom of Buganda. On January 25, 1971, following Idi Amin's military coup against Milton Obote, they adorned their Makerere University gowns and rode in the Kampala city festive street processions of cars, taxis, lorries, buses and motorcycles, with people waving branches of trees, flowers, and Buganda Kingdom flags and singing in jubilation of the downfall of Obote's Government.

Some students had joined the local Baganda people, and were all cheerfully hailing Idi Amin as the coming "saviour of Uganda and the saviour of Buganda Kingdom!" Some of them were shouting: *"Down with Obote the Dictator! Up with Idi Amin the Saviour!"* Some Makerere University students in the procession also ceremoniously tore up pages of the deposed President Obote's manifesto, *The Common Man's Charter*, and tossed them up into the air with cheers of joy.[16]

Many of the Baganda and Makerere faculty members had experienced Obote's repression when he had abolished their kingdom in 1967, and they felt free to express their joy at his downfall. Some leading Church leaders and intellectuals welcomed Idi Amin with great enthusiasm and anticipation for the beginning of a more democratic Uganda. Most conservatives and traditionalists did not like President Obote's new leftist and socialist socio-economic principles and policies. This was particularly true of many conservative Christians in Uganda, especially the Catholic Church leadership which was influenced by North Americans, who had already denounced Obote's socialist policies as "a move toward communism."

However, their own optimism and hopes for a brighter and more prosperous future were misplaced. President Idi Amin's promises were a well-constructed illusion as a facade for seizing political power. The people had been deceived. Many people in Uganda had supported Idi Amin mainly due to the apparent soundness of his eighteen reasons for removing President Dr. Milton Obote from office by force of arms.

16. I was an eyewitness to these dramatic and tragic events! I was both an Assisting Chaplain in St. Francis Chapel and a student at Makerere University. On January 25, 1971 at 10:00 AM, I went to Wandegeya in Kampala to watch street mass celebrations and processions, including the Makerere University students in academic regalia.

These eighteen reasons were read on both Uganda television and the Radio of Uganda, and were also published in *The Voice of Uganda* [later known as the *Uganda Times*], the government-owned newspaper. They are as follows:

1. The unwarranted detention of people without trial.
2. The continuation of the state of emergency.
3. Lack of freedom to air political views.
4. The frequent loss of life and property from armed robberies.
5. The proposals for National Service.
6. Wide-spread corruption in high places, especially [cabinet] ministers and civil servants.
7. The failure by political authorities to organize an election and the proposed "three plus one" electoral method which would only favor the rich.
8. Economic policies that had caused poverty and unemployment.
9. High taxes, e.g. Development, Graduated, Sales, and Social Security Fund.
10. Low prices for crops as opposed to high cost of food and education.
11. Isolating Uganda from East Africa by sending away Kenyans and refusing Kenyan and Tanzanian currencies.
12. The creation of a wealthy class of leaders.
13. Failure of the Defense Council to meet under its chairman, the President.
14. Training of a secondary army of people from Akokoro County where Obote and Akena Adoko come from.
15. The Lango Development Master Plan was designed to give all key positions in politics, the army, and commercial/industrial sectors to people from Akokoro in Lango.
16. Dividing the army and giving the Langi top positions.

17. Using the Cabinet Office to downgrade and divide the army through bribery.
18. All the matters mentioned were leading to bloodshed.[17]

Without realizing that all these publicly stated reasons for Gen. Idi Amin's military coup and violent takeover of the Government of Uganda were merely matters of public relations, some people took them seriously as new political truths.

Many Ugandans positively accepted the above reasons for the military coup, as political promises, and the manifesto for political and economic reforms in the country. As a result, these trusting people were disillusioned when these principles were completely violated and negated. These were many politically marginalized Ugandans, including the intellectuals and some religious leaders, who had truly found Gen. Idi Amin's eighteen reasons, as politically justifiable and morally acceptable.

On the surface, these eighteen reasons, that were declared to the public as the justification for Gen. Gen. Idi Amin's military coup and violent overthrow of President Obote's elected civilian government, seemed to be noble, virtuous, democratic, peaceful, and justified, until they were fully examined within the Ugandan political, religious, historical and cultural context.[18] Most people in Uganda wanted civil liberties, and democracy, and Gen. Idi Amin promised to deliver them, but he lacked the necessary education and political skills to accomplish that important task, especially given the complex nature of Uganda's political history, kingdoms and diversity of ethnic groups, sectarian religions and Anglican political hegemony.

Subsequently, General Idi Amin, became Uganda's president, established a military government, and actually managed to convince many people that he was their political and cultural "messiah." As president, Amin promised to deliver them from the evils of oppression and dictatorship of President Obote and his Anglican dominated government. Idi Amin had declared that his fundamental objective was

17. *Voice of Uganda*, January 26, 1971, 1.
18. Some Baganda religious leaders hated President Milton Obote because he had in 1967 abolished their most valued cultural and political institution of the monarchy (*Kabakship*). Therefore, most of the Baganda, including religious leaders and the elites were ready to welcome Gen. Idi Amin, as their political messiah. They erroneously hoped that Amin would restore their ancient monarchy.

merely to establish "a caretaker military government to bring peace, order and security to the country, while arrangements were made for a peaceful transition to an elected government."

The aggrieved Baganda and the traditionally disenfranchised religious and political groups, particularly the predominantly Catholic DP members, finally, saw their opportunity to rise and come into political power. Subsequently, they cautiously tried to support Idi Amin's Government until they realized that they were merely being used for Idi Amin's own political agenda to gain absolute power unopposed. Most Catholics became disillusioned when they finally realized that Idi Amin had already concentrated considerable political power into his office as military president and dictator, as well as accomplishing a significantly high degree of consolidation of wealth and power in the hands of the semi-illiterate Muslim soldiers, greedy merchants, and Nubian Muslim mercenaries from Southern Sudan.

Some educators and religious leaders were very pessimistic about the future of the nation. They knew that "power corrupts and that absolute power corrupted absolutely." They knew that President Idi Amin was not an exception to this moral predicament. Their fears for his power included the fact that he was an elementary school dropout and did not know much about world affairs, economic systems, democracy and human rights. They also knew that he was an intolerant and brutal man both by nature and his military training. These concerns were expressed in the classrooms, lectures, sermons and writings.

President Idi Amin responded by declaring harsh decrees of censorship of the media, press, the Church, and limitation of the academic freedom in the classroom, research and publications. On Sundays, President Amin sent his informers and Muslim spies into major Christian churches and university or college chapels to monitor sermons[19] preached there and note which priest or minister criticized him or the government. He also sent his spies and informers into university and college classrooms to listen to lectures for any criticisms of his government.

Idi Amin made it clear that those who dared to challenge his power or question the government policies or decision through criti-

---

19. We (the clergy and college teachers) learned to spot spies and intelligence agents because they often were strangers and came into the Church or lecture rooms wearing dark glasses, and looked around quite a lot. On spotting them, we modified our sermons and lectures accordingly.

cism were "traitors" and "unpatriotic" dangerous people. He declared that they were "guilty" of both "treason and sedition." He also declared that they would be punished severely according to the discipline and regulations of the military concerning "rebellion," "treason" and "sedition." The penalty for those guilty of these crimes against the state was public execution by a firing squad. Subsequently, President Idi Amin became notorious for stage-managing these public firing squads as a means to eliminate dissent, demoralize the public, intimidate and censor public freedom of speech, and silence opposition to his dictatorship and reign of terror.

Makerere University in Uganda, which was East Africa's highly esteemed center of excellence in education, research, scholarship, and tropical medicine, and also had the best educated professionals, which made Uganda, a well-run civil country with some of the most excellent services in Sub-Saharan Africa, was quickly disseminated. The country soon became both completely corrupted and economically ruined by President Idi Amin. As a result, Uganda will take a long time to recover from Idi Amin's destructive and tragic institutional culture and legacy of corruption and violence in government related agencies and the military.

In fact, Idi Amin feared the potentially combined opposition of the Anglican and Catholic churches. As a result, he tried to ensure that such a combined opposition did not arise. He deliberately tried to keep the two denominations in competition for his favor, attention, foreign exchange, permits for importation of goods such as cars, machinery, equipment, books, and missionaries or permits for visits abroad. In order to monitor this carefully, he created a new ministry of Religious Affairs. He filled the position at the level of Permanent Secretary for Religious Affairs. Its main hidden agenda and political mission seem to have been to weaken the Church, and promote his Islamization program in Uganda.

Idi Amin planned to accomplish this, partly by killing the Christians. He also sought to oppress Christians through systematic persecution, assassinations, censorship, control of the Church and Christian leaders. He planned to achieve these objectives through intimidation, surveillance, and restrictions on the essential foreign exchange allocation needed by the Church for the purchase of essential equipment or books, and also by limiting the Church's fund-raising activities, and freedom of the Church leaders to travel abroad.

Like Makerere University to which they were affiliated, Mulago Medical School and the university hospital also were negatively affected. Most professors at the medical school and the hospital's senior medical consultants fled from Uganda to Kenya, South Africa, and the United Kingdom. This exodus was so great that in the 1980s and early 90s, there were more Ugandan doctors practicing in England, Kenya, and South Africa than the total number of doctors in Uganda.

As a result of this exodus of doctors and other medical professionals, there was an acute shortage of doctors in Uganda, and Idi Amin's government tried in vain to fill these important medical positions with expatriates. In fear of their own safety, the foreign doctors declined President Idi Amin's invitation to come to Uganda. Because of Idi Amin's reign of terror, today, there are still more Ugandan professors and technical experts working in the United States, Canada and Britain than the total number working in Uganda. This "brain drain" came about as a result of Idi Amin's military coup and the subsequent reign of terror.

In 1967, Buganda Kingdom, along with the kingdoms of Bunyoro, Ankole, and Toro, were abolished by President Milton Obote, who was an Anglican anti-monarchist and anti-federalist from Lango in Northern Uganda where there were no established kingdoms. This was done by President Obote in order to eliminate the intrinsic threat of Buganda's politics of separatism and potential for violent secessionism. The abolition of kingdoms in Uganda deeply offended the Baganda. The Baganda's repressed nationalism, frustration, and hate for President Obote and his repressive government, to some great extent explain why the Baganda welcomed Idi Amin's military coup with a great public show of jubilation and support for Amin. Unfortunately, the Baganda had tragically both misjudged and seriously underestimated Idi Amin's real political and religious ambitions to rule Uganda, as a Muslim head of state and military dictator, for life.

The Baganda ethnic nationalists later came to realize their mistake. For instance, the Baganda Anglican Christians came to a rude awakening when Idi Amin squashed Namirembe's Diocese's attempt to secede from the rest of the Anglican Church of Uganda in 1971. This Baganda Anglican ecclesiastical secession attempt took place after the Anglican Church of Uganda had elected Bishop Eric Sabiti to become the first African Archbishop of Uganda to replace the retiring Archbishop Leslie Brown, the English missionary Bishop and first Archbishop of the Anglican Province of the Church of Uganda.

The Anglican Christians and Bishops from Buganda had preferred the election of Bishop Dunston Nsubuga, the Bishop of Namirembe Diocese, as the first African Anglican Archbishop of the Anglican Church of Uganda. The Baganda Christians had become offended and discriminated against by non-Baganda Anglican bishops. President Idi Amin's intervention was greatly appreciated by non-Baganda Anglican bishops. Bishop Festo Kivengere had even declared that in this intervention, President Idi Amin, though a Muslim, had in essence become God's chosen divine instrument for the healing and unification of the Anglican Church of Uganda.

Though correct in this particular case, what Bishop Kivengere may not have realized was that Idi Amin was not doing the Anglican Church of Uganda any favor. Like Emperor Constantine's intervention in the Church's Christological controversies of 324–25 CE in order to keep his Roman Empire united and strong, Idi Amin had also in 1971 shrewdly intervened in the Anglican Church's affairs in Uganda for well calculated political reasons. He had actually carried out a well calculated political plan and strategy to win the Bishops and the Church's support to help him keep Uganda as a united republic under his rule.

Idi Amin correctly realized that if he allowed the Baganda to secede from the rest of the Anglican Church of Uganda and force the Archbishop out of the Namirembe Cathedral from his Archbishop's throne, the second step would be for the same Baganda nationalists to demand secession from the rest of the country of Uganda, as they had done in 1966. He knew that the Baganda ethnic nationalists wanted to restore their pre-colonial independent state, which had been incorporated into the colonial state of Uganda as a main independent kingdom within the federation of Uganda.

In his fight against Buganda's ethnic nationalism and separatism, President Milton Obote had sent Gen. Idi Amin in 1966 to quell the attempted Buganda military coup and secession from the rest of Uganda. Idi Amin had succeeded in his military mission to quell the Baganda secessionist rebellion at the cost of hundreds of fatalities, negative press coverage, and mass protest from Baganda nationalists.

As such, in his new difficult role as the President of the Republic of Uganda, Gen. Idi Amin was not about to create future political and military troubles for himself from a restored, nationalistic and separatist Kingdom of Buganda.

President Idi Amin's assassination of Benedicto Kiwanuka, the Chief Justice and esteemed former Prime Minister of Uganda, was another public attempt to intimidate and control the Baganda nationalism. The Baganda had hoped in vain that Idi Amin would step down and give Benedicto Kiwanuka the opportunity to be elected, or appointed as the new President of Uganda. His brutal murder was meant to silence all opposition and dissent in Uganda.

On September 31, 1972, the Chief Justice was dragged from his chambers by Idi Amin's assassin squads during a session of the East African Court of Appeal. He was murdered one week following his ruling against the Uganda Government in "writ of *habeas corpus*," which had been brought by the British High Commission concerning the illegal and unconstitutional detention of Donald Stewart, who was being held in military custody by the Ugandan military. This tragic murder of the Chief Justice Benedicto Kiwanuka, reportedly by both torture and beheading, also was meant to warn, intimidate, censor and silence all those people, regardless of whether they were judges, professors, bishops and clergy, or other groups of people who intended to oppose or criticize the actions of Idi Amin and his government.

Increasing Tension between President Idi Amin and Anglican Archbishop Janani Luwum

On February 16, 1977, Janani Luwum, the Anglican Archbishop of Uganda, also was arrested and symbolically silenced, as a warning to his political enemies, especially the Anglican politicians and the Church. He was executed, by being shot once in the mouth, and twice in the chest area. This was President Idi Amin's most gruesome, symbolic and public message that those who dared to oppose him, and his military government, would likewise, be hunted down, arrested, and permanently silenced. Their own hearts would be either stopped with bullets, or ripped out with machetes, or rifle bayonets! It is not surprising, therefore, that there were rumors that Idi Amin was a cannibal who tortured and killed his chief opponents, then ripped out and ate their hearts and livers so as to incorporate their own *"manna"* or spiritual energy, and to prevent possible supernatural retaliation for their murders.

Logically, this unorthodox belief meant that in order for Idi Amin to become stronger, he would have to kill his most powerful opponents in the military, government, Church, educational institutions, business community, and the rest of Uganda. As a result, Idi Amin's first and most important political strategy was to divide the Christians along traditional rivalries and hostilities. This was designed so that he could enlist even the Catholics' support in his bloody mission to exterminate the Anglican elites as their enemies and oppressors in order to appoint Muslims and Catholics in their positions!

Amin's real goal was to get rid of the Anglican elites through isolation, extermination, and dismantling of the Anglican political power structure, without the Catholics joining them to oppose him. And then, Amin's strategy was to turn against the Catholics and exterminate them, too, unless they converted to Islam. His final goal was to turn Uganda into a Muslim country like the northern neighbouring countries of the Sudan, Egypt, and Libya. To this end, in 1973, Idi Amin applied to Muslim countries for economic aid and for Uganda to be officially recognized among the Muslim countries by the Arab and Muslim International Alliance.

President Khadafi of Libya came to visit Uganda in 1973, in support of Idi Amin's regime. He arrived with the false assumption that the majority of the people in Uganda and the students at Makerere University were Muslim. He was subsequently very surprised when many students walked out in protest during his speech instead of the expected cheers of joy and thanks!

In the course of his speech about friendship and cooperation between Libya and Uganda, Khadafi had indicated that he would give the Ugandan Government sufficient funding to complete Idi Amin's noble mission of transforming Uganda into a Muslim country. Professor John Mbiti, the Head of the Department of Religious Studies and Philosophy at Makerere University, an Anglican priest, preached a critical sermon in St. Francis Anglican Chapel at Makerere University in response to Khadafi and Idi Amin's plan for a forced Islamization of Uganda. In his address, Professor Mbiti rejected the state repression of

Christianity and condemned the official state policy for the promotion of Islam in a predominantly Christian nation.

To the fully packed congregation at Makerere University, Anglican Francis Chapel, whose membership included the university community of professors, lecturers, clergy, students, and the ever present group of secret police and State Research Bureau intelligence officers, he boldly declared from the pulpit: "Christianity and Africa have fallen in love with each other, and intend to live in bonds of a lifelong marriage. Christianity is here to stay." For this criticism and similar ones conveyed within his lectures, the classroom, and sermons, he became a marked professor and clergyman to be harassed and silenced. He joined the watched groups of professors like Ali Mazrui of the Political Sciences, and several other censored and harassed faculty members of Makerere University. Finally, Professor Mbiti and his family fled the country to Europe.[20]

The main blows of Idi Amin's censorship and Christian persecution was at first directed mainly against the Anglican Church's hierarchy. This was mainly because of the hegemonic nature of the Anglican political power. This sectarian role of religion was deeply rooted within pre-colonial, colonial, and postcolonial religio-political history of Uganda. The Anglicans had become the privileged class and ruling elite. Due to their alliance with the British Colonial Government of Uganda, the Anglicans had become the established Church in Uganda, following the political and religious model of the Anglican Church establishment in England.

Subsequently, the Ugandan Anglican Christians had by mere chance and power of Lord Lugard's maxim gun won the religious-political war, thereby, permanently coming into power, and thereafter, attaining the domination of the Ugandan politics and the Civil Service. They also had monopolized the key positions in the Civil Service since the time of the religious wars in Buganda and the final Anglican victory of 1892 in which Lord Lugard had come to the aid of the local Anglican British allies. He had deployed his awesome power of the machine-gun (maxim gun) and the cannon, to mow down the numerically superior Catholics, who were armed with mere rifles and some ineffective, or inferior muzzle-loaders.

---

20. See Ford, *Even Unto Death*, 65–66.

Consequently, the major traditional political positions and chieftainships in Buganda had been reassigned to the Anglicans, with the Catholics getting the less powerful positions, and the Muslims who had been defeated by the combined force of Anglicans and Catholics getting the least powerful chieftainship as a mere token, since it carried very little political power and negligible influence. This three-tier hierarchical power structure, which was based on religion, remained the primary societal paradigm and *"operandus modus"* (mode of operation) in Uganda through the colonial and postcolonial eras. This remained the case until January 25, 1971 when Idi Amin, a Muslim military general, came to power in Uganda, and tried to destroy it.

As a formerly marginalized and oppressed Muslim, at the urging of local Muslims and rich foreign Muslim Government leaders like King Faisal of Saudi Arabia and President Khadafi of Libya to the north of Uganda, Idi Amin declared Uganda a Muslim country. Subsequently, he embarked on a reign of terror and forced the program of Islamization of Uganda. He worked hard by all the means he could think of regardless of their consequences, in order to transform Uganda from a predominantly Christian country into the true Muslim nation of his dream.

President Idi Amin's Islamic religious mission was in that sense that of the "Ugandan Madhi" or "Messiah." He was perceived by Muslims as God's instrument to reverse the historical religious trends in Uganda. He was supposed to return Uganda to an Islamic and traditional era, like that which had prevailed in the pre-colonial and pre-Christian Buganda. This was the period prior to the arrival of the English Church Missionary Society (CMS) Anglican missionaries in Buganda in 1877, at the invitation of Kabaka Mutesa I, as well as the subsequent arrival of the uninvited Roman Catholic White Fathers in 1899.

The arrival of the Catholic missionaries at Kabaka Mutesa's court in the spirit of rivalry and hostile competition with the Anglicans for Christian converts, and the charge that Anglicans were Protestant heretics who preached a false and non-redemptive form of Christianity, caused permanent religious confusion in Buganda and later in the rest of Uganda.

King Mutesa I and his cabinet chiefs were greatly amused as they marveled at the vicious rivalry and hostility of the European Christian missionary groups, at the king's court, palace and the country. The king and his chiefs also wondered how they could figure out which group of Christian missionaries was teaching the truth about God and needed to stay; and which group of two competing Christian missionaries was teaching falsehoods. They wanted to promote religious truths and therefore, wanted to punish the foreign Christian missionary group that both preached a non-redemptive false religion, and promoted falsehood, as God's redemptive revelation, and to evict the religious frauds from the country! But they had no way to tell who was teaching the truth and who was teaching falsehoods, and so they reluctantly tolerated the two cankerous Anglican and Catholic missionary groups.

However, these mutually hostile and intolerant British Anglican and French Catholic missionaries sowed the evils of religious mutual intolerance, rivalry, hostility, and confusion in the country. These European Christian missionaries' vices were transferred to politics and the political parties based on this sectarian form of Christianity. This religious and political fusion and traditional hostilities had created King Kalema, a short-lived Muslim king, and his persecution of Christians. It also created King Mutesa II, and presidents Milton Obote and the reprehensible Idi Amin! President Idi Amin, a Muslim head of state of Uganda by means of a military coup, was a second King Kalema! Idi Amin's determination and strategies to Islamize Uganda by both force and persuasion led to his colonial-like policy to "divide, conquer, isolate and exterminate the opposition leaders." President Idi Amin's strategies also included censorship and surveillance in order to intimidate, and control the religiously and politically divided, confused, and discouraged Ugandans.[21]

President Idi Amin was a brutal dictator, who tragically invoked the name of God to do so! He was also an ambitious and comical military general who proclaimed himself "the Conqueror of the British Empire." As a ruthless and fundamentalist Muslim leader, President

---

21. There is a common saying that "history does not repeat itself." In the case of Uganda, history has repeated itself. After a century of Christianity in Uganda, a Muslim President came to power and persecuted the Christian Church in the same way that King Mwanga had done in 1883–88. Ugandan martyrs were created by King Mwanga and a century later, new Christian martyrs were, again, created by President Idi Amin. The most internationally celebrated of these recent Christian martyrs is Janani Luwum, the Anglican Archbishop of Uganda 1973–77, and my own immediate Church superior in Kampala Diocese.

Amin also set out to exterminate the numerically superior Christians in Uganda. Logically, Idi Amin began with the Anglicans, whom he perceived to be the immediate threat, having been the ones traditionally set in power by the British Colonial Government of Uganda, and having been the local British agents for conquering and administering Uganda on behalf of the British Colonial Government. For instance, Kakungulu, a Muganda Anglican chief, and military general, had conquered most of Eastern Uganda for the British Empire.

In order to appreciate the problem of Idi Amin encountered in terms of the Anglican powerful machine which he had to destroy through the extermination of Uganda's intellectuals and important political leaders, one must look at the history of Uganda, the Church, religion and politics. Therefore, it is of great political and historical significance that we should note that during the colonial and postcolonial eras, all the kings in Uganda and their major chiefs were Anglicans. Furthermore, the greatest number of highly educated people in Uganda, were also Anglicans. The Catholics still had an advantage in terms of a higher number of masses of converts, especially the politically marginalized, powerless, peasants and poor people (*Bakopi*) in rural areas.

Unfortunately, due to Uganda's unique religio-political history and elitist Anglican missionary strategies, most of these masses of rural Catholic converts, consisted of the underprivileged, disenfranchised, poorly educated illiterate masses, and lower class people. The Anglican elitists were Uganda's upper class, professional groups, and the ruling elite. The Anglicans, as former British allies and colonial collaborators, were regarded as neocolonial agents and traitors.

Subsequently, Idi Amin subjected these Christian religious leaders to surveillance as spies for foreign powers, arbitrary arrest, torture, and cruel and inhumane punishment, as well as complete censorship of speech. Furthermore, in addition to killing Christians, President Idi Amin's regime also obtained money from Saudi Arabia and Libya in order to bribe and pay some Christians with that money, and gave them important positions in his Islamic Military Government, as inducements for them to convert to Islam. The illiterate Muslims became so rich and politically powerful to the extent that they degraded and despised education and the educated people.

The popular saying in President Idi Amin's reign of terror and Muslim economic privilege was: "*Nasoma wa? Eyasoma ansinzaki?*" (Look! I did not go to school! What does the educated person possess that I need?) This was indeed a tragic and a morally corrosive dramatic reversal of the traditional roles of the educated elite class as opposed to the uneducated masses of the poor class. President Idi Amin had given "*mafuta mingi*" (a lot of wealth) to the less educated Muslims so as to create an economic elite group that would permanently wield power and influence in Uganda. The kings of Buganda had played a similar political game of political patronage with the assignments of major chieftainships in the kingdom.

Like King Mwanga a century earlier, President Idi Amin did not like the foreign Christian missionaries. These foreign Christian missionaries, both Protestant and Catholic, were marked for deportation as potential foreign governments' spies and informers. He believed that the American Christian missionaries were CIA (Central Intelligence Agency) agents, and feared them. The Christian missionaries were counted, and work permits and new visas for Christian missionary entry into Uganda were denied. Subsequently, many of those work permits and entry visas which were previously issued by his Military Government were abruptly revoked and cancelled.

In August 1975, President Idi Amin deported sixteen Verona Missionaries from Northern Uganda and four Anglican missionaries on charges of being agents of foreign governments and spies. Idi Amin also had accused Dennis Hills, a British lecturer in the Departments of English at Makerere University and Education, at the National Teachers' College at Kyambogo of treason, sedition, defamation, and spying. President Amin sentenced Hills to death. President Idi Amin's outrage had been provoked by the fact that Hills had written a book entitled, *The White Pumpkin*, which was very critical of his government. In 1978, President Idi Amin, banned more than 27 small Protestant sects and denominations from Uganda and expelled their foreign Christian missionaries from the country. The Anglican and Catholic Church leaders did not defend the banned Protestant Christian groups mainly because they too perceived them negatively as sectarian rivals and a religious nuisance.

Uganda's Christian missionaries had also come from England and Ireland. Tragically, they also had brought along with them their own culture of mutual distrust, mutually exclusive religious doctrines, bigotry, mutual intolerance, and armed violence.[22]

Therefore, to a great extent, Uganda's case of fusion of Christian denominational rivalry, politics, and armed violence is similar to that of Northern Ireland and the Middle East. Like Uganda, these are the countries where serious political, military, moral, social, economic, and religious problems have constantly erupted into violence due to the failure to have an effective constitutional separation of Church and State affairs. Just like Islam, African Traditional Religion does not divide human matters into the Western familiar dualistic paradigm of "the sacred realm" (Church and all the spiritual matters) and "the secular realm" (the State, commercial and other mundane affairs).

In most of ancient and pre-colonial Africa, pharaohs, kings, chiefs, patriarchs and elders, were believed to be endowed with God's own delegated divine power, and obligation to rule society humanely, benevolently and orderly in God's name. Just like the divine kings or the pharaohs of ancient Egypt to the north, the Nile Civilization and kingdoms of the inter-lacustrine region at the source of the Nile, to the upper Nile region or the south of Egypt, also were ruled by both religious and political nature "divine kingdoms," whose divine kings were regarded as God's agents in the world.

Accordingly, the saying in Buganda was that if the "Kabaka sneezed, the whole of Buganda Kingdom sneezed, and if the Kabaka limped, the nation limped!" This was also true of the Bunyoro, Toro, Ankole, Mpororo, Karagwe, Rwanda, and Burundi kingdoms, as well as Ethiopia, which is to Uganda's north east. This being the case, religion and politics or Church and State were by nature, intrinsically linked and were going to remain inseparably linked during the colonial period as well as during the post-colonial period. As such, for such African kings and their societies, religion and politics were God's inseparable twin gifts.

Within this African-religious view and theocentric value system, a good king or queen is regarded as God's chosen special agent to rule, protect and deliver his people from poverty, chaos and evil. As God's divine chief representative and moral agent in society, the traditional

---

22. Because of these religiously prejudiced and intolerant Catholic Christian missionaries from Ireland and anti-Catholic Anglican (Protestant) missionaries from England, Uganda was nearly transformed into another religiously and politically violent state like Northern Ireland!

king or queen is one who also either serves as a priest to God or a devout religious compassionate person.

Similarly, priests also were regarded as God's special people who possess some essential royal and divine qualities. In Uganda, most priests and bishops also were members of the royal families. This was partly because education was originally a privilege for the royal family, sons, and daughters of chiefs and the privileged royal or rich class. Accordingly, good original Anglican boarding schools like Kings College Budo and Gayaza high schools, were established by the Anglican English Christian missionaries in order to serve for the education and training of future kings and chiefs, as well as queens and princesses.

In a spirit of competition, the Catholic missionaries also established Namilyango as a school for boys, and both Nabbingo and Namagunga as schools for girls. These were supposed to be the counterparts of the Anglican royal schools of Budo and Nabbingo. Since the Catholics had fewer chieftainships and no royal positions to fill, naturally, they opened their own schools to cater for children of a lower class, or those who were predominantly of non-royal or chieftainship political origins.

Those children of political ambitions were very often sent to the Anglican schools even when their parents were non-Anglicans. Later, other Anglican schools of similar caliber and objectives were opened in the other kingdoms and districts of Uganda with great political impact on Ugandan political affairs and Anglican establishment in these areas.

Consequently, because of the practical nature of the political training emphasized and virtues of good governance in the Anglican schools, naturally, most of the future leaders of Uganda and founders of the country's nationalist political parties were the graduates of these Anglican schools in Uganda. Examples include people like I. K. Musazi who founded the pan-Uganda nationalist political party, *The Uganda National Congress* (UNC) in 1952, which was the forerunner of Milton Obote's *Uganda People Congress*, which was founded in 1958; and E. K. Mulira, who founded the *Uganda Progressive Party* (UPP) in January 1955.[23]

---

23. See Karugire, *A Political History of Uganda*, 177–97; E. Makubuya, Mwaka and Okoth, *Uganda*, 1–90.

Similarly, most of the membership of these political parties, which had been founded by Anglican nationalist politicians, was predominantly composed of Anglican elites, of which the majority were graduates of Budo. Non-Catholics were recruited into these Anglican Christian founded national political parties. However, they remained in the minorities, and some of them may have felt marginalized or like outsiders. As a result, in 1956, the Catholics founded their own political party called, "*The Christian Democratic Party*."

The *Democratic Party* (DP) as Uganda's Christian political party was formed with the political and religious guidance of some Roman Catholic bishops with the hope that other Christians, particularly the Anglicans, would join it. However, DP was unfortunately permanently negatively viewed by the Anglicans and stigmatized as a Roman Catholic political party. As a result, most Protestants, Muslims and other non-Christian groups avoided DP due to its alleged Catholic Church association, in its foundation, mode of operation and leadership. Later, this was to be the same fate for those Christian leaders who supported President Idi Amin, and failed to condemn him for his terrible abuses of power, human rights, persecution of Christians, censorship of the truth, censorship of ideas and the press, torture, and tragic mass murders of innocent people.

How could Christian leaders keep quiet and not become a part of Idi Amin's support? How could the majority of the good people of God keep silent while evils were perpetrated in their country? How could God's holy or good people remain silent in the face of evil, and yet claim not to be accessories to the evil? By remaining silent in the face of evil, don't they become silent partners with the evildoers through apathy, fear, cowardice, anxiety, and lack of positive action to either prevent, or stop the commission of the destructive societal evils? Don't they, by their own silence and omission to act to prevent societal evils around them, become guilty, for being accessories to crime, injustice and other evils, such as corruption, tribalism, racism and sexism?

Those were some of the fundamental moral questions some of us as religious leaders, educators, and community leaders had to confront and answer. If evil is perpetrated by commission of negative acts, or performance of evil deeds, as well as by omission to do the good, such as the opposition of evildoers like Idi Amin and Adolph Hitler and their evil regimes, then, apathy, fear and cowardice that lead to silence or non-action to prevent or stop these evil men and their regimes, is evil in itself. Silence in the face of evil may constitute support for those committing those horrible evils! There is no neutral moral ground in these tragic cases of moral evil, violence and genocide. You are either for it or against it.

President Idi Amin made it clear that those who are guilty of opposing his government would be severely punished, without any exception. This was repeated several times in 1971–1973, by the so-called "Government Spokesman." It was reported that, his Excellency, Gen. Idi Amin, the President of Uganda, wished to warn Makerere lecturers, other teachers, religious leaders, the clergy, and the public "from teaching and preaching lies, treason, and sedition against the President or the Government." These words were read on the Government Radio of Uganda and the government owned and operated television station. These official government decrees of censorship carried severe punishment for violations of the decree on limitations to free speech and religious freedom. It also limited academic freedom in the classroom, research, and publications. The sanctions also were published in the *Voice of Uganda* which was a government owned and controlled newspaper.

Great emphasis was placed on the fact that those caught doing so would be "very severely punished," which was a known local euphemism for extrajudicial government political killings, clandestine abductions, "disappearances of people," torture and murders by the State Research Bureau intelligence officers or those of the Public Safety Unit. Lectures and religious services at Makerere University and the National Teachers' College at Kyambogo, and Church religious services in Kampala and other major municipal areas, such as Jinja, Mbale, Masaka, Mbarara, Gulu, and Kabale, were closely monitored by the government intelligence officers and informers.

Due to President Idi Amin's overt persecution of the Christian Church and its members, no bishop or clergy person felt safe in the country. A number of Anglican priests were killed in Buganda, Ankole and Kigezi. They were arrested and never seen alive, again, by their congregation and family members. More dramatic was the case of Father Mukasa, a Catholic Priest in Masaka who was tragically dragged away from the altar while celebrating mass and executed for having preached what was regarded to be both an inflammatory and an anti-Government sermon!

On Christmas Day 1976, the live broadcast sermon on Radio of Uganda, by the Archbishop Janani Luwum of the Anglican Church of Uganda was abruptly cut off from the air. Instead of the Archbishop's sermon, President Idi Amin came on the air, and in a strict act of official government censorship of Christian Church and religious freedom of speech, including that of the Church sermons, declared that there would be very severe punishment for the Church leaders. He went on to clarify that the punishment was especially for "those religious leaders of the Church, who were preaching bloodshed and treason."

Idi Amin fulfilled this deadly threat against the Church within a month and half and killed the Most Rev. Janani Luwum, the Anglican Archbishop of Uganda, whose Christmas sermon he had interrupted to denounce Christian leaders of the Church as "preachers of bloodshed, sedition and treason," who would be "very severely dealt with, and punished" by his military government.

Later, the "Government Spokesman" repeated the same message which was previously delivered by the President. He went on to elaborate that "the government would not tolerate such religious leaders of the Church who falsely criticize the government, tell lies about Idi Amin, and cause fear, panic, and unnecessary confusion in the country." He warned that these religious leaders of the Church would be punished very severely if they did not stop those dangerous lies and attempts to overthrow the government.

These threats were repeated on Uganda television. They were also reported by the *Voice of Uganda*, the government-owned newspaper, on December 26, 1976. To the surprise and irritation of many Ugandans, who traditionally celebrate Christmas for about a week, the government-owned Radio of Uganda also had announced that the Government of Uganda had canceled the Christmas holidays. It was emphasized that all people had to report for work; and must be in their offices for regular work the following day, as a normal work day.

However, many people had already gone upcountry for the expected traditional long Christmas holidays. Moreover, not every Ugandan was listening to the news broadcast on the radio and announcements. In any case, following the British tradition, Christmas Day and the day after were legal holidays in Uganda. The day after Christmas was known as "boxing day." As a result of President Idi Amin's threats against the Church leaders, and the demand for the cancellation of Christmas holidays, most Christians began to wonder whether President Idi Amin had finally decided to ban Christianity and its holidays in order to Islamize Uganda by decree, force, and bloody persecution of the Christian Church and its members.

However, this was part of Idi Amin's strategy for artificially stage-managing a deadly confrontation between his pro-Islamic military government and the Anglican Christian Church in order to provide the Christian public and the world with some bogus, but plausible reason to cancel the Anglican Church's Centenary Celebrations already planned for the second-half of 1977. President Idi Amin had been falsely telling the Muslim world leaders that Uganda was a Muslim country. But now the reality of the local, noisy, festive, mass Christian and international celebrations of the Christian centenary threatened to reveal the truth, namely, that Uganda was, indeed, a predominantly Christian country. As a result, President Idi Amin's political strategy was to prevent these Christian Centenary Celebrations from taking place.

In addition, President Idi Amin dreaded the international press coverage of the Ugandan Church in the Ugandan context of political and economic affairs. He realized that this was bound to take place due to foreign Christian dignitaries who had been invited by the Anglican Church of Uganda to come for these celebrations in 1977, and it worried him very much.

Fearing the inevitable failure and loss of control of his Islamization agenda for Uganda, Idi Amin tried to increase the censorship and intensity of persecution of the Church and to kill the various Christian leaders of the Centenary Celebration Committees. These marked Christian leaders and moral activists included Byron Kawadwa and his actors in the *Martyrs of Uganda Pageant*,[24] and the Rev. Emmanuel Twesigye, its main playwright. As expected, Kawadwa was finally arrested and killed and Rev. Twesigye went into hiding and finally fled into exile.

However, the list of the leading clergy marked for surveillance was long. It included most bishops, particularly Janani Luwum the Archbishop of Uganda, Bishop Yona Okoth of Bukedi, Festo Kivengere

---

24. The Rev. Emmanuel Twesigye did not discuss this inner conviction for fear of being arrested and charged with treason or sedition. It remained part of the hidden agenda in urging the Archbishop to convene the House of Bishops to write a public letter of protest against President Idi Amin's repressive government. This hidden agenda also shaped the nature and content of the *Uganda Martyrs Play*.

of Kigezi, Bishop Melchizedek of Lango, and Bishop Benon Ogwal of Northern Uganda. These Anglican bishops were called the main troublemakers and traitors. Rev. Twesigye was monitored by President Amin's Intelligence Agents, on suspicion that he was the dangerous brain behind many of the Church's ideas of peace and justice, protest policies and political strategies to overthrow President Idi Amin's repressive regime. He was denied travel papers outside Uganda and his moves were monitored until the day he fled to Kenya in 1977, shortly after the murder of the Archbishop Janani Luwum, on February 16, 1977. [25] Likewise, the bishops Okoth, Kivengere, Ogwal and Otim, fled into exile. They wanted to avoid being arrested, tortured and killed, by President Idi Amin, or his hired assassins. They returned to Uganda after the liberation of Uganda in 1979 by Tanzanian troops and Museveni's liberation army.

The Assassination and Martyrdom of the Archbishop Janani Luwum

Ultimately, the Anglican Bishop's protest letter of February 10, 1977, finally provoked President Idi Amin's blind rage that led to the tragic arrest and assassination of the Anglican Archbishop. After the bishops had met and carefully analyzed and evaluated the great crisis confronting them and the Church, especially President Idi Amin's policy of Christian persecution, they decided to unite and launch a very loud official and public ecclesiastical protest to his repressive Military Government.

Subsequently, these Anglican bishops wrote and signed a very strong letter of protest to President Idi Amin. They also decided to distribute copies of the Church protest against the repressive government's abuses of human rights, the policy of Christian persecution, and genocide, to all cabinet ministers and religious leaders of the Catholic Church, Greek Orthodox Church, and the Sheik Mufti of the Muslim Supreme Council of Uganda. The main body of the Anglican bishops' formal protest letter is very poignant and prophetic. In part, the historic Episcopal letter reads as follows:

---

25. See Ford, *Even Unto Death*, 78–85.

Your Excellency,

We the Archbishop and the Bishops of the [Anglican] Province of Uganda, Rwanda, Burundi and Boga-Zaire are meeting at Namirembe on Tuesday, 8th February, 1977, humbly beg to submit our most deeply felt concern for the Church and the welfare of the people whom we serve under your care. . . . We are deeply disturbed to learn of the incident which occurred at the Archbishop's official residence in the early hours of Saturday morning, 5th February 1977.

In the history of our country, such an incident in the Church has never before occurred. Security officers broke through the fence and forced their way into the Archbishop's compound. . . . First, we want to register our shock and protest at this kind of treatment of the leader of the Church of Uganda, Rwanda, Burundi and Boga-Zaire. Then, we shall draw out the implications of this incident for the rest of the Bishops and all the Christians of the Church of Uganda. . . .

Now that the security of the Archbishop is at stake, the security of the Bishops is even more in jeopardy. Indeed, we have a case in point. The night following the search of the Archbishop's house, one of us, the Bishop of Bukedi was searched and arrested. . . . The Christians are asking: "If this is what is happening to our Bishops, then where are we?" The gun whose muzzle has been pressed against the Archbishop's stomach, the gun which has been used to search the Bishop of Bukedi's houses, is a gun which is being pointed at every Christian in the Church. . . .

The security of the ordinary Christian has been in jeopardy for a long time. It may be that what has happened to the Archbishop and the Bishop of Bukedi is a climax of what is consistently happening to our Christians. We have buried many, who have died as a result of being shot, and there are many more whose bodies have not been found, yet their disappearance is connected with the activities of some members of the Security Forces. Your Excellency, if it is required, we can give concrete evidence of what is happening because widows and orphans are members of our Church.

Furthermore . . . in some parts of Uganda, members of Islam who are in leading positions are using these positions to coerce Christians into becoming Muslims. . . . There is also a war against the educated which is forcing many of our people to run away from the country in spite of what the country has paid to educate them. This brain drainage of our country, the fear and mistrust, make development, progress and stability of our country almost impossible.

> The gun which was meant to protect Uganda as a nation, the Ugandan as a citizen, and protect his property is increasingly being used against the Ugandan to take away his life and his property. . . .
>
> Indeed we were shocked to hear over the radio on Christmas day, Your Excellency saying that some Bishops were preaching bloodshed. . . . An action such as this damages the good image of our nation. It also threatens our preparations for the Centenary Celebrations. Christians everywhere have become very cautious about taking part in the fund raising activities of the Church for fear of being misrepresented and misinterpreted. The ban on sales of things donated for fund-raising in aid of the Church is a case in point. This too, could have been cleared, if only Your Excellency had given the Archbishop an opportunity to brief you on the matter.
>
> In addition to the concern of the Christians in the Anglican Communion, there is also the concern of the Christians of other denominations in Uganda and all over the world with whom we are in fellowship. . . .[26]

Tragically, President Idi Amin, as a dictator that resented any challenges, or opposition to his military government, negatively perceived the Anglican Church's protest letter, and strong condemnation of his military government and its murderous activities. He treated it as the Anglican Church's formal declaration of war on him and his repressive regime. Subsequently, as a Head of State and the military, President Idi Amin tragically responded in a characteristic military manner. He swiftly and brutally mobilized the military to defend him and his reign of terror, falsely alleging that the Anglican Archbishop

---

26. The letter was only signed by the Anglican bishops. The Catholic bishops, though approving of the protest letter, and the issues it raised, viewed the issues and contents of the letter, as being fundamentally Anglican matters of ecclesiastical conflicts with the state and therefore regarded them to be of less concern to the Roman Catholic Church.

However, this assessment of the matter was only partially true. All Christians were subject to censorship and oppression, although the Anglicans received the brunt of it because they symbolized elitism, privilege, political power and hegemony in Uganda. All the governors, kings and most major chiefs in Uganda had been Anglicans! Catholics, Muslims and Traditionalists resented that privileged Anglican Church establishment and monopoly of power and resources. Some of them saw President Idi Amin's persecution of the Anglican Church and its leadership as God's judgment and punishment for the Anglican sins of arrogance and exclusion of people of other religious traditions from sharing political power and its privileges.

Janani Luwum, the bishops, priests and their Anglican followers were plotting a military coup to overthrow his military regime.

The Anglican Archbishop Janani Luwum was arrested, publicly tried by the military troops, and murdered that fateful evening of February 16, 1977. Amin's government refused to release the body for burial at Namirembe Cathedral. The memorial service had been planned to take place on Sunday in the Namirembe Cathedral in Kampala, including many foreign dignitaries and bishops, of whom many had already gathered in Nairobi, Kenya in order to travel in a long convoy from Kenya to Kampala led by the Anglican Archbishop of Kenya.

However, the convoy of Christians from Kenya was barred from entering the country by President Idi Amin's Government. President Amin also issued a decree that canceled the memorial service for the martyred Anglican Archbishop. However, there was a smaller alternative memorial service held at the All Saints Cathedral in Nairobi, in Kenya, where the convoy to Kampala had already gathered in order to travel together to attend the slain Anglican Archbishop's memorial service, in Kampala, which had been previously ceremoniously planned to take place in Namirembe Cathedral, the official seat for the Anglican Archbishop of Uganda.[27] Meanwhile, the Rev. Twesigye held a local memorial service at Kyambogo University. Surprisingly, the intelligence officers attended the somber service and did not stop it.

With Idi Amin's declaration of war on Christians and the Church, most of the Anglican bishops and Christian leaders found it prudent to go into hiding, or flee into exile. Many of the Bishops, clergy and leading Anglican professionals fled into exile in Kenya, Tanzania, Zambia, Europe, Canada and the USA. In exile, they mobilized political resistance, public opinion against Idi Amin and encouraged an armed struggle to topple President Idi Amin's murderous and repressive regime. Most of these leaders in exile returned to Uganda after the triumphant overthrow of President Idi Amin and his repressive government, and his Libyan allies. This benevolent military task for the deliverance of Uganda from Idi Amin's reign of terror and Christian persecution, was heroically accomplished, by a "Ugandan Coalition of [Christian] liberation armies" and President Julius Nyerere's Tanzanian military forces, in 1979.

---

27. See Ford, *Even Unto Death*, 86–92.

Conclusion

In Uganda, the overt and public tragic history of Church and State conflicts formally ended with the overthrow of President Idi Amin, and his repressive Islamic Military Government in 1979. The religio-political wars, such as the Muslim's armed radical group called the ADF (*Allied Democratic Forces*) have militarily continued to resist and fight against President Moseveni's predominately Christian government. Likewise the predominantly Catholic militant groups like Alice Lakwena's *Holy Spirit Movement Forces* (HSMF) 1986–1987 and Joseph Kony's *Lord's Resistance Army* (LRA) 1987–2010,[28] have waged brutal holy wars in a quest to overthrow President Museveni's Anglican based *National Resistance Movement* (NRM) Government, in order to establish theocracies in Uganda. These forms of religiously armed resistance and holy wars provide a clear indication that President Museveni's NRM Government has not resolved all forms of Church and Sate conflicts and hostilities. This is especially true for the traditionally marginalized religious traditions, including the Roman Catholic Church and Islam.

However, despite the occasional publicly expressed continuing dissatisfaction by many Catholics, including bishops and leaders, such as the Cardinal Emmanuel Wamala,[29] have significantly diminished, despite the self-evident fact that many forms of the colonial Anglican hegemony have been revived and perpetuated by President Museveni, as an Anglican politician. This is partly self-evident by his failure to appoint qualified Catholics to cabinet positions, in the same numbers as the Anglicans. Nevertheless, religious freedoms and the rule of law were once again reestablished in the country, in 1986, when Yoweri Museveni came to power as an enlightened Pan-Africanist leader, and as president, worked hard to reverse Uganda's tragic history of religious and political conflict, censorship, bigotry, intolerance and violence. Political parties were abolished by the 1995 Constitution

---

28. Joseph Kony has failed to sign the negotiated peace treatises with President Museveni's NRM Government. He has demanded the withdrawal of the ICC (International Criminal Court) indictment against him for war crimes before he would sign the treaty and cease to attack civilians in Uganda, Sudan and the Democratic Republic of the Congo.

29. Based on an interview with the Cardinal Wamala, on August 7, 2007, at Rubaga Cathedral, Kampala, Uganda. The *New Vision* and *The Monitor* newspapers also report the bishops' statements and protest sermons from time to time.

because they had been based on religious and ethnic sectarianism, but they were restored in 2005.

Freedom of religion, press, education, and ideas were reestablished as the basis of President Museveni's Government. Religious leaders are again regarded with respect as important national and community leaders. No person is harassed on the basis of religious affiliation. Education has been encouraged so much that universities have increased from two, when President Museveni came to power in 1986, to a new total of nine in 1998! Most of these new private universities were both founded and supported by the Christian Church and other various Christian communities within Uganda.

Idi Amin's persecution of Christians and repression of the Church failed to transform Uganda into a Muslim country. Even when, in September 1977, Idi Amin banned twenty-seven Christian sectarian groups and other religions, leaving only the Anglican Church, the Roman Catholic Church, the Greek Orthodox Church, and Islam as the "recognized religions" in the country, there were no Christian defections to Islam.

Ultimately, prosperity, meaningful and lasting peace will not come to Africa, especially Uganda until corruption, bigotry, intolerance and violence rooted in religious sectarianism and ethnic nationalism (or tribalism) have been fully transcended, and negated. Some practical remedies, or lasting solutions for some major African problems may be found in religious ecumenism, joint or interfaith activities and democratic organizations. Above all, an inclusive religious, cultural, and political paradigm as well as an ideal federation, and constitutional practical model for the Africans to follow, are those of the United States of America. Similarly, within a future United States of Africa, an inclusive and secular based American constitutional model of separation of Church and State, and the constitutional equality of all people before the law, most of pressing problems and evils of parochialism would be finally overcome. Through this approach, some pressing African problems of poverty, corruption, tribalism, injustice and religiously based politics and violence will be, either eliminated, or completely minimized.[30]

---

30. See: the *American Constitution*; the UN 1948 *Universal Declaration of Human Rights*; Twesigye, *Global Human Problem*; Twesigye, *God, Race, Myth and Power*; Twesigye, *Religion & Ethics for A New Age*.

Bibliography

Anglican Church. *Book of Common Prayer*. New York: Seabury, 1977.
Coomes, Anne. *Festo Kivengere: A Biography*. Sussex, England: Monarch, 1990.
Ford, Margaret. *Even Unto Death: The Story of Uganda Martyr Janani Luwum*. Elgin, IL: David Cook, 1978.
Gonzalez, Justo L. *A History of Christian Thought*. Vol. 1. Nashville: Abingdon, 1989.
Hansen, Holger Bernt. *Mission, Church and State in a Colonial Setting: Uganda 1890-1925*. New York: St. Martin's, 1984.
Hansen, Holger Bernt, and Michael Twaddle. *Religion & Politics in East Africa*. London: James Currey, 1995.
Karugire, Samwiri Rubaraza. *A Political History of Uganda*. Nairobi: Heinemann, 1980.
Kivengere, Festo. *I Love Idi Amin*. Achimota: CP, 1977.
Kiwanuka, Semakula. *History of Buganda from Foundation to 1900*. London: Longman, 1972.
Makubuya, E. Khiddu, V. M. Mwaka, and P. G. Okoth, editors. *Uganda: Thirty Years of Independence 1962-1992*. Kampala: Makerere University Press, 1994.
Museveni, Yoweri Kagutai. *Sowing the Mustard Seed: The Struggle for Freedom and Democracy in Uganda*. London: MacMillan, 1997.
Twesigye, Emmanuel Kalenzi. *African Religion, Philosophy, and Christianity in Logos-Christ: Common Ground Revisited*. New York: Peter Lang, 1996.
———. *Common Ground: Christianity, African Religion and Philosophy*. New York: Peter Lang, 1988
———. *The Global Human Problem: Ignorance, Hate, Injustice and Violence*. New York: Peter Lang, 1988.
———. *God, Race, Myth and Power*. New York: Peter Lang, 1991.
———. *Religion & Ethics for A New Age*. Oxford: American University Press of America, 2001.
Tuma, Tom, and Mutibwa, Phares, editors. *A Century of Christianity in Uganda*. Nairobi: Uzima, 1978.
Tumusiime, James, editor. *Uganda 30 Years: 1962-1992*. Kampala: Fountain, 1997.

PART THREE

Religion and State Formation in the Shadow of Apartheid in South Africa

7

From Apartheid's Christian Hegemony to Religious Pluralism

SAMUEL PAUL

> One day while the Buddhist nun was chanting, beating her drum which apparently annoyed the parliamentarians, and holding her vigil which apparently annoyed the police, I stood watching the responses of pedestrians passing on Government Avenue. Some stopped, some passed, some gathered around the sound, the incense, the flowers, and the small shrine. One woman, a grey-haired, conservatively attired, South African senior citizen, stopped, stared, and demanded of the nun, "What are you doing?" Receiving no response, she turned to me and shouted, "What is she doing?" I replied, "She is praying for the release of children from detention." The woman looked back at the nun. Then, turning her attention again to me, she posed what struck me as an unexpected, impossible, but, on further reflection, a particularly revealing question: "Is she Colored or European?" "She's a Buddhist," I quickly answered. This stopped her. She glared at me for what seemed like a very long time, and then, as if in resignation, she concluded, "Well I guess you can have European Buddhists."
>
> —David Chidester

Introduction

INTENSE NEGOTIATIONS BETWEEN THE AFRIKANER NATIONAL Party and the African National Congress gave birth to a South African democracy in 1994 setting the stage for the Truth and Reconciliation

Commission through a liberative process of confession, forgiveness, repentance, reconciliation, and re-membering back into one society. The spirit of ubuntu is woven into the tapestry of this community's constitution demonstrating egalitarian concepts of freedom and equality while also promoting religious pluralism from Christian hegemony. This chapter will elucidate the elitism and exclusivism of Christianity. Christianity has been a dominant influence in the South African community having been used to support oppression on the one hand, while believers on the other side have been trying to make sense of how this same faith can also be utilized to support oppression of the other. In this chapter I will review the current principles that govern the church-state relationship and show that these principles do not require a separation of church and state. South Africa confidently seeks to uphold religious practices in conformity with the egalitarian foundations of its new constitution. It is not a secular state either because religion is not perceived as taboo. In this chapter I will examine, evaluate, and critique the American establishment and free exercise clauses against the 1996 South African Constitution as well as other African countries' constitutional provisions relating to religious freedom.

The attitude of the Western Church in the 15th century toward other religions such as Islam, Hinduism, and Buddhism, were seen as enemies to Christ that must be destroyed. With the arrival of Muslims in South African slaves and Christian settlers in the 17th century, religious pluralism became more pronounced. Then in the 19th century, Indians brought Hinduism with them and the East European Jews added more facets to the religious scene. Religious pluralism has always been a feature and a social reality of South Africa and is even reinforced by the fact that Christianity itself is plural in its methodology, theology, liturgy, and practice.[1]

Even though South Africa is a plural country the apartheid government enforced separation, prevented inclusion, and suppressed necessary inter-religious, inter-faith pluralism in this society. If their policies were dedicated to maintain integrity of cultural, social, and religious difference, this would require the theo-politics of religious pluralism. For David Chidester a religious studies theorist, this was a lie and is clearly exposed in the Dutch Reformed church's rigid theo-

---

1. Lubbe, "Religious Pluralism" 208–9.

logical exclusivism. Difference was not of value. Greater interest was in the economic, political, and military domination of a majority by a minority. Chidester suggests that this exclusive political domination of the majority could be seen as a theological extension of the exclusivist Christian conviction that the vast majority of humanity will be condemned to hell.[2]

It was Calvinist Reformed Christianity that first found its roots in South Africa and was protected by the occupying Dutch East Indian Company. Lutherans were given freedom to worship in 1780. It wasn't until 1804 when religious freedom was granted to all. Muslims were not allowed to practice their religion in public, offenders were punished by death, but if they showed any interest in converting to Christianity, they were welcome to join Christian churches. It was only in this potential of conversion to Christianity that Muslims received any respect, dignity, and freedom to worship. This reflects the government's influence on the Church with regard to people of other faiths. Even so, people of other faiths were regarded as objects of evangelism. White Christians had to come to grips with the otherness of people of different faiths. With the exception of a small number of Jews, White Muslims, and White Buddhists, all members of religions other than Christians were regarded as Black, including Coloreds and Indians. White Christians had to face the challenge that the otherness was both color and creed, it was political and religious.[3]

The exclusion of other religious voices was clearly seen in South Africa's public education system. Christian nationalism and Christian values were impressed upon all through Christian National Education. Chidester proposes that the underlying element, utilized through Christian National Education to maintain control and prevent religious pluralism, was hegemony. Religious symbols that represent the political interests of one group is hegemonic domination and determines the religio-political order. This hegemonic domination leads to privileged access to shared legitimating sacred symbols, and other religio-political interest groups are forced to subservience, marginality, and exclusion. It does not welcome integration within a community, but instead isolation. The hegemonic appropriation of Christian sacred symbols enjoyed by Afrikaner nationalism established privileged

2. Chidester, "Christians, Buddhists, Muslims," 81.
3. Lubbe, "Religious Pluralism," 209–10.

claim to biblical symbols, sacred history, and legitimacy with sacred authority to rule in South Africa.[4]

Two subjects were of importance in public school education, Religious Education and Biblical Studies. M. C. Kitshoff and W. B. van Wyks' teacher-training manual, *Method of Religious Education and Biblical Studies* offers an explanation of the differences of these two subjects. Biblical Studies is described as a subject that, "busies itself with the Bible . . . to facilitate Christian maturity." It encourages respect for the text as the authoritative word of God. It instructs one for reverence, obedience, and submission to biblical demands that fulfills cultural and religious destinies. While Religious Education appears as an introduction to the literature and histories of world religions in American and British public schools, this was not the case in South Africa. Religious Education meant instruction in the Christian religion based on the Bible. This was state policy, (Act 90 of 1979), the Act for Education and Training, that education should be Christian in character. While Jews, Muslims, Hindus, Buddhists, traditional African and other religious symbols are present in South African society, it disappears in Christian National Education, it is invisible in the hegemonic domination of sacred symbols, because Biblical Studies and Religious Education is all about the Bible.[5]

M. C. Kitshoff and W. B. van Wyk provide three reasons as to why Biblical Studies and Religious Education busy themselves with the Bible. The manual states that, "this is a Christian country." The 1984 Constitution affirms this in its opening. But what does the label "Christian country" mean? Does it automatically imply that the political order operates on Christian principles? Or is it hegemonic domination to prevent all possibilities of religious pluralism? The manual also asserts that, "without knowledge of the Bible the lives of people would be much the poorer." It is not very difficult to recognize the hegemony in which students in black schools and the dispossessed are forced to accept the very sacred symbols which have given legitimacy to their dispossession. In other words, the riches of the Bible are all that is needed to nourish the hunger of the dispossessed. A third reason provided by the authors makes the claim that, "a child who follows the Christian faith is more likely to behave in a moral way than a non-

---

4. Chidester, "Religious Studies," 6.
5. Ibid., 7.

Christian or an unreligious child." A substantial explanation as to how this could be convincingly argued in the company of Jews, Muslims, Hindus, Buddhists, Humanists, traditional Africans, and others in the country is not offered. This once again could be interpreted as a way Christian National Educational (CNE) utilized hegemony to prevent possibilities of an integrated society, which would demand conversations for religious pluralism.[6]

While I am in agreement with Chidester's hegemonic theory utilized in Christian National Education, I must now consider another possibility. Was this in fact purely a political tool to prevent religious pluralism, or could this have been a profound religious conviction of the Afrikaner deeply rooted in Dutch Calvinism? Theologian Irving Hexham draws from the work of Brian Bunting's, *The Rise of the South African Reich*, in reference to the "received opinion," on Christian National Education. The cultural arm of the Broederbond, the Federation of Afrikaans Cultural Societies, reinstated the CNE in 1939 following the Second Anglo-Boer War, and its main purpose was to indoctrinate the young. He asserts that the term CNE was a way to evoke an emotional response and to revive the memory of post-war resistance movement affirming continuity with the Afrikaner past. Its desire was to resist British political domination and served the needs of the militant Nationalist. The received opinion claims that at a time when opposing British rule was difficult and impractical, the CNE was a means of expressing dissatisfaction and indirect political pressure to Britain.[7]

While this may have satisfied the militant Nationalist by stirring indirect pressure on the British authorities without direct confrontation, there were other Calvinist preachers who saw the CNE as more than the received opinion. S. J. du Toit (1847–1911) introduced the CNE in 1870. Jan Lion-Cachet (1838–1912) and leaders of the Reformed Church further developed it. Du Toit sought to apply the teachings of Calvinism into all areas of life acknowledging a debt to Dutch Calvinism and the success of nineteenth century revival that produced a Christian school movement, trade unions, and a political party in the Netherlands. It was through the success and direction of Groen van Prinsterer (1801–1876), and Abraham Kuyper (1837–

6. Ibid., 8.
7. Hexham, "Religious Conviction," 13–14.

1920), that du Toit and other Calvinists introduced CNE to South Africa. Hexham contends that if the CNE in South Africa was a result of its development and practice in the Netherlands then the "received opinion" becomes untenable. It did not originate in South Africa following the Second Anglo Boer War as the received opinion posits and it was not an extension of the pre-war educational system.[8]

The Reformed Church and fellow Afrikaners joined to establish the CNE system as a way to resist the Anglicization of Minister Lord Milner's policies. The Reformed Church and other leaders of the Afrikaner played a key role in training the teachers in the theories of Christian Nationalism to further the cause of CNE. If the CNE was not a tool produced by the Afrikaner to further its political objectives, then for Hexham it was an important element in the creation of the Nationalist ideology itself. It helped create the distinctive features of Nationalism. The effectiveness of the CNE as an ideological factor in the creation of Afrikaner nationalism can be seen in the way Reformed Church members identified with the Nationalist cause which was deeply rooted in the church's understanding of Calvinism. Van Prinsterer, who had a great influence on Dutch Calvinists in the nineteenth century called his members to the source of their religion; the Bible, and challenged them to apply the source to all areas of their life. In his opinion, only a thorough Christian way of life could resist unbelief and revolution. He charged, "if Christian parents wanted their children to grow up as true Christians they could not entrust their education to deceptive liberal teachers who would undermine the power of the Gospel by their rationalism." Therefore parents had to make sure that their children were educated in accordance with Calvinist truths. Negligence of this serious parental obligation means a betrayal of their baptismal promise to God in rearing their children in the knowledge and fear of God.[9]

Dutch Calvinists spent the latter half of the nineteenth century fighting the State on what became known as the School question. They took their Christian parental duty serious. They did not want to send their children to public schools and fought the state for subsidies for private schools. They claimed as taxpayers, they had the right to educate their children according to what made them feel safe and comfort-

8. Ibid., 14–15.
9. Ibid., 16–17.

able, not according to what the government prescribed. They wanted schools to be controlled by the parents of the children who attended them. In sending a child to school they argued a parent delegated their God-given authority over the child to the schoolteacher. The liberals in Dutch politics resisted this narrow minded ideology, which led the Calvinists to form a united political front, which then gave rise to the first modern political party in the Netherlands under the leadership of Abraham Kuyper in 1879, the Anti-Revolutionary Party. Kuyper developed van Prinsterer's theories. Kuyper's charisma, creativeness, organized ability, and vision made him popular among his followers. They felt a sense of unity and a conviction that they would win, and which they did. Thus, when Kuyper entered Dutch parliament in 1901, he passed the school legislation and changed the structure of Dutch education.[10]

The school question in the Netherlands was an important element in Dutch society, because it focused on a whole range of developments and changed the character of this culture. Calvinists now had control of their children's education. This was a huge achievement, because the freedom of their children's education identified with their freedom of religion. All opposition was seen as an attack to their faith. Therefore in South Africa the need for CNE became an accepted part of Calvinist faith for the Reformed Church. The Nationalist Party was founded in 1914 and the support of the Reformed Church for the Nationalist cause was a great boon to the party. In response, the party made concessions to the convictions of the church. *The Program of Principles* published in 1914 shows the Party's support for CNE. Reference is made to "the guidance of God," and the "people's life along Christian national lines." In the education section, reference is made to, "the right of parents to choose the direction of their children's education." The "sphere of work" and "sovereignty in each sphere," derived from Kuyper's theory of "sphere sovereignty" justified his political stance. *The Program of Principles* was published by Willem Postma. It was revised by a committee, which included Postma and Professor Jan Kamp who was on Kuyper's editorial staff of the daily newspaper *De Standaard*, before emigrating to South Africa. Therefore one should not be surprised of the strong Calvinist influence in National Party policy.[11]

10. Ibid., 18.
11. Ibid., 19–20.

Hexham believes that the main purpose of the CNE was to promote the interests of Calvinism, it was not intended as a device to indoctrinate the young in apartheid theory. He contends that one of the most valuable elements of the CNE both in the Netherlands and South Africa is that it incited Calvinists into political action. He proposes that while the CNE may have given legitimization to aspects of apartheid through its close ties and support of the National Party, it may have also contributed to the development of Afrikaner racial attitudes. However, the primary focus of the CNE, was the preservation of Calvinism, and only to the extent of this identifying with the Afrikaner has it been a factor in the development of apartheid. In other words for Hexham, CNE in South Africa was truly a religious conviction rooted deeply in Dutch Calvinism.

I think there is validity to Hexham's proposal and accept that the CNE was initially a strong religious conviction. However, I think that somewhere along the process, through their close ties with the policies of the National Party it lost its initial purpose. As they got more involved in the politics of the National Party they gave legitimacy to the policies of apartheid and racial discrimination. As one having been raised in this context, I can attest to the role of the CNE in its validation of apartheid and racial attitudes from experiences of this educational system. What better system is there to instruct, control, and indoctrinate the youth of all races that you actually believe for a fact that the White race is in fact the superior race and most suited to rule and dominate? I believe that the Afrikaner became more comfortable with its exclusive separatist ideology and the CNE was utilized purely as a strategy for hegemonic domination. Therefore I now want to pursue Chidester's proposal of a religio-political imperative toward otherness to show how embracing and inclusive this proposal is in the spirit of ubuntu.

In Chidester's disposition toward otherness, he concludes that, "every us has a disposition toward them . . . what any us cannot do is ignore them. An intrinsic religio-political imperative requires every us to somehow come to terms with them."[12] Us-ness is contingent to our relationship with them. He proposes three orientations as a strategy in adopting a religio-political imperative, beginning with the most violent and concluding with the least violent disposition toward

---

12. Chidester, "Religious Studies," 12.

otherness. He believes first that the strategy of *exclusion* is a violent method of elimination. Us becomes an exclusive, single group, where the group believes that they are the chosen race, they belong to the one true church, and that there is only one biblical salvation and that unity in a world of religio-political multiplicity is dealt with violent methods of exclusion. This aversion to otherness is a violent strategy to eliminate all possibilities of pluralism.[13]

Other faiths are seen as nothing but objects for Christian mission. With the divisive ideology of Apartheid in 1948 Muslims, Buddhists, Hindus, and traditional Africans were not only separated spiritually but also physically. The only evidence of any vague form of religious pluralism was due to the Jewish presence in which otherness was based on creed and not color. The largest group of Christians in South Africa is Black, but political agendas were more important than religious aspects because they were excluded due to their color, although they were the very products of White missionary effects.[14]

Second, the strategy of *hegemony* is a less violent method toward otherness and is accomplished overtly. As seen in the public education of South Africa the violation of difference is achieved by the sacred symbols of one particular group. Religious plural beliefs of otherness, is explained with hegemonic terms by the ideology of the dominant group. Ancestors are replaced by demons, other religious beliefs become superstitions and foreign. Hegemony is established by giving validation to the dominant political interests with Christian religious symbols.[15] The preamble of the apartheid Constitution read: "In humble submission to Almighty God who controls the destinies of peoples and nations . . . to uphold Christian values and civilized norms, with the recognition and protection of freedom of faith and worship."[16] This is a clear example of hegemonic domination of one religio-political group. In 1985 hundreds of Muslims joined Blacks on the streets of Cape Town in protest against the totalitarian government. Several Muslims were detained and a year later the DRC warned against Muslim involvement in revolutionary action. In 1986 the DRC

---

13. Ibid., 13.
14. Lubbe, "Religious Pluralism," 211.
15. Chidester, "Religious Studies," 13.
16. Lubbe, "Religious Pluralism," 211.

pronounced that Islam was a false religion and a threat to Christianity in South Africa and the world.

The strategy of *toleration* toward otherness is a religio-political compromise, which no one group is more powerful to establish any form of dominance over others. In the U.S., religious toleration embodied in the First Amendment is a negotiated compromise that guarantees religious freedom and liberty so that no one group can enforce its will and power over another. Therefore in order to protect the rights and liberty of one it is necessary to ensure the freedom of all.[17]

In South Africa though tolerance is perceived, not intended, since other religions consider themselves as being tolerated, but not free, Lubbe contends that religion and racism is closely connected in theory. Every experience of race is also interpreted as an experience of religion. Members of other faiths contend that as long as they are not politically free, they are not religiously free. The perceived attitude of the State toward these members is that they are religiously tolerated, but not religiously free. Once again, the religious tolerance that existed during the apartheid era was in fact yet another mode of exclusion and avoidance of religious pluralism.[18]

These three strategies seem to represent different aspects of one over-arching strategy in the context of South Africa. "Hegemony . . . extended through . . . hegemonic explanations of otherness by which plural religious beliefs, practices, and experiences are forcibly re-explained in terms by the singular ideology of a dominant group."[19]

Apartheid's Revelation of Christianity

Three quarters of South Africa's population attest to some form of Christianity presently and has played a significant factor in the post-apartheid era since 1994 in its search for providing equal rights, equal opportunities, and freedom for all. Undoubtedly however, since Christians were involved in the creation of the apartheid regime a critique must be applied to bring light to the credibility of this religion. Only in a constructive critique that demands liberation of Christianity, can it then fulfill its true potential as a force to humanize and provide

17. Chidester, "Religious Studies," 13.
18. Lubbe, "Religious Pluralism," 212.
19. Chidester, "Religious Studies," 13.

greater justice to society. Any form of legalized and enforced discrimination based on the color of one's skin and is shaped and supported by Christian principles is a violent denial of the egalitarian and universal love message of its founder Jesus. I wish to illuminate these problems within the teachings of Christianity in light of its support of apartheid as a Christian country and provide examples of how Christians in its new democracy has helped in the healing of this broken country. Sincere and authentic healing cannot be achieved in any society unless truth of the past and present is exposed, faced, and dealt with, as shown with the Christian influence in the South African TRC. I believe the enormous success of the TRC was due to the strong positive influence of Christians in the country and on the TRC Commissions, unlike that of the apartheid era.

History and Philosophy of Religion scholar Martin Prozesky says that, it is one thing to declare apartheid a heresy in that it condemns a system as morally offensive. But that does not provide answers as to how an orthodox group with orthodox convictions can devise, implement, and support a system that seem to be a major departure from their orthodoxy. The declaration of apartheid as heresy speaks to the effect but not to the cause. He believes further that without a sincere search for the cause, Christianity could be prevented from being a positive influence in society. To the extent that people of other faiths and religions would be less apt to support it because of its undesired ethical quality and a loss of credibility.[20]

Prozesky's criteria for critiquing Christianity are formulated around the universal love of the founder, Jesus. Therefore he contends that White Christians must come to grips with the fact that apartheid South Africa failed disgracefully and was incompatible with the basic tenets that factored the common elements of Jesus' universal love. The commitment to loving ones fellow beings as oneself involved equality, care, support, and wellbeing for all South Africans. Anything short of this cannot be real love and contradicts the central message of the founder. This is not a problem for White Christians in South Africa only. Some White Christians colonized the world, introduced slavery, almost made the Native Americans extinct and possessed their land, they gave us the Holocaust, they gave us Hiroshima, and the list goes on. The point here however, is that this religion which claims to have

---

20. Prozesky, "Implications of Apartheid," 125.

salvation for all of humanity through Christ, with its scriptures as the truest living Word of God, the Logos, has been associated with some of the world's worst atrocities and human rights violations. Not to forget though, this is the same religion that condemns those without salvation through Christ to hell.[21]

In the preface of Immanuel Kant's *Critique of Pure Reason,* he wrote:

> Our age is, in a special degree, the age of criticism, and to criticism everything must submit. Religion through its sanctity, and law-giving through its majesty, may seek to exempt themselves from it. But they then awaken just suspicion, and cannot claim the sincere respect which reason accords only to that which has been able to sustain the test of free and open examination.[22]

Words written over two centuries ago very aptly describes what the Christian religion and the government in South Africa sought to do, that is, exempt themselves from criticism, and in the process arose suspicion and disrespect. Instead it divided and almost destroyed this society. Prozesky contends that "apartheid shows just how easily even devout believers in a heavily Christianized culture can unwittingly make their faith into an effective component of group self-interest in the forms of nationalist domination and economic exploitation."[23] When one reads the Bible at face value without the luxury of sophisticated tools for varying interpretations, it does not give a clear egalitarian treatment of humanity. Rather it focuses more on conquering and domination. What one concludes from biblical history is that survival depends on domination. If the Bible was clearer on egalitarian social teaching then opposition to slavery and other social inequalities would have taken place a lot sooner than it has. Instead, the Bible is loaded with models of domination that seem to further discourage an egalitarian message of universal love that embrace all. Israel from Moses to the Jerusalem fall, nations from the Egyptians to the Canaanites is repeatedly seen as Israel's enemies. Israel suffered oppression from many of these nations and to free themselves from slavery the first born Egyptian children were put to death. This hardly constitutes a

---

21. Ibid., 128.
22. Kant, *Critique of Pure Reason*, 7.
23. Prozesky, "Implications of Apartheid," 129.

move toward universal egalitarian benevolence. One concludes from this type of domination model and Israel's violent successes as the chosen nation that believers could very well accept this as God's way of accomplishing things and will have no reason to choose a different approach. If the Bible is the authoritative word of God, divinely inspired and written, then one cannot blame its followers to take these models seriously and apply it to their history.[24]

Prozesky makes another intriguing point regarding Christianity and its salvific emphases, which is very crucial to this chapter. He finds a serious problem with Christianity's traditional view of salvation and a contradiction to Jesus' message of universal love for all. Prozesky finds the Christians view of salvation to be elitist and exclusivist which is in contradiction to the spiritual model of embracing all, since they claim to be the only religion blessed with the keys to eternal life through Christ. I believe that any religion that claims that their way is the only true way to believe and non-acceptance of this faith will lead to condemnation and damnation, then they must be viewed with extreme suspicion and caution. To say that God's gift of salvation to all human beings can be only received through Christianity is elitist. It's exclusivist to further admit that this free salvation is through Christ alone. That is an audaciously bold claim. Christian pluralists reject this form of elitism and exclusion. One must reject this form of spiritual apartheid. If Jesus taught of unconditional and universal love, why is His salvation limited to just those who accept His teachings only?

In the discussion of Korean minjung theology, one of the strengths of the people hermeneutic is in its redemption of the prominence of the historical Jesus, because it is much easier to identify with Jesus as a human person rather than a deified anthropomorphic personification. This can be viewed as a weakness or distortion to Evangelical theology because it seems to take significance away from the resurrected Christ. The importance of the historical Jesus is that people can identify with this Jesus of suffering and pain and his mission to alleviate the class, gender, and social barriers, which much of his presence on earth was attributed to. Evangelicals however, are consumed with the afterlife and their security of salvation in heaven through Christ therefore the resurrected Christ is tantamount to their worldview and spirituality. This can explain why some Christians like the Afrikaners, could sin-

---

24. Prozesky, "Implications of Apartheid," 130–31.

cerely support the injustice of their policies of apartheid with sincere religious convictions.

Further, to say that Jesus Christ is the unique salvific mediator denies salvific roles of other religions like Buddhism, Hinduism, Islam, and Judaism. It is not difficult to see why these exclusivist and elitist teachings could lead to the Afrikaners discriminatory and non-egalitarian methods to control since they believed like Israel, they were the chosen. The egalitarian and universal concepts of Jesus' teachings did not fit well with the architects of apartheid, because they understood Christianity in non-egalitarian, elitists, and exclusive terms.

Constitutional Implications for Religious Pluralism

> The political and legal system of pre-1994 South Africa was particularly noted for the totalitarian interference of the state in the private sphere of people's day-to-day lives. In apartheid South Africa, the state prescribed, with race as the prime criterion, whom one could marry, where one could reside and own property, which schools and universities one would be allowed to attend, and which jobs were reserved for persons of a particular race. The state dictated to sports clubs whom they could admit as members, and against whom they were permitted to compete. The sick had to be conveyed in racially exclusive ambulances, could only receive blood transfusions from donors of their own race, and only qualified for treatment in racially defined hospitals. The state even regulated, with race as the primary criterion, who would be allowed to attend church services in certain regions, and where one could be buried. These racist appendices of a totalitarian regime did not reflect the spirit of, at least, the victims of their practical impact, which-as everyone knows-constituted a vast majority of the South African nation. Nor were they supported by the religious convictions of the people, or of a majority of the people, or for that matter of any distinct section of the people.[25]

The new South Africa attempts to Africanize the country from the Western and European model which only benefited the White elite minority. It seeks to uphold African values in its institutions. In South Africa's totalitarian regime, two factors monopolized the country, namely:

25. Van der Vyver, "Constitutional Perspective," 2.

Institutionalized discriminatory structures by the state and,
A bias to one religion, Christianity.

The power of the sword to enforce a dominant religion was a distinct feature of this regime. Although there wasn't an established state church, there were laws that gave the state a right to interfere in the affairs of religious institutions, to repress the total freedom and full practice of these religions under the Internal Security Act 21. If the Minister of Law and Order was of the opinion, that an institution upheld communist influences they were subject to banning and had their privileges to worship denied. The history of apartheid was a repression of religious pluralism with an agenda to preserve the national, ethnic, cultural and religious identity of its own people only.

Therefore, the transitional Constitution of April 1994 was constructed under the rubric to eliminate such hegemony and provide social, political, and legal structures different from its past. In a way, it may have been designed as a reactionary response to its predecessors. Therefore, it states:

> While thus recognizing the injustices of our past . . . the new South Africa is an open and democratic society based on human dignity, equality and freedom . . . Any institution associated with the discrimination and repression of apartheid must be taken to be incompatible with the values embodied in the kind of society the country now aspires to be.[26]

South Africa's new Constitution was written with the intent to draw from its tragic past and to avoid its repetition. Its history was one of repression, oligarchy, inequality, and secrecy. Its new Constitution set the foundation that made for a peaceful transition from oligarchy to democracy. Its ultimate goal is to look forward by recognizing the evils and injustices of the past. After intense negotiations, a transitional Constitution resulted in 1993. It was enforced on April 27, 1994, coinciding with the country's first democratic elections. This transitional Constitution served as a bridge of its repressive, unjust, and painful past, to a peaceful, democratic future, as the nation looked forward to a final Constitution. The 1993 transitional Constitution laid a solid foundation for the protection of rights in the final 1996 Constitution. The right to equality, freedom of expression, religious

26. Ibid., 3–4.

freedom, and freedom of association, were all part of this impressive catalogue of rights. Unlike the apartheid Constitution, religious rights were not subject to suspension during a state of emergency. The 1996 Constitution was set into action in February 1997. It was to impress upon all South Africans, tolerance. Affirmative tolerance, according to Lourens du Plessis means that people make a concerted effort to understand a desire to accept, and appreciate one another, while passive tolerance is people just putting up with one another. However, passive tolerance is more welcome than no tolerance at all.[27]

There has been an escalating trend for conflicts along the lines of religious, ethnic, and civilizational lines that has surfaced following the post Cold War. A resurgence of nationalism is a considerable factor toward this increasing aggression internationally. Nationalism spun the two great world wars and the more recent conflicts in India, Pakistan, Palestine, Israel, Lebanon, Kosovo, Sri Lanka, Afghanistan, Iraq, Iran, and the United States. Nationalism promotes the idea that one particular nation is superior to other nations and the United States is a fine example of this. Tolerance encourages the idea that all are equal, that no nation, race, or religion is superior to another, while nationalism manipulates the feelings of inferiority through conversion to a superiority mentality.[28]

The 1996 Constitution aims at a high level of affirmative tolerance, because it foresees a jubilation of religious pluralism, since special provisions are made for particularities that arise out of a diversity of religious individuals and communities. Because reconciliation is a high priority to South Africa for nation building, the preamble of the final Constitution alludes to this significance and connotes positive or affirmative tolerance. The era of Christian dominance ended with the enforcement of the 1996 Constitution. The conciliatory preamble reads:

> We, the people of South Africa, Recognize the injustices of our past; Honor those who suffered for the freedom in our land; Respect those who have worked to build and develop our country; and believe that South Africa belongs to all who live in it, united in our diversity.

---

27. Du Plessis, "Freedom of or Freedom from Religion?" 2.
28. Smith, "Protecting the Weak," 6.

We therefore, through our freely elected representatives, adopt this Constitution as the supreme law of the Republic so as to: Heal the divisions of the past and establish a society based on democratic values, social justice and fundamental human rights; Lay the foundations for a democratic and open society in which government is based on the will of the people and every citizen is equally protected by law; Improve the quality of life of all citizens and free the potential of each person; Build a united and democratic South Africa able to take its rightful place as a sovereign state in the family of nations. May God protect our people.[29]

The 1983 Afrikaner Constitution proclaimed; "The people of the Republic of South Africa acknowledge the sovereignty and guidance of Almighty God." Arguably, the Almighty God could have been a reference to the Holy Trinity as in Reformed theology. In the 1996 Constitution, the name of God is used only in the closing phrase of the preamble. God is called to protect. In the opening lines of the national anthem God is asked to bless Africa and is repeated in the six official languages of the country. However, du Plessis contends that, this reference to God in the closing of the preamble seems to favor a monotheistic belief and he makes a valid point. While tolerance and reconciliation is a high priority to this new democracy as discussed above, this favoring of monotheism could be intolerance toward polytheists and atheists.[30] While this religious favoritism might well be against non-theists, Christians could find the reference to God offensive in that it seeks to maintain neutrality in respect to all religions and this belittles their divine deity, which leans toward idolatry. But maybe this is exactly what the Constitution attempts to achieve, religious practices in conformity with egalitarian foundations.

The change from Christian hegemony, which stifled religious pluralism to religious freedom, demonstrates the importance of fundamental human rights in the Constitution to embrace ubuntu being true to African spirituality. The drafting of the Final Constitution consisted of a Constitutional Assembly (CA), which comprised of the National Assembly and the Senate. Four hundred and ninety representatives from seven political parties made the CA. The public was involved in the negotiation process toward the final Constitution. To make this

29. Du Plessis, "Freedom of or Freedom from Religion?" 3–4.
30. Ibid., 4.

a true democratic process the CA made a working draft available to the public in October 1995 with requests to receive submissions from the public about their Constitutional concerns. The CA decided to use language that was understandable by its citizens. They published a newsletter called Constitutional Talk, and this informed the people on the progress of the process. People were invited to discussion groups to clarify misunderstandings. A useful Internet homepage included CA minutes and reports, databases of submissions, issues of previous newsletters, media statements, and draft texts were made available to the public. A Talk-Line provided information by telephone. The public involvement with the Constitutional process proved to be successful in the constructing of the Final Draft.[31]

The Constitution endorses human rights over popular majority concerns. As examples, it is believed that over 80% of South Africans favor capital punishment, but the Constitution does not endorse the death penalty. Almost the same percentage disagrees with abortion but again the Constitution provides for the right to ones choice. Since Christianity has enjoyed a major influence with a more conservative evangelical bent in the country, it would be safe to say that a greater percentage reprehend the idea of homosexuality, but the Constitution protects discrimination based on sexual orientation.[32] The largest number of submissions from the public revolved around the guarantee of equality based on sexual orientation. Section 9 of the Constitution sees the Church as a juristic person. Although homosexuality maybe a violation to a Church's doctrine, it will be in violation of human rights if membership is denied to a person of the gay or lesbian orientation. A more controversial issue arose around the gender of clergy. Many churches still discriminate clerical roles based on gender. Women may not be allowed to enter the vocation of ordination in some denominations due to its biblical beliefs and church bylaws. A recent lively debate evolved around the Roman Catholic Church and their refusal to ordain women as priests and discrimination against gays and lesbians. A strict reading of Section 9 would impose that the Roman Catholic Church's practice would be illegal under the South African Constitution. The Church cannot discriminate on any ground unless they can prove that such discrimination is fair. The Church is then

---

31. Blake, "Religious Freedom in Southern Africa," 4.
32. Van der Vyver, "Constitutional Perspective," 6.

required to prove in a court of law, fairness. Albeit the equality section in Section 9 may be at odds with the rights associated with freedom of religion, "no person (including juristic persons) may unfairly discriminate directly or indirectly on any ground."[33]

The union between the church and state during apartheid certainly provided legal preferences for the DRC. However, it is interesting to note that the 1996 Constitution does not make a separation between church and state and had no intention to do so either. Given the historic past of the Afrikaner government, one would think that the average South African would call for a total separation of church and state. During the Constitutional drafting, controversy erupted around the issue of separation of church and state. Archbishop Desmond Tutu called for a secular state. It should not come as a surprise that Tutu would call for a secular state, since the history of the previous Christian State was a tragic one. However, 3,000 Christians marched to parliament to protest against a proposal to separate church and state. Protesters included Christians from Charismatic denominations to the DRC. Consequently, God was mentioned in the preamble, which makes Zambia the only other country in Southern Africa to discuss religious themes in prefatory language.[34]

Christo Lombaard provides two trends of policy on religion which he calls first, a flat view of religions and second, a non-American type of separation of church and state which he terms a home-grown separation of church and state. The first trend suggests that all religions are equal not only by law but also in its essence in the presence of God. Only extremists will promote the idea that one religion should be given preference over others. If all religions are equal in the eyes of the state then philosophically the state sanctions that all religions provide ways to the same deity such as Indian and Eastern Religions promote. This would be a comfortable trend for most governments to adopt especially if their citizens represent a broad variety of religious beliefs and practices. This flat view of religions will not be bogged down with issues of history, dogma, and liturgy. Rather it will focus on similarities to urge dialogue and harmonious co-existence in the interest of democracy.

---

33. Blake, "Religious Freedom in Southern Africa," 4–5.; Van der Vyver, "Constitutional Perspective," 14.

34. Ibid., v 3–7.

Lombaard's second trend of a homegrown separation of church and state is similar to the US' position which calls for a total separation of church and state. He posits that the American policy in practice echoes traits of fundamentalism and possible authoritarianism. Absolute church-state separation has to be adhered to the extent that the minutiae of public life have to be legislated. This just accentuates an extreme form of nationalism where prayers are replaced with patriotic singing of the national anthem and religious symbols are substituted with the display of the national flag. This is seen as a gesture of nationalist support and a theological apologetic. Due to the importance of religion to South African citizens it is incorporated rather than excluded and most visible in state functions. The state does not remove itself but gives religions equal space without religious preferences to one over the other.[35]

Religious Rights and Freedom

Discriminatory state polices and religious persecutions resulting in atrocious human rights violations have occurred even in more secure countries in 1998. These policies are in violation of the freedom of thought, conscience, and religion principles of the 18th Article of the Universal Declaration. Almost six million Coptic Christians faced threats in *Egypt,* resulting in the attack of several Coptic businesses and churches and the deaths of eight people by extremists. *Iran's* government executed one Bahai, detained fourteen, including six awaiting the death penalty for the practice of their faith. Religious leaders and Christians, particularly those ascribing to the Greek Catholic Church were targets of bombings, violence, and the murder of a priest in *Turkey.* The Ahmadis in *Pakistan* are sentenced to life imprisonment, since the preaching of their faith is considered an attack and blasphemy to the Islamic religion. Buddhism enjoys preferential treatment and the practice is compulsory for all in the schools of *Bhutan.* Protestants, Catholics, Tibetans, Buddhists, and Muslims continue to face religious repression and official control from the *Chinese* government. Shiite teachings in *Malaysia* are considered a national security threat to Islam, which results in imprisonment. The Buddhist state in *Myanmar* practices discriminatory and intolerant policies toward

---

35. Lombaard, "Left Governing Hand," 2–3.

Muslims and Christians by destroying mosques, schools, denying healthcare, civil service employment, education, and a revocation of citizenship. *North Korea* discourages religious activities unless it serves the interests of the state. *Uzbekistan* prohibits Christians to proselytize except in churches. *Vietnam* opposes unofficial religious activities.

In 1997, *Russia* adopted the limited citizen's religious freedom law imposing severe limitations on minority religious groups including some mainline Orthodox groups. A wait period of fifteen years for full legal status had been imposed on these groups, which is a requirement to obtain property, publish, operate schools, and conduct charitable activities. Many nations in Europe have set up enquiry commissions to investigate the spread of cults and sects with an increased attitude of xenophobia and hostility toward new religious movements. *France* identified 172 groups as sects in 1996, including Jehovah's Witnesses and the Church of Scientology. The report that identified these groups was formulated and publicized without the full knowledge of these minority groups. This contributed to an atmosphere of media libeling, circulation of false information and religious intolerance. *Germany's* commission investigated so-called sects and psycho-groups with an emphasis on the dangers of Scientology, but failed to recognize them as a religion.[36]

The death toll of March 2002 Hindu Muslim riots in *India* had reached over 1,000 in one week. This was instigated by Hindu leaders who went on a rampage, looting, killing, raping Muslim victims, and destroying mosques, while the police stood by and watched. The Indian government by way of its inaction seemed to condone these acts of barbarism. The Indian Muslim forms part of India's economically depressed minority, within the voiceless millions. The states apathy was seen in its failure to respond to these victims of hate.[37]

Section 15 of the South African Final Constitution categorically mandates the right to religious freedom: "Everyone has the right to freedom of conscience, religion, thought, belief and opinion."[38] This does not just protect freedom of religion, but guarantees freedom of thought, belief, opinion, and conscience. It also makes room for those who choose to not believe in any religion at all. It entitles one

---

36. Smith, "Protecting the Weak," 7–9.
37. "Where is World Conscience?" 1–2, online in Dawn Editorial.
38. South African Constitution, Section 15, 1996, 1.

to believe in whatever they decide to.[39] The freedom of religion clause includes, "forbidding discrimination on the basis of religion, a clause discussing religious education, a provision dealing with oaths contrary to religious beliefs, and a freedom of association clause." This covers freedom for a potpourri of thoughts.[40]

This is conspicuously different to the American Constitution establishment clause in the First Amendment; "Congress shall make no law respecting an establishment of religion, or prohibit the free exercise thereof." What the amendment simply says is twofold: first, there shall be no official governmental action, which promulgates the establishment of a particular religion (establishment clause). Second, the government shall not interfere with an individual's right to practice his or her religion as he or she sees fit, (free exercise clause). The religious influence during the colonization of America profoundly impacted the establishment of religious liberty in its Constitution.[41]

There is a differing of opinion on the language of Section 15 of the South African Constitution. Does this include establishment proscriptions as understood in the American Constitution, or is the protection of religious rights and freedom better off than the establishment clause? The establishment clause calls for a strict separation of church and state as well as a separation of politics and organized religion. Du Plessis informs that such a separation promotes freedom from religion rather than freedom of religion.[42] The establishment clause in the US Constitution serves to prevent advancing or inhibiting religion by the State, while the free exercise clause is to allow members of all religious backgrounds to pursue their faiths without any interference from the State. The essence of the notion of religious freedom is having the right to religious beliefs, to be able to declare these beliefs openly without fear of being intimidated, or repressed. It also guarantees one the right to demonstrate this belief by worship, practice, teaching, and that this freedom will be stifled by forcing people to act in ways that will be contrary to their common beliefs and practices. Therefore, it is argued that Section 15 of the Constitution does not attest to an establishment clause but rather it deals with free exercise.

39. Du Plessis, "Freedom of or Freedom from Religion?" 6.
40. Blake, "Religious Freedom in Southern Africa," 3.
41. Smith, "Protecting the Weak," 5.
42. Du Plessis, "Freedom of or Freedom from Religion?" 6.

For example, all religions with a substantial following are allowed to buy equal time to broadcast their religious services via the state controlled Radio and Television Corporation. Institutions, who can afford to buy extra airtime, are not permitted since this will defeat the egalitarian intent. In an attempt to understand and support African values and African customary marriages, evidence is seen by legislation that legalizes present and future marriages that is and will become polygamous.[43] Section 15(3) of the Constitution recognizes marriages under systems of religious, personal, or family law, however it was traditionally held that Muslim marriages are polygamous and therefore should not be recognized legally whether the marriage was polygamous or not. The courts deduced that the very potential of a monogamous union could result in polygamy and concluded that it did not follow the mainstream jurisprudence. In a case regarding a divorced Muslim woman's claim for alimony, the Constitution still prejudiced with its conventional language maintaining that the contract in a Muslim marriage violated good morals therefore any claim for alimony could not be enforced. This seems rather preferential and contradictory. While the courts attempt to understand and maintain African values and African customary marriages the verdict of the Muslim trial indicated that the Constitution recognizes but does not guarantee the rights of persons cultural, religious, and community practices. One can only conclude that this case questioned a public policy that tends to favor the preferences and prejudices of one group over the other.[44]

Religious Freedom Clauses in Southern Africa

Many countries in Southern Africa turned toward democracy in the 1990s. South West Africa became Namibia after South Africa ended its rule there. Multiparty elections took place in Zambia in 1991 after a history of one party rule, Malawi moved in the same direction in 1993, and free elections took place in Lesotho. Five southern African countries improved freedom for its citizens and approved new constitutions. Many African constitutions include clauses promoting religious liberty covering; *general freedom of religion, discrimination on the basis of religion, religious education, and oaths contrary to religious*

43. Van der Vyver, "Constitutional Perspective," 17.
44. Du Plessis, "Freedom of or Freedom from Religion?" 11.

beliefs. Many African countries define the *general freedom of religion right* from a negative approach. The Zimbabwean Constitution is one such example as it reads:

> Except with his own consent or by way of parental discipline, no person shall be hindered in the enjoyment of his freedom of conscience, that is to say, freedom of thought and of religion, freedom to change his religion or belief, and freedom, whether alone or in community with others, and whether in public or in private, to manifest and propagate his religion or belief through worship, teaching, practice and observance.[45]

Other countries define it in a positive light as "everyone has the right to freedom of conscience, religion, thought, belief and opinion." The negative type is understood as, no one's freedom of religion can be hindered, while the positive type reads as, one has the right to freedom of religion. One grants freedom affirmatively and implies that hindrance of that freedom is strictly forbidden, while the other prohibits the hindrance of freedom, which can be interpreted as a right to which one is entitled in order to be hindered. In defining the scope of religious liberties of the negative type, it includes the right to change, practice, and share religious beliefs. It also provides for one to consent to a derogation of one's religious rights and allows parents to limit their children's rights through discipline. While these limitations are absent in the positive type, the scope of religious liberties are by no means restrictive or narrow.

Most southern African constitutions prohibit against *discrimination on the basis of religion,* or creed. The distinction however is between whether protection from discrimination is based on creed or religion. Namibia, Lesotho, Malawi, and South Africa forbid discrimination based on religion, while other countries protection in the region is based on creed. No African court has defined creed, although Botswana's highest court argues, that it is different from religion. Webster's 3rd edition defines creed as a, "formulation or system of religious faith." Five American courts and one Canadian court define creed in religious terms. It could be that Botswana, Swaziland, Zambia, and Zimbabwe, include political, social, and economic aspects to encompass a broader definition of creed. Therefore, the absence of the word

---

45. Blake, "Religious Freedom in Southern Africa," 5.

religion not appearing in the discrimination clauses of these countries could also mean that discrimination based on religion is accepted.

There are two types of clauses, relating to *religious education*; one protects the right for an institution to establish their own schools and provide religious education, and the second clause addresses compulsory religious education in public schools. Constitutions differ though, in the right to establish religious schools. Three countries grant the right to establish and maintain religious schools at their own expense, two countries do not grant this right, but does not prevent religious education to take place within that religious community. Three other constitutions include, "any person or everyone to establish private schools at their expense," providing that these schools, maintain government educational standards. No reference is made to compulsory religious education or observances in the Malawian and Namibian constitutions. South Africa and other constitutions promote freedom of choice, making attendance to religious ceremonies free and voluntary if it relates to a practice other than one's own belief. This is opposite to the American proposal, opposing religion in school as you will note in the section below. Most African constitutions also allow for the protection from taking *oaths,* if it is contrary to ones religious belief. South Africa allows one to take an affirmation such as "so help me God," rather than an oath when being sworn into political office. Taking of an oath is not prohibited, but taking an oath that is contrary to one's own religious convictions could be seen as a violation of one's religious liberty and state coercion.[46]

President Kenneth Kaunda of Namibia since 1964 was replaced by President Fredrick Chiluba in 1991 through the ratification of a new Constitution, which resulted in a multiparty democracy. After five years Chiluba amended the preamble of the Constitution to read, Zambia a "Christian nation but upholding the right of every person to enjoy that person's freedom of conscience of religion." This amendment was a constitutional breach and antithetical to the equality of peoples religious beliefs. Since then, there has been a number of recent incidents were Hindus have been the targets of hate crimes. Hindus have been ostracized and this only further encourages antagonism by Christians, therefore excluding the amendment in the prefatory language will help promote religious liberty in Zambia.

46. Ibid., 5–7.

South Africa may be the strongest democracy in the area. Provisions are made to protect the rights of persons to practice culture and religion, with freedom. Though they are not perfect models for the rest of Africa and the world to immediately muster, the direction is admirable and desirable. While Hindus and Muslims are still persecuted in many southern African countries by members of other religions, and countries are regressing on democratic commitments, South Africa seems to be leading the path for other southern African countries to follow. [47]

The American Establishment Experiment

America's commitment to religious freedom must be understood within the framework of its historical struggle for this very freedom. During the settlement in the 17th century, several colonies were established as sanctuaries for the different sects and denominations. This plurality laid the foundation for religious freedom in the United States. *Massachusetts* and *Connecticut* were established by puritans seeking reform from the Church of England along Congregationalist lines. Although the New England Congregationalists and Puritans favored political freedom, they did not possess a good record when it came to religious tolerance. In fact, they resorted to similar forms of religious intolerance that they fled from England for. Roger Williams, Anne Hutchinson, and other non-conformists were expelled from the colony. Baptists were not allowed in the colony, four Quakers were hung after insisting to return after being expelled. Roger Williams founded *Rhode Island* in 1630 on the principle of freedom of conscience and complete separation of church and state. Later other evangelicals and Baptists followed in the path of Williams' separation of church and state. *Maryland* and *Pennsylvania* soon incorporated the doctrine of free exercise of religion.[48]

Maryland was founded as a haven for Catholics from Protestant England in 1625, by George Calvert and his son Cecil. George Calvert was a convert to Catholicism. It was Calvert's request from the new Protestant governor of Maryland to promise not to disturb Christians and Catholics specifically that the term free exercise first appeared in

47. Blake, "Religious Freedom in Southern Africa," 2.
48. Smith, "Protecting the Weak," 4.

an American legal document in 1648. William Penn, a Quaker was committed to finding a safe place for religious minorities, settled Pennsylvania in 1681. The great diversity of religions in Pennsylvania was indicative of its tolerance. In 1776, there were 403 different congregations in Pennsylvania. *New York, New Jersey, and Pennsylvania* became prominent Presbyterian colonies due to the influx of Scotch-Irish immigrants.

The rationalist ideas of the Enlightenment no doubt represented Thomas Jefferson's thoughts on free exercise. He wanted a wall between church and state, so that there would not be a corrupting influence from either. Therefore, the establishment of freedom of conscience was fundamental to him in that it guaranteed to free the mind from outside bondage. At the end of the colonial era, there were many different religious sects that existed, with no one sect large enough to establish a public state church. In the absence of this majority, the non-religious state provided the ideal situation for diversity and unity to take place among the colonies in the quest to protect religious liberty. James Madison who championed this sentiment at the constitutional convention said, "In a free government the security for religious rights consists in a multiplicity of sects." These practical considerations contributed to the strong separation of church and state, which guaranteed religious freedom in the United States Constitution.[49]

For Jefferson, the establishment of religious freedom, which prescribed religious liberty for all, was a fair and novel experiment. Jefferson was proposing that all religions should be in equal footing with Christianity. Christianity and all its forms must learn to stand on its own feet, he said, "on equal footing with the faiths of the Jew and the Gentile, the Mahometan, the Hindoo, and the Infidel of every denomination."[50] This proposal was very different to the Western model, which proscribed that Christianity, as an established community must be protected from all other religions by the state. In other words, he wanted the growth of a religion to survive by its power to compel and convince, rather than by coercion of the state, and support by law.[51]

---

49. Smith, "Protecting the Weak," 4–5.
50. Jefferson, *The Complete Jefferson*, 1147.
51. Witte, *Most Mild and Equitable Establishment of Religion*, 1.

John Adams political experiment on religious liberty was engineered through the 1780 Constitution of Massachusetts. Like Jefferson, he wrote with equal inspiration that, "authority in magistrates and obedience of citizens can be grounded on reason, morality, and the Christian religion without succumbing to other forms of ecclesiastical or civil tyranny." While the Constitution guaranteed equal liberty and security of property for all people of all religions, it instituted a mild establishment of religion with special protection, preference, and privilege for types of Christian piety, morality, and charity. Both Jefferson and Adams were consciously involved in a new religious liberty experiment. The American Declaration of Independence, which they both drew, articulated the framework of their values. All are created equal with certain unalienable rights. Every religion should be constitutionally recognized, protected, and possess essential rights and liberties.[52]

Jefferson's model of religious liberty involved two factors, disestablishment and free exercise of all religions. The state could not show special preference, or privilege to any one religion, nor should they make or affirm laws or policies on explicit religious grounds. The state should not depend on religious institutions to perform or carry out their functions and should refrain from getting involved with the doctrines and disciplines of these institutions. The state should respect freedom of conscience and free exercise of all its subjects as inalienable and the most sacred of all human rights. Jefferson's experiment on religious liberty did not only influence Virginia but the entire nation.[53]

> Almighty God hath created the mind free, Jefferson wrote therefore:
>
> All attempts to influence it by temporal punishments, or burdens, or by civil incapacitations, tend only to beget habits of hypocrisy and meanness, and are a departure from the plan of the holy author of our religion . . . no man shall be compelled to frequent or support any religious worship, place, or ministry whatsoever, nor shall be enforced, restrained, molested, or burdened in his body or goods, nor shall otherwise suffer, on account of his religious opinions or belief, but that all men shall be free to profess, and by argument to maintain, their opinion

---

52. Ibid., 1–2.
53. Jefferson, *The Complete Jefferson*, 957.

in matters of religion, and that the same shall in no wise diminish, enlarge, or affect their civil capacities.[54]

Adams' model of religious liberty involved establishment of one public religion and the freedom of many private religions. He believed that every state needed to establish some form of public religion by law. Adams saw Jefferson's model as a philosophical fiction because he felt it was impossible to imagine that a state can successfully remain neutral and removed from religion. Yet, at the same time he was cognizant to the notion that it would be philosophical fiction for a state to successfully coerce all people to one common public religion alone. Therefore, he proposed that people should be able to make their own private decisions regarding matters of faith, for he regarded the rights of conscience to be indisputable, unalienable, indefeasible, and divine. He envisioned the creed of this public religion to be:

> . . . honesty, diligence, devotion, obedience, virtue, and love of God, neighbor, and self. Its icons were the Bible, the bells of liberty, the memorials of patriots, the Constitution. Its clergy were public-spirited ministers and religiously-devout politicians. Its liturgy was the public proclamation of oaths, prayers, songs, and election and Thanksgiving Day sermons. Its policy was state sanctions against blasphemy, sacrilege, and iconoclasm, state sponsorship of religious societies, schools and charities.[55]

Religious pluralism was essential in the maintenance and protection of religious and other forms of liberty. His 1780 Constitution aimed at striking this balance between establishment of one public religion and the freedom of all private religions. When asked about his personal religious affiliation, Adams responded, "Ask me not . . . whether I am a Catholic or Protestant, Calvinist or Armenian. As far as they are Christians, I wish to be a fellow-disciple with them all." As a fierce patriot, and a vigorous moralist he knew that some would insist on establishment and others on freedom, therefore he sought to appease both interests, by proposing a tempered religious freedom with a slender religious establishment. He was convinced that the establish-

---

54. Edwin S. Gaustad, *Sworn on the Altar of God: A Religious Biography of Thomas Jefferson*, (Grand Rapids: Eerdmans, 1996), 13.
55. Witte, *Most Mild and Equitable Establishment of Religion*, 2–9.

ment of one common religion alongside other plural private religions' was fundamental for the survival of society and the state.

We must certainly begin, Adams wrote:

> ... by setting our conscience free. For when all men of all religions consistent with morals and property, shall enjoy equal liberty ... and security of property, and an equal chance for honors and power ... we may expect that improvements will be made in the human character, and the state of society. But we must just as certainly begin by setting religion at the fore and floor of society and government ... without religion, this world would be something not fit to be mentioned in polite, I mean hell.[56]

Conclusion

In this chapter I highlighted the elitism and exclusivism of Christianity in its use of Christian National Education by the Afrikaner to educate, propagate, and influence young South African children to grow up with the same ideologies of their parents and maintain an exclusive race, Afrikanerdom. I examined the American establishment and free exercise clause in comparison with the 1996 South African Constitution and conclude that even though religion played an integral part in South Africa's oppressive past in supporting oppression, she did not call for a separation of church and state but rather embraced religious pluralism in its Constitution to promote egalitarian values to all of its community in true ubuntu spirituality.

America and South Africa lament a similar past and often this history will instruct how they illuminate and modify their current laws and Constitutions to overcome rather than repeat. In response to colonialism, the American Constitution forges a "preferential status to the First Amendment freedoms and accordingly instilled essentially libertarian values in the fabric of all constitutional arrangements." South Africa's past is one of institutional discrimination therefore human dignity and equal protection is a priority for the construction of this new Constitution. While the sentiments of libertarianism can be found in America's separation of church and state, South Africa strives for egalitarianism with hopes to provide a lucent model for its

---

56. Witte, *Most Mild and Equitable Establishment of Religion*, 9–10.

neighboring countries to follow. Therefore religion is not treated as a government taboo for religious institutions to work out the details of its place in society, but rather the Constitution calls for an evenhanded treatment in official dealings.[57]

John Adams' 1780 Constitution strove for a balance between establishment of one public religion, namely Christianity, and the freedom of all private religions. Jefferson's model at the core was one of separationism and religious individualism. This is the American model, a separation of church and state. Adams proposed a more inclusive and embracing model, which at the heart aimed at accommodationism and religious communitarianism. Whenever a state establishes a public religion such as the Christian worship of God by civil authority, it essentially hopes to promote happiness, order, and preservation of that state authority. However, it turns out that invariably it promotes impiety, hypocrisy, and other oppressive evils, and South Africa's past is one such example.[58]

Therefore, Jefferson's model of separation and religious individualism would not have worked in the South African theme of ubuntu because it would have enforced a more rugged separation that already existed through apartheid. Separation compounded with isolation would result to the extreme form of individualism that would result in an Americans' extreme nationalist and patriotic pride. Adams model of establishment of one public religion and the freedom of many private religions would not work in South Africa either. Christianity was the established public religion under apartheid. Which other religion would be the new public established religion in the new democracy, or would want to follow the tragic legacy of Christianity? Accommodation and community are essential elements to the new democracy, which are elements of Adams model, but religious equality was also fundamental to this new democracy. Therefore it is not a separation of church and state or a secular, but an egalitarian religious state promoting diversity, inclusivity, and community.

I have shown that Christianity has been a dominant influence although South Africa is a religiously plural country. The Afrikaner used this religion to separate, prevent inclusion, and suppress pluralism. The exclusion of otherness and other religious voices was clearly vis-

57. Van der Vyver, "Constitutional Perspective," 16–17.
58. Witte, *Most Mild and Equitable Establishment of Religion*, 3, 13.

ible through Christian National Education. This was used as a political tool to procure hegemonic domination. I have shown why religious pluralists would be suspicious with the traditional elitist salvific view that most evangelical Christians hold to. It is not difficult to see why exclusivist and elitist teachings like this could lead to the Afrikaners discriminatory and non-egalitarian methods to control because they believed like Israel, that they were the chosen race.

South Africa's new Constitution drew lessons from its past, an unjust, painful past, therefore the right to equality, freedom of expression, religious freedom, and freedom of association, were prioritized in the new Constitution. It was set in place to promote affirmative tolerance with a celebration of religious pluralism, inclusivity, diversity, and community for healing, nation building, and national reconciliation for ubuntu to weave its presence into the fabric of this once demoralized segregated society to now in the present South Africa embrace all of humanity as persons interrelated together into one common society. Therefore, it is not a separation of church and state, because she fervently seeks to uphold religious practices in conformity with the egalitarian foundations of its new Constitution. It is not a secular state either, because ubuntu is necessary for this community's survival, growth, and maturity. It was once a broken nation and now is on its way toward healing, reconciliation, repentance, forgiveness, and embraces democracy with egalitarian values. Ubuntu is the cement that holds this community together.

Bibliography

Blake, Richard Cameron. "Religious Freedom in Southern Africa: The Developing Jurisprudence." *Brigham Young University Law Review* (1998) 4.

Dawn Editorial, The Internet Edition. "Where is World Conscience?" Online: http://www.dawn.com.htm.

Chidester, David. "Christians, Buddhists, Muslims, and Others." *Journal of Theology for Southern Africa* 60 (1987) 81.

———. "Religious Studies as Political Practice." *Journal of Theology for Southern Africa* 58 (1987) 6.

Du Plessis, Lourens. "Freedom of or Freedom from Religion? An Overview of Issues Pertinent to the Constitutional Protection of Religious Rights and Freedom In the New South Africa." *Brigham Young University Law Review* (2001) 2.

Gaustad, Edwin S. *Sworn on the Altar of God: A Religious Biography of Thomas Jefferson*. Grand Rapids: Eerdmans, 1996.

Hexham, Irving. "Religious Conviction or Political Tool?" *Journal of Theology for Southern Africa* 26 (1979) 13–14.

Jefferson, Thomas. *The Complete Jefferson: Containing His Major Writings*. Edited by Saul K. Padover. Freemont, NY: Books for Libraries, 1943.

Kant, Immanuel. *Critique of Pure Reason*. Translated by N. Kemp Smith. New York: Palgrave MacMillan, 2003.

Lombaard Christo. "The Left Governing Hand and the Right Governing Hand: Begging for a Church without Public Hands?" *Journal of Theology for Southern Africa* 109 (March 2001) 2–3.

Lubbe, Gerrie. "Religious Pluralism and Christianity in South Africa." In *Christianity amidst Apartheid*, edited by Martin Prozesky, 208–16. New York: St. Martin's, 1990.

Prozesky, Martin. "Implications of Apartheid for Christianity in South Africa." In *Christianity amidst Apartheid*, edited by Martin Prozesky. New York: St. Martin's, 1990.

Smith, Gordan. "Protecting the Weak: Religious Liberty in the Twenty First Century. *Brigham Young University Law Review* (1999) 6.

South African Constitution, Section 15, 1996, 1.

Van der Vyver, Johan D. "Constitutional Perspective of Church-State Relations in South Africa." *Brigham Young University Law Review* (1999) 2.

Witte, John, Jr. "A Most Mild and Equitable Establishment of Religion: John Adams and the Massachusetts Experiment." *Journal of Church and State* (Spring 1999) 1.

8

Instruments or Inhibitors of Civil Society?
The Role of Christians in the Formation of Public Policy

JAMES R. COCHRANE[1]

AT A LECTURE, ON "RENEWAL AND RENAISSANCE-TOWARDS A NEW World Order," given at the Oxford Center for Islamic Studies in England, Nelson Mandela noted that it was five hundred years ago that year (1997) that the Portuguese explorer Vasco da Gama set out around Africa "in search of Christians and spices."[2] South Africa was one of da Gama's stopping points, and the names of many places still testify to his visit. It was not, of course, the first imprint of Christianity on Africa—that honour belongs to the early churches established in North Africa long before much of Western Europe could be regarded, in its later language, as "civilized."[3]

Da Gama's voyage signaled the arrival on the African continent: of the forces of modernity through the processes of conquest and colonization. The impact upon African peoples of this development is well-documented and needs no comment here. But Mandela interrogates that history with a provoking thought: "I come to pose the

---

1. The University of Cape Town Research Committee provided financial support for this paper, though the author bears all responsibility for its content.

2. Mandela, "Renewal and Renaissance."

3. The Coptic Church in Egypt claims ancestry dating to the first disciples of Jesus of Nazareth, for example, and was certainly in existence by the second century of the Christian era. See Partrick, *Traditional Egyptian Christianity*. From a Coptic perspective, cf. Iris Habib el Masri, *Story of the Copts*.

question whether our generation has the capacity to close the circle on these five centuries."

In this context, Mandela points to the very real possibilities for regeneration or renaissance in Africa as a whole, particularly sub-Saharan Africa, noting as "outward signs" of this hope that democratic elections have been held in more than twenty-five countries in this decade alone and that average GDP growth since 1995 has more than tripled from 1.5 to over 5 percent per annum.

Religion is necessarily part of this transformation in his view. He draws on a perception that strong "inter-religious solidarity in action against apartheid, rather than mere harmony or co-existence, was crucial in bringing that evil system to an end." He thus suggests that interaction and cooperation between "the three great religions of Africa [Islam, Christianity, African Traditional Religions] . . . could have a profound bearing on the social space we create for the rebirth of our continent." Indeed, he adds, rather grandly, that such a process might even assist in the establishment of a world order "based on mutual respect, partnership and equity."

The possibility of religions contributing significantly to the social space necessary for renewal in African nations is the backdrop of the question I pose about the relationship between religion and civil society, or more narrowly, between Christian churches and civil society. I begin by discussing the notion of civil society in relation to Africa, arguing that it is an important concept for contemporary African societies as long as it is properly located.[4] I then problematize the role of religion in civil society under the conditions of a plural democracy. The challenge of democratization, in turn, is brought up against the experience of popular religion in (South) Africa, notably in respect of the rise of African initiated churches (AIC). The final section attempts to relate these issues to the engagement of churches or Christians per se in processes of public policy formation.

---

4. I do not, in this paper, detail the reasons why civil society itself is an important construct under conditions of modernity (or postmodernity, for that matter). This I have done elsewhere; see Cochrane, "Religion and Civil Society: Readings from the South African Case."

Civilizing Africa: A Colonial Curse or a Double Emancipation?

Africa has in the past been viewed by mainstream Northern cultures as "uncivil," or in more recent negative terminology, as "undeveloped." The "civilizing" mission of the original European colonial representatives, despite its positive aspects, left a negative heritage whose effects are still apparent. Thus, it evokes suspicion when outside forces push for democracy in Africa expecting to see, alongside a market economy, a civil society emerge which acts as a bulwark against "tribalism," "nepotism," "corruption," "one-party states" and similar terms frequently applied to African nations.

There is a play on words when one brings the notion of civil society into relation with ideologies framed around ideas of civilization or civil behavior. But it is not merely a play. The notions of civilization and civil behavior have arisen in conjunction with the modern use and understanding of civil society, attached quite directly to the history of particular (European) cultures. This history, in turn, relates to the substantial changes in European economic processes with the rise of mercantile capitalism, and more importantly, industrial capitalism and the bourgeoisie.

That South Africans, particularly representatives of the black working class and their dependents, are suspicious of talk of civil society reflects the emergence of the concept in the rise of bourgeois led nation-states. Similarly, in South Africa as elsewhere, the call for a process of Africanization arises as a term of opposition to the dominant and still historically efficacious forms of discursive, political and economic practices of the early colonial powers.[5] What exactly Africanization should or could mean remains disputed, even vague in its practical meaning.[6] Nevertheless, the call itself signals a protest against the hegemonic discursive and rhetorical practices of the past,

---

5. Of course, most of Africa was decolonized in the late 1950s and the 1960s. South Africa is a latecomer in this respect, though it must also be made clear that the nature of colonization and the way in which it remained efficacious differs across the continent and over time. Thus in South Africa one frequently encountered theories in the two decades before the collapse of apartheid of "internal colonization," referring to rule by settler whites no longer linked to an imperial metropole.

6. In academic circles, the claim has been put forward most publicly in recent times by William Makgoba of the University of the Witwatersrand; cf. Mokoko, *Makgoba Affair*.

and a challenge to concepts associated with modernity and Western thought in particular.

A hermeneutic of suspicion is inevitable, therefore, when an African is confronted by the demand to pay attention to "civil" society. The hermeneutic of suspicion must remain, because the genealogy of civil society is particular, because it is historically and sociologically located in a specific class discourse, and because it is philosophically located in the nexus of Western national and imperial epistemologies.[7]

But suspicion alone will not resolve the question of how we might define practical relationships of political life in the context of the plural life worlds, powers and practices, which is essentially what we identify through the notion of a differentiated civil society. Differentiation in the articulation of political, economic and social dynamics in African states is an important issue, particularly given the sad history of African demagogues and tyrannies in the last half of this century (repeating, of course, what has happened in other parts of the world as well), and the increasing evidence of differentiation (both political and economic) at all levels in many states. This forces upon us some clarification of the idea of civil society, even if the term arose elsewhere under different conditions.

Civil society as such cannot be conceived in Africa without reference to the way in which modernity impacted upon Africa. The historical link seems obvious. The famous "scramble for Africa," a colonial venture, coincides with the formal separation of spheres of society into political, economic and civic domains of authority elsewhere, most notably in France and North America. De Tocqueville's description of the United States of America presents the classic paradigm case of this tripartite conception of society.[8]

Yet in Africa the formation of colonial (and later, neo-colonial) constructs of society represents something else than a tripartite construction of social authority and power. As Mahmood Mamdani has

---

7. Notwithstanding the later transformations of the term offered by Antonio Gramsci, among others.

8 As an aside, we might note that this tripartite differentiation of society was accompanied by liberal, humanist and romanticist attacks on the authority of religion in society, and over political and economic life in particular. Religion tends, therefore, to disappear from notions of public life with increasing rapidity, giving rise in the 1960s to the famous, though partly misplaced, "secularization debate."

shown in a seminal study on citizens and subjects in Africa,[9] late colonial practices of direct and indirect rule left a legacy of bifurcated societies, with massive historical consequences.

Urban areas, conceived as directly under the control of metropoles or their agents, were regulated through modern notions of civil society and citizenship (even if citizenship status might be differentially accorded to colonizers and indigenous people). Rural areas, in general, were governed by indirect rule—also called "association" among the French—through secondary agents, particularly local tribal authorities, who acted on behalf of the colonial power.

But these tribal authorities were, firstly, always constructs in part: the colonial establishment drew on traditional foundations of political life in ways that made them useful for indirect rule while simultaneously altering their meaning under conditions of tribal political economies.[10] Secondly, they were agents of the urban based colonial authority but practitioners of a different structure of law and practice (usually called "customary law" in English colonies), under which local people were governed as subjects without the rights of the citizens of urban areas. In the process civil society is racialized (predominantly an urban experience) and native authorities are tribalized (predominantly a rural experience of the peasantry).[11]

This classic contradiction is reflected in the disjunction between contemporary reformers in Africa. Modernists, Mamdani argues, seek a political solution to Africa's problems in the development of a vigorous civil society in which individual rights are protected, while Africanists wish to place communitarian politics at the center where culture is defended. Mamdani himself believes that both options must be sublimated under a critique of each.

The main point of Mamdani's analysis, carried out in relation to the cases of Uganda and South Africa (the latter now being seen as the exemplary case of the paradigm rather than an exception or an aberration), is that the contradictions between urban and rural politics,

---

9. Mamdani, *Citizen and Subject*.

10. In South Africa, from well back in the nineteenth century, this meant promoting to chieftanships particular parties seen as compliant or cooperative over against others with perhaps stronger traditional claims. In this century, this practice was formalized by allowing magistrates to appoint and pay chiefs, often with no reference to tribal custom at all.

11. Ibid., 18–19.

between direct and indirect rule, have led to the incomplete democratization of African nations. This is less because Africa resists democracy of one kind or another, and more because the dualist legacy of colonial policy prevents it. Democratization in Africa remains a vital and burning project, but it must entail both "the deracialization of civil power and the detribalization of customary power..."[12]

If Mamdani is correct in his analysis,[13] then the issue of culture and inculturation must take on a very different form than it is often given. Detribalization seems to imply a movement against attempts to re-establish tribal authorities and practices, as well as tribal identities. Indeed, as many black South Africans can testify, tribal identities are often fictions, in part fabrications of colonial mythologies of subjecthood or reconstructions of African myths to support a particular power base, besides the fact that such identities inevitably undergo all kinds of changes under the impact of modern economic and social exigencies.[14]

Similarly, the notion of civil society must include some revitalized sense of the importance of the local and rural polities which incorporates into any framework of rights and law a rich acknowledgement of differentiation, even as it encourages alliances which transcend the local and the particular. The key for Mamdani, which I take to be programmatic, lies in a democratic appreciation of both the civil and the customary which is able to "disentangle authoritarian from emancipatory possibilities in both."[15]

The question of what constitutes an emancipatory possibility as opposed to an authoritarian one still has to be disentangled. It must be done so, I suspect, aware of the well-established warnings against the destruction of tradition ("prejudice," and a positive meaning of au-

---

12. Ibid., 25.

13. One should point out here, as is implicit in his conclusions, that Mamdani's analysis is predicated upon a conviction that democracy in some strong form is necessary to Africa, and that some form of "modernization"—an acceptance of social structures and economic practices which transcend the local or the tribal and thus require other forms of organization—inevitably accompanies the process.

14. The point here is not to erase identity, as it is carried in enduring wisdom and values (conserving politics in part), but to see it move away from particular—now distorted—forms of social organization which cannot meet the demands of a transforming society without retreating into reactionary politics.

15. Ibid., 299.

thority) from Gadamer. For the moment, however, let us connect this discussion to the matter of religion.

Civil Society and Religion in Africa

The relationship between religion and society in Africa is as complex as anywhere. In South Africa it takes the form of a rich mix or religious traditions (African, Christian, Muslim, Hindu and Jewish in particular), alongside strong secular or non-religious traditions (liberal humanism and revisionist Marxism perhaps being the most influential). Inevitably these traditions sit within the contradictions of economy and politics common not only to South Africa but to many African countries, particularly in the articulation of different modes of production and social organization some call modern and traditional, and the patterns of direct and indirect colonial rule to which I have already referred.

Contemporary debates thus characteristically include controversies over traditionalism versus modernization, inculturation versus liberation, postcolonialism versus postmodernism. The notion of civil society sits within the parameters of meaning usually given to the second term in the above polarities. One must therefore expect a challenge from traditionalists, supporters of inculturation and some postcolonial theorists to the idea that the development of civil society is vital to Africa. Instead, it is often argued, the key to the future lies in recovering from the subjugated knowledges of African peoples those experiences, sources of wisdom and constructions of lifeworld which will offer a counter to the dominant hegemonies of colonial and neo-colonial powers.

This dichotomy between two paradigms—previously noted in Mamdani's distinction between rights-oriented modernists and communitarian Africanists—enters into the way in which religion is analyzed as well. Thus the dominant dialectic in contemporary discourse on Christianity in Africa probably emerges in the debates between those who champion inculturation versus those who promote liberation as the hermeneutic keys to the theological task. Despite attempts to unify these poles—some more successful than others[16]—the dichot-

---

16. One of the better attempts may be found in a recent work by Bediako, *Christianity in Africa*.

omy remains significant, perhaps inevitably. It reveals different visions about what the problem is and how to address it.

Mamdani's analysis of the contradictions of the late colonial legacy of a divide between urban and rural (directly and indirectly ruled) contexts suggests that the construction of civil society in African nations must go via the integration of the emancipatory aspects of law and practice in both contexts. Applied to religious constructs (worldviews and institutions), this analysis pushes us in a direction which challenges the most central terms of reference of both liberationist and inculturationist approaches to religion.

In the case of the approaches of liberation theologians, the modernist foundations of concepts of autonomy, rights, will, power, and history (usually theorized in terms of some grand narrative) tend to make it difficult to appreciate local, particularized patterns of culture which are not overtly or consciously political. In South Africa, this lacuna is seen most obviously in a widespread inability—among black theologians as much as among any others—to find an adequate relationship to the most populous and most popular forms of religion: the Zionist and Zionist-Pentecostal churches.[17] If, however, these are the churches of the poor, the communal centres of participation which give meaning and organizational substance to struggles for survival or for carving out a protected site of existence, then the contradiction becomes almost fatal to liberation theology movements.

On the other hand, inculturation approaches, at least as I have read them in South Africa, emphasize concepts of community, duty, authority, obligation, and spirituality. This tends to accent the local, particularized patterns of culture and tradition in ways which make it difficult to theorize, let alone contest, the structural, systemic and developmental dynamics of a political economy. Thus one reason black theologians (and others) find it difficult to deal with popular, African initiated forms of religion (including the African initiated Christian churches), lies precisely in the lack of any obvious relationship on the

---

17. Perhaps the leading contemporary black theologian in South Africa who is beginning to find ways of overcoming this pattern is Tinyiko Maluleke of the University of South Africa. On the side of those who represent Zionist or Zionist-Apostolic churches, there are signs of a shift as well, as in the Spiritual Churches Institute of Bishop Ngada, or since the transition in South Africa, in the work of Bishop Ntongana and Revd S. Molisiwa at the Khanya Theological College, both in Johannesburg.

part of AIC's to the concerns of the public sphere (other, perhaps, than those that have do with cultural polity or morality).

Are we then left with an irresolvable dilemma? Must we assume that some Christian positions will be overtly engaged in the public sphere, many others not, and that between them we face a gap that cannot be bridged? If so, then the prospects of a significant contribution on the part of Christian churches, taken as a whole, to the reconstruction of Africa is unlikely. Denominationalism, historic alienations between mission churches and African initiated churches, substantial differences in understandings of the meaning of the gospel, and the like, all contribute further to what might be a bleak picture. In short, the contestations and contradictions within Christianity itself, to limit myself to this tradition, inhibit the chances of a strong engagement and contribution in the public sphere, and thus in the development of a civil society.

Yet this is not the whole picture, as far as I can judge. There are practical and theoretical reasons for thinking that other possibilities exist and will or do materialize. Clearly, church leaders in many parts of Africa are taking a direct interest in the public sphere, particularly in regard to the protection of important elements of civil society. Thus, for example, in recent times the Roman Catholic Bishops of Kenya have issued a statement condemning killings they blame on a government unwilling to reform,[18] while the Archbishop of Monrovia, Michael K. Francis, issued a Pastoral Letter early in 1997 aimed at conscientizing the population about the importance of participation in the looming elections.[19]

Such advocacy at the level of public leadership has always been vital, even if not always present. This we know in South Africa. But we

---

18. Kenyan Catholic Bishop's Statement, Episcopal Conference, Waumini House, 9th July 1997.

19. Among other things, the Archbishop pointed to that state of the nation as being characterized by "corruption and trickery, false elections, ethnocentrism, nepotism, use of office for self aggrandizement, distinctions of privileged and underprivileged, settlers and indigenous, total lack of distributive justice, denial and infringements of human rights" where "cleverness has come to be prized more than wisdom, manipulation preferred to administration." This catalogue of vices offers one argument in the negative for the importance of a robust civil society founded on a vision of the common good and a workable, well-founded set of civic virtues, neither of which are likely without recourse to a retrieval of reinvigorated traditions and their emancipatory elements. We shall return to this theme below.

also know that advocacy at the level of "the diplomatic," if I may so describe it, does not necessarily translate either into the growth of civil society or into the rooting of public life concerns and practices among ordinary people who make up local Christian or other religious communities. Thus we must revisit, it seems, the importance of locally rooted movements, even though they might use patterns of discourse not easily integrated into public sphere activities. Despite this, they hold an important space open for the development of a civil society capable of affecting the directions that the steering media of money and power take in the economy and politics.[20]

One example of such movement to attract the attention of scholars is found in Southern Zimbabwe, among the followers of Mbuya Juliana.[21] The movement arose out of an ecological crisis, and it follows the pattern of similar earlier movements.[22] Mbuya Juliana claims to be a rainmaker, sent to lead people back to traditional values. In fact, the values she proclaims are a mix of African traditional and Christian ideas. The occasion of her prophecy lies in a severe drought, which she blames in part on modernization processes in the region (such as the "cementing of holy places" to make dams). Her mission is the restoration of the land.

The point for our purposes is that Mbya Juliana's movement challenged the powers of both the state, business, church and indeed traditional authorities, in the process helping restructure social relations on the land and land-use practice.[23] Wilson and Ndhlovu, whom Ranger quotes in his article on the movement, develop an analysis that fits what I am trying to say here. Noting that the Juliana movement builds a new sense of community which may reintegrate the "disparate and conflictual social field within the villages, between the villages in the wider region, between the people and the government structures, and ultimately between people and the natural order," they argue that "The continuing constraints on rural participation in 'civil society'

---

20. The terms "steering media of money and power" are of course drawn from the social theory of Jurgen Habermas.

21. See Mafu, "The 1991–92 Zimbabwean Drought."

22. I follow here a discussion by Ranger, "Religious Pluralism in Zimbabwe," which surveys and comments on several presentations given to the Society.

23. Ibid., 239. One example of the restructuring of social relations is the imposition by Mbuya Juliana of price constraints on local stores.

will clearly require generations of innovators of the caliber of Ambuya Juliana."[24]

Possibilities for the Construction of Civil Society

The example of Mbuya Juliana enables us to pay attention to two things simultaneously, which I will express in the form of claims. First, the construction of a strong and healthy[25] civil society must include the institution of processes and mechanisms which allow popular, particular marginalized voices their proper place and dignity. Second, the injection of virtues and values by which a civil social consensus on the common good becomes possible must draw on the traditions with which people identify and which shape them.

It is worth commenting on these two claims in order to unpack some possible foundations for them in social theory, and to open up further options for a reinsertion of reflected practice into social life. To do this requires a return to the notion of civil society, first to expand our understanding of it, and second to propose a particular version of it. We will begin by relating the significance of civil society to the question of the sources for its virtues and values.

As Cohen and Arato make clear,[26] the contemporary idea of civil society points to the ineluctable shift in power under conditions of modernity, now global in their influence, from small centralized political authorities to large, mostly independent economic agencies with whom nation-states and international political bodies must come to terms. In this shift, the realm of citizen activity increases in complexity, and under democratic conditions, enters directly as a "third" partner into public life alongside economy and polity.

---

24. Ibid., 241.

25. By "healthy" I mean 'inclusive of all who have a stake in what happens to them politically and economically, such that their voices and experiences are taken to be part of the body politic and not seen or treated as marginal or parasitic.' I regard this as healthy because it prevents "dis-ease" growing among groups and communities, and manifesting itself in actions aimed at destroying civic life. Of course, this implies too that civic life is so ordered that it allows for meaningful participation (which could be defined in many ways, probably best in terms of "spheres of justice" as Michael Walzer suggests) by all stake-holders.

26. Cohen & Arato, *Civil Society and Political Theory*.

Thus, as a first step, our consideration of the role of Christian churches, or religion generally, drives us to assume a separation between the spheres of the civic, the economic and the political. In modern states, religious bodies usually (though not always) find themselves out of the centres of power, having neither economic clout nor political muscle.[27] Civil society becomes—by a kind of secularizing process of reduction—the prime sphere within which to consider the role and significance of religion.

There is a danger here: that of conceiving the spheres of political and economic activity to be outside of the realm of church or religious life, not only practically but also theoretically, that is, theologically. Where societies are in rapid and dramatic transition, as is the case in South Africa and many other parts of Africa, the forces of privatization reach not only into government and civil society generally but also into the religious self-understandings of churches and/or individual Christians. Faith becomes privatized, at least in principle.

But there are counter-forces to this trend. One of these counter-forces is precisely a holistic understanding of the range of religious imagination and practice as incorporating the material, social and spiritual well-being of persons, communities and nations. Religious bodies such as Christian churches must come to terms with the separation of powers, spheres, and responsibilities characteristic of democratic political arrangements. Yet politicians, business-people, and the like cannot be allowed to function as if their spheres of activity were immune to or free of the demands for a holistic view of the life of a people, including the spiritual and relational values and practices necessary to the construction of well-being.

In short, a privatized religion must be seen not as a result of the development of civil society under modern conditions, but as an abdication of a role in civil society. It leaves concerns for the material and relational well-being of citizens in a plural context to other interests and forces than those motivated by the transcendentals of truth, goodness and beauty, or holiness, justice and love.[28] In Christian terms, this would be an abdication of the gospel itself.

27. The examples of Poland, of Israel and of Egypt, to name three disparate locations, suggest that religious bodies continue to have some substantial direct influence on politics, though perhaps less so on economics.

28. In using these particular terms, I am thinking of the work of Hans Urs von Balthasar on theological aesthetics and the fundamental link between aesthetics, eth-

The link I am arguing for here is not invisible to wise politicians either. In a recent address on "nation-building and spirituality" to a group meeting under the auspices of the South African chapter of the World Conference for Religion and Peace, Deputy President Thabo Mbeki began by quoting scripture, specifically the well-known text, "What shall it profit a person to gain the whole world but lose his or her soul."[29] Of course, the devil may quote scripture too. But Mbeki's point throughout was that social and economic transformation would not succeed unless it had spiritual foundations. Crime, corruption, graft, a culture of egoism and individual entitlement, violence against women and children and the like are for him, as for others, fundamental threats to the construction of a just and whole society. These threats cannot be countered by political or economic policies alone or even in the first instance. It is the degeneration of the moral fiber of society as a whole that is the problem, and its regeneration is the task.

Equally, as is widely argued in the theory on civil society, a strengthening of civil society in a plural context also acts as a counter to the domination of the institutions of state and economy over others, a dominance usually secured through the exercise of substantial financial, legal, organizational and human resources. It would necessarily be in the interests of churches (and other religious bodies) to enter into civil society for this reason alone, both for theological reasons and for reasons of religious freedom.

Some Tentative Judgments

Clearly, then, religious institutions and personalities have a critical role to play, and Mbeki would not be the first, nor will he be the last, to note this. The challenge is there. The question is how religious institutions are to meet it, and whether or not they can.

The question itself must be posed in the knowledge that religious institutions may well enter into public life by obstructing the development of civil society rather than encouraging it. Further, the very contradictions they usually represent within their own tradition

---

ics and authentic being for which he argues, a link essential to a holistic conception of both human life and divine presence. To break this link by leaving out anyone of the terms would be to produce a truncated reality, a flawed human—and thus social—existence, an argument he carries out by reference to historical examples.

29. Mbeki, "From Liberation to Transformation," 11–16.

specific heritage—as appears in the divisions between denominations, between mission and indigenous churches, between conservative and progressive theories and practices, between conflicting interpretations of sacred texts or foundational creeds—often function to inhibit a constructive role in the public sphere. Finally, under certain conditions, civil society may well seem to be what in fact it was in part, namely, a Western invention, linked to a particular religious tradition (Christianity), which is fundamentally contradictory to specifically religious claims for authority, even sovereignty over public life.[30]

It does not seem to me fruitful to pursue such possibilities at this point, however. Rather, I wish to ask how one may conceive of religion in civil society such that religious discourse and practice becomes integral to public life. Here I will accept that some concept of civil society is necessary to a plural context in a democracy. I would also argue that very few national contexts, if any today, are not plural, even if the extent to which they are democratic varies.

Cohen and Arato, I think, help us to analyze the place and significance of religion in civil society, though I might add, astonishingly, that they pay no direct attention whatsoever to the question of religion in society in over seven hundred pages of discussion.[31] In the first place, civil society should not be conceived as a privatized sphere but a realm of communicative action based on mutually achieved agreements about norms and goals. These agreements may be minimal but sufficient for some action to become possible; or they may be temporary, based on a single issue around which a particular coalition or cooperative action becomes possible; they may also be deeper and more durable.

Cohen and Arato are at pains to recover this normative dimension to civil society against what they see as destructive tendencies

---

30. This was of course the case in the Holy Roman Empire in respect of Roman Christianity. But it would also be the position of a Muslim fundamentalist, to name but one other example.

31. One reference to the Roman Catholic Church in Italy, as viewed by Gramsci, is in the index. Otherwise religion does not feature, while the concepts of lifeworld, family, gender, sexuality and the like do appear. No references to a possible analogue of religion, namely "tradition," appear either. I find this astonishing because it ignores completely the practical impact of religious institutions and worldviews on billions of those who make up civil society, as it does the many ways in which religious claims and motivations are often embodied in practices which, while recognizing distinctions, seek a fusion of the spheres of society (Cohen and Arato support a fusion model of civil society, following Habermas's discourse theory).

to surrender it to administrative bureaucratization and market economic mechanisms. They seek thereby to rescue a politics of social solidarity and social justice. This, then, is a vision of civil society which takes as central "patterns of normative integration and open-ended communication"[32] that may confront and challenge the strategic and instrumental criteria of bureaucracies and markets. The only way in which this vision can be made socially fruitful is if one is able to institutionalize the necessary patterns through "structures of socialization, association and organized forms of communication of the lifeworld."[33]

The link posited here between lifeworlds and civil society, as well as the emphasis on the institutionalization of claims arising out of the lifeworld in civil society, points to the place religion may occupy—and, indeed, does occupy in my own analysis of local religious phenomena and movements.[34] For it is very often the case, particularly in less urbanized areas, that a religious worldview and tradition is central to the lifeworld of particular persons or groups. Moreover, a religious worldview and tradition more often than not (a) make quite direct claims upon persons in the practical negotiation of relationships in civil society, and economic and political life, and (b) provide for the values and virtues which are essential to civic life.

Put simply, religious communities have quite a lot to do with offering the resources for the patterns of normative integration and open-ended communication that Cohen and Arato see as the necessary foundations of civil society. Equally, by insisting on exclusive control over particular norms, by refusing to take into account the norms of other traditions, or by undermining open-ended communication

---

32. Cohen and Arato, ix.

33. Ibid., x.

34. Elsewhere I have explored these links via the historical- and social anthropological theories of Jean & John Comaroff, *Of Revolution and Revelation*, and of Scott, *Domination and the Arts of Resistance*. The Comaroffs, in particular, have shown how religious constructs among the Tshidi clan of the Batswana in South Africa operate to allow them, first, to come to terms with a context of colonization and modernization, and second, to contest and transform the terms of their engagement in that context. The dynamic, historically precise understanding of culture, tradition and power which results lends itself to a reconsideration of the place of local religious communities, whether shaped by African traditional religions, Christianity, Islam or any mix of them, in the emergence of civil society. In both cases, the Comaroffs and Scott, we are forced to reconsider classic understandings of hegemony and the making of social (public) discourse.

through an aggressive attack or denial of other norms, particular religious communities may well damage the emergence of a healthy and strong civil society.

A further corollary of this argument must be stressed. This is simply that the introduction of the norms derived from tradition into attempts at normative integration and open-ended communication is "normal," indeed, essential. To be most meaningful, such norms should be solidly grounded in their traditional matrices in a way that makes them available as inputs into a plural, public process of constructing more general civic virtues and values. In short, religious communities best serve a strong and healthy civil society—in its necessary differentiation—if they enter into it with a "strong sense" of their own tradition and its claims as they see it.

Clearly, such an argument suggests that the claims of those normally marginalized by the forces of modernization or the structures of dominant powers must be foregrounded at least as much as any other. They represent otherwise subjugated knowledges, and these knowledges often contain a store of local, appropriate practical experience and wisdom necessary to a well-rooted civil society. Further, they have important inputs to make into political and economic policy—not in terms of generalized theory or analysis but in terms of the actual constraints and possibilities which confront policy makers on the ground.[35]

I would support such claims more generally by reference to the argument put forward by Vaclav Ravel, as summarized by Jean Elshtain,[36] that "one must begin from the bottom, from the humbly respected boundaries of the natural world, rather from behind a veil of ignorance where one enacts a project of justice as a noumenal moment."[37]

---

35. We may think back to the earlier example of Mbuya Juliana's movement as a test case of this claim. But the claim can be more generally substantiated simply by referring to current "fourth generation" development theories which provide persuasive evidence of the need to incorporate ordinary people and their lifeworlds, particularly those most marginalized from centres of power and money, into the development process as active participants. See, for example, Korten, *Getting to the 21st Century*.

36. Jean Elshtain, "Political Theory and Moral Responsibility," 51.

37. The reference to a "veil of ignorance" points of course to the theory of justice offered by John Rawls, in which some universalized general principles, derived from a consideration of a context-free idea of the ideal society, operationalize what we mean by justice. In this framework, a contextually derived notion of justice is prohibited, except in the (dubious) sense in which Rawls believes his universal norms may be assented to by any human being who thinks about his or her true interests.

As Elshtain puts it, this is an approach to public life in which one tries to demystify and diversify our sense of reality, "to look at the messy, complex realities of *this* situation, here and now, as that which requires our attention and calls forth our very best and clearest attempts at thick description laden with moral notions."[38]

> A "thick description" of moral life in the public sphere depends not on a kind of rationality abstracted from the particular, but on bonds of affection, on the imitation of significant others who embody or express "how it is to live, on stories which narrate the point of a moral life together—"narratives of possibility" rather than of closure which help us to see the vitality and importance of everyday life and "the connection of small events to wider streams of life and thought."[39]

For Elshtain, such a theory is the necessary foundation of political life (she is a political theorist, though one interested in religious phenomena). In my view, such a theory opens up the possibility of reconceiving the importance of the everyday life of ordinary religious communities for the polis.

Narratives, however, are not necessarily public. They may be hidden in secluded, secure places, or silenced by others. Even when such narratives enter into the public sphere (or "transcript")[40] it is often the case that they do so in coded ways (with double meanings, or through mechanisms such as trickster tales, irony, etc.). In large part, the history of African initiated churches—the popular form of Christianity, the "churches of the people"[41]—in South Africa represents a range of such narratives which are absent from the public sphere.[42] They thus enter into the life of civil society only indirectly.

---

38. Elshtain, "Political Theory," 51.

39. Ibid., 54. "Narratives of closure" are for Elshtain those which freeze history and politics into theories in which everything is known in advance, all categories are specified, and all the possibilities are laid out. They bear some relation to the "grand narratives" which postmodernists attack, though Elshtain sees herself as a "moral realist" rather than as postmodern.

40. James Scott, op. cit.

41. This is the self-description of many of these groups.

42. In the first two decades of this century, the Ethiopian Movement, partly linked in some of its early origins to the AME in the USA (cf. Campbell, *Songs of Zion*), caused considerable public ferment among whites who ruled the country and dominated mission church leadership because of its overt claims to justice, freedom and full participation in citizenship on religious/theological grounds. But once the

Given the ambiguous character of actual historical narratives in the public sphere, we need to ask how civil society may be conceived so as to take into account this ambiguity or contradictory reality. How, in short, does space become available for excluded, suppressed, hidden or diminished narratives to enter into the construction of a fully differentiated, healthy civil society? One may put the question in terms of traditional Catholic social theory as well: How is the principle of subsidiarity—the proposition that governance should maximize the healthy participation and the exercise of freedom in civil society of particular groups in accordance with their level of specific, inherent competencies[43]—to be given flesh?

There are some clues available to us in answering this question. John Coleman, summarizing Scott Mainwaring's analysis of base community experience in Latin America in terms quite appropriate to our South African experience, notes that religious communities empower civil society by "training ordinary, even poor people in transferable leadership skills . . . : skills of speaking, convoking a meeting, gathering a people together, pursuing public discussions about issues of concern and moment in their society," as well as "by outreach through popular organizations" which enables people to learn how they might "have a voice in the decisions about their life in their neighborhoods and places of work."[44]

That this has happened in South Africa is perhaps most visible in the extraordinarily significant presence of clerics or lay church people with a strong Christian activist record in all sectors and levels of the

---

movement waned and it became clear that it would not constitute any direct political threat to white dominance, both political and ecclesial leaders among white settlers lost interest in the movement. By and large, the absence in "mainline" church circles of any significant interest in such forms of Christianity, or in the later emergence of Zionist and Zionist Apostolic churches (a good analysis of which is provided in Kruss, *Religion, Class and Culture*), characterizes church history in South Africa until the present, bringing into question the meaning of ecumenism in a country where the ecumenical movement has played a significant political role, but largely at the behest of the mission- or settler-origin churches.

43. McLean, "Philosophy and Civil Society," 16, 21–22. McLean interprets subsidiarity in contemporary pluralist societies to mean "not deadening the initiative of other groups by holding power to oneself, but enlivening and empowering the multiple communities to direct or govern their own life or area of activity and to train people . . . to live and exercise responsibility in their own sphere of community life."

44. Coleman, "Civil Society, Citizenship and Religion," 6.

new government.[45] Such people, in turn, are important fulcrums of activity within political and economic society around which organizations of civil society may generate knowledge, experience and influence—what Cohen and Arato, following Habermas, call the necessary role if civil society is to impact directly on politics and economics of "sensors."[46] Such sensors organically connect the rooting of civil society in "ordinary, everyday life" to the institutions of political and economic life and open them to the processes of civil society. It is in this context, I believe, that we may best understand the importance and the nature of the role of church leaders, synods and the like when they address government, business, and so on—they may enable and facilitate the kind of interaction that sensors require in relation to the organs of civil society.

Still, the insertion of religious institutions in civil society remains unstable. This is firstly so because many religious institutions are unclear about their role in the public sphere, or if clear, then often by abrogating any such role. Second, they are often marginalized within their own public contexts, both ecclesially in the ecumene and socially in the polis. Third, civil society—because it requires normative integration and open-ended communication and because these practices are frequently institutionalized

> for pragmatic and strategic reasons in new, non-religious or non-traditional ways—tends systematically to undercut precisely the particular religious and philosophical visions upon which it depends.[47]

Fourth, civil society contains its own negativities and deformations; it can degenerate into a mess of private interests and factions, "[evacuating] the larger social world of any sense of truly public or

---

45. The list includes members of cabinet, senior party leadership who function as national or regional MP's, provincial premiers, top administrators in government institutions, key members of new constitutional bodies such as the Truth and Reconciliation Commission or the Human Rights Commission, and the like.

46. Sensors are elite allies in state and economic systems who are supportive of programs of democratization or cultural revision initiated by social movements or institutions within civil society; cf. Cohen and Arato, op. cit., 471–72 *inter alia*.

47. This point is strongly made by Seligman, *Idea of Civil Society*; Seligman's point is developed in relation to faith communities by Mudge, "Traditioned Communities and the Good Society."

common goods"[48] (as citizen militias tend to do, for example).[49] Fifth, civil society itself is unstable, threatened by the colonization of life-worlds, by the imperatives of the steering media of politics (power) and economy (money), or (as in parts of Africa) by the assertion of traditional patterns of authority and identity against the plurality of actual nation states (thus Mamdani's call for "detribalization" of the subject in the context of the bifurcated legacy of colonial rule).

We are faced, therefore, with a situation where civil society remains fragile, in which religious communities may well fail to play the role for which they are—in some respects, at least—well-equipped. Yet that does not diminish the importance either of civil society or the potential of religious communities as part of civil society. In Africa it is a truism to say that people are strongly religious; moreover, the demographic reach of religious communities exceeds that of any other institutional form of life. Couple this with a view on civil society which emphasizes a multiplicity of voices as essential to the health of the body politic, add to it a religious/theological conviction that has roots in social experience of the importance of making space for the voices of those who are silenced or marginalized, mix it with the view that civil society is the bed-rock upon which a social morality must be constructed under modern conditions, and the task becomes immediately obvious.

How to give effect to this task is less obvious. To understand this better will clearly require the identification of particular religious movements and programs in concrete contexts where everyday life and the life of the polis come together. To some extent it is also outside the hands or control of anyone—there is a serendipitous element to the construction of generalizable values and virtues in civil life by

---

48. Coleman, op. cit., 21.

49. In recent history in South Africa, this danger was visible in the rise of an organization called PAGAD (People Against Gangsterism and Drugs), overtly religious in its origins and orientation (it was formed around, and backed strongly by, a particular militant grouping of Muslim organizations in the Western Cape that challenged the authority of the Muslim Judicial Council in the region). PAGAD formed an armed wing, and then waged a deadly war that raged in black townships around Cape Town where drugs and gangs are a particular problem (in part as a result of the heritage of apartheid social engineering). Authorities had great difficulty managing this situation because PAGAD, with wide public support, was engaged in a highly popular campaign, one that, however, became increasingly contradictory to the values and virtues of civil society as vigilanteism and indiscriminate violence grew.

which particular possibilities are realized by particular people and actions at particular times, an eschatological reserve in the making of the common good.

Nevertheless, we are not consigned to fate nor the impotence of those who only wait for God. The engagement of religious communities in the construction of the values, virtues and practices of civil society is a moral task as much as it is a public one. As Cohen and Arato put it: "It is on this terrain that we learn how to compromise, take reflective distance from our own perspective so as to entertain others, learn to value difference, recognize or create anew what we have in common and come to see which dimensions of our tradition are worth preserving and which ought to be abandoned or changed."[50]

I would only add to this positive claim a caution: "One must continue to think political thoughts and to do political deeds, not knowing how the story ends, nor with any finality who or what is its author."[51] In this sense, the engagement of religious communities in public life, as a project of ethical formation, begins and ends in an act of faith.

---

50. Cohen and Arato, 23.
51. Elshtain, 55.

Bibliography

Bediako, Kwame. *Christianity in Africa: The Renewal of a Non-Western Religion*. Edinburgh: Edinburgh University Press, 1995.

Campbell, Joseph T. *Songs of Zion: The African Methodist Episcopal Church in the United States and South Africa*. New York: Oxford University Press, 1995.

Cochrane, James R. "Religion and Civil Society: Readings from the South African Case." In *Sameness and Difference: Problems and Potentials in South African Civil Society*, edited by J. R. Cochrane and Bastienne Klein, 15–53. Washington, DC: Center for Philosophy and Values, 2000.

Cohen, Jean L., and Andrew Arato. *Civil Society and Political Theory*. Cambridge, MA: MIT Press, 1992.

Coleman, John A. "Civil Society, Citizenship and Religion," Unpublished manuscript, 6.

Comaroff, Jean & John. *Of Revolution and Revelation: Christianity, Colonialism and Consciousness in South Africa*. Chicago: University of Chicago Press, 1991.

Elshtain, Jean Bethke. "Political Theory and Moral Responsibility." In *Schools of Thought: Twenty-five Years of Interpretive Social Science*, edited by Joan W. Scott and Debra Keates, 315–29. Princeton, NJ: Princeton University Press, 2001.

Iris Habib el Masri. *The Story of the Copts: The True Story of Christianity in Egypt*. 2 vols. Kenya: Coptic Bishopric for African Affairs, 1987.

Kenyan Catholic Bishop's Statement, Episcopal Conference. Waumini House, July 9, 1997.

Korten, David C. *Getting to the 21st century: Voluntary Action and the Global Agenda*. West Hartford, CT: Kumarian, 1990.

Kruss, Glenda. *Religion, Class and Culture: Indigenous Churches in South Africa, with special reference to Zionist-Apostolics*. MA thesis: University of Cape Town, 1985.

Mafu, Hezekial. "The 1991–92 Zimbabwean Drought and Some Religious Reactions." *Journal of Religion in Africa* XXV/3 (1995) 288–308.

Makgoba, William. *Mokoko—The Makgoba Affair: A Reflection on Transformation*. Florida Hills, South Africa: Vivlia, 1997.

Mamdani, Mahmood. *Citizen and Subject: Contemporary Africa and the Legacy of Late Colonialism*. Kampala: Fountain, 1996.

Mandela, Nelson. "Renewal and Renaissance- Towards a New World Order." Lecture given at the Oxford Centre for Islamic Studies, U.K., July 11, 1997.

Mbeki, Thabo. "From Liberation to Transformation." Address to the World Conference on Religion and Peace Consultation, in Spiritual Power for Nation-Building, Report on Seminar, Goethe Institute, Johannesburg, June 14–16, 1997, 11–16.

McLean, George F. "Philosophy and Civil Society: its Nature, its Past and its Future." In *Civil Society and Social Reconstruction*, edited by George F. McLean, 16–22. Washington, DC: Council for Research in Values and Philosophy, 1997.

Mudge, Lewis S. "Traditioned Communities and the Good Society: The Search for a Public Philosophy." Address to the Center for Hermeneutical Studies, USA, April 1993.

Partrick, Theodore Hall, *Traditional Egyptian Christianity: A History of the Coptic Orthodox Church*. Greensboro, NC: Fisher Park, 1996.

Ranger, Terence. "Religious Pluralism in Zimbabwe: A Report on the Britain-Zimbabwe Society Research Day, Oxford 1994." *Journal of Religion in Africa* XXV/3 (1995) 226–51.

Scott, James. *Domination and the Arts of Resistance: Hidden Transcripts.* New Haven, CT: Yale University Press, 1990.

Seligman, Adam. *The Idea of Civil Society.* New York: Knopf, 1991.

9

Bahia and Zion

The Eruption of New Religions of the Poor, Political Implications of Afro-Brazilian and South African Independent Churches

IAIN S. MACLEAN

THIS ESSAY SEEKS TO EXPLORE THE POTENTIAL POLITICAL IMPLICAtions and influences of African religions often assumed to be apolitical, namely the African Indigenous or Independent Churches of Southern Africa ("Zionists") and the Afro-Brazilian religions and their offshoots of North-East Brazil (centered in Bahia). While one is partly a consequence of colonialism and the other of the African slave trade, they both show structural similarities in the places they have traditionally occupied in their societies and in the ways they have been understood and interpreted by researchers. Suffice to state at the outset that this study suggests that these religions have always been "political," in that while not institutionally visible earlier, as they lacked connections or linkage to other societal sectors, they did promote participants' self-awareness, and so the political impact of these religions might only now be emerging as democratization occurs in Brazil and South Africa and they are now free to create linkages with other social actors and institutions. Further it is argued, utilizing the work of Pierre Bourdieu, that religions are always in creative process and only to be understood, not only within discrete socio-political contexts, but also within their particular religious fields.[1] In addition, any potential political impact is always dependent upon the linkages that religious sectors forge with

---

1. Bourdieu, *Language and Symbolic Power* as well as his *Outline of a Theory of Practice*, 78–87.

other social actors.² Using such criteria for instance, the results of this provisional investigation indicate that the AIC's will have a greater and more immediate political impact than the Brazilian ABR's.

South Africa and Brazil are part of what Samuel Huntingdon has described as the "Third Wave of Democracy," one which has been particularly marked by the prominent role of religion in the democratization process.³ Prior to democratization, the religious field of each of these countries was characterized by a dominant, institutional religion as well as a variety of predominantly African-originated religions. Thus in Brazil there is the majority Roman Catholic Church and the Afro-Brazilian religions (ABR's), while in South Africa there is a dominant Protestant and Reformed tradition and the African Independent or Indigenous Churches (AIC's). In both countries elements of the Roman Catholic Church (Brazil) and of Protestantism (South Africa) actively opposed oppressive regimes and prepared the way for peaceful transitions to democracy in the late Eighties and early Nineties respectively. Further, the ABR's and the AIC's, characterized as predominantly religions of the poor, oppressed, black and or darker-skinned inhabitants, were typically stigmatized by both Protestants and Roman Catholics as somehow impure or inauthentic since they represented syntheses (to varying degrees) of the dominant religious tradition and African religions. Thus in Brazil, the country with the second largest Black population in the world outside of Nigeria,⁴ Afro-Brazilian religious traditions had been marginalized or demonized by the dominant religions (Roman Catholic, Protestant or Pentecostal⁵) or regarded as politically acquiescent (Brazil and South Africa). Consequently, during these countries' periods of political oppression, religious and social scientific researchers focused on the political roles of the dominant institutional opposition religions. Thus until recently, researchers in Brazil focused almost exclusively upon

---

2. I am referring to the political science theory of strategic linkages between social sectors, utilized for instance by Vallier, "Roman Catholic Church," 129–52, and by the Brazilian political scientist Luis Bresser Pereira in his *Pactos Políticos: Do Populismo à Redemocratização*.

3. Huntingdon, *Third Wave*.

4. Lewu, "Negros e Política," 36–40, 39.

5. Mariza da Carvalho Soares, "Guerra Santa no País do Sincretismo," 65–74. For the official Roman Catholic position, one of grudging acceptance only since 1992, see the introduction to Berkenbrock, *Die Erfahrung der Orixás*.

the political stances of the Catholic Church or of segments within it such as the *igreja popular* (the "popular Church" supported by liberation theologians).[6] Researchers in Southern Africa, while concentrating on the role of mainline Churches (the so-called "English Churches"[7]) in opposing apartheid, have not ignored AIC's, but have concluded almost unanimously that they are politically irrelevant since they focus almost exclusively on ritual matters, exorcisms, and healings.[8] Thus there exists a large lacuna in research on the specific subject of both ABR's and AIC's and politics. Have these perceptions and realities changed as both Brazil and South Africa have undergone democratization?

In the Nineties this question becomes appropriate since, contrary to expectations, both the dominant Protestant churches in South Africa and the Roman Catholic Church in Brazil, in the forefront of the struggles against oppression through to the end of the Eighties, are currently witnessing sharp membership decline while both the AIC's and the ABR's (and Pentecostals) experience phenomenal growth. Some statistics are instructive: In South Africa, while AIC's numbered but 32 denominations in 1913, this number had increased to 3,270 denominations (with 6 million or 29.3 percent of the black population) by 1980 and to about 4,000 (with 46 percent of the black population) according to the 1991 census. Meanwhile, just in the period from 1960 till 1990, Protestant Church black membership had dropped over fifty percent, from seventy percent to thirty-three percent of the total black population.[9] In Brazil, despite definitional problems, racial categories and dual memberships, by the early 1990's it is believed that 30 millions or one fifth of the population of 150 million, was involved in Candomblé, Umbanda, or one of its offshoots.[10] While regarded as a Catholic nation, nominalism is a great problem and it is estimated that

---

6. This recent transition is observable in the periodical literature and in anthropological studies such a Burdick, *Looking God in Brazil*, and Ireland, *Kingdoms Come*.

7. On this terminology and the history of this opposition, see de Gruchy, *Church Struggle in South Africa*, 85–96.

8. See the works by Daneel, *Old and New in Southern Shona Independent Churches*, Vols. 1 and 2; Kiernan, "Poor and Puritan," 31–41, and "The Healing Community," 49–64; and Oosthuizen, *Religion Alive*.

9. See Kitshoff. "African Independent Churches." 155–64; and Kritzinger, "Development of African Independent Churches," 291–312.

10. See Berkenbrock, *Die Erfahrung der Orixás*, chapters 2 and 5, for details.

on Sundays there are more worshippers in Protestant churches than Catholics attending mass.[11] In addition, definitional problems arise in the Brazilian case from the complexity of the Brazilian racial dynamic and the difficulty of separating into discrete categories the adherents of popular Catholicism, spiritism, and Afro-Brazilian religions.[12] While a "syncreticism" between traditional African religions and Catholicism was the only viable option, under slavery, for slaves to preserve their own religions, it was only after the independence of Brazil in the early Nineteenth Century and the abolition of the Inquisition, that Afro-Brazilian religions were able to organize in some fashion, though still largely proscribed by state civil codes as "injurious to public morality." Thus participants in ABR's were simultaneously baptized Catholics and participated in catholic ceremonies in addition to specifically ABR rituals often performed immediately prior, post, or even simultaneously with Roman Catholic ceremonies (the latter option of course often earning the ire of the local clergy).[13] In addition, while Brazil has often been described as a "racial democracy," in contrast to the USA. and South Africa, the dominant ideology of branquemento[14] results in participants of Afro-Brazilian religions disavowing as far as possible, all associations with Africa. Thus while according to the 1853 census, 2 millions of total population of five millions was black, somehow, without any intervening catastrophes, the 1991 census records that only 6% out of a population of 150 millions describes themselves as "negro."[15] This process is most clearly witnessed in the forms of Umbanda presently flourishing in Rio de Janeiro.[16] Consequently, this "branqueamento" ideology, as the pre-eminent scholar of Brazilian racial affairs, Carlos Hasenbalg declares, "has contributed in no small

---

11. Cox, *Fire From Heaven*, Introduction and 167–68.

12. See in particular Pinto, "Negro," 116–25 and Luz, "Ideologia Da Cidadania e a Comunalidade Africano-Brasileira," 108–15.

13. In addition to Berkenbrock, *Die Erfahrung der Orixás*, chapter 1, see also Ferretti, "O Negro e o Catolicismo Popular," 66–75.

14. The term "racial democracy" was popularized by the early Brazilian social scientist, Gilberto Freyre in his classic work, *Casa Grande e Senzala*, by which the gradual "whitening" of the Brazilian population through intermarriage was contrasted positively with other racially hierarchialized societies.

15. Lewu, "Negros e Politíca," 39.

16. See the outstanding survey and analysis by Brown, *Umbanda*, and by Pordeus Jr., "De Indio a Caboclo," 113–26.

part to the difficulties that negro movements have experienced in mobilizing the support of the masses."[17]

The similarities in the history and the scholarly interpretation of AIC's and ABR's are striking. Both religions emerged under oppressive conditions and with the suspicion of both colonial administrators/rulers and missionaries/clergy that not only were they corruptions of the true Christian religion, but that they were also political threats. This latter suspicion arose or was confirmed especially after a series of slave revolts (the Quilombos for instance) in Brazil[18] or in Southern Africa, through confrontations with authorities such as that between Enoch Mgijima's "Israelites" and the military in the Eastern Cape.[19] Such perceived political threats, if not suppressed by force, were in addition usually circumscribed by legal and civil restrictions. As the political threat subsided, scholars focused in the early part of this Century on such movements as examples of "syncretism." Research thus focused on the syncretistic (read "exotic") elements of these religions and their deviance from an accepted religious norm. Much of this work typically served to delegitimize ABR and AIC claims to authenticity either as Christian or as African religions. For if religion scholars found the "syncretism" unacceptable, anthropologists found that the "syncretism" obscured allegedly earlier or more genuine African traditions. In Southern Africa then, AIC's were regarded by many missionaries and scholars alike as regressions to primitivism suitable only for underdeveloped peoples, while in Brazil ABR's were viewed as but "superstition," or more negatively as "witchcraft."[20]

An unfortunate result of such research focusing on the atypical in ABR's or AIC's was that their possible political influences were obscured or at best described as proto-nationalist. However, with the decolonization of most of Africa underway, social scientists of the Fifties onwards shifted from viewing these religions as "havens of the masses" to viewing them as religions of resistance, whether that was openly articulated or submerged and only expressed symbolically.

17. Hasenbalg, "Entre o Mito e os Fatos," 20.
18. For information on the Quilombo and other slave revolts, see Rodrigues, *Os Africanos no Brazil*, 70ff.
19. On this famous incident, in which over two hundred unarmed "Israelites" were shot by troops, see Edgar, *Because they Chose the Plan of God*.
20. See Brandão, *Os Deuses do Povo*, and Landim, *Sinais dos Tempos*.

These theorists argued that the oppressed, lacking legitimate political expression, expressed such religiously. This approach however, failed to explain why ABR's did not decline after Brazil abolished slavery in 1881 or AIC's after African independence or after the collapse of South African Apartheid from the Nineties onwards, precisely the period which has witnessed dramatic growth of AIC's. A far more significant trajectory for scholars has been (and still is) that of examining these religions for their function in preserving authentic, though fragmentary, voices from past African traditions and more recently, their role as healing and divining cults.[21] The focus on healing and divination and on the role of the spirit/s emphasizes the place and status of the individual participant and this, this paper argues, both in Brazil and in Southern Africa, has mistakenly been interpreted as proof of the apolitical nature of such religions. That both ABR's and AIC's emphasize healing and divination is not denied. However it is the conclusion that is questioned. In many cases such close and excellent studies of individual religions have occluded the wider religious field and the structural and political contexts which might further explain such emphases. For religions such as the AIC's and ABR's emphasizing precisely these features of individual healing and divination in Brazil and in Southern Africa are growing most rapidly, and in urban not rural areas. Recent field-work by anthropologists in Brazil and in Southern Africa has led to attempts to combine symbolic/cultural analyses with the wider religious and socio-political power structures, precisely the linkage absent from earlier studies of such "syncretistic" religions.[22]

The reasons given for the alleged lack of political involvement by AIC's can be summarized as including pietism, fear of the authorities, poverty, Black separatism, sectarian division and most recently, that they represent individualized responses to suffering and so focus on individual healing rather than on political structures causing suffering.[23] With very little modification these reasons could apply to the

---

21. While such foci are evident in both African and Brazilian contexts, such an emphasis has declined as both AIC's and ABR's are being recognized as religions in their own right. See Berkenbrock on the Brazilian case and on the African, the recent works by Oosthuizen and Daneel.

22. For recent examples, see Comaroff, *Body of Power*, and Ranger, "Religious Movements and Politics," on Africa, and Burdick, *Looking for God in Brazil*, and Ireland, *Kingdoms Come*, on Brazil.

23. Schoffellers, Daneel and others claim that the focus on healing effectively

case of the ABR's. Here additional reasons include the social ostracism often associated with "blackness," the diverse and unassociated local groupings of terreiros (Candomblé cult centers)[24] and the ABR's leadership's role in perpetuating political patron-client relationships. However, these studies, while valuable and insightful in their own rights, have unfortunately sundered these religions from their often conflicting religious field, their interaction with other religions, and their impact upon the dominant or historical religions. Thus, scholars such as the Comaroffs, Glenda Kruss, and Terence Ranger on African AIC's, and Degroat Brown, Ireland and Burdick on Afro-Brazilian religions have sought to clarify both the wider religious fields and sociopolitical contexts. The question remains though as to how a primarily religious group impacts the political arena. A comparative examination of AIC's and ABR's will point to the importance of these religions' creating and maintaining (or losing) linkages, either symbolic or institutional (or both) as a critical variable in their actual or perceived political influence.

African Indigenous Churches

Of the African initiated Indigenous or Independent Churches,[25] two major groups are distinguished, namely the earlier Ethiopian and the Spirit type Churches. The former aspired to ecclesiastical and political freedom, while the latter (arising from the Zionist and Apostolic movements of turn of the twentieth century in a creative synthesis of elements of African traditional religion and Christianity) offer personal, spiritual and physical healing. The earliest AIC is generally recognized as the "Tembu Church" led by Nehemiah Tile in 1884,[26] though State recognition for such churches came slowly. While the Zuid Afrikaansche Republiek (ZAR) recognized (in 1893!), the Ethiopian Church of Mangena Mokone, prior to the South African Union in

---

precludes active political participation. See Schoffeleers, "Healing and Political Acquiescence in African Independent Churches."

24. This criticism does not apply to Umbanda, as noted below.

25. See the discussion on nomenclature by Hayes, "African Independent Churches," 139–46.

26. According to a recent article, a seccesion twenty years earlier from the Dutch Reformed Church might be the earliest independent Church. Kitshoff, "Between Mainlinism and Independentism," 3–15.

1910, official recognition policies depended on each colony, and later province. Thus while the Methodist Episcopal Church (AME) was recognized by the Cape Colony in 1901,[27] the Ethiopian movement was denied official status in both Orange Free State (OFS) and Natal, where it was linked to African nationalism and in Natal harshly repressed.[28] The Bulhoek massacre in 1921 led to official investigation and the setting down, for the first time, rules for recognizing AIC's.[29]

The first studies of AIC's, primarily by missionaries, understood these movements as basically syncretistic[30] or as bridges[31] between Christianity and traditional religions, functioning as a "nativistic- syncretistic interpretation of the Christian religion." This interpretation was followed by one which understood AIC's as reactions to conquest, an approach powerfully developed by Sundkler who saw the root of Ethiopianism in the 1913 Native Land Act and Protestant denominationalism. According to this understanding, with few avenues of political expression open, AIC's served as alternatives and as psychological safety valves and so move from resistance to accommodation.[32] Sociological research in urban areas, concluded that AIC's represented adaptation to urbanization and modernization.[33] Variations on this

27. By Cape Premier John X. Merriman, on the grounds that "Repression will be like the "blood of the martyrs, the seed of the Church."

28. Reasons were the Zulu war of 1881, the Mambata Rebellion of 1906, racial bars, and the visit by Rev Joseph Booth, an early proponent of "Africa for Africans." From 1902 onwards restrictive laws against Black independency were passed. Sundkler, *Bantu Prophets*, 68–69.

29. These rules laid down the institutional and ministerial requirements for legal recognition. However, so stringently were these applied that by 1945 only 1 percent of AIC's were officially recognized. That is, about eight out of eight hundred. Claasen, "Independents made Dependents," 25.

30. A more positive approach to "syncretism" emerged at the WCC conference at Mindolo, 1962. See the articles by Nussbaum and Daneel in *Missionalia* (1980–84). Kruss, "A Critical Review of the Study of Independent Churches," 21–32.

31. A helpful typology of syncretistic models is offered by authors noted in footnote 30.

32. Sundkler, *Bantu Prophets*, 179. This approach is followed by Schutte, "Die politischer Funktion religiöser Bewegnungen"; Mills, "The Fork in the Road"; and Etherington, "Historical Sociology." These studies focused on types of Ethiopianism and rural movements.

33. Interestingly, a similar thesis is argued by Brazilian theologian João Comblin, to explain the Ecclesial Base Community Movement in the late 1980's. See his, "Algumas Questões a partir da Prática das Comunidades Eclesiais de Base no Nordeste." 335–81.

approach are studies that argue that AIC's provide security in the face of the collapse of traditionalism[34] and as a replacement for kinship groups.[35]

The most prominent post-colonial interpretation though, has been to understand AIC's as forerunners of African nationalism. However, by the mid-Eighties the scholarly consensus held that most AIC's were historically neither nationalist nor even proto-nationalist. The underlying presuppositions of such an approach was that all that happened under colonialism was caused by it, that nationalism is the political movement. This form of scholarly and political myopia, while understandable, actually served as a form of reductionism which failed to account for religious motivations and the African religious past. It actually reduced or narrowed the definition of "politics" to nationalism simpliciter. Thus despite the absence of nationalistic emphases, the AIC's were not thereby apolitical, but rather their political activity was taking differing forms![36] By the Seventies however, the research focus had moved almost entirely to AIC's emphasis on healing and to the conclusion that AIC's were politically acquiescent.[37] Scholars have been loath to give up such an attractive nationalist or proto-nationalist thesis, and so Buijtenhuijs[38] argues that AIC's are counter-cultural while Comaroff argues that political resistance is implicit rather than explicit.[39]

While earlier studies had examined the role of healing as symbol (Comaroff), as a recruitment mechanism (Daneel) and its consequences upon AIC's (Kiernan), little had been done on political aspects if any.[40] Schoffeleers sought to verify the connection between healing

---

34. West, *Bishops and Prophets in a Black City*, 190–203.

35. For example, Kiernan, "Poor and Puritan," who sees Zionist bands as urban responses of the "poorer than the poor."

36. Ranger, "Religious Movements and Politics," 31.

37. A controversial conclusion given the emphasis on AIC's during this time as forms of people's resistance, especially for those denied regular political channels.

38. Buijtenhuijs, "Messianisme et nasionalisme"; Mills, "Fork in the Road," 51; De Beer, "Kerkelijk verzet teen apartheid."

39. Comaroff, *Body of Power*. However, Werbner regards her concept of "protest" as too general. For while symbols (uniforms etc) could be signs of resistance, they could also represent accommodation to Western values.

40. Comaroff, *Body of Power*; Daneel, *Old and New*; and Kiernan, "Poor and Puritan."

and political acquiescence, arguing, with H. W. Turner, that healing has wider connotations than in the accepted Western medical understanding of the term. According to Turner's pioneering anthropological work, "illness is conceived as a species of misfortune alongside other species as bad luck at hunting, reproductive disorders, physical accidents and loss of property,"[41] thus calling for healing in the discrete spheres of life, society and psyche (in Schoffeleers' terms biotherapy, sociotherapy, and psychotherapy respectively). Schoffeleers concludes that all three medical systems he discerned fostered political acquiescence because all tended to individualize-and thus depoliticize -problems which are to a large extent political. Thus healing excludes critical politics.[42] Yet it is significant that the ailments requiring healing include drug addiction, poverty, alcoholism, and criminality, problems normally associated with urbanization. South Africa, it should be noted, has one of the highest African urban populations, a population that has dramatically increased over the past thirty years. Likewise, Brazil has been experiencing, since the beginning of the "Brazilian economic miracle" in the Sixties, a dramatic if not overwhelming urbanization rate. It is precisely among the newly urbanizing classes and among their lowest strata that AIC's are flourishing and in Brazil, the ABR's and Pentecostals. The AIC's understanding of healing as defined above certainly "overlaps" the Western divisions typically made between the individual and society, illness, healing, and the wider community. Thus it is doubtful that such AIC's' healing practices signify purely an individualized political acquiescence. If healing is, in Comaroff's terms, the "reconstitution of physical, social and spiritual orders," then healing does have implicit political meanings, though perhaps not immediately evident.[43]

While the dichotomy between political and cultural analyses still remains in many studies, research of AIC's is exposing how symbolic and ideological usages of power serve as implied resistances to pow-

---

41. Turner, *Forest of Symbols*, 300.

42. Schoffeleers distinguishes the "healing" from the "prophetic" role. The latter when dominant, causes the other to recede. According to Schoffeleers, the disappearance of one creates the conditions for the re-emergence of the other. This is rather similar to function of the "Prophet" in Nuer society as described in the pioneering anthropological work of E. E. Evans-Pritchard on the Nuer.

43. Comaroff, "Healing and the Cultural Order," 639.

er.[44] Are AIC's then a form of bricolage between forces of colonialism/ modernity and traditional culture, creating associations /meanings / structures oriented to meet newer needs, in particular the immediate survival (on all levels) needs of urbanizing workers through healing practices? Thus, contrary to initial appearances and assumptions, the AIC's' practices reflect elements of adaptation to and resistance to the dominance of modernity and its particular ideology and power.[45] What this all too brief survey indicates is that in the instance of healing practices, a more complex pattern of religious activity with political implications exists. Research now needs to relate this to the broader religious field, in particular examining the linkages between religious groups, and to the changing political situation. AIC's have now become majority religions in Southern Africa and are free from legal restrictions. Linkages have existed for a considerable time between them and some mission/mainline churches.[46] They are also beginning to address broader societal issues. This is clearly revealed in the actions of the largest AIC, the Zion Christian Church (ZCC), which created a stir in 1985 by invited the then State President, P. W. Botha to address Easter services at Moria in the Transvaal. In the post-1991 period AIC's were courted by political leaders, both M. De Klerk and N. Mandela spoke at AIC Church gatherings, while in February, 1997, the ZCC called for the return of the death penalty.

A comparative study with ABR's in Brazil can be fruitful at this juncture as they also represent a synthesis of African traditions with Christianity, occupy a similar structural position, and emphasize divination and healing. It is ABR's (and Pentecostalism) that represent the fastest growing sectors in the contemporary Brazilian religious field, precisely it seems, because their emphasis on healing enables individuals to control immediate survival needs in a rapidly changing society.

---

44. Hobsbawm and Ranger, *Invention of Tradition*; Field, *Revival and Rebellion*.

45. Comaroff, *Body of Power, Spirit of Resistance*, 237–38; Kiernan, "Poor and Puritan." This is precisely what Cecilia Mariz reported about poor urban Pentecostal and Afro-Brazilian women in Rio de Janerio's periphery "Religion and Coping with Poverty in Brazil." Similar conclusions were reached by Ireland, *Kingdoms Come*, and Burdick, *Looking for God in Brazil* in comparative studies of the Brazilian religious field.

46. The AIC's formed their own Council of African Independent Churches and in addition have shown their wider religious acceptance by recently joining the South African Council of Churches.

Afro-Brazilian Religions

Afro-Brazilian religions refer to those religious groupings whose practices and rituals can be linked to lesser or greater extent, with the diverse ethnic origins, gods, rituals, practices such as divination, magic, and healing, originating in Africa and brought from there to Brazil by enslaved Africans. These religions then entered Brazil almost simultaneously with the first colonists and were largely confined to the North and North-East regions (except for later, diverging forms such as Umbanda). Today these religions, diffused throughout large parts of Brazil are known by differing regional terms. Thus ABR's in Bahia and surrounding regions are known as Candomblé and, in a post-Second World War migration, are now strongly represented in Rio de Janeiro and São Paulo. They are known as Xangô in Pernambuco, as Tambor de Mina in Maranhão, as Batuque in Pará and also, with a derogatory connotation, as Macumba in Rio de Janeiro and São Paulo. ABR's survived in part due to colonial policy, its association with Roman Catholicism, particularly in lay brotherhoods which served as friendship associations, mutual-aid societies, burial societies and also, as Roger Bastide suggested, served as means of protection and manumission.[47] This resulted in a fusion of both Catholicism and indigenous African beliefs and practices, syntheses which were not initially prohibited as long as they were not publically practiced. This regional accomodationism led to the development and maintenance of independent local religions marked by diverse practices, by Yoruba/Ewe and Sudanic (nagô) elements and specific African and Christian beliefs.

By the Twentieth Century such Afro-Brazilian beliefs and practices were widespread, with adherents in addition to their devotion to ABR's, cheerfully claiming adherence to Catholicism. This common practice of "syncreticism" led to increasing pressure from the Church, especially from 1916 onwards and indeed to the proscription of public ritual activity. The 1934 Constitution recognized Roman Catholicism as the dominant state religion and the 1937 Vargas coup led to greater repression, especially amongst the popular classes where ABR's flourished. Surprisingly, it was this period which saw the first major works on ABR's, such as those of Edison Carneiro and Gilberto Freyre.[48]

---

47. Bastide, *As Religões Africanas no Brasil*.
48. Carneiro, *Candomblés da Bahia*; and *Religiões Negras*; and Freyre, *Casa-*

With the shift, largely attributed to Gilberto Freyre's efforts in redefining Africanness as a positive source of an unique Brazilian national identity, research on ABR's took on new directions.[49] Roger Bastide, in his classic *Religiões do Brasil* argued that ABR's such as Candomblé, and later Umbanda, were means for people of color to express themselves against dominant white society. The work of Bastide, like that of Camargo, Willems, and Birman, conceptualizes ABR's as classical religions of the oppressed, which serve as alternatives for repressed political action.[50] However, as in Africa, extensive fieldwork in the Northeast, led the Leacocks, to conclude that it would be difficult "to accept Bastide's interpretation that religions such as Umbanda and Batuque represent a Negro Protest or that of a color class, against their low class status." In fact, they state:

> We did not encounter any evidence ... of a movement of protest ... little if any explicit expressions of hostility towards any social or racial elite, even less exists a symbolic subversion of the traditional structure of power which Willems seemed to encounter among Pentecostals.[51]

The study of ABR's during the Seventies focused on discovering pure Afro-Brazilian religious elements in Candomblé and other regional manifestations of ABR's, since these religions were seen as spontaneous creations or survivals of African, lower class, or repressed elements.[52] They were thus understood to be:

1. Symptoms of psychological maladjustment;
2. an escape valve from everyday realities;
3. or as symbolic reversals of such realities.

Grande e Senzala source. Freyre was the organising founder of the first *Congresso Afro-Brasileiro*, held in Recifé in 1933.

49. Such as Ramos' 1934 *O Negro Brasileiro*, which moved the emphasis in ABR's from race to culture. This was the first attempt at a country-wide study, one not limited to Bahia as earlier works such as Nina Rodrigues. See also Gonçalves Fernandes' *Xangôs do Nordeste*.

50. Birman, *Comentários* sourcesource; Camargo, *Kardecismo e Umbanda*; Willems, *Followers of the New Faith*.

51. Leacock, *Spirits of the Deep*, 123.

52. Thus as expressions of negritude, taking up again Roger Bastide's work, as Juana Elbein dos Santos, *Os Nâgo e a Morte*, and others have done.

This explains in part the relative paucity of political analyses of Afro-Brazilian religions. In Candomblé, African gods are transformed from lineage or local deities into personal gods, received by each participant in their bodies as a protector. In Kardecism, the spirits of the dead are received by the mediums, in order to accomplish some charitable deed. They are thus spirits of individuals and recognized as such. In Umbanda the divinities are situated somewhat intermediately between the gods of Candomblé and the spirits of Kardecism. It is difficult to generalize about Afro-Brazilian religions as there are such diverse beliefs, practices and each center is independent. Further, since 1983, a re-Africanization has been underway in sectors of Candomblé, as a radicalized and younger generation of leadership sought to remove all Christian elements and re-define it as a purely African religion. Some scholars have begun to examine ABR's within the broader religious field and understand them as expressing the independence of Afro-Brazilian traditions and of the lower classes.[53] Consequently it was often assumed that elite or middle class participation was peripheral or insignificant. However as researchers in the Eighties began to observe how such religions functioned in context, they realized that ABR's served the oppressed by re-creating new identities,[54] providing individual survival mechanisms through the means of spirit possession, divination, and healing for dealing with the present, and for creating linkages with participants from other classes.

Such participation (and subsequent adaptation) across class and racial lines is most clearly discerned in the development of Umbanda, mainly in Rio de Janeiro from the Thirties onwards, from a synthesis of Kardecism and Macumba, with a largely urban, lower-middle class white leadership and black, lower-class adherents.[55] Umbanda tends to focus on both African and Indian spirits and mediums and reflects to some extent the prevalent Brazilian ideology of itself as a "racial democracy" and thus aspires to be, like the Catholic Church, a national religion. However despite its claims to be egalitarian, Umbanda's hierarchy of spirits, mediums and *chefes* (leaders) of the *centros* (cult centers), reflect the dominant religious form of divine-human and thus patron-client relationships found in rural Brazil. Under the

---

53. Ireland, "Catholic Base Communities."
54. See Hobsbawn and Ranger, *Invention of Tradition*.
55. The definitive study is Brown, *Umbanda*.

military dictatorship which ruled from 1964 onwards, legal sanctions were lifted, registration of umbandista centers moved from police to civil control, and Umbanda was able to legitimatize and expand its organization. The first public display of Umbanda ritual occurred on 31 December, 1967 on Rio de Janeiro beaches, and by 1976, public officials were dedicating statues in São Paulo state.[56] While issues and problems are conceived of and conceptualized individualistically by participants, the rapid hierarchicalization of Umbanda Federations has led to some attempts to influence local or state officials or to direct voting patterns. Here is evidence of linkage between levels of the lower classes and an ABR enabling some political activity at the local level.

However scholars remain divided on the significance of ABR's for the wider Brazilian political sphere between those who approach religion as a dominating and hegemonic power and those who emphasize religion's anti-hegemonic and liberatory potential.[57] Thus while scholars in the Seventies sought to understand popular forms of religion such as ABR's as representing opposition to dominant systems of power, more recent fieldwork during the late Eighties revealed that many of the so-called "religions of the oppressed" such as ABR's (such as Candomblé and Umbanda in particular) were as hierarchical and clientelistic as rural or popular Roman Catholicism. This result in turn questioned the claims that non-Catholic popular religions or lower class social movements such as ABR's or even Pentecostalism were more egalitarian or democratic than Brazilian Roman Catholicism. Thus the results are ambiguous and call for caution in claiming that as ABR's are a "religion of the oppressed," they necessarily reflect liberatory political and social alternatives. What the research does reveal is the deep influence of dominant religious and social structures. Further, the idea of religion as a compensation or as an alternative to politics, while valid in specific instances, tends to obscure ABR's (and Pentecostalism's) actual political impact. Afro-Brazilian religions serve to provide the newly urbanizing poor with immediate individual assistance and thereby assist in re-orienting and re-constructing new identities and expressing such, in the case of Umbanda in particular, in new organizational structures. The studies by Ireland and others show that ABR's authen-

56. da Silva, *Candomblé e Umbanda* source.
57. Birman, *O Que é Umbanda?*; Burdick, *Looking for God*; Ireland, *Kingdoms Come*; Seiblitz, "A Gira Profana."

tically express lower class autonomy, values and interests.[58] These in turn indirectly contribute to the political realm. However, the linkages that make this possible are not clearly delineated for ABR's (though connections can be made more distinctly in Umbanda Federations) primarily due to the ongoing racism of Brazilian society by which ABR participants from other social classes will deny association with a "*religião negra.*"

Conclusions for Further Research

Both AIC's and ABR's emerged then as "religions of suffering" from black peoples under slavery or colonialism. Both represent to varying degrees the synthesis of African religions with Christianity within their specific contexts. Both have been subject to legal proscription, in most cases only recently lifted as democratization has begun.

The history of scholarship on both these religions is extensive and illuminating, but to a great extent reflects the interests of the researchers, who often sought, in the political realm, something comparable to resistance or proto-nationalistic movements. Later scholarship has revealed, in both cases, the limits and strengths of such approaches. The increasing complexity of the religious fields in both Brazil and Southern Africa challenge broad generalizations, but nonetheless, the comparative approach can suggest possible lines of inquiry.[59]

First, both the AIC's and ABR's are what has until recently been described as "syncretistic" (for want of a better term) religions. What this has often meant is that they are regarded by those in religious and political power as impure, imperfect and inferior forms of religion. However, they are now recognized as religions in process as they interact with their religious and social contexts. This raises the need for further examination of these religions and their often non-institutional forms of politics (positive or negative), especially as focused on the individual. Second, anthropological field research has shown the comprehensive role of healing, divination or possession among both ABR's and AIC's, within surprisingly similar social strata (lower class

58. Ireland, *Kingdoms Come*. Thus is contra Umbanda which tends to be individualized, clientelistic and verticalistic in relations. Is this too sharp a distinction between Umbandista and other Afro-Brazilian groups?

59. West, *Bishops and Prophets* did suggest comparative studies with similar movements in Africa, while more recently Kunnie, "Black Churches in the United States and South Africa," compared AIC's and Afro-American Churches in the USA.

to "poorest of the poor") and in similar stages of urbanization on the periphery of large cities. In Brazil at least, work by Burdick, Ireland and Mariz, have shown that ABR's or Pentecostals, who emphasize such healing, are both growing rapidly and creating new subjects in their converts. This is a conclusion reached by, for instance, Kiernan and others in their observation of the "puritan/ascetic" work ethic as a corollary to the AIC's healing emphasis. This emphasis on healing has certainly led to an emphasis on the individual, but for those whose personhood is denied by society, this is perhaps not an unwelcome emphasis. The Brazilian case in turn, with some ABR's involved in local community activity, questions Schoffeleers and others' conclusions that healing leads to individualism, which in turn leads to political acquiescence. Was "political acquiescence" in the South African scene then but just a sensible survival tactic for the individual? Third, such provocative research results suggest a reason for the dramatic increase in membership for both AIC's and ABR's during the last decade. This period was one of worsening socio-economic opportunities for the urban poor in both contexts and with increasing demand for immediate survival mechanisms. The mainline Protestant (or "English-speaking") Churches in Southern Africa and the liberation theologians of the Roman Catholic "popular Church" in Brazil were all advocating long-term structural and rational changes at the national level. While these goals were exemplary, they did not meet the immediate survival needs of individuals and thus their adherents, it now seems, migrated to AIC's or ABR's (or Pentecostals) respectively.

However, having noted this shift in the religious field, the actual and potential linkages with other, perhaps more powerful groups need to be noted as indicators of the potential political implications of these recent and dramatic shifts. Here a comparison with AIC's and ABR's within a wider context becomes instructive. In Southern Africa AIC's and older mission or mainline Protestant Churches are moving closer together. The AIC's have sought to be considered Christian, and this has led to greater institutional affiliation with mainline religions, the formation of an AIC council, shared theological training facilities, and membership in the South African Council of Churches. The linkages thus being formed by AIC's will probably lead to greater visibility and institutional political impact. In Brazil however, the ABR's are either moving to an anti-syncretistic position as is the case with radical "Afro-centric" adherents of Candomblé in Bahia post-1983 for instance, or they are content to remain as they are with a dual ABR and Roman Catholic membership. These diverging movements have differing political implications however. The more radical ABR's will certainly foster an alternative, and positive, African-Brazilian identity, but depending on their size, without clear linkages to other social actors, could be marginalized. In addition, they, as well as the rest of the ABR's (except Umbanda perhaps), lack linkages to other institutions and face the increasing pressure from both official Catholicism and Pentecostalism. The Roman Catholic hierarchy, while recognizing ABR's as a New World religion, are demanding that baptized Catholics withdraw from such religions. This is placing great strain on the traditionalist ABR's at present. The greatest challenge in this respect comes not from the Roman Catholic Church but from the Pentecostals, especially Pastor Macedo's *Igreja Universal do Reino de Deus* (The Universal Church of the Kingdom of God), who regard ABR's as satanic. This has led to sharp confrontations between Pentecostals and ABR's which some scholars have dubbed a "holy war" (*a guerra santa*).[60]

Finally, despite the Freyrian "racial democracy" thesis, race remains a sharp class marker in Brazilian society. The Roman Catholic Church, even in its "popular" or "liberatory" forms has not adequately reached the Afro-Brazilian population (75 percent of the populace being in North-East). The Afro-Brazilian religions and the Pentecostals are the active religious actors here. Further research needs to pursue the role of ABR's in fostering (as they already have) positive Afro-Brazilian identities, especially through the rituals of healing and divination. Both in the South African and Brazilian contexts, the AIC's and ABR's are reaching the dislocated populations on the margins of modernity and in their own ways are asserting and recreating individuals in dramatically shifting social locations. This might not be a direct political function, but indirectly such self-formation is fostering an active and participatory citizenship, without which no political system, democracy in particular, can survive.

---

60. Though officially the Roman Catholic Church, for the first time, recognized ABR's as legitimate religions at the fourth CELAM, in Santa Domingo in 1992. See Berkenbrock, *Die Erfahrung der Orixás*, "Introduction," for details. On the "Holy War" being waged against ABR's, see Soares, "Guerra Santa no País do Sincretismo," 65–74.

Bibliography

Bastide, Roger. *As Américas Negras. As Civilizações Africanas no Novo Mundo*. São Paulo: DIFEL/USP, 1974.

———. *As Religões Africanas no Brasil. Contribução a uma Sociologia das Interpretações de Civilazações*, 2 vols. São Paulo: Editora Pioneira, 1971.

———. *O Candomblé da Bahia, Rito Nâgo*. Brasiliana, vol. 313. São Paulo: Companhia Editora Nacional, 1961.

Berkenbrock, Volney. *Die Erfahrung der Orixás. Eine Studie über die religiöse Erfahrung im Candomblé*. Bonn: Borengässer, 1995.

Birman, Patricia. *O Que é Umbanda?* São Paulo: Brasiliense, 1983.

Bourdieu, Pierre. *Language and Symbolic Power*. Cambridge: Harvard University Press, 1991.

———. *Outline of a Theory of Practice*. New York: Cambridge University Press, 1977.

Brandão, Carlos R. *Os Deuses do Povo*. São Paulo: Editora Brasiliensis, 1980.

Bresser Pereira, Luis. *Pactos Políticos: Do Populismo à Redemocratização*. São Paulo: Editora Brasiliense, 1985.

Brown, Diana deGroat. *Umbanda: Religion and Politics in Urban Brazil*. New York: Columbia University Press, 1994.

Brumana, Fernando Giobellina, and Elda Gonzales Martinez. *Spirits from the Margin: Umbanda in São Paulo. A Study in Popular Religion and Social Experience*. Stockholm: Almqvist & Wiksell, 1989.

Burdick, John. *Looking for God in Brazil. The Progressive Catholic Church in Brazil's Religious Arena*. Berkeley: University of California Press, 1993.

Buitenhuijs, R. "Messianisme et nasionalisme en Afrique noire: une remise en question." *African Perspectives* 2 (1976) 25–44.

Carneiro, Edison. *Candomblés da Bahia*. (Retratos do Brasil, Vol. 106) Rio De Janeiro: Civilização Brasileira, 1986.

———. *Religiões Negras: Notas de Etnografia Religiosa*. Rio de Janeiro, 1936.

Claasen, J. "Independents made Dependents." *Journal of Theology for Southern Africa* 91 (June 1995) 15–34.

Comaroff, Jean. *Body of Power, Spirit of Resistance: The Culture and History of a South African People*. Chicago: University of Chicago Press, 1985.

———. "Healing and the Cultural Order: The Case of the Baralongboo Ratshidi." *American Ethnologist* 7/4 (1980) 639.

Concone, Maria Helena Vilas Boas, and Lísias Negrão. "Umbanda: uma Representação à Cooptação. O Envolvimento Político partidário da Umbanda Paulista nas eliçoes de 1982." In *Umbanda e Política*. Edited by Marco Zero, 43–80. Cadernos do ISER 18. Rio de Janeiro: ISER 1985.

Congresso Afro-Brasileiro, *Anais do IV Congresso Afro-Brasileiro*. 4 Vols. Recife: Fundação Joachim Nabuco, Editora Massangana, 1995–96.

Cox, Harvey G. *Fire from Heaven: The Rise of Pentecostal Spirituality amd the Reshaping of Religion in the Twenty-First Century*. Reading, MA: Addison & Wesley, 1995.

De Beer, David. "Kerkelijk verzet tegen apartheid." *Het Uur van de Waarheid: het Kairos Document van Zuid-Afrikaanse Christenen*. Edited by De Beer et al. Baarn: Ten Have, 1986.

De Carvalho Soares, Mariza. "Guerra Santa no País do Sincretismo." In *Cadernos Do ISER*, Vol. 23, edited by Leilah Landim, 65–74. Rio de Janeiro: ISER, 1990.

de Gruchy, John W. *The Church Struggle in South Africa*. 2nd ed. Grand Rapids: Eerdmans, 1986.

Da Matta, Roberto. *Carnavais, Malandros e Heróis*. Rio de Janeiro: Zahar, 1979.

Da Silva, Vagner Gonçalves. *Candomblé e Umbanda: Caminhos da Devoção Brasileira*. São Paulo: Editora Atica, 1994.

Daneel, M. L. *Old and New in Southern Shona Independent Churches*. Vols I–II. The Hague: Mouton, 1971, 1974.

Edgar, Robert. *Because They Chose the Plan of God: The Story of the Bulhoek Massacre*. Johannesburg: Ravan, 1988.

Etherington, Norman A. "The Historical Sociology of Independent Churches in South-East Africa," *Journal of Religion in Africa*. 10:2 (1979) 108–26.

Fernandes, Gonçalves. *Xangôs no Nordeste. Investigações sobre os Cultos Negros-Fetichistas do Recife*. Rio de Janeiro: Civilização Brasileira, 1937.

Fields, Karen. *Revival and Rebellion in Colonial Central Africa*. Princeton: Princeton University Press, 1985.

Freyre, Gilberto. *Casa-Grande e Senzala*. Rio de Janeiro: Livraria José Olímpio, 1934.

Hayes, Stephen. "The African Independent Churches: Judgment through Terminology?" *Missionalia* 20:2 (1992) 139–46.

Hobsbawn, Eric, and Terence Ranger, editors. *The Invention of Tradition*. New York: Cambridge University Press, 1983.

Huntingdon, Samuel. *The Third Wave: Democratization in the Late Twentieth Century*. Norman: University of Oklahoma Press, 1991.

Ireland, Rowan. "Catholic Base Communities, Spiritist Groups, and the Deepening of Democracy in Brazil." Vol. 131, Working Paper, Latin American Program of the Woodrow Wilson International Center, Washington, DC, Smithsonian Institute, 1983.

———. *Kingdoms Come: Religion and Politics in Brazil*. Pittsburgh: Pittsburgh University Press, 1992.

Kiernan, Jim. "Poor and Puritan: An Attempt to View Zionism as a Collective Response to Urban Poverty." *African Studies* 36:1 (1977) 31–41.

———. "Variations on a Christian Theme. The Healing Synthesis of Zulu Zionism." In *Syncretism/Anti-Syncretism*, edited by Charles Stewart and Rosalind Shaw, 69–84. New York: Routledge, 1994.

Kitshoff, Mike C. "African Independent Churches. A Mighty Movement in a Changing South Africa." *South Africa International* 21 (1991) 155–64.

Kritzinger, J. J. "The Development of African Independent Churches." In *Empirical Studies of African Independent/Indigenous Churches*, edited by G. C. Oosthuizen and Irving Hexham, 291–312. Lewiston, NY: Edwin Mellen, 1992.

Kruss, Glenda "A Critical Review of the Study of Independent Churches in South Africa." In *Religion Alive*, edited by G. Oosthuizen, 21–32. Johannesburg: Hodder & Stoughton, 1986.

Landim, Leilah. *Sinais dos Tempos: Igrejas e Seitas no Brasil*. Rio de Janeiro: ISER, 1989.

Leacock, S. and R. *Spirits of the Deep*. New York: Doubleday, 1972.

Mills, W. G. "The Fork in the Road: Religious Separatism and Nationalism in the Cape Colony, 1890-1910." *Journal of Religion in Africa* 9 (1978) 51-61.
Mariz, Cecilia. "Religion and Coping with Poverty." PhD diss., Boston University, 1989.
Motta, Roberto. "A eclesificação dos cultos afro-brasileiros." *Comunicações do ISER* 7:30 (1988) 31-43.
Nye, Joseph H., and Robert O. Keohane, editors. *International Organization.* Cambridge, MA: Harvard University Press, 1972.
Oosthuizen, G. C. "Divine-Prophet Parallels in African Independent Churches and Traditional Religion." In *Empirical Studies of African Independent/Indigenous*, edited by G. C. Oosthuizen and Hexham Churches, 163-94. Lewiston, NY: Edwin Mellen, 1992.
———, editor. *Religion Alive: Studies in the New Movements and Indigenous Churches in Southern Africa.* Johannesburg: Hodder & Stoughton, 1986.
Oosthuizen, G. C., and Irving Hexham, editors. *Empirical Studies of African Independent/Indigenous Churches.* Lewiston, NY: Edwin Mellen, 1992.
Oosthuizen, G. C., M. C. Kitsoff, and S. W. D. Dube, editors. *Afro-Christianity at the Grassroots: Its Dynamics and Strategies.* Leiden: Brill, 1994.
Ranger, Terence. "Religious Movements and Politics in Sub-Saharan Africa." *African Studies Review* 29 (1986) 1-69.
Rodrigues, Nina. *Os Africanos no Brasil.* São Paulo: Cia. Editora Nacional-INL, 1976.
Santos, Juana Elbein dos. *Os Nâgo e a Morte. Pàde, àsèsè e o Culto Egun na Bahia.* Petrópolis: Editora Vozes, 1977.
Schoffeleers, M. "Healing and Political Acquiescence in African Independent Churches," in *Religion and Politics in Southern Africa.* Edited by Carl Fredrik Hallencreutz and Mai Palmberg. Uppsala: Scandinavian Institute of African Studies, 1991.
———. "Ritual Healing and Political Acquiescence: The Case of the Zionist Churches in Southern Africa." *Africa* 61:1 (1991) 1-25.
Schutte, G. "Die politischer Funktion religiöser Bewegnungen in Südlichen Afrika." *Zeitschrift für Evangelische Ethik* 17:1 (1973).
Seiblitz, Z. "A Gira Profana." In *Umbanda e Política*, edited by Marco Zero, 43-80. Cadernos do ISER 18. Rio de Janeiro: ISER 1985 122-54.
Sundkler, Bengt G. M. *Bantu Prophets in South Africa.* Cape Town: Oxford University Press, 1961.
Turner, V. W. *The Forest of Symbols.* Ithaca, NY: Cornell University Press, 1967.
Vallier, Ivan. "The Roman Catholic Church: A Transnational Actor." International Otganisation 25.3 (Summer 1971) 129-52.
Van Binsbergen W. M. J., and M. Schoffeleers, editors. *Theoretical Explorations in African Religion.* London: Routledge, 1985.
Velho, Yvonne Maggie Alves. *Guerra de Orixá. Um Estudo de Ritual e Conflito.* Rio de Janeiro: Zahar Editores, 1975.
Werbner, R. P. "The Argument of Images: From Zion to the Wilderness in African Churches." In *Theoretical Explorations in African Religion*, edited by W. van Binsbergen and M. Schoffeleers, 1-49. London: Kegan Paul, 1985.
West, Martin. *Bishops and Prophets in a Black City. African Independent Churches in Soweto, Johannesburg.* Cape Town: David Philip, 1975.
Willems, Emilio. *Followers of the New Faith.* Nashville: Vanderbilt University Press, 1967.

PART FOUR

Religious Pluralism and Social Change in West Africa

10

Religion and Social Change in Multi-Ethnic Nigerian Society

UKACHUKWU CHRIS MANUS AND BOLAJI OLUKEMI BATEYE

Introduction

FROM TIME IMMEMORIAL, RELIGION HAS THRIVED AS A LIVED PHEnomenon in the social cultural history of humankind. Religion of all sorts, and in the Nigerian context; namely the African Traditional or Indigenous Religion, Islam and Christianity, to just name the rather popular faiths in our environment, constitute one of the living springs of human life which influence the course of people's lives in diverse ways. On the interface between religion and the forces of social change, George Bernard Shaw in his work, *Getting Married: The Play* (1914) had this to say:

> Religion is a great force—the only real motive force in the world; but what you fellows don't understand is that you must get at a man through his religion and not yours.

Bernard Shaw's vision is true of Nigeria, a multi-ethnic nation, where it has so overwhelmingly become acknowledged that religions have been operative in ushering social change in multifaceted forms.[1] In the wake of the intellectual godlessness prevailing in our tertiary institutions, some intellectuals consider it fashionable to reject religion and trivialize its appeal to liberatory values in the "city of man".

---

1. Manus, "Relevance of Religious Studies in Nigerian Universities Today," 35–36.

But throughout human history, the positive values of religion than its dysfunctional role have copiously been acknowledged.²

Was it not Polybius, the second century Greek historian who, in his work, *Histories* 6.56, had informed us that the source of the social political genius of the Roman Empire was due to the overarching influence of their national religion? According to Polybius, Rome's constitutional system, a perfect balance of the monarchic (Consulate), the oligarchic (Senate) and the democratic (Assemblies) were structures solidly welded together by the fear of the gods and their capricious determinations.³ In addition to this, it is on record that the superior social engineering achieved in the Roman commonwealth had been realized through religious convictions and the practice of popular piety. Research on the Greco-Roman religious history reveals that the Romans quickly absorbed foreign religions and cults. The religion of ancient Egyptians and Osiris, their god of the underworld, and his consort Isis, the benefactress of devotees, and their stupendous festivals had attracted the Romans that they altogether egyptianized their faith. In the ceremony of the *Evocatio*, the Romans, on arrival at the gate of an enemy city readily invoked the local deities to change sides and grant them victory. They promised that they would give dutiful worship and respectable socially oriented *Leitourgeia* (services) to the deities than the stale homage of the inhabitants. The gregariously consented appeal must have received the favor of the gods as the Romans had always been victorious in the wars.

Religion

Let us first begin by navigating through some of the definitions of religion proffered by representatives of nineteenth and twentieth century scholarship whose thoughts have influenced scholars of religion who had worked or are still doing research in Nigeria. Most of the authors agree that religion is the belief in an ever-living God, or seen from the philosophical point of view, it is the belief in a Divine Mind and Will (*Nous*) ruling the universe and holding moral relations with mankind. Rudolf Otto had declared that, "Religion is that which grows out of, and gives expression to experience of the holy in its vari-

---

2. Huxley, *Religion without Revelation*, 110.
3. Ferguson, *Backgrounds to Early Christianity*, 20.

ous aspects." Emil Durkheim, a sociologist had defined religion as a system of beliefs and practices, which cluster around the sacred and unite the followers into a single community. Bolaji Idowu, the doyen of African Traditional Religious Studies at Nigeria's premier university, the University of Ibadan, had defined religion as the means by which God as spirit communicates with man's essential self. Francis Cardinal Arinze, the Nigerian prelate at the Vatican, Rome had defined religion both subjectively and objectively. According to him:

> Subjectively, religion is the consciousness of one's dependence on a transcendent Being and the tendency to worship Him. Objectively, religion is the body of truths, laws and rites by which man is subordinated to the transcendent Being.[4]

According to H. O. Anyanwu, of the Religious Studies Department at the University of Uyo, religion is "human interaction with the supernatural in order to cope up with life's crises."[5] Among other functionalities of religion, Anyanwu includes the fact that religion "is really a social phenomenon which has both philosophical and social dimensions."[6] For me, it is obvious that "life's crises" and the "philosophical and social dimensions" of religion that Dr. Anyanwu describes is, by no means, exclusive of social engineering in a multi-ethnic society peopled by multi-faith communities. For our present purposes, John Dewey's psychologizing definition of religion hits the nail at the right point. According to him, "the religious is any activity pursued on behalf of an ideal end . . . because of its general and enduring value."[7] This definition indicates that "the religious" includes a quality of activity that is found in many human pre-occupations among which the forces of change are primary. By this understanding, the social critical activist, whose commitment represents a state of being grasped by an ultimate concern for his or her unionists, is a *religious* being. Further expatiating, Livingston deposes that in Dewey's perception, "everything and anything is capable of being religious" and that "if everything human is religious, then it would seem to be synonymous with politics."[8] Neil Omerod corroborates this assertion

---

4. Arinze, *Sacrifice in Ibo Religion*, 8.
5. Anyanwu, *African Traditional Religion from the Grassroots*, 4.
6. Ibid.
7. Livingston, *Anatomy of the Sacred*, 7.
8. Ibid., 7.

when he says: "all human activities have a social political dimension"[9] thus including by inference religion, which in itself is a superb human activity.

There is no doubt accepting the verdict of most scholars of religion "that religion is a universal and abiding dimension of human experience."[10] Unfortunately the knowledge of what religion is all about is what many Nigerians do not realize. Many people do not submit the phenomenon to a "second activity order" rather they dismiss in depth study of religion with the wave of the hand. Such people readily classify religion as one of those issues that cause palaver in our world; especially since the attacks on September 11, 2001 in The United States of America. They do not even take stock of the consequences of the *Al Qaeda* prowls and the *Boko Haram* sect's terrorism in Nigeria. There is no doubt that definitions of religion are many and varied. But the question remains as to why do Nigerians appear to be very religious people in the world and oftentimes the most irreligious. What many analysts do not comprehend is that there is need for a critical examination of some unique characteristics of the Nigerian peoples' self consciousness. On this, attention may be drawn to the Nigerian peoples' obsession to "shop" for spiritual wholeness and self transcendence in the midst of the human experience of exploitation, suffering and oppression from the ruling elites. While there is no modern society where people are without religious beliefs and practices, there are individuals who refuse to exhibit conventional religious tendencies. They suppress or hide their innate inclinations to tend towards the divine in adoration and supplication. Many of our colleagues from the academia do not realize that their preferred agnostic attitude is derived from their exposure to early Marxist ideology. It is held by many that "religion has no content of its own but is simply the illusory articulation of the divisions and contradictions of society in its secular basis."[11]

No matter who we are, where we are, and how we may wish to figure out what religious people are doing, one thing that is certain is that religion is one universal human phenomenon that manifests itself as a pervasive and permanent reality. Phenomenology of religion, "one of the more recent and, in some respects, the most illuminating

---

9. Ormerod. *Introducing Contemporary Theologies*, 126.
10. Livingston, 3.
11. Davis, *Toward a Marxist Theory of Nationalism*, 134.

approaches to the study of religion" points up to religion as constitutive of "the data of experience that directly presents itself to human consciousness."[12] Thus the phenomenological approach takes serious interest in the morphology of religion, that is, in the structures or forms of religion as manifested in and across different cultures and temporal periods. Generally speaking, the forms differ. They might be the aspects of creation myths, rites of sacrifice, prayers, or even forms of religious leadership and administration. It is by the combination of the *noema* (the object of intentionality, content of experience; namely that which immediately appears to consciousness) and the *noesis* (the subject's experience and intention towards the object of consciousness) in the process of understanding religion as a phenomenon that the knowing subject after careful *epochetic analysis* (suspension of judgment or the bracketing of previous beliefs) and *eidetic reduction* (reflection on the essences of the believing consciousness) can come to a rigorous description of religious experience as it appears to him or her.

This task of isolating and describing the specific forms of religion using comparison and contrast is what great phenomenologists, represented by G. van der Leeuw (1890–1953), Mircea Eliade (1907–1986) and others had excelled in and had bequeathed to Religious Studies research in the postmodern academy. Thus phenomenology of religion does not interest itself in the study of the origin and content of religious dogmas but it is a stakeholder in the *how* questions, that is, in the morphology (structures and forms) of religions in the peoples' cultures and any value or good it portends to society. Much earlier than these later exponents of the methodology of religious studies, Rudolf Otto in his book, *The Idea of the Holy*, had described the numinous as the actual object of faith. The holy is, for him, *mysterium tremendum et fascinosum*—a majestic and ineffable Being—that which strikes awe and fascination—in any serious adherent. In the opinion of a recent commentator, it is an "experience, which falls into a category that is qualitatively different from all others."[13] And for Schmidt such an experience is "the primary religious category."[14]

---

12. Livingston, 39.
13. Ott, "Does the Notion of 'Mystery'?" 10.
14. Schmidt, *Exploring Religion*, 367.

To sum up this section, we dare say that, this feeling of the "uncanny" is the beginning of religion in which the "Holy," this "totally other" manifests itself as the sacred in human life. It can therefore be argued that every human person is a *Homo religious*. And as John S. Pobee, a Ghanaian scholar of religion strongly affirms and with special reference to Africans: "an *homo Africanus (est) homo religiosus radicaliter*—an African person is a radically religious being—for African cultures have a religious epistemology and ontology" that is nondescript, except perhaps, in the Asian continent.[15]

Generally, the faith of the religionists translates into belief in a transcendent (supernatural) God. Already in Nigeria, Traditional Religion, Islam and Christianity garner such adherents whose belief systems acknowledge the existence of a transcendent Supreme Being known and addressed variously as *Allah, God, Olódùmare, Chukwu, Oghene,* and others by various ethnic groups who constitute this geographical expression, Nigeria. Certainly, given such a situation, the political community is polarized on faith traditions. Such a religious landscape grounds the political society in a transcendent order. It is the task of the enlightened political class that their political agenda penetrate the faith communities and positively influence the populace to adopt democratic principles that reject and oppose the absolutization of any single will and the introduction of immanentist forms of religion for the people. In an ideal political community, religion with its faith in a transcendent order constitutes the foundation of the ethos of the community particularly in the quest for the attainment of a set of teleological values otherwise today "baptized" as the "dividends of democracy" which many Nigerians have hardly benefited from.[16]

Ethnic and Religious Pluralism as Forces for Social Change

With over 130 million people, Nigeria is Black Africa's most populous nation and the tenth largest in the world. The U.S. Library of Congress has directed attention of historians that Nigeria

> represents only about 3 percent of the surface area of Africa, and contains about 20 percent of total African population. In

15. Pobee, "Africa's Search For Religious Human Rights," 391.
16. Manus, "Religious Values, Social Justice and Peace," 41–44.

this and other respects, it is arguably the single most important country in the continent. The population of Nigeria is composed of over 370 ethnic groups. Three of them—the Hausa in the north, the Igbo in the southeast, and the Yoruba in the southwest—are the major groups and make up over 40% of the population. The country is equally a nation of diverse religious beliefs; Muslims account for 50% of the population, Christians 40%, and those holding indigenous beliefs 10%.[17]

Both the ancient and modern stand side by side in the suffocating climate of changes visiting the nation. The changes are due, mainly, to the encounter between colonialism, Western culture, Christian culture, Islamic culture and other social political factors. In spite of all these external influences, Nigerian cultures, with their strong religious features still remain unshaken. Besides this, there is a plurality of peoples composed of nations, races, and ethnic groups with own religions. These peoples had, since 1914, been amalgamated into this one nation-state. "Nigeria's fragile diversity has begun of recent to fray seriously at the many seams that join it together" submits the author of the U.S. Library of Congress. As shown in that Library's assessment, the Nigerian situation is a pluralism that does not exclude religious, cultural, ethnic or racial considerations.

At this juncture, we wish to address ourselves to five concrete sets of ethnic pluralisms in Nigeria. In the North, the Hausa-Fulani race (27.1 percent) dominates and Islam is the major religion. In the Middle belt, the Tiv and the Idoma outnumber the rest of the inhabitants with Islam and Christianity neck and neck in the race for supremacy and hegemony over the population. In the southwest, the Yoruba nation (17.8 percent), a tolerant Islam lives side by side with Yoruba Traditional Religion and Christianity. Quite often the faith communities collaborate to douse causes of tensions and conflicts. "Settler" Muslims freely practice their religion. In the southeast and the littoral towns across the Niger, the Igbo (17.5 percent) practice Christianity, which claims the majority of adherents. Among the Igbo, there is little room for conflicts except occasional revenge skirmishes when their kith and kin are massacred because of their faith in the north. In the Niger Delta area, more than two hundred ethnic groups with own ver-

---

17. These figures can be controversial. Christians in the land do not agree with the enumeration. We hope the planned head-count will, if carried out religiously, reveal comfortable results.

nacular languages exist in tensions and share horrendous experiences of sporadic ethnic conflicts sometimes caused by oil driven politics. In spite of the persistence of indigenous belief in the Mermaid cults (Owu Mmiri), Christianity remains the dominant religion.

With the free movement and settlement of peoples in Nigeria, Christians and Muslims stand almost equal in numbers in any given township or urban area. None of the thirteen Shari'ah states are composed only of Muslims. The problem, among others, has been whether or not the Shari'ah Law should apply to every resident in those states irrespective of their religious beliefs. These divergent scenarios indicate different dynamics in peoples' interpersonal relationships. Such dynamics are equally acerbated to a large extent by non-religious factors such as ethnically inherited struggle for political leadership, resource control, power sharing, inter-ethnic and sub-ethnic rivalries arising from border disputes when either side remains unwilling to give up its ancestral land. Thus the problem of welding a nation out of these disparate ethnic numbers and religious pluralism dispose the country to social upheavals. It can now be asserted that religiously inspired social changes remain the biggest challenges facing the Nigerian polity when the elite derail the nascent democracy.

In the light of the foregoing discourse, we want to observe that one of the most important challenges Nigeria faces as a multi-cultural polity is the challenge of religious pluralism. Evidence from contemporary Religious Studies research reveals that more than ever before Nigerians are becoming seriously aware of their being religiously pluralistic. Pluralism means the acceptance of the other as an other with all his or her uniqueness. Once pluralism is accepted as a basic reality of our world and its attendant historical processes at all levels, it becomes much easier for Nigerians to see the very legitimacy of the other to exist and to operate at all levels of life. World religions are beginning to experience the fact that their future does no longer consist in any kind of domination but in their readiness to respect each other and to engage in constructive dialogue. This developing phenomenon should positively influence Nigeria's self-understanding as a pluralistic state and help re-position her mission to the citizenry.

One may not fully grasp the interface between religion and social change in Nigeria without the religio-political context in which Nigerians live. Allow me to provide you with the judgment of John S.

Pobee, though an outsider but a neighbor from Ghana with interest in the Nigerian geo-political engineering. According to him:

> Nigeria has for long been religiously pluralistic. In 1921, tribal religions comprised 56.8% of the population, Islam 39%, and Christianity 4.3%. These ratios have changed dramatically over time. In 1931, tribal religions comprised 50% of the population, Islam 43.6%, Christianity 6.3%. In 1953, the ratios were 32.8% tribal, 45.3% Islam and 21.9% Christian; in 1963, 18.7% tribal, 43.4% Islam, 37.9% Christian; in 1975, 8.0% tribal, 44.5% Islam, 47.2% Christian; and in 1980 5.6% tribal, 45% Islam, 49% Christian.[18]

The following data though not yet reviewed and updated to reflect the realities on ground *per* the present administration, indicate that Islam and Christianity are key players in the Nigerian national life. Indeed, in all the political struggles and upheavals Nigeria has had in recent history, it is on record that they have in part been struggles between the Islamic North and the Christian south whose various agendas have been used to control these large geo-political zones. We still hear of the Northern Governors' forum as a group cemented together by, among other considerations, political traditions and world outlooks of the Islamic religion.[19] In other words, the two religions find themselves in perpetual competition for the souls of Nigerians within the same political system. Thus it has to be argued that the Nigerian multi-ethnic differences determine to a large extent the use and abuse of religion in Nigeria. Have we so quickly become ignorant of the furor the enrollment of Nigeria into the Organization of Islamic Countries (OIC) without debate by the administration of General Ibrahim Babangida was raised in the nation? Have we forgotten that in the ensuing riots in the North many Christians and Muslims died and property worth millions of Naira was destroyed? Have we not read from late Justice Aniagolu's work, *The Making of the 1989 Constitution in Nigeria,* how Clause Six in the 1989 Draft Constitution on the proposal to introduce the Shari'a Law into the Constitution rankled the Christians and left the matter implacably undecided? If any one doubts that religion and politics are mutually interrelated; especially in

---

18. Pobee, "Africa's Search For Religious Human Rights," 403.

19. This establishment had given birth to a parallel Forum in the south by the Southern Governors, indeed a balkanization of the country on political and perhaps, religious grounds.

Nigeria, how may s/he explain why each time the proposal to incorporate the Shari'ah is discussed, a lot of steam, often irrational, is let out? Suffice it to state that the two received-religions now predominant in Nigeria, which had originated from the Ancient Near East, had been long-standing rival ideologies with a horrific history of ethno-political antagonisms in their native lands. Unfortunately Nigerians have allowed themselves to be drawn into that imbroglio. In this light, Bala J. Takaya warns that "religious creeds excite and extract the deepest possible emotional and physical loyalties from their adherents when in political competition with people of other faiths."[20] Such indices indicate that "religion is, at some point, politics and the most potent and long lasting political association." This notion is exemplified in his objection that "the politicization of religion (is) most objectionable in a multi-faith society like Nigeria because the objectivity of "brothers" in public offices are likely to be blurred by religious considerations in serving a heterogeneous community."[21]

Religion and Social Change in Nigeria

From the definitional notions of religion offered above, one can argue that religion, on its own, cannot provide a roadmap for the trajectory of social change in Nigeria. From the cultural perspective, religion is indeed a constitutive ingredient in the valorization of society. Such a role of religion must be evaluated from the liberative praxis of the adherents as indicated in their expressions and religious activities towards the pursuit of peace, justice, solidarity and charity in any community. Such actions translate exactly into an understanding of how religious institutions and leadership can engage the public arena.

In many areas of Nigeria, traditional religious symbols and personages have provided and still provide varying degrees of the interface between religion and the web of social interactions. Audacious and aggressive steps to initiate social metamorphosis in traditional African societies are known to have been engineered by some valiant women. The mythology and social order of the Yoruba people in southwestern Nigeria reveal that women had excelled as power-brokers because of the "dual gender system of the social political organization in which

20. Takaya, "Religion, Politics and Peace" 110.
21. Ibid., 112.

they had maintained equal standing with men. On further and in depth research, we discover that Yoruba traditional civil society had provided women the space to share power with men and that the equal standing they had enjoyed with men of their communities had empowered them to advance the fortunes of women in order to find their feet and fulfillment in the religio-cultural setting of pre-colonial society. These aspects of the traditional life of the people had promoted the fabric that cemented society together.

In pre-Christian Igbo society, the position occupied by priest-kings, the likes of *Eze Ulu,* in Achebe's novel, *Arrow of God,* and the curators of *Ibini Ukpabi* of the Aro in northern Igboland of Nigeria, were the central religious symbols that resonated the religiosity of the people. It is well accepted that prophets, diviners, priests, and herbalists sit upon the ancestral stool of time from which they derived their powers and authority to enact and exact moral laws and probity in the communities. Such potentates had their powers conferred on them at the public installations and enthronement ceremonies before the people. Such official enstoolement had empowered them to serve the people with diligence in both social and religious affairs. They had sworn an oath of office, oftentimes in the ancestral shrines, to ever remain responsible to the people. Nowadays when Western-type democracy is failing in many parts of Africa, it seems that the retrieval of the traditional religio-cultural institutions which still have overriding influence in many a leader can donate realist and pragmatic insights on the development of modern political culture in Nigeria and Africa at large.

Given the Nigerian political climate since independence, the Christian Religion has, through its organization, the Christian Association of Nigeria (CAN), an interdenominational forum for Christian action, had created forums for the emergence of a crop of counter-elites that do galvanize mass social protests when the policies of Government become anti-people. In its execution of the functions of civil society, CAN has provided a formidable avenue for opposition to questionable characters in politics. In such cases, the organization has been able to garner broader social support. It has constantly acted in the prophetic tradition as the emboldened voice of the voiceless, the liberator of the marginalized, and the defender of the rights of women. Christian women have not remained silent. We have been intrigued by the discovery of "the impact of contemporary female religious leaders on their followers that yield into positive gender relations in the church and society."[22] Our findings draw attention to "the positive influence of female religious leaders to liberating women from oppressive socio-cultural norms.[23] The CAN has consistently challenged the structures that have promoted poverty and the deprivation of the masses of the People of God. Its arsenal of courageous and outspoken prelates as custodians (*episkopoi*) of Christian orthodoxy have, through their Lenten Pastoral Letters, Synodal Exhortations, and the Declarations of various Episcopal Conferences, denounced politics of bitterness and acrimony that are so rife in the Nigeria nation-state. These princes of the Church have castigated political leaders who have resisted constructive criticisms and have staunchly held on to the Machiavellian credo that the "end justifies the means." Many of these "masters" cling on to political power as the only means to gain entry to wealth, influence and authority in an oil rich nation, Nigeria.

As an organization that is peopled by clerics who minister to the pastoral and spiritual needs of the people, CAN has supported the development of grassroots Christology through which lens the faithful have come to see their affirmative actions as a replication of Christ's liberatory role according to the lessons of Luke 4:16–30.[24] In their sermon profiles, they have enjoined congregations to engage in participatory democracy, to vote wisely, and to shun the "bribes" of those who come to power to rape the nation's economy, loot the treasury, and to enslave the people. For CAN members, those are political robbers who should be resisted and fought against with the last blood of the Christiadelphians of Nigeria. CAN's prelates and clerics like the Catholic and Anglican Archbishops of Abuja, Most Reverend John Onaiyekan and Rt. Reverend Peter Jasper Akinola, Anthony Cardinal Olubunmi Okogie of the Catholic Archdiocese of Lagos and Pastor Ayo Oritsejiofor, Chairman of the Pentecostal Fellowship of Nigeria (PFN) are trail-blazers in the process of mass conscientization and the awakening of an ethical civil society. These Churchmen and other lay leaders of the faithful have established themselves as men of God who exude the moral courage against Government violations of its own

---

22. Bateye, "Female Religious Leaders of New Generation Churches," 227.
23. Bateye, "Impact of Female Leaders," 229.
24. Manus, 116–43.

rules and policies. They call for a revisionism that is in deep search of politics with a human face. They insist that Christians in politics should be committed to a faith that promotes justice, care of and service to the poor as well as the democratization of the society so that members become committed to the service of others.

CAN leadership recognizes that the Churches in Nigeria are not Government institutions and parastatals, which Government can close down at will. These men of God do mobilize their followers to recognize the need to organize potty protests through which they express their resistance intelligently as they show no fear of being banned or closed down. Christians in Nigeria look up to the Churches as divine establishments and as such that they possess an aura of fear and reverence which daunt the authorities to dare consider sanctions.

The vast population of Christian adherents and their umbrella organization, CAN, constitute a united front. Their interventions do send shockwaves to the "wicked" in power to dread the possibility of Church-led uprisings. The candlesticks march by Christians that led to the overthrow of President Marcos in the Philippines are still very recent to be forgotten by both the "ruled" and the "rulers." The teeming number of Christians in Nigeria signifies a force to reckon with in terms of their material and human resource output, which the administrators can only overlook at the detriment of their own positions. In the membership of CAN are other social groupings cut across ethnic divides. There are lawyers, journalists, liberation theologians, medical and health professionals, and business moguls; these are people who drive the non-oil sector of the national economy. There are academics and amongst them are many who are today pastors, priests, and Christian laity, that belong to the Academic Staff Union of Universities (ASUU) whose restless and inquisitive minds and activism have been dreaded by successive Governments as an influential member of the civil society in Nigeria. CAN draws courage and inspiration from the manifestoes of these organizations and work through their members in the unions to demand change and resist Government tyranny and exploitation, as has been the case in both the health and education sectors. In Nigeria today, there is a growing recognition of the moral dimension of citizenship reaching out to the emergence of an "ethical model of civil society" that must continue to press for due process, the rule of law, constitutionality and probity in all aspects of our national life.²⁵ The promoters stress the moral implications of politicking and governance in such a way that adherents are equipped to make responsible choices. Through the pulpits, the open-air rallies, the numerous crusade grounds, and redemption camps, the various Christian establishments under the umbrella of CAN wield enormous clout as alternative change agents in situations when structural injustices not only "go against the Christian faith but also are at variance with the Christian conception of the human person and his or her ultimate vocation."²⁶ In this respect, CAN finds no evil in galvanizing the public to tackle corrupt leaders in office. The contemporary media reports of impeachment sagas of Governors, Deputies, and Speakers in some states of Nigeria is stunning even though their overthrow has not been engineered by Christian organizations but many of the motivators are from the circle of the "born-agains," a zealotical group in CAN. Indeed the Churches have much larger constituencies that any politician can boast of at any given time. The members of the Christian elites penetrate various social strata and thus have a lot of interest groups such as the market women, young farmers' clubs, schoolteachers and their teeming pupils. Many Nigerians have not yet forgotten the Aba Women's Riot of 1927 against the colonialists' oppressive tax laws.²⁷ Female religious leaders have become active change-agents as "there is reason for optimism that Nigeria is arriving boldly toward the vision of a society where all are regarded as equal irrespective of gender."²⁸ In contemporary times, the religious organizations use these resources to resist Government tyranny.

Islamic Approach

In the light of the above information, certain fundamentalist understanding of religion had occurred in Islamic circles in Nigeria. In 1977, the *Izala Movement* was founded by Sheikh Abubakar Mahmud Gumi. The movement, which had its ambition to restore Islam to its ancient practices and to expunge of all forms of modernizations and innovations, provoked the anger of the *darika*—the current Islamic

---

25. Wnuk-Lipinski, "Vicissitudes of Ethical Civil Society," 2–3.
26. Oraegbunam, "Doing Liberation Theology in Nigeria," 103.
27. Njoku, "Eastern Nigerian Women War," 123.
28. Bolaji, 234.

leadership. Since 1977, the execution of the strategic design of the *Izala* group had wreaked much havoc in many cities of the North. In a joint force with the Maitatsine Islamic group, a political plot that hit Kano in 1980, Kaduna in 1982, Maiduguri in 1982, Yola in 1984, and Gombe in 1985, was hatched.[29] Real secularization of the Islamic religion as a means for social change happened in the same year the transition to the Second Republic civilian administration under Alhaji Shehu Shagari, a Northerner himself, came on board. The *Izala* group added fuel to the fire already started by both the pro-Shagari and anti-Shari'ah extremist groups whose emotional outbursts trailed the 1977–1978 Constitutional debates. The *Izala* bandied a fanatical slogan: *Islam Kawal* (Islam Must Rule) thus calling for the establishment of an Islamic state system for Nigeria as the only activist change-agent. Since that time, the secularization of religion has grown stiffer and stiffer in the North of Nigeria. This scandal has compelled both Christian and Muslim leaders, as J. Takaya would have us believe, "to weigh every government decision in terms of their respective religions; calculating there from, their possible gains and losses."[30] Here, we must not fail to discuss the role of the *Khilafat* (the political extremists) who believe that because Islam is a total way of life, social political change is desirable. For this faction, Islam must be seen as a religion of power and glory as it had been lived by the founder, Muhammad, who was himself the first Muslim Head of State. For this reason, Muslims must work towards the establishment of a *dar al Islam* (Islamic State). Muslims of this credo, do not believe that it is possible to practice Islam when a non-Muslim holds political power. They can only obey a secular leader when the size and strength of the Muslim *Ummah* (brotherhood) is too weak for them to bring about the change to an Islamic State or when the social political and economic conditions of the state where they live make it inadvisable to attempt to do so. This was the situation of Muslims in Kenya, especially under the administration of President Daniel arap Moi of KANU for twenty-eight years.

29. Takaya, "Religion, Politics and Peace," 113. Still in the last few years, Muslim fanatics have continued to attack and kill Christians, burn their churches buildings and business premises. Last February 2006, violent clashes erupted in the Northern cities of Maidugiri, Kano and Kaduna with reprisal killings which spelled doom to the Muslims of Northern origin in Onitsha, the commercial nerve-centre of Anambra state in the largely Christian east of Nigeria.

30. Takaya, 114.

This mentality of some Nigerian Muslims shows how precarious religion can sometimes manifest itself as an agent of social change in a multi-ethnic and a multi-faith society. Apart, however, from this sort of dysfunctional role of the Islamic religion in the Nigerian society, elsewhere in the world it is honestly known that "the Islamic faith has functioned as a primary tool to confront and to overthrow oppressive regimes, and to bring about desired social changes."[31] The Qur'an categorically denounces *zulum* (oppression) and shows great interest in the protection of the poor and the weak in the community. Islam is known to encourage the weak and the subjugated to use "liberative violence" to defend themselves and for the faithful to use such violence to liberate those who are being oppressed."

The Christian Approach

Apart from the time of Constantine the Great and the medieval period when Western Christendom had controlled both the political and the religious affairs of the society, Christian religion has consistently made a distinction between what belongs to Caesar and that which belongs to God (Mark 12:17; Matt 22:21; Luke 20:25). This longtime injunction attested in the three Synoptic Gospels, draws the attention of Christians to their dual heritage in the world. As it has been argued elsewhere, the text reminds them to "fulfill their civic obligations in the city of man . . . as well as an injunction to do works that help 'pile up' treasures of eternal reward in the city of God."[32] There are hardly any lessons from the Bible that yield into doctrines that confer worldly power to Christians not even Matt 28:16–20—the Great Commission—even if some colonial masters had read such meanings into the text.[33] Scholarly reflections on the Bible belong to the domain of the theological enterprise. Mainline Christian traditions manifest a strong belief in the relationship between religion and social change; especially in its objective understanding of salvation as inclusive of liberation and transformation of society. There is, among other currents, a political theology, one inspired by the struggle to get rid of the squalid socio-political conditions of the people of God. The gen-

---

31. Fabella, *Dictionary of Third World Theologies*, 125.
32. Manus, "New Testament Theological Foundations," 8, 11.
33. Dube, "Rereading the Bible," 57.

esis of political theology can be traced to Karl Marx's concept of the unity between theory and practice, which marked a turning point in the history of Western thought. Johan Baptist Metz, the originator of political theology in its German complexion had acknowledged the Marxian correlation between theory and practice as the essential ingredient in contemporary liberation theological discourse. According to him, "Political theology claims to be a basic element in the whole structure of critical theological thinking, motivated by a new notion of the relation between theory and practice, according to which all theology must be of itself "practical," and oriented to action."[34] As he argues, theology must turn to the concrete subject and the praxis of subjects.[35] Charles Davis goes further to add that political theology is "faith brought to expression in and through political practice"[36] especially when viewed in the context of "the relation between faith and social practice."[37] Ormerod admonishes us that political theology is "a theology which examines social structures, cultural movements, economic philosophies in the penetrating light of the Gospel."[38] This praxis-driven theology is predicated upon the fact that "Christian practice has to concern itself above all with those who are prevented by social conditions from becoming fully mature as human subjects. For that reason, Christian practice cannot be merely ethical, but must also be social and political."[39]

The earliest and most eloquent representatives of this sort of doing theology in an oppressed environment are the African-American James H. Cone,[40] the Latin American theologian, Gustavo Gutiérrez.[41] For Cone, liberation is sanctification. "To be sanctified is to be liberated, that is, to be politically engaged in the struggle for freedom."[42] According to Fabella, freedom of the oppressed who lives in history becomes a reality when s/he can see beyond it and be able to recognize

---

34. J.B. Metz, "Political Theology," 47.
35. Metz, *Faith in History and Society*, 7.
36. Davis, 3.
37. Davis, 5.
38. Ormerod, 124.
39. Ormerod, 124.
40. Cone, *A Black Theology of Liberation*.
41. G.A. Gutiérrez, *A Theology of Liberation*.
42. Fabella, 123.

that "salvation or liberation is not simply freedom in history, (but) freedom to affirm that future which is beyond history—God's own eschatological future."[43] Gutiérrez asserts "that the historical process in which Latin America has been involved, and the experiences of many Christians in this process, led liberation theology to speak of salvation in Christ in terms of liberation."[44] For Gutiérrez, there are different aspects of liberation: "liberation from social situations of oppression and marginalization; liberation from all forms of inner servitude; and liberation from sin which breaks human friendship with God and other human beings."[45] For comparative religion scholars, this is the equivalent of *Jihad* in Islam. Latin American liberation theology therefore employs the language of prophecy to denounce unjust political situations, its structural causes of injustice and the marginalization of women and men.[46]

Inspired by these foreign movements, there has began to emerge a growing literary corpus on Nigerian Liberation Theology.[47] The practitioners have made Nigeria's socio-economic and political struggles their primary agenda.[48] Poverty, gender inequity, and mounting health problems and the HIV and AIDS epidemic are defined in anthropological terms. Efforts are being made to critique all unjust situations: political, governance, economic, corruption, nepotism, religious, and labor related issues, in fact, all that dehumanize and impoverish the African person created in the image of God. The prevalence and ravages of the HIV/AIDS pandemic in the African continent have been recognized as the consequences of national and international injustice.[49] Homegrown liberation theology in Nigeria is fully interested in anti-people policies of the state. Its goal is to redress the oppressive and exploitative socio-economic and political conditions that have been rearing their ugly heads in the nation since independence. Do the current political class not see itself as a functionary within the so-called "wide authority of the state"? In his diatribe on Hon. Titi Oseni's

43. Fabella, 123.
44. Fabella, 123.
45. Fabella, 123.
46. Boff and Boff, *Introducing Liberation Theology*.
47. Cf. Oraegbunam.
48. Cf. Martey, *African Theology*.
49. Manus, "Theological Perspectives on Gender, Human Rights and HIV/AIDS."

lecture titled: *"Corruption in Public Service: Antecedents and Role of the Legislature and the Civil Society in Challenging it"* recently given at the Dominican Community,[50] Ibadan, Fr. Tony Akinwale berates the Honourable Speaker of Ogun State Assembly of Nigeria on her coinage of the slogan: "wide authority of the state." Fr. Tony considers the term as "another name for . . . big government" by the powers that be. In his words:

> Big government is megalomaniac, ubiquitous and ultimately inefficient. Big government is megalomaniac because, in violation of the principle of subsidiary, it nurses the illusion that it can and must do everything for the people. Instead of securing the environment so that the people are enabled to take care of themselves, big government accumulates power and uses its officials to make the environment insecure thus disabling the people from taking care of themselves. In the final analysis, big government neither takes care of the people nor allows the people to take care of themselves because big government stifles the potential and initiative that it has pleased the Creator to give to the citizens. It is this megalomania of government in Nigeria, this illusion that it can do all things for the people, that encourages big government to be ubiquitous. It is ubiquitous in the sense that it seeks to be present by commanding and controlling every sector of the economy. In concrete terms, big government dispossess the people of the wealth of the land under the pretext that it will use the wealth to take care of people. But the wealth of the land ends up in the hands of government officials. The government controls the oil sector, and whoever finds his or her way into government by election or by appointment is in control of the wealth. That is how big government provides a fertile soil for corruption. Big government runs many parastatals because it pretends to take care of the people when in fact it does not. In Nigeria, we have NEPA (PHCN), NITEL, NNPC etc. In a big government, it does not matter whether such parastatals work. What matters is that they provide jobs and opportunities for the enrichment of people who know people in government.

Critical interventions as the above quote from Christian theologians are how the Christian faith may be said to inspire and promote

---

50. Hon Titi Oseni, Speaker of the Ogun State House of Assembly, delivered a lecture at the Dominican Community, Samonda, Ibadan, April 29, 2004 which Fr. Dr. Anthony Akinwale offered a critical response.

change by engaging in the quest for social justice and ethics of good governance in Nigeria.

Conclusion

This paper has commenced with a disquisition on the interface between religion and social change. We tried to define religion in the perspectives in which it is studied in the academy all over the civilized world and reached out to its application in the Nigerian context. We briefly explored the importance of the phenomenological approach to the study of religion and upheld it as a methodology that can still help researchers to objectively determine the morphology of religions in Nigeria in order to expatiate on what exactly distinguishes religion from other disciplines. To comprehend religion as a motive force in human history, we rummaged through different perspectives of religion to come to an understanding of what are implicated in the concept "religious" and argued that it includes a set of human activities in which interest in the social engineering of society is paramount.

We have seen that Nigeria is comprised of a plurality of peoples. This pluralism, which does not exclude religion, impacts seriously on the ethos of society. Besides this, it is observed that the socio-economic conditions of the people inspire religious organizations and leaders to fight on the side of the downtrodden. In view of these findings, the paper went further to explain the nexus between theory and praxis was examined. It is found that reflections on the duo yielded into the emergence of the theology of struggle against man's inhumanity to man and the total liberation of humankind from oppressive and exploitative systems.

Apart however from the dysfunctional role of religions when they are "pushed" irrationally, we have seen that a study of religion and social change in the Nigerian context reveals a plethora of values that need to be embraced as relative to the development of authentic Nigerian religiosity, good governance and an ethical civil society. The valorization of the Nigerian civil society must be founded on an inclusive understanding of human existence in communion with others; especially in the sense of the Muslim idea of the *Ummah* where *Zakatu (charity)* must be given to the less privileged after Ramadan. In this perspective, the Christian religious term, *koinonia (fellowship)* readily calls to mind. *Koinonia*, in its Greek sense, means fellowship. It supposes active participation in the faith community. All Nigerians live out their humanity to the fullest in communities where they participate in and share common destiny, diverse cultures, customs and other symbols of unity in diversity. Implicated in the concept, *koinonia* amounts to the Christian desire for "participatory democracy"; one that can dispose the citizenry towards a better appreciation of a patriotic sense of belonging. Participatory democracy will involve all the stakeholders and inspire them to become agents in quest for good governance and one that is devoid of religious bigotry. This leads us to make the suggestion that Nigerian leaders should adopt the *polycentric approach* as an alternative mode of governance. With the approach, the political class can curb unhealthy upheavals religions tend to engender in the Nigerian socio-religious terrain. The model emphasizes the need to nip in the bud the pluralistic power bases religions tend to establish in the country.

Genuine liberation theology as is cultivated in both Islam and Christianity today must be let to offer Nigerians the capability to reposition and to recreate the religio-political order in their local communities. The condition of the poor, the exploited, women and minors, the oppressed and those trafficked into slavery and prostitution must continue to remain top on the preachment profiles of the religious leaders and clerics. Given Nigeria's religious pluralism and the tendency to reject toleration, religious institutions must rise to the challenge to defend religious human rights and the right and freedom to live one's faith and beliefs without molestation in any part of Nigeria. The anti-corruption campaigns of the present administration must be cautioned to mean well for the citizenry and to continue to receive the support of religious organizations and traditional rulers who are duly recognized as Royal Fathers of both the secular and faith communities. As key players in critiquing the Nigerian polity, religious leaders must continue to fight against corruption, which undoubtedly robs many Nigerians of their dignity. Religious institutions should be seen as the moral conscience of the society and the voice of the voiceless against unjust policies. Members of the CAN have been called upon to play the Amos of modern Nigeria. Both Islamic and Christian religions, even African Traditional Religionists, have strong prophetic traditions. They should retrieve their prophetic heritage, sharpen their prophetic utterances and rise to defend the weak and the marginalized in the society. What have the religious authorities and their organizations said about the callous demolitions of houses and homes of the poor for real estate developers in Kubwa district of Abuja? They should preach and canvass the need for open and transparent governance, free and fair elections come 2007, civil and political rights, respect for labor rights, pension and gratuity rights and the promotion of the emergence of a well-informed and articulate civil society.

As change agents, Islam and Christianity should be held as equal actors in the quest for justice and the rule of law in a fledgling democracy as Nigeria. They must be partners in the development of genuine politics and be disciplined operators of social ethics, equity and public policy. Religious leaders, away from the divide and rule policy of some states, should foster inter-religious harmony, initiate constructive dialogue, preach the constancy of peace and explore alternative ways by which our diversity must be respected without destabilizing different communities who wish to collaborate in building one nation under God. Inter-ethnic and inter-religious rivalries, competition and conflicts must be dreaded as counter-productive in nation building. Religious leaders, theologians and scholars of religion must decisively work together to produce a holistic vision of *re-awakening* for Nigeria in the twenty-first century. It is time Nigeria has a Ministry of Religious Affairs as religion has come to assume a center stage in deciding and resolving several matters in the country. Such a ministry shall have the responsibility of regulating pilgrimage operations for both Muslims and Christians and at home organize from time to time inter-religious dialogues and arrange meetings between Muslim Ulamas, clerics and Christian pastors and Bishops. Such meetings should aim at dousing fundamentalist tendencies that tend to divide a people under the One God.

In a culturally and religiously pluralistic society as Nigeria where the religions produce teachers and nurturers of *conscience* (synedesis); freedom of conscience must be respected, fostered and defended by the rule of law. Religious leaders and scholars should create possibilities to ensure that freedom of conscience is consistent with religious doctrines that affirm the dignity of all persons: big or small, high or low.[51] In all political activities, adherents of all religions in politics must

---

51. This is in accord with the spirit of Art. 8 of the *African Charter on Human and*

aspire to engage themselves in positive praxis that foster development of an ideal ethical civil society.

Bibliography

An-Na'im, A. A. editor. *Proselytization and Communal Self-Determination in Africa.* Religion and Human Rights. Maryknoll, NY: Orbis, 1999,
Anyanwu, H. O. *African Traditional Religion from the Grassroots.* Lagos: Minder, 2004.
Arinze, F. *Sacrifice in Ibo Religion.* Ibadan: Ibadan University Press, 1970.
Bateye, B. O. "Female Religious Leaders of New Generation Churches as Change-agents in Yorubaland." PhD diss., Obafemi Awolowo University, 2001
———. "Reclaiming a Lost Tradition: Nigerian Women in Power and Resistance." In *Women and the Culture of Violence in Traditional Africa,* edited by D. O. Akintunde, and H. Labeodan, 79–91. Ibadan: Sefer, 2002.
———. "The Impact of Female Leaders of New Generation Churches on their Followers Among the Yoruba of Southwestern Nigeria." In *Women and Gender Equality for a Better Society in Nigeria,* edited by A. Ojo, 219–34. Lagos: Federal Government, 2002.
Boff, L., and C. Boff. *Introducing Liberation Theology.* Maryknoll, NY: Orbis, 1987.
Brandon, S. G. F. *Man and His Destiny in the Great Religions.* Toronto: Toronto University Press, 1962.
Brede, K. W. *The Meaning of Religion: Lectures in the Phenomenology of Religioni.* The Hague: Martinus Nijhoff, 1960.
Cochran, C. E., and D. C. Cochran. *Catholics, Politics, & Public Policy: Beyond Left and Right.* Maryknoll, NY: Orbis, 2003.
Cone, J. H. *A Black Theology of Liberation.* Maryknoll, NY: Orbis, 1990.
Davis, H. *Toward a Marxist Theory of Nationalism.* New York: Monthly Review, 1980.
Dube, M. W. "Rereading the Bible: Biblical Hermeneutics and Social Justice." In *African Theology Today,* edited by Emmanuel Katongole, 57–68. Scranton: University of Scranton Press, 2002.
Durkheim, E. *The Elementary Forms of the Religious Life.* New York: Free, 1969.
Eliade, M. *The Quest: History and Meaning in Religion.* Chicago: University of Chicago Press, 1969.
Fabella, V., and Sugirtharajah Fabella, editors. *Dictionary of Third World Theologies.* Maryknoll, NY: Orbis, 2000.
Ferré, F. "The Definition of Religion." *Journal of the American Academy of Religion* 38 (1970) 5ff.
Ferguson, E. *Backgrounds to Early Christianity.* 3rd ed. Grand Rapids: Eerdmans, 2003.
Glottal, N. K., editor. *The Bible and Liberation: Political and Social Hermeneutics.* Maryknoll, NY: Orbis, 1983.
Gutiérrez, Gustavo. *A Theology of Liberation.* Maryknoll, NY: Orbis, 1988.
Huxley, J. S. *Religion without Revelation.* New York: Harper, 1957.

Peoples' Rights, January 7–19, 1981.

Idowu, E. B. *African Traditional Religion: A Definition*. London: SCM Press, 1973.
Jeffery, A. *Islam: Muhammad and His Religion*. New York: Liberal Arts, 1958.
King, W. L. *Introduction to Religion: A Phenomenological Approach*. New York: Harper & Row, 1968.
Lerner, N. *Religion, Beliefs and International Human Rights*. Religion and Human Rights. Maryknoll, NY: Orbis, 2000.
Livingston, J. C. *Anatomy of the Sacred: An Introduction to Religion*, 4th editor. Upper Saddle River, NJ: Prentice-Hall, 2001.
Manus, C. U. "New Testament Theological Foundations for Christian Contribution to Politics in Nigeria." *Bulletin of Ecumenical Theology* 2:1 (1989) 7–30.
———. "Religious Values, Social Justice and Peace in the Nigerian Context." In *Religion and Peace in Multi-Faith Nigeria*, edited by J. K. Olupona, 40–53. Ile-Ife: Obafemi Awolowo University Press, 1992.
———. "The Relevance of Religious Studies in Nigerian Universities Today." In *African Cultural Revolution Islam & Christianity in Yorubaland*, edited by E.O. Babalola, 34–40. Lagos: Eternal Communications, 2002.
———. "Theological Perspectives on Gender, Human Rights and HIV/AIDS." A Commissioned Paper Read at the 11th Spiritan International School of Theology Missiological Symposium, Attakwu, Enugu, April 20–23, 2005.
Martey, E. *African Theology: Inculturation and Liberation*. Maryknoll, NY: Orbis, 1993.
Metz, J. B. *Faith in History and Society: Towards a Practical Fundamental Theology*. New York: Seabury, 1980.
———. "Political Theology." In *Sacramentum Mundi: An Encyclopedia of Theology*. Vol. 5. London: Burns & Oates, 1970.
Njoku, U. J. "The Eastern Nigerian Women War of 1929 as a Model for the Role of Women in the African Church." *Journal of Inculturation Theology* 7:2 (2005) 118–35.
Oraegbunam, I. K. E. "Doing Liberation Theology in Nigeria Today in the Light of *Octogesima Adveniens*." *Journal of Inculturation Theology* 7:2 (2005) 99–117.
Ormerod, N. *Introducing Contemporary Theologies: The What and the Who of Theology Today*. Maryknoll, NY: Orbis, 1971.
Ott, H. "Does the Notion of "Mystery"—As Another Name for God—Provide a Basis for a Dialogical Encounter Between The Religions?" In *God: The Contemporary Discussion*, edited by F. Sontag and B. M. Darrol, 5–17. New York: Rose of Sharon, 1982.
Otto, Rudolph. *The Idea of the Holy*. New York: Oxford University Press, 1958.
Pobee, J. S. "Africa's Search For Religious Human Rights Through Returning to Wells of Living Water." In *Religious Human Rights in Global Perspective: Legal Perspectives*. Edited by J. D. van der Vyver, and J. Witte, 391–415. The Hague: Martinus Nijhoff, 1996.
Reader, J. *Beyond All Reason: The Limits of Post-Modern Theology*. Aureus: Cardiff, 1997.
Sharpe, E. *Understanding Religion*. New York: St. Martin's Press, 1983.
Schmidt. R. *Exploring Religion*. Belmont, California: Wordsworth Publishing Company, 1980.
Smart, N. *Beyond Ideology: Religion and the Future of Western Civilization, Gifford Lectures, Edinburgh, 1979–1980*. San Francisco: Harper & Row, 1981.

Smith, C. *The Meaning and End of Religion.* New York: New American Library, 1964.
Takaya, Bala J., "Religion, Politics and Peace: Resolving the Nigerian Dilemma." In *Religion and Peace in Multi-Faith Nigeria,* edited by J. K. Olupona, 109–23. Ile-Ife: Obafemi Awolowo University Press, 1992.
Turaki, Y. *Foundations of Traditional Religions and Worldview.* Nairobi: International Bible Society Africa, 2001.
Van der Leeuw, G. *Religion in Essence and Manifestation.* New York: Harper & Row, 1963.
Witte, J. Jr., editor. *Christianity and Democracy in Global Context.* Boulder, Colorado, 1993.
Wnuk-Lipinski, E. "Vicissitudes of Ethical Civil Society in Central and Eastern Europe." Paper read at the *Society for the Study of Christian Ethics* on the theme: Political Ethics and International Order, Wadham College, Oxford, August 23–27, 2006, 1–8.
Yinger, J. M. *The Scientific Study of Religion.* New York: Macmillan, 1970.

11

Shari'a, Democracy, and Civil Society
The Case of Northern Nigeria

Umar Habila Dadem Danfulani

Introduction

Some of the indices for measuring and determining the level of civil society are the presence of democracy and good governance, the enhancement and maintenance of high levels of human rights, respect for rule of law, transparency and the due process in economic matters and decision making, political stability, and the achievement of Human Development Index (HDI) in the living conditions of citizens. Democracy promotes and enhances the human rights of citizens and it supplies regular constitutional opportunities and level playing ground for peaceful competition to political office among different groups without forcefully excluding any significant sector of the populace.[1] Democracy evolves and sustains a number of institutions guaranteeing freedom of political choice, a high level of civil and political liberties, multi-party political electoral system, institutionalization of the opposition, and sustenance of the rule of law.[2]

However, most ordinary Nigerians will likely define democracy, not along the line of Platonian, Aristotelian and/or Athenian conceptions, but with cynicism and derision. This is more a reflection of its failure; that is, the fact the democratic experiment has so far failed to

---

1. Nnoli, "Ethnicity and Democracy in Africa," 4.
2. Nwokedi. "Democratic Transition and Democratization," 4.

provide food on the table:³ political, economic, social and religious stability, peace and progress in Nigeria. This notwithstanding, the clamor for democracy by Nigerians is based more on the desirability rather than feasibility of the system, in the belief that it will nurture peace and transparency and thus sustain a healthy economic growth and national development.

Shari'a is the general normative system of Islam as historically understood and developed by Muslim jurists from the first to the third, and from the eighth to the tenth centuries EE. *Shari'a* includes a much broader set of principles and norms than legal subject matter.⁴ Spelt as *"shari'ah," "shari'a," "shariah," "sharia," "Shariÿah,"* and *Sharîcah*, it emanates from the root word *At-Tashri'*, which is the abstract form of *Sha-ra'a*.⁵ *Shari'a* is the divine law guiding the affairs of the Muslim faithful from birth to death.⁶ *Shari'a* is based on the interpretation of the *Qur'an* and *Sunnah* (traditions), as supplemented by juridical techniques, such as *ijma* (consensus of the jurists) and *qiyas* (analogy). The *shari'a* developed as a systematic body of theology and jurisprudence during the first three centuries of Islam, making it over twelve centuries old, as a body of law divinely revealed by Allah for the governance of *dawla* state and *duniya* society.⁷

Shari'a is defined as "a way, course, rule," "a path, or tract; a path leading herds of animals to a large stream of water" or "the way to a watering place."⁸ "It is [. . .] the path believed by all Muslims to be the path shown by Allah, the creator himself through his messenger, Prophet Mohammed."⁹ It is a body of rules and regulations—a body of laws, in the form of commands and prohibitions, prescribed to govern and guide all spheres of human life—in religion, politics, commerce, social interaction and culture. *Shari'a* refers to criminal *hadd/hudud* aspects of life.¹⁰

---

3. Kukah, *Democracy and Civil Society in Nigeria*, 1ff.

4. An-Na'im, *Islamic Family Law in a Changing World*, 1.

5. Ambali, *Practice of Muslim Family Law in Nigeria*.

6. Yusuf, "An Overview of Shari'a Law and Practice in Nigeria," 129.

7. An-Na'im, *Toward an Islamic Reformation*, 12ff; "Islam and Human Rights in Sahelian Africa," 89; cf. Bouslimani, "Islamism in Algeria," 301n. 2.

8. Isma'il, "Shari'ah Sources and the Defence of Women's Rights," 140.

9. Doi, *Shariah*, 2; Nasirm, "Cedaw and the Women Under Sharia," 20; cf. Byang, *Sharia in Nigeria*, 36; cf. Wakili, *Sharia and OIC in Nigeria*, 4.

10. Isma'il, "Shari'ah Sources and the Defence of Women's Rights," 140.

In Nigeria, the conflict over the expansion of *sharia* laws beyond civil matters to cover criminal issues generated a great deal of controversy in recent times. This gave birth to so-called *sharia* compliant states in twelve out of nineteen states of the defunct Northern region of Nigeria, which include Zamfara, Jigawa, Kano, Katsina, Kebbi, Sokoto, Niger, Borno, Kaduna, Gombe, Yobe and Bauchi from October 1999. The exercise was accompanied by a great deal of violence across the northern states, particularly in Kaduna (from March 2000) and Jos (since September 2001).

This chapter examines four areas in the interaction between religion and politics in Northern Nigeria. First, it concerns itself with the interplay between democracy and *sharia* in Northern Nigeria, which led to the expansion of *sharia* to cover criminal aspects of law as well. Secondly, the chapter discusses political *sharia* and human rights with particular focus on the rights of women, Christians (*Tamani* Association of Hausa-Fulani Christians and other Christians in Northern Nigeria, including those from the Middle-Belt and those from Southern Nigeria), and the rights of persons living on the fringes of Hausa-Fulani Muslim society, such as the *Maguzawa* who actively participate in mediumistic spirit possession (*wasan bori*). The paper opines that from its expansion in 1999, *sharia* has had a tremendously negative impact on Christians living in the *sharia* compliant states contrary to the claim of political *shariarists* that *sharia* will not affect Christians.

Thirdly, the paper provides an analysis of political *sharia* as a tool employed either for the emancipation of the masses (*talakawa*) or for the negation of same. The clamor for, and employment of *sharia* law is examined in relation to the establishment and promotion of civil society in Northern Nigeria. It questions the validity of the emancipation slogan of *sharia* propagandists by asking whether indeed the *talakawa* are yearning for *sharia* or for something else. For instance, have the living conditions of the *talakawa* improved with the expansion of *sharia* law according to the belief that it will usher into being a utopian world in Northern Nigeria? What are the social-economic, industrial, educational, literacy, and health conditions in Northern Nigeria today? Fourthly, and finally, what are the implications of politicians presiding over *sharia* expansion in Northern Nigeria? Can extremists ever have enough of *sharia*, or to what extent can *sharia* be expanded to the satisfaction of anti-establishment Muslim extremist groups? The paper examines the possibility of the establishment of an Islamic theocratic state against the backdrop of *shari'a* as a "Self-Determination" Movement in Nigeria as proposed by Lubeck, Lipschutz and Weeks.[11]

A Brief History of Shari'a in Nigeria

A revolutionary Fulbe led the *jihadic* reform movement from 1804 that greatly transformed and northwestern Nigeria and introduced *shari'a* in the area.[12] A similar development also occurred in the northeast under the Kanuri. Islamic law was exclusively enforced in both the Sokoto and Borno emirates.[13] Shehu Uthman bin Fodiye was a fiery and radical Muslim preacher and charismatic leader/scholar, who, together with his son Muhammed Bello and brother Abdullahi, carved out a geographically vast, multi-ethnic Muslim empire extending across northern Nigeria, Niger, and Cameroon, known as the Sokoto Caliphate—the largest and most complexly organized pre-colonial African states. He was influenced by Islamic revivalism that was centered around Mecca and Medina.[14]

Therefore, Uthman bin Fodio and the El-Kanemi forged two extensive and complexly organized highly bureaucratic Islamic states in both Sokoto and Borno prior to British conquest. These caliphates prospered and expanded under British rule, while Islamic law provided cultural cohesion prior to and throughout the colonial period. The British:

> Indirect rule introduced—borrowed from India—by rationalizing the existing policies and practices of the *jihadic* or pre-colonial administration at the lowest cost to the treasury of the Crown. The British outlawed slave raiding and trading (not slavery), initiated and buttressed higher poll tax, forced labor, powers of the ruling class over *talakawa* commoners. Muslim district heads were placed over non-Muslim subjects, Christian

---

11. Lubeck, Lipschutz and Weeks. "Globality of Islam."

12. See Steed and Westerlund, "Nigeria"; Stamer, *Islam in Sub-Saharan Africa*, 19ff.; Clarke, *West Africa and Islam*, 77ff; and Rosander, "Introduction," 1–27, 115 for details.

13. Ostien, *A Study of the Court Systems of Northern Nigeria*, 5; Schacht, *An Introduction to Islamic Law*, 86.

14. Lubeck, Lipschutz and Weeks, "Globality of Islam," 14.

missionaries were banned from proselytizing in Muslim areas; traditional juridical checks on autocratic power were eroded; and most importantly, Islamic law was institutionalized and rationalized throughout northern Nigerian usually by borrowing from British legal institutions already established in Sudan and Egypt.[15]

Anderson asserted:

> At present ... Islamic law is more widely, and in some respects more rapidly applied in Northern Nigeria than anywhere else outside Arabia ... [T]he case of Northern Nigeria was, indeed, almost unique, for up till [1960] this was the only place outside the Arabian Peninsula in which the Islamic law, both substantive and procedural, was applied in criminal litigation—sometimes even in regard to capital offences ... This is due to the fact that the orthodoxy of the Fulani Jihad has been preserved first by a century of virtual isolation and then by half a century of colonial administration; for the Muslim Emirates have naturally tended to take refuge in an almost fictitious orthodoxy and rigidity in the in the face of any un-welcomed demands or innovations, while Protecting Power has almost invariably respected this attitude in return for the willing co-operation otherwise forthcoming.[16]

The introduction of English law in colonial Nigeria did not lead to the abolition of "such local laws and customs as were found good."[17] (Thus, the Nigerian legal system emerged from a colonial legacy that recognized, besides English Common Law, the equity and statutes of general application and growing bulk of locally-enacted laws, various bodies of customary law throughout the country, which includes *shari'a*, where applicable.[18]) So, from colonial period to contemporary times, *shari'a* has always been placed at the disposal of Muslims in the North, and it has to a large extent governed their mode and conduct of life, with the exception of matters placed within the jurisdiction of Federal and State high courts.

---

15. Ibid., 15.

16. Anderson, "Law and Customs in Muslim Areas of Africa," 116 and Lubeck, Lipschutz and Weeks, "Globality of Islam," 15.

17. Elias, *Nigerian Legal System*, 3.

18. Elias, General, *Law in a Developing Society*, 128.

By 1900, the British Native Court Proclamation placed the *shari'a* courts at a par with Customary courts, stating that "these courts are to administer native law and custom prevailing in the area of jurisdiction and might award any type of punishment recognized thereby, except mutilation, torture, or any type of punishment, which is repugnant to natural justice and humanity." This notwithstanding, the Muslim North saw native laws as synonymous with Islamic law—a dual system of law functioned where the *shari'a* continued to deal with matters affecting the personal status of Muslims. This was applied in adjudication of cases amongst Muslims concerning marriage, divorce, family relations, inheritance, land ownership, custody or guardianship of infants, *wakf* endowment of wills and succession, debt, slave emancipation, and other questions relating to Muslim personal law. Business transactions in markets, sale and pledge of land (except those subject to Right of Occupancy granted by the governor), are also regulated by *shari'a*. This way the British merely modified and sustained *shari'a* law administered by courts of emirs and alkalis, which hitherto entertained both civil and criminal cases. Under a modified *shari'a* law, the British made a distinction between homicide and manslaughter, repelled the *shari'a* ruling of *rajm* (stoning to death) in the case of *zina* (adultery), upheld imprisonment for theft instead of amputation/mutilation of the hand, and abolished the payment of *diya* indemnity in lieu of capital punishment. The modern *shari'a* politicians have returned to the legal system which the colonial masters met and modified from 1900.

This implied that the British in practice suspended the punishment for *hudud* crimes (stoning for adultery, amputation for theft, etc), while the emirs and their clients continued to administer *shari'a*-based civil and criminal court system. This meant that Islamic social movements, educational institutions and cultural practices thrived under the improved security, transportation infrastructure, commercial protection, and the *Pax Britannica* provided by colonial power. This provided conducive atmosphere for the emergence of popular Islamic revivalist *turuq* led by *Sufi* brotherhoods among the urban-based Muslims scholars, the commercial classes infiltrating the trading networks and cells of merchants, craftsmen and artisans, transforming education, female seclusion, mysticism, pilgrimage, and public piety. The *Tijaniyya* and *Qadiriyya turuq* led this Islamic revivalist movement, taking advantage of a more efficient transportation system to establish and extend the frontiers of their network of scholars, schools, and mosques throughout the commercial and cultural networks of West Africa.[19]

From 1955, profound statutory and constitutional changes with far-reaching implications for Northern Nigeria made it possible for appeals hitherto impossible to be made against the decision of alkali *sharia* court judges. The emir's court was originally the final court of appeal. Henceforth, appeals from Area Courts lie in *sharia* Court of Appeal on Muslim personal law and to the High Court on all other *sharia* matters.[20] Thereafter, appeals go to the Court of Appeal and finally the Supreme Court from both lower courts. The Court of Appeal was welcomed by Muslim jurists as a means of protecting Muslim law from the intrusion of English law.[21] When the politicians at the pre-independence conference of 1958 decided the 1960 constitution should have a provision that "a person shall not be convicted of any offence unless the offence is deemed and penalty therein is prescribed in a written law.[22] Under the new Procedure Code passed in 1960, courts were no longer permitted to exclude the testimony of non-Muslims or women. A *sharia* Court of Appeal was established in Kaduna, the regional headquarters of the North on October 1st, 1960. It was composed of a *Grand Qadi*, a Deputy Grand *Qadi*, and two other judges trained in Islamic law.[23]

This integrative bond of Islam and the Fulani and Kanuri empires gave a large part of the north a certain feeling of identity that has lasted to contemporary times. This feeling of identity is because "a policy of preserving the very special identity of the Northern Province was consciously followed by [the British]" and under Indirect Rule, "the north entrenched itself in a policy of self-protective withdrawal from Western culture." This policy of self-withdrawal is described as *Jihadin Nafs*, since Western political models and bureaucracy were then regarded by the Muslims as *bid'a*, an innovation "in the hands of blue-blooded aristocracy, a narrow based oligarchy whose legitimacy as members of the ruling class derived from membership of the royal

19. Lubeck, Lipschutz and Weeks, "Globality of Islam," 15.

20. Kukah, *Religion, Politics and Power*, 116, cf. Kumo, "Organisation and Procedure of Shari'a Courts," 49.

21. Kukah, *Religion, Politics and Power*, 117.

22. Bello, "Obstacles before the Shari'a."

23. Keay and Richardson, *Native and Customary Courts of Nigeria*, 74.

nobility.²⁴ This laid the foundation for the rejection of colonialism together with its whole premise of civil society—Western education, capitalist economy, social and legal institutions as *bid'a*, an innovation of the "Christian West," and therefore an attempt to return the high level Islamic civilization back to the *jahiliyya* period of ignorance. The ideal and most acceptable civilization is *shari'a*, which possesses more suitable and better institutional counterparts than those of the West. Such belief is still held by most of the Muslim north even to contemporary times. Many Muslims saw Christianity as the underlying fabric of Western and secular culture introduced by the British, regarding it as a foreign encroachment that should be resisted at all costs.²⁵

The colonial *modus vivendi* gave Islam great prestige in Northern Nigeria, thus making emirs and imams quite powerful. In doing so, they used Islam as an insulated spring board for legitimizing their position as spiritual and political leaders,

> at various times the emir has served as imam, leader of the dominant brotherhood, as final *shari'a* court of appeal, as chief repository of religious symbols, as maintainer of the Islamic constitution, and as contact with international and political culture in Kano.²⁶

Indirect Rule, therefore, enhanced the status and vast unchecked powers of the emirs, while chieftaincy institutions were based on Hausa-Fulani emirate model. This emirate model was imposed everywhere in the Middle-belt and, in some instances, the emirs of the North sent Hausa-Fulani rulers to govern some Middle-belt ethnic minorities. This continued well after colonial take and deep into the period of independence. The inclination to manipulate religion for economic gain, power, and authority, was thus built into the body politic of Northern Nigeria at quite an early stage.²⁷

The colonial decision to keep Christian missionaries out of areas claimed by the Caliphates as Muslim areas, otherwise known as the 'non-interference' policy, gave Islam an added advantage and served

24. Kukah, *Religion, Politics and Power*, 17; cf. Whitaker, *Politics of Tradition*, 420
25. Bello, "Obstacles before the Shari'a." 19.
26. Paden, *Religion and Politics in Kano*, 367; cf. Williams and Falola, *Religious Impact in the Nation State*, 4.
27. Illesanmi, *Religious Pluralism and the Nigerian State*, 112; cf. Usman, *Studies in the History of the Sokoto Caliphate*.

to widen the gap between Muslims and non-Muslims in the region. It further boosted the idea of "the Muslim North," an ideology once sown in the hearts of northern Muslims caused them to consider all non-Muslims in the area as outsiders, strangers, and non-indigenes. This mentality led to the confinement of non-Muslims to the *sabon garis*, "stranger's quarters" or new towns. It is an ideology that prevents the north from proper integration with the rest of Nigeria and such a mentality certainly birthed the clamor for the implementation of *shari'a* law in *shari'a* compliant states in Nigeria today.

Shari'a and Democracy

With the successful return of Nigeria to multi-party democracy in 1999, there have been two national elections (in 1999 and in 2003), with both witnessing mass irregularities. With a high youth bulge and high level of unemployment and unemployables, youth restiveness, violence, and vigilantism, voting processes in the north witnessed cross-state and cross-border voting (with influx of youths from Chad and Niger Republics), mass rigging, intimidation of party opponents and women, and the open operation of money bags, among others.

The politics of passing the *shari'a* Bill into Law in Nigeria started from 1999 to 2002, when twelve Muslim governors in Northern Nigeria passed bills that introduced the *shari'a* Penal Codes in their State Houses of Assemblies and signed the bill into law as a result of direct electioneering campaign promises. Thus the entry of political *shari'a* in Nigeria's body politics from 1999 is not by accident. Politicians used the *shari'a* issue to gain popularity, votes, and praises from praise singers. In September 1999, Governor Ahmad Sani, the democratically-elected Governor of Zamfara state, introduced a bill containing proposals for making *shari'a* the official law into his state House of Assembly for debate. He also pronounced the adoption of *shari'a* law, as well as the Muslim code of conduct, in a public ceremony that received emissaries from Saudi Arabia and other Muslim countries on October 27, 1999.[28]

This gave birth to a feverish rush of core Muslim states in the North towards following suit. For instance, Niger state, with 47 percent Christian population, declared *shari'a* the official state law in

---

28. Danfulani, *Sharia Issue and Christian-Muslim*, 13ff., 52ff.

November, 1999, in the same manner with Zamfara state. Other *shari'a* states were to follow the same way, until all twelve *shari'a* compliant states had emerged by 2001.[29] In all these states, the executive and legislative arms of government formulated the *shari'a* Law Bill, passed it through their respective Houses of Assemblies, and the governors put in place *shari'a* Implementation Committees. Those who championed the cause of *shari'a* re-implementation were not only politicians, as opposed to the *ulema*—the cleric, but like the *Hamas* government of Palestine, they used the democratic institution and process to achieve this feat towards theocracy. Some scholars believe that since state governments in Nigeria today retain all powers not formally allocated to the federal government, sub-national states possess the right to implement *Shari'a* law at the criminal level and to create local *shari'a* police (*hisba*) and courts to enforce *Shari'a*.

However, a section of the Nigerian society regard *shari'a* as being inconsistent with the constitution of the Federal Republic of Nigeria, since Section 38(1), states, "If any other law is inconsistent with the provisions of this constitution, the constitution shall prevail and that other law shall, to the extent of the inconsistency, be void."[30] It is because of this belief that the re-implementation of *shari'a* is seen as totally unconstitutional by a section of the Nigerian society that is calling for a constitutional review. Their goal is to limit the powers of state houses of assemblies to promulgate and bring into existence what in effect is the equivalent of a state religion or theocracy.

The role of youths in fueling the Shari'a riots, Miss World, the Prophet Muhammad Cartoon, and other riots related to religion are not in doubt. Youths are found everywhere in Northern Nigerian towns and villages, staying idle because of lack of any gainful employment. There are four categories of youths in Nigeria. First, secondary school and university graduates that are unemployed. They may remain idle for long before getting any form of gainful employment. Second, are early leavers ("drop outs") at various level of the school system. They are unemployable since they are without any specific form of training and may remain idle for long before being employed in low job areas. Third, are the *almajirai* pupils of both mobile and static Muslim Koranic (*madrassa*) schools, typical of Northern Nigerian Muslim

29. Ibid., 52ff.
30. Ibid.

communities. The fourth group is the *Yan Cirani* (seasonal unskilled migrant labourers), mainly from the far or core North, with some of them coming from neighbouring countries such as the Chad and Niger Republics. They roam about major cities of Nigeria trying their hands at menial jobs such as brick-laying, well sinking, shoe polishing, or the peddling of water, petty foodstuff and/or household equipment. They also provide ready muscle for carrying out attacks and mayhem on members of other religions in the case of conflicts such as the *shari'a* riots. This way *Shari'a* re-implementation in twelve states has been associated with rioting, mayhem, pogroms, break down of law and order, fanaticism, and intolerance. These multi-faceted and complex factors birthed a general shift to Islamism.[31]

There has been an unhealthy youth bulge, which has given birth to youth restiveness and violence vigilantism, mass vote rigging, cross-state and cross-border voting, intimidation of party opponents and of women politicians, emergence of money bags and money politics throughout Nigeria. Unfortunately, the *shari'a* proponents gloss over the destruction of life and property, claiming that no revolution is expected to come without the shedding of human blood. All that matters is that the laws of Allah are reinstated in such a manner that they take pre-eminence over the laws of human beings—the Constitution of the Federal Republic of Nigeria.

The legal system introduced by the British is discredited by the *shari'a* proponents who consider it a Christian and Western legal system. The *shari'a* movement in the core Muslim northern states and the restoration of *shari'a* criminal law is widely popular. It is so popularly legitimated that it would win by a landslide if put to the vote on the ballot.[32] According to Lewis, he discovered in a survey he conducted that the clamor for *shari'a* in the area is so popular that 66.3 percent of northern and 38 percent of southwestern Muslims favor the expansion of *sharia* law.[33]

---

31. Lubeck, Lipschutz and Weeks, "Globality of Islam," 6.
32. Ibid., 13–14, 18.
33. Ibid., 18.

Political Shari'a and Human Rights

Nowadays, Islam gains publicity in relation to catastrophes, terrorism, fundamentalism, and fanaticism. Such labeling for distinct Muslim movements possessing articulate political objectives gained credence worldwide particularly after the Islamic revolution in Iran in 1972.[34] This produces and elicits preconceived attitudes that strongly affect our way of reacting towards Islamic culture. However, the association of catastrophes and fundamentalism with worldwide Islamic resurgence does not necessarily preclude the fact that there are some Christian, Hindu, and other religious groups sharing similar characteristics. Furthermore, this negative picture of Islam in the public domain does not imply that most Muslims are fanatical, quite on the contrary only a small number of Muslims are terrorists, fundamentalists, and fanatics.

This notwithstanding, the expansion of *shari'a* law in Northern Nigeria has tended to generate a number of violent crises in some of the states, such as the one that occurred in Kaduna in 2000. In addition to the violence it has triggered, the re-implementation of *shari'a* in the manner in which it is being carried out in Nigeria has the capacity and tendency of trampling upon the rights and human dignity of citizens (see Danfulani, *forthcoming* for details).

An-Na'im asserts that *shari'a* seeks to secure certain rights for specific groups of people as typologised by religion and gender, rather than apportioning equality in rights and status for all. *Shari'a* law discriminates between men and women (in terms of serving as witness before the courts) and between Muslims and non-Muslims.[35] For instance, in Jaafar Mohamed Nimeiri's Sudan, there is a polarization of the Arab and Islamic north against the African and Christian south, which suffered increasingly from the grand scheme to ethnically cleanse out and annihilate the Southern black Christian population out of Sudan. Furthermore, the introduction of *shari'a* in Sudan, Pakistan, and Afghanistan under the Taliban regime only left behind poverty, a lack of civil society, economic crisis, violations of the rights of women and children, hunger, disease, etc. An-Na'im states further:

---

34. Holm, "Introduction," 16, Hallencreutz, and Westerlund, "Introduction," 5.

35. An-Na'im, *Toward an Islamic Reformation*, 74–94, 170–79; "Islam and Human Rights," 88.

> Many traditional formulations of *shari'a* are fundamentally inconsistent with universally accepted principles of international law. It would therefore follow that even if *shari'a* can be enforced by the state, those problematic principles are morally untenable and practically impossible to maintain. It is not therefore surprising that there is no state in the world today, including self-proclaimed so-called Islamic states like Iran, Saudi Arabia and Sudan, that is practically capable of actually living by all the dictates of *shari'a*, as commonly understood by Muslims everywhere.[36]

Human rights very often find its most fundamental theoretical expression in religion. It implies the existence of human beings and the fact that humans naturally possess inalienable and individual rights.[37] Human rights are based on insights that human beings are capable of exterminating life on earth, which is against the justice, peace, and the integrity of creation.[38] While human rights are universal since they are due to every human being by virtue his/her humanity and are not restricted by race, gender, religion, language and/or nationality, *shari'a* law suffers restriction.[39] A part of the political mess we are seeing in Northern Nigeria today is as a direct result of fifteen years of continues military (mis)rule and dictatorship. This long period of military misrule in Nigeria systematically battered human rights for a very long period, thus making Nigerians wake up feverishly towards embracing democracy in 1999 to protect their fundamental human rights[40]

With reference to *shari'a* in Nigeria, and based on the experiences of the past, the human rights of women, non-Muslims and minorities, apostates, and persons living on the fringes of Muslim societies in the north should be of utmost concern. For instance, liberal Muslims regard *shari'a* as a private and spiritual issue that should be individually and not collectively enforced. Can the rights of such liberal Muslims that are not in full support of the re-implementation of a *shari'a*, pro-

---

36. An-Na'imm, *Shari'a and Positive Legislation*, 39.

37. Haar, *Rats, Cockroaches and People Like Us*, 3–5; cf. Tergel, *Human Rights in Cultural and Religious Traditions*, 22.

38. Tergel, *Human Rights in Cultural and Religious Traditions*; cf. Nash, *Rights of Nature*, 22ff.

39. An-Na'im, "Islam and Human Rights," 85.

40. Federal Republic of Nigeria, *Report of the Presidential Committee on the Review of the 1999 Constitution*, 55.

mulgated by politicians, be guaranteed under the same law they seem to be rejecting? This notwithstanding, critical intellectuals amongst *shari'a* propagandists do not identify with human rights concerns and progressive politics. They criticize only interpretation of *shari'a*, the ignorance of the judges, the *hizbah* or vigilante police, the outrageous gender bias in *shari'a* enforcement, the interest of the poor, the lack of preparation, absence of codified law, etc.[41]

Concerning the gender question, the rights of women, the current stress of *shari'a* law, both in theory and practice marginalizes women. This is because Islamization of tradition eradicates and even denigrates education for females.[42] This is exemplified and experienced in the public whipping of women under the Taliban regime of Afghanistan, for what is referred to as indecent dressing, lack of decorum, and other such flimsy excuses. The subordinate status of women is linked with the *Qur'an*, the *Sunnah*, and *shari'a*.

The truth is not in doubt that women from the *shari'a*-compliant states are among the mass populace in Nigeria that cannot exercise their fundamental rights and freedom effectively because of their poverty and low social status. Women here live in a male-dominated society, where gender disparities in economic and political power sharing are important factors constituting towards poverty of women in the North. Despite the fact that poverty affects households as a whole, women bear an extra and disproportionate burden of managing the household consumption and production under conditions of increasing scarcity. Poverty is particularly acute for women living in rural households because they lack economic opportunities and access to resources, including credit lines and the ownership of land.[43]

Girls' access to education is even worse—being characterized by customary attitudes, early and/forced marriage, high incidence of teenage pregnancy, inadequate gender sensitization, gender biased teaching and educational materials, sexual harassment, and inaccessible educational facilities. Girls' and womens' poor performance in school results from heavy domestic work. The dropout syndrome among girls is very high since they leave early to marry as this is their station in life according to Hausa/Islamic tradition of Northern Nigeria.

41. Lubeck, Lipschutz and Weeks, "Globality of Islam," 13–14.
42. Rosander, "Introduction," 7.
43. Ladan, "Women's Right and Access to Justice," 78ff.

This is because the readiness of girls for marriage and therefore conjugal/sexual obligations, child birth, and motherhood is not only decided by the growth of the body, since the *Maliki* school of Islamic law that dominates in Northern Nigeria holds the view that a girl of five years may be fit for sex, though other schools place it at nine.[44] The problem of early marriage is also accentuated by the issue of *tallah* (street hawking). It causes a great deal of problems for the young Muslim girl who is very often forced to marry early, with no skill she becomes economically weak, and she may be the victim of Vesicovaginal fistula among other problems.

Thus sexuality remains, in general, a very significant public (and hence, by extension, political) issue in most Muslim societies,[45] where girls pay the cost of being born female. Though the woman is correctly viewed as benevolent wife/mother, her picture as destructive sexual creature that is present, in varying degrees, in the ideology, culture and symbolic system of Muslim Northern Nigeria marginalizes and dehumanizes women. This, however, is based on a striking preoccupation in Islamic discourse with female sexuality, and especially with its regulation and control.[46] Even the famous Islamic philosopher from Al-Azar University, Hassan Hanafi admits that one of the characteristics of the Islamist approach is that it is dominated by:

> A sexual perception of the world: they start with the veil, with segregation and turning the eye away and turning the voice down. [Yet] the larger the veil, the greater the desire to recognize what it hides! There is more to social and political life than such a sexual perception of social relations that classifies a citizen [only] into man and woman, male and female... Such a classification might not signify a virtue, but may indicate a repressed sexual desire and a sublimated sexual deprivation.[47]

Next is the knotty problem of guaranteeing the human rights of minorities under an Islamic theocratic government in Northern Nigeria. During the colonial period, the Middle-Belt wanted a separate region carved out for them because they felt their political future

---

44. Bambale, *Crimes and Punishments under Islamic Law*.

45. Ayubi, *Political Islam*, 45.

46. Moghadam, "Women, Work and Ideology in the Islamic Republic," 225; cf Ayubi, *Political Islam*, 45.

47. Hanafi, *Al-Turath wa al-tajdid*, 42, cf. Ayubi, *Political Islam*, 45.

was in jeopardy if they were left together with the Muslim North. They complained that Muslim emirs imposed rulers upon them in total disregard for their traditions and treated their rulers with levity, since they could be dismissed or retired on the slightest excuse. They feared that Muslim prohibitions on alcohol may be extended to them. They found distinctions between the sexes unnatural, since their women normally played important political roles, owned property, and even took titles. They complained of difficulties experienced in obtaining permission to build churches, mission compounds and schools and C of Os for their landed properties. They complained over restrictions placed on the sale of religious literature and permission to freely preach the gospel of Christ, lopsided allocation of radio and television air time for religious broadcasting in favor of Islam, and extreme pressure placed upon chiefs from the Middle-belt to change their religion to Islam.[48]

They greatly feared the *shari'a* law and the *siyasa* politics operating in the region that distinguished between a Muslim and non-Muslim, since the evidence of a male Muslim was greater than that of a Christian or animist, while sometimes the only evidence admissible in any degree was that of a devout male Muslim. An accused Muslim could swear by the *Qur'an* and be freed, while the non-Muslim had no such alternative before a *shari'a* Court. In matters of indemnity for manslaughter, the beneficiaries of the victim got full compensation where he was a Muslim, only half in the case of a Christian, and only one-fifteenth in the case of an animist. In the case of homicide, *shari'a* law took no account of intention or provocation.[49]

In the period of politicking of the first republic, a woman politician from the Middle-belt who had contributed greatly to the development of the north had cause to complain that "people of the far or upper north were considered 'proper northerners', better still if you were a Muslim, but Middle-beltan, Muslims and non-Muslims alike were 'another class of northerners.'"[50] If non-Muslims are considered an inferior class of northerners, the rights of Christians living in the twelve *shari'a* compliant states of Northern Nigeria cannot be guaranteed. There are two major categories of Christians living in the *shari'a* compliant states. First are Christians that are indigenous to the *shari'a*

---

48. Williams and Falola. *Religious Impact in the Nation State*, 131ff.
49. Ibid.
50. Kukah, *Religion, Politics and Power*, xi.

compliant states. These are composed of the *Maguzawa* (traditional Hausa people that were practicing bori mediumistic or spirit possession cult initially found in Kano, Jigawa, and Katsina), the Dukkawa (found in Kebbi and Sokoto), Kanuri Christians, and the TAMANI which stands for *Tarayyar* or *Ja'amiyar Masihiyawan Nijeria* (meaning Association of Hausa, Fulani and Kanuri Christians). The second category is composed of Christians that have migrated to the *shari'a* compliant states from other parts of Nigeria prior to the re-implementation of *shari'a* law in the area. They migrated from the Western, Eastern, South-South and the Middle-Belt areas of Nigeria to the far North. Under theocratic Islamic government, their rights can never be guaranteed.[51]

Furthermore, there are minority Christians living on the door steps of the *shari'a* compliant states. These are the Middle-Belt Christian minorities. For most non-Muslim minorities of the Middle-belt, the introduction of indirect rule was simply a rubber stamp of the emirate system in the North. The imposition of indirect rule on diverse ethnic groups where it did not exist, merely confirmed Hausa-Fulani domination, while it at the same time institutionalized the inferiority status of Middle-beltans.[52] In 1958, some minorities, particularly Christians and animists from the Middle-belt, who were agitating for separation from the Islamic North prior to independence, complained that *shari'a* was unfair to those of them it covered and might be extended further after British hand over.[53] There has been great apprehension in the Middle-belt, since the expansion of *shari'a* law in twelve states of the north, because the Christians fear the institution of the unfavorable *dhimmi* status on Christians in the region. Concerning this, Deng asserts:

> At best, non-believers may be allowed to stay under the terms of a special compact which extremely restricts their civil and political rights. Believers who are not Muslims, mainly Jews and Christians, are allowed partial citizenship under *shari'a* . . . and are disqualified from holding any position of author-

---

51. See Danfulani, "Responses of TAMANI and Other Christian Groups," 183–92, for details.

52. Turaki, "Socio-Political Role and Status."

53. Bello. "Obstacles before the Shari'a."

ity over Muslims. As such [they] are disqualified from holding general executive or judicial office in their own country.[54]

There are other human rights issues such as capital punishment meted out to apostates under *shari'a* law.[55] There is also the fundamental tension, for example, between *shari'a* notions of the Muslim state (the *umma*, which is the exclusive community of Muslims) and national unity amongst Muslims and non-Muslim citizens of the modern state.[56] These positions cannot be acceptable if national unity is to be achieved in Nigeria.[57] Thus:

> The prospects of human rights in the region are inversely related to the dominance of *shari'a* values and institutions. The more Islam is identified with *shari'a* in popular belief and practice under an 'Islam in Africa' model, the less likely will human rights norms be accepted and implemented by the Muslim population at large.[58]

Finally, the rights of persons living on the fringes of Muslim society, for instance, the *Maguzawa* members of the *bori*-spirit possession cult—*masu wasan bori* (women of low status)—*karuwai* (the prostitutes), *bazawara* (divorcees), and *yan daudu* (homosexuals), can never be guaranteed. The attempt of *shari'a* here to get rid of moral decadence is only at best-skin deep, since the privacy of rich men, who hide in five star hotels with their concubines and prostitutes, is guaranteed. At the end, there is an attempt to cleanse only the moral conscience of the poor and not that of the rich and powerful, while the sin of immorality becomes a class or VIP sin and changes venue, from hotels found in the ghettoes and other such facilities to five-star hotels and private or government guest houses.

Shari'a, the Talakawa Masses and Civil Society

Contemporary Muslim politicians strive to be guided by the *shari'a* like previous reformists or *Mahdis*, such as Shehu Uthman bin Fodiye,

54. Deng, "Scramble for Souls, 221–22.

55. An-Na'imm, "Islam and Human Rights,"88–89; cf. "The Islamic Law of Apostasy.

56. Ibid., 89.

57. An-Na'imm, "Introduction," 222.

58. An-Na'im, "Islam and Human Rights," 90.

Sultan Bello, and the Sardauna of Sokoto, Sir Ahmadu Bello. The present champions of *shari'a* regard themselves as emancipators who want to use Islamic law to transform society into a theocratic state by bringing them into conformity with the laws of Allah. Furthermore, a great number of Muslims in Nigeria believe that the re-implementation of *shari'a* will solve all intractable social, economic, moral, political, ethnic and spiritual problems,[59] and usher into existence a Utopia in *shari'a* compliant states. Thus the masses (*talakawa*) view it as the vehicle that will create a utopian society, free of immorality, material want, theft, and such other vices.

Unfortunately, however, most of the masses do not see through the hypocritical life of their *shari'a* governors—their luxurious life styles, massive corruption, looting of the treasury, adulterous life, obstruction of justice, and lack of respect for the rule of law. Others who can see through the thickness of this whole charade of hypocrisy are powerless to change the status quo, while the rich continually grow fat on the peoples' collective wealth, leaving the majority of the masses to live in abject poverty. They ride over the masses in style, promising what they know the will never give. Such is the characteristic of a utopia, where we very often know how things should be, far more than describing how things are in reality.[60] It can, however, be argued that "the more unrealistic, the better, for the more unattainable the utopia appears to be, the greater the readiness on the part of the people to accept the reality as unavoidable."[61]

Today, *shari'a* law has been operational for six years in most *shari'a* compliant states of Northern Nigeria. How are these states fairing? What is the relationship between the political *shari'arists* and the *talakawa*? What are the living conditions of the *talakawa* masses in *shari'a* compliant states of Northern Nigeria? Concerning the Islamic principles of poverty and redistribution of wealth, the *Qur'an* and traditions of the Prophet (SAW) enjoins the Muslim *ummah* to develop the spirit of brotherly love and sisterhood towards fostering an egalitarian existence.[62] Islam encourages the redistribution of wealth through the *Zakat* institution, which most of the *shari'a* compliant

---

59. Hunwick, "Sub-Saharan Africa and the Wider World of Islam," 50.
60. Ayubi, *Political Islam*, 17.
61. Ibid., 25.
62. Qur'an 57, 7.

states of Northern Nigeria have established. This is in accordance with *Hadith* of the Prophet that says, "He is not a true Muslim who eats his fill when his next door neighbor is hungry,"[63] the administrator who rules over the affairs of Muslims but remains indifferent to their plight, needs and poverty, Allah will also be indifferent to his own plight, needs and poverty.[64] The responsibility for the collection of *zakkat* and its redistribution is supposed to rid the *ummah* of poverty because the *ummah* including the caliph, have equal rights in the wealth of the community.

It is however, difficult to rid the North of its general abject poverty. This is because, aside from its backwardness in terms of education, industrial infrastructure, economic strength, general development and civil society, the economy and religious map of the North have been systematically devastated by years of ethno-religious riots and civil unrest that consistently moved from one city to the other from the 1980s to the 1990s and into the millennium. This has had the net effect of creating an atmosphere of desperation, socio-political and economic instability, personal and collective insecurity, general individual and collective poverty and increased criminality.[65]

This rather unpleasant situation was made worst by the riots that greeted the re-implementation of *shari'a* by politicians in Kaduna, Plateau, Niger, and Gombe states. The situation is certainly not helped by the Miss World and the Prophet Muhammad Cartoon riots in parts of Abuja, Maiduguri, Bauchi, Kano and Kaduna. Furthermore, the expansion of *shari'a*, together with the institutions and reforms that it has birthed, have not substantially improved the living conditions of the *talakawa* masses in the *shari'a* states. It is therefore, clear that:

> ... the fundamental issues of the relationship between reforms and the living conditions of the tens of millions of Nigerian citizens of the Muslim faith who are mostly directly affected are almost completely ignored. Many of the politicians, journalists and clerics on both sides of the controversy seem to want to turn the whole matter into one of a "jihad" or a "crusade," in wanton disregard of what will be the grim consequences to millions of innocent men, women and children of

63. Al-Bukhari, al-Adal al-Mufrad, 52, quoted in Yusuf, "An Overview of Shari'a Law and Practice in Nigeria."

64. Abu Dawood, *Sumaa*, vol. 2, 481.

65. see Danfulani, *Expansion of Sharia Criminal Law*.

both the Muslims and Christian faiths who have been living together peacefully, amicably and fraternally, and whose living conditions are daily deteriorating irrespective of their religious faiths.[66]

The enormity of the challenges of justice as envisaged by the *shari'a* is still to be fully grasped and appreciated by Nigerians, including Muslims themselves who have chosen to live under it. The impression received from many current advocates of *shari'a* is that it is essentially a punitive political arrangement put in place to deal with partakers of alcoholic beverages, enforce the Islamic dress code, amputate the limbs of thieves, refurbishment of mosques,[67] flogging of fornicators, and the stoning of adulterers. Compared to the grim realities of the poor living conditions of the *talakawa* masses in Northern Nigeria, these moral problems and *shari'a* measures to curb them are quite beside the point. The works of Mohammed, Adamu and Abba[68] and Lubeck, Lipschutz and Weeks[69] have provided numerous facts and figures concerning the daily lives of the *talakawa* masses that militate not only against the peoples' ability to meet the stringent moral conditions of *hudud* related punishments, but also constitute obstacles towards fulfilling the religious obligations of millions of Muslims. There is a great deal of poverty, hunger and destitution, ignorance, illiteracy and educational backwardness, lack of basic health facilities, inadequate housing, economic crunch, and political instability. The living conditions of Muslims have been largely ignored by the *shari'a avant garde* and swept under the carpet once power was secured and the spoils of office were being enjoyed. *Shari'a* defines the Islamic faith, it spells out how, when, and where a Muslim prays. It goes beyond faith to define the basic requirements for existence of a Muslim, covering education, health, housing, nutrition, employment, environment, commerce, neighborliness, transportation, and communication, among others.

Despite the fact that every Local Government Council in Nigeria receives anywhere between 20 and 30 million naira per month or even more from the Joint Federation Account, with state government getting almost 2 billion naira monthly, there is hardly any meaningful

66. Mohammed, Adamu and Abba, *Living Conditions of the Talakawa*, 2.
67. Ibid., 8.
68. Ibid.
69. Lubeck, Lipschutz and Weeks, "Globality of Islam."

development recorded in the majority of LGCs and states, including *shari'a* compliant areas. On the contrary, economically there is a great deal of chaos, human misery, economic mismanagement, economic anarchy, lawlessness and disorder, technological incompetence (petrol, electricity, and water supplies), overdependence on petroleum rents, numerous Muslim-Christian riots, ethnicity (over 300 ethnic groups) and inter-ethnic divisions and conflicts, settler/indigene fights, and competition over other scarce resources. The third republic, though democratic, is widely corrupt, incompetent, and incapable of managing Nigeria's vast economic resources, security, and social problems. Salaries are paid, civil society groups are thriving, and press/media freedom in guaranteed.[70]

The economy is controlled by a few rich people, while 70 percent of Nigerians live in abject poverty, that is, on less than one dollar a day, yet the States and Local Governments Areas receive huge allocations from the Joint Federation Account and there have been remarkable increases of these allocations since 1997. In fact, a survey shows that the figures literarily doubled between 1997 and 1999. For example, Kano received 2.0 billion naira in 1997, but in 1999, it was 4.3 billion naira, while the Ogun State allocation almost tripled from 1.4 billion naira in 1997 to 3.1 billion naira in 1999. Niger State received 1.5 billion from January to March 2000, almost representing the total figure it received throughout 1997.[71] The increase in budgetary allocation is even higher for local government councils in Nigeria, recording first a doubling, then a tripling and finally almost a quadrupling. For example, between June 1999 and May 2000, the fourteen LGs of Zamfara State shared 77.5 million naira in June 1999, 150.9 million naira in September 1999, 207 million naira by December and 229.8 million naira by May 2000—an almost 300% increase. This is besides many other internal sources of revenue accruing to the states and LGCs from industries located in the states, vehicle registration and particulars, fees charged for stores in both urban and rural markets, and the poll tax among others.[72]

Heavy economic and social problems have increased since the diminishing of the petroleum boom in 1981. This is evident in the

---

70. Ibid., 5.
71. Mohammed, Adamu and Abba, *Living Conditions of the Talakawa*, 26.
72. Ibid., 26.

widespread criminality, police corruption, vigilantism, truncating of the rule of law, misadministration of public services, and political corruption. In 2000, 70.2 percent of Nigerians lived under $1/day and 90.8 percent live under $2/day.[73]

The poverty rates reveal that Northern *shari'a state* rank among the poorest with less access to amenities, health facilities and other government services.[74] From 1980 to 1996, poverty increased from 17.7 million to 67.1 million, relative proportion of poverty-stricken Nigerians rose from 28.1% to 65.6% within the same period. The Middle class—the non-poor—declined and diminished from 72.8% down to 34.4% of the population from between 1980 and 1996. The incidence of poverty is generally higher in the *shari'a* states than non-*shari'a* states, reaching 83% of the population in the five poorest states.[75]

This has proven sufficiently that the states are in a good position to substantially improve the living conditions of the *talakawa* masses in the North. It is well-positioned to provide better education, good road networks, basic health facilities and services, essential infrastructure for economic improvement, and regeneration and subsidised inputs for the agricultural sector, which employs the bulk of the *talakawa* masses, for example, irrigation and dry season farming equipment. It is also clear that the bulk of the wealth and resources are in the hands of the state. However, the principles of the redistribution of wealth as laid down by in the *Qur'an* and the *Sunnah* of the Prophet (*SAW*), encapsulated in the institution of *Zakat*, are completely negated and subverted by the political *Shari'arists*, while they grow rich daily on the public treasury, fueling crises and creating chaos to cover their tracks. In fact, the numerous ethno-religious conflicts that ensued (in 1999) have diverted attention of the public from where these huge funds are being channelled providing a clear coast for these political *Shari'arists* to loot and empty the state treasury for their own benefits. They hinged this on so called security votes and other such empty contingencies, whereas for the majority of ordinary folks—the *talakawa* of the north—living in abject poverty in *Shari'a* compliant states has been accepted by faith, since they have been taught to consider poverty as

---

73. Lubeck, Lipschutz and Weeks, "Globality of Islam," 5–6.

74. FOS, 1999.

75. Sokoto, Kebbi, Zamfara, Bauchi, Gombe. See Lubeck, Lipschutz and Weeks, "Globality of Islam," 6, 22.

an act of God. Sanusi Lamido is not a prosperity Christian gospel preacher or Pentecostal Church founder, but a good Muslim, yet he declared:

> Against this background we see the error of those who insist that "poverty is from God" and pretend that Islam does not give attention to material well being. I have myself heard scholars argue that our masses should not expect material upliftment as a "dividend" of *Shari'a*. "The *Shari'a* is the law of Allah," they say, "and people should obey leaders who implement it without expecting material results." Umar wrote in his letters to Abu Musa: "The best of men in authority is he under whom people prosper and the worst of them is he under whom people encounter hardships."[76]

In fact, a great number of Muslim women that become pregnant out of wedlock and thus constituting threatening targets of *shari'a* stones were victims of abject poverty who, like Safiyyatu Hussaini, were enticed into committing *zina* (adultery) by the "occasional gifts" of their more economically buoyant boyfriends. For instance, Safiyyatu Hussaini was sentenced to death by stoning by the very society that was unable to cater for her because it does not run a social welfare scheme for the less privileged. However, Safiyya's farmer-fisherman boy went away scot-free from *shari'a* stones.

The wretched living conditions of most Muslim families militate against any application of *shari'a*. Most Muslim families live in such appalling and poverty-stricken communities that it is impossible for them to live according to the tenets of their religion and embrace *shari'a* in its totality as a way of life. The majority of the Muslim population of the North lives in squalid ghettoes, which are well-known for their lack of decent housing and privacy. This tends to promote immorality and indecency. In such ghettoes,

> it is common to see . . . a Muslim family of seven living in a dilapidated two-room apartment and sharing a compound with several other Muslim families in similar circumstances. In the first place, there cannot be any privacy in such a situation, as husbands and wives are forced to be intimate with each other within the sight, or hearing, of their children, some of whom might even be grownups. The children are thus forced to become adults before their time. No wonder, the growing

---

76. Abu Yusuf, kitab al-Kharaj.

incidence of incest, pre-marital sex and homosexuality in our urban areas. In such circumstances, it is also obvious that the incidence of adultery will be very high.⁷⁷

The seeds of moral decay and decadence are thus sown in homes even before the children are ripe for sex education. Some of the *shari'a*-compliant states have a high rural population of subsistent farmers that live without adequate health care facilities, water, electricity, and education—a zone of high incidence of poverty, ignorance, disease, poor diet and poor shelter, and high unemployment among the youths, with the majority of them remaining unemployable.⁷⁸

Illiteracy is high—95%—and the mean years of schooling is very low: between 0.43 and 1.52. Secondary school enrollment is low. The tertiary institutions in the region are inadequate to contain the teeming number of youth. The incidence of stunted growth in children and wasting, "acute under-nutrition," "under-weight" and under nutrition on the parts of mothers in is highest in the region. This is not due to lack of agricultural resources since a substantial proportion of food and meat is produced in the North. A high number of children suffer from diarrhea resulting from poor sanitary and toilet conditions, poor water supply, lack of safe water. Prenatal care for expectant mothers is scanty and the North is disadvantaged in access to modern healthcare, ignorance made male parents in the area oppose inoculation and vaccination for children in the false belief that some Western agents want to kill them or control the population. The area registers higher infant mortality rates than the Southern part.⁷⁹

Though the UNDP registers a very low Human Development Index (HDI) for Nigeria, the states with low HDI are concentrated in the North, while states in the South have generally higher HDIs.⁸⁰ In the area of industrialization, less than 20% of industries are located in Southern Nigeria.⁸¹ Most facilities for generations, energy, power, and

---

77. Muhammed, Adamu and Abba, *Living Conditions of the Talakawa*, 32.

78. Ladan, "Women's Rights under Shari'a in Northern Nigeria," 78.

79. FOS, "Demographic and Health Survey," 38, 101 and UNDP, "Nigeria: Selected Health Indicators by Region," 108; USAID, *USAID Integrated Baseline Health Survey*, 36. Yazid, "Role of Agriculture in the Development of Nigeria," 142.

80. UNDP, "Nigeria: Selected Health Indicators by Region," 4.

81. Ibid., 101.

electricity are located in the South. In the North, less than 8% of the vast rural population has access to electricity.

The Expansion of Shari'a as a "Self-Determination" Movement

Lubeck, Lipschutz and Weeks[82] proposed the thesis that the clamor for the re-implementation of *shari'a* in Northern Nigeria is a "Self-Determination" Movement. They cast the *shari'a* re-implementation exercise in twelve states of Northern Nigeria within the framework of "striving for a major change in the values and organization of society" and identity construction.[83] For An-Na'im,

> Muslims have the right to self-determination, including the right to define and express their Islamic identity as they deem fit. But that cannot be on the basis of the enactment and enforcement of *shari'a* as such, because whatever norms are enforced as positive law is the political will of that state, and can never be *shari'a* as commonly understood by Muslims to mean the expression of divine will. Consequently, I hold, the pretence of enforcing *shari'a* through positive legislation (as claimed by the present governments of Iran, Afghanistan, Pakistan, Saudi Arabia and Sudan or advocated by Muslim political activists in many other countries) is dangerous naivety, if not cynical manipulation of the sentiments of Muslims.[84]

I stated elsewhere that the clamor for *shari'a* may well be a Muslim response to the rise and predomination of Pentecostal Christianity and together with its 'born again' cliché among a large sector of Nigerian Christianity, including the President Olusegun Obasanjo who publicly declared that he is a born-again Christian.[85]

Northern Muslims claim autonomy and self-determination based on *shari'a* re-implementation as a means of achieving a major change in moral/spiritual values and the way in which they believe their society should be organized.[86] Thus in his *Ten Good Things About*

---

82. Lubeck, Lipschutz and Weeks, "Globality of Islam."
83. Ibid., 2
84. An-Na'im, *Shari'a and Positive Legislation*, 30.
85. Danfulani, "Sharia Issue and Christian-Muslim," 54ff.
86. Lubeck, Lipschutz and Weeks, "Globality of Islam," 6.

Shari'a, Ostien sees in *shari'a* re-implementation attempts by Northern Nigerian Muslims to reclaim their past/pre-colonial heritage.[87] *Shari'a* advocates argue that *shari'a* law has been the basis of civil and personal law among consenting Muslims prior to and since independence and that the Nigerian criminal law is largely derived in part from it. They appeal to populist, anti-imperialist sentiments by arguing that the postcolonial secular state was imposed upon Nigeria by colonial powers that introduced Western/Christians laws (the English Common Law) in the northern region regardless of the desire of the Muslim majority in the region. They point to the failure and dismal performance of the Nigerian court system, referring to the obstruction of justice resulting from massive corruption of judges, slow trials often resulting in long periods of imprisonment, or imprisonment without trial, and failure to uphold the rule of law, etc that very often characterizes the legal system in Nigeria. They however forget that the *shari'a* system was guilty of these same offences and even more prior to the colonial period, during the colonial period, and after independence. They also argue that *shari'a* should be re-implemented because there is a widespread knowledge of the principles of Islamic law jurisprudence (*fiqh*) among the general Muslim population. Again, this clearly is not the case as has been exemplified in numerous misapplications of *shari'a* law in cases handled by ignorant jurists presiding as *qadis* over *shari'a* courts.[88]

Lubeck, Lipschutz and Weeks, state that the *shari'a* movement as self-determination can be comprehended against the backdrop of the practices of the *sufi/turuq* and the conflict and opposition their praxis elicited and incited among the contemporary *salafi*-inspired Islamist mms, of the late 70s and early 80s in Nigeria.[89] Their intense discursive struggles involved a great deal of violence, blood shed, mass movement, and declaration of apostasy (*takfir*), especially targeted against Sufi *turuq*. This led the *Salafi*, or anit-*turuq* movements such as the JIBWIS, alias *Izala* and *Ikhwan*, to launch their anti *bid'a*, innovation movements. They describe this position thus:

---

87. Ostien, *Ten Things about Shari'a*, 1.

88. See, for example, Ladan, *Women's Rights under Shari'a in Northern Nigeria*, 67–78.

89. Lubeck, Lipschutz and Weeks, "Globality of Islam," 16.

Charismatic leaders of the *Sufi* movements/*turuq* claim mystical insight into the experience of the divine, realized through dreams and/or supernatural experience. *Muqaddams* ritually initiate members into the *turuq*, with their lineage of initiation being ranked according to proximity to the *turuq* founder or his *zawirah*, or the Prophet and multiple lineages are eagerly sought by *turuq* members. Membership of a *tariqah* entails the acquisition of secret/Gnostic knowledge, secret prayers, chants, trances, drumming and claims of special meditations through their founder to Allah or the Prophet.[90]

They opined that the *salafi* reformats recognize only *Qur'an*, *Sunnah* and the legitimacy of the four rightly-guided caliphs, rejecting all others, including ritual trappings, dancing, chanting, and Gnostic claims as *bid'a* innovation. They reject belief in saints and intermediaries between individuals and Allah, including apportioning sainthood to the Prophet Muhammad and the founders of the *sufi-turuq*. They also reject as *bid'a* innovation the belief in mystical powers and insights of charismatic *Sufis*, veneration of *Sufi* saints, the observation of their birth days, founding dates, and visits to their tombs. They also reject the belief mystical powers and use of charms, amulets, relics, water, *Qur'anic* erasure, and other magical forms. The *salafi* therefore viciously attacked Sufi leaders and their followers "for tolerating, promoting and sustaining the popular industry of itinerant, uneducated *ulama* (*mallam*) who earned a living by making and selling charms, amulets or *Qur'anic* erasure, that is, the writing of verses on wooden slates, which are then washed off and consumed as a religious portion."[91]

However, despite controversies that has trailed the relationship between the *sufi turuq* and the *salafi* movements, it is not true that the one is in support of *shari'a* re-implementation, while the other is totally opposed to it as claimed by Lubeck, Lipschutz and Weeks when they asserted, "On the other hand, the *shari'a* movement is promoted by groups like JIBWIS, alias *Izala* with strong linkages to the global Islamic networks operating within Nigeria."[92] This implies that the current public discourse concerning the establishment of an Islamic state amongst Muslims in Nigeria is hinged on the belief that Islamists, traditionalists or fundamentalists, in Nigeria represented by the *Izala*

90. Ibid.
91. Ibid.
92. Ibid., 18.

and *Ikhwan* (The Brothers), are the proponents of an Islamic state, which will systematically and comprehensively implement *shari'a*. Those opposed to it are seen as the secularists, liberals, or nationals, in Nigeria represented by the *turuq* such as *Qadriyya* and *Tijaniyya*. Considering the Nigerian case as a classic example, this Islamist/secularist dichotomy and the assumption on which it is based is much more complex than the position being canvassed.[93]

Islamist/*salafi* groups such as Izala and Ikhwan (The Brothers) have not been peculiar in their pursuit for *shari'a* re-implementation in northern Nigeria anymore than the Sufi sects. On the contrary, the older *Sufi turuqs* such as the *Qadriyya* and *Tijaniyya* pursued a hard line approach towards *shari'a* re-implementation. Led by *Alhaji* Mustapha Jokolo, the deposed emir of Gwandu, the emirs in the north garnered a firm populist support for it by mobilizing scholars and their subjects. Together with their clerics, they fully participated in the rallies, seminars and conferences that culminated in widespread public demand for and general re-implementation of shari'a in twelve states of the north.[94] Thus the *shari'a* expansion project enjoyed wide grassroots support throughout the Muslim north.

In fact, *Sheikh* Mallam Ibrahim El-Zakzaki (of Zaria), the radical leader of the *Ikhwan* (The Muslim Brothers) is, for instance, not in support of *shari'a* re-implementation in Northern Nigeria. Though an Islamist sect, the leader argues that it is too early to introduce *shari'a* in the manner in which it is being pursued because Nigeria is not ripe for it, the non-Muslim population is still too large and it is impossible to achieve the desired goal because theocracy cannot be successfully imposed on a secular state. He argues further that the majority of Nigerian Muslims are not theologically educated enough to understand and follow the tenets and demands of *Shari'a*. He is of the opinion that Muslim theologians should rather give more time to engage in thorough awareness campaign and education of the Muslim masses, both males and females, before the full introduction of *shari'a*. This will make it easier for the operation of *shari'a* in all its ramifications and the masses will not be unduly manipulated by operators of the system. Such a programme would also allow for the training and

---

93. An-Na'im, *Shari'a and Positive Legislation*, 36.

94. See Danfulani, "Sharia Issue and Christian-Muslim Relations in Contemporary Nigeria," 15ff.

recruitment of judges educated in *shari'a* law. El-Zakzaki also regards mass poverty and institutionalised corruption as detrimental to the immediate re-implementation of the full corpus of *shari'a*. Mass abject poverty, he opines, ensures that the control of the enormous wealth of the country is in the hands of only a small percentage of the population, leaving aside the vast majority of the people impoverished. This gives rise to increasing crime rate in a society where many "genuinely steal" for the mere sake of surviving and not just for the sake of it. He thinks it is unfair for a thief to be punished under the *shari'a* if he had stolen out of dire need. He clearly saw through what is, in effect, a charade of *shari'a* re-implementation since the champions of *shari'a* re-implementation are politicians instead of the *ulama* Muslim jurists and scholars. He criticized the hijacking of the process by politicians, the low level awareness of *shari'a* law among lower cadre jurists and the *talakawa* masses and called for the intensification of Islamic *da'awah* towards Islamizing Nigeria as a precondition for *shari'a* re-implementation.

It should, therefore, be noted that though Islamist groups such as the *Yan Izala* and El-Zakzaki's *Ikhwan* (The Muslim Brothers) are largely anti-*Sufi* in character,[95] the mother branch of the *Ikhwan* did not support *shari'a* re-implementation for reasons given above, while it was a splinter or breakaway group from the *Ikhwan*, known as the *Jama'atul Tajdidil* Islam (JTI), based in Gusau, the capital of Zamfara, with small branches in Zaria, Kaduna, Katsina and most especially Kano gave their full support to the *shari'a* re-implementation. The JTI, in fact formed the support base of Ahmed Sani, Yariman Bakura and the former executive governor of Zamfara who initiated the whole *shari'a* palaver in his states in 1999. However, this does not in anyway imply that the older *Sufi turuq* were left behind in desiring and campaigning for the re-implementation of *shari'a* in Nigeria.

The Problem of Viewing *Shari'a* as Self-Determination Movement

There are attendant problems and dangers trailing the use of the *shari'a* re-implementation by propagandists as a self-determination movement. First, it is evident that such militant Muslim groups in Northern

---

95. Lewis, Robinson and Rubin. *Stabilizing Nigeria*, 77.

Nigeria, as the *Ikhwan* of Zaria led by El-Zakzaki and the *Hijra* or *Taliban* group that emerged for a short period in Kanamma of Yobe State, long for the re-enactment of the golden epoch of Islam in Nigeria. As already indicated by the *Hijra* or Taliban group of Kamanna of Yobe State, can extremists ever have enough of *shari'a*, or to what extent can it be expanded to the satisfaction of anti-establishment Muslim extremist groups?

The second problematic refers to the question whether the Muslim masses *talakawa* of Northern Nigeria are really yearning for *shari'a* or are they are hungry for something else which *shari'a* law may well never satisfy? If they are indeed clamoring for *shari'a* law, one is tempted to ask the question, which *shari'a*? This is because, though Northern Nigerian Islamic law is based on the *Maliki* School of jurisprudence, there is so far no uniform application of *shari'a* law in the area. For instance, the application of *shari'a* law in the *Shari'a* compliant states vary significantly as one moves from one state to the other. This is notwithstanding the position of groups that reject the present *shari'a* as political *shari'a* and therefore not meeting their own stricter standards. For instance, El-Zazaki, the leader of the *Ikhwan*, believes that *shari'a* cannot and should not be applied in a multi-religious Nigeria until the whole of Nigeria becomes an Islamic country.

Thirdly, there is the question concerning the implications of politicians presiding over *shari'a* expansion in Northern Nigeria. Where is the authority of the *ulama*, jurist and Islamic scholars who are the spiritual leaders? Even if they have participated as chairmen and members of committees set up by various states to oversee the embedment of *shari'a* re-implementation, they are not the ones in the driving seat. Thus the scenario presented to us is that of a traumatized, poverty-stricken people, plagued and haunted by disease, (among myriads of other problems, some of which are enumerated above), shaken by a self acclaimed born-again Christian President (Olusegun Obasanjo). In their response towards containing such a threatening Pentecostalism in a country experiencing an upsurge of within Christendom, Muslims in the north had to look elsewhere for emancipators, in the process the *talakawa* masses, together with the political system were hijacked by political *shari'arists*. The *Ulama* were sidelined, pocketed and silenced into doing the bidding of the political class and the voices of the few who smelled a rat were muffled by the political juggernauts of the North, who promised that with the laws of God governing human beings, "things will be better." Most of the *talakawa* masses cannot see through the hypocritical life style of their *shari'a* governors, their lush lifestyles which can only be supported by massive corruption, looting of the treasury and money laundering at home and abroad, and their total disregard for the rule of law and deliberate obstruction of justice. They grow fat on the collective wealth of the people leaving the majority of the people living in abject poverty and squalid ghettos. They ride over the masses in stylish motor vehicles, sprawling mansions while promising what they know they will never give.

Fourthly, it should be recognized that demands for *shari'a* have been on the political agenda of Nigeria in various forms since the Constitutional Assembly debates of 1976–77. If the view that the *shari'a* imbroglio emanated as a response to the demands of southern groups for greater regional autonomy, as exemplified in the demands for a Sovereign State of Biafra in the East, and similar agitations in the south-south, then it must be accepted that the sovereignty and unity of Nigeria as a nation is not only being tested to the extreme, but that its demise as a nation may well occur very soon.[96]

Conclusion

The challenge facing *shari'a* critics is to modernize Islamic law.[97] The conditions for the full implementation of the *shari'a* corpus are clear. The one hundred stripes prescribed for fornication and stoning for adultery applies only in a society where lewdness and mixing of the sexes have been removed and where women find it easy to marry, people are God-fearing. *Shari'a* stones and whipping cannot take place in a filthy society where sexual excitement is rampant, pornography is available, the cinema and other amusement spots have been taken hostage by sexual perversion, and a society where mixed, semi-nude parties are accepted as the acme of social progress.[98]

Such conditions were totally absent in the Muslim societies of Northern Nigeria prior to the re-implementation of *shari'a* from 1999

---

96. Lubeck, Lipschutz and Weeks, "Globality of Islam," 18.

97. An-Na'im, *Islamic Family Law in a Changing World*, 14.

98. Ladan, "Women's Rights under Shari'a in Northern Nigeria," 75; Cf. Maududi, *Islamic Law and Constitution*, 55.

and they are absent in contemporary Northern Nigeria about seven years after *shari'a* re-implementation. Some *shari'a* compliant states such as Kano, Bauchi, Kaduna, and Katsina have no doubt taken giant strides towards the provision of housing for civil servants in the urban areas, electricity and water to some of their rural societies, but this constitutes a mere drop of water in the Sahara Desert. All of the *shari'a* states have created *Zakat* boards for the collection and redistribution of the poor tax to Muslim beneficiaries, with small Christian populations enjoying such allowances in Kano state, but the compliant among the poor still remains the same: as the *zakat* collected is far too small compared with the magnitude of poverty facing it. Moreover, officers of the *Zakat* boards are faced with various problems of collection ranging from refusal to conform with the new tax regime in preference to the traditional system of self disposal of *zakat* to outright reluctance to even give out *zakat* to the board.

Furthermore, Ministries of Religious Affairs, the *hisbah* local or *shari'a* police, Liquor and Drug Abuse Boards, and Committees for *da'awah* (the building and repair of mosques), among others have been created. However, there have hardly been substantial changes. The major change is that of a change of venue for "physical sins" to the effect that prostitution, the sale and drinking of alcoholic beverages, gambling, homosexuality, substance/drug abuse, and mediumistic or trance/spirit possession performance of the *bori* cult have all gone underground. This goes a long way to confirm the fact that human moral character cannot be changed by legislation. I thus agree with An-Na'im when he stressed, "In my view, *shari'a* cannot be enforced as positive legislation and remain the source of a religiously sanctioned normative system . . . Moreover, in view of the nature and role of the state in the modern global context, an Islamic state would not be practically viable."[99]

> Accordingly, past or present claims or demands to enforce *shari'a* through positive legislation by the state are based on a historical fallacy because that is inconsistent with the nature of *shari'a* itself, and impossible for the state as constituted today in any country in the world. In other words, it is neither possible to conceive of this possibility in theoretical terms, nor is

---

99. An-Na'im, *Shari'a and Positive Legislation*, 29.

it true that such a model existed in the past so that it can be re-enacted today.[100]

The *Shari'a* Penal Code existed in 1958, several decades before the clamor for the full embedment of *sharia* witnessed in 1999. The Penal Code was executed under the supervision of Sir Ahmadu Bello, the Sardauna of Sokoto and the then premier of the North. He did this in consultation with a panel led by Professor J. N. Anderson of SOAS, who carried out research in Pakistan, Sudan and the Middle-East. The consultants in 1958 did not prescribe *rajm* stoning for adultery, amputation for theft, or crucifixion for armed/highway robbery. Those who prescribed the *Shari'a* Code back in 1958 were not bad Muslims, and the political *sharia* propagandists of today are not better Muslims than them.[101]

Sharia sanctions concerning the cutting of hands and limbs of thieves/armed robbers, caning for fornicators and for those who patronize alcoholic beverages, stoning for adulterers, and the capital punishment for apostates, are not enough for the *talakawa* masses to celebrate the success of the restoration of the laws of Allah. This is because aside from the inability of *sharia* compliant states to strive towards poverty reduction, good governance for their citizens and the development of a civil society, even by Muslim standards, most of the governors of these states led very corrupt governments. In fact, if *sharia* were to be thoroughly applied in these states, most of the *sharia* governors will have their hands and limbs chopped off for theft, money laundering, and massive corruption, which very often leave their state treasuries empty. "The enforcement of a so-called Islamic state through positive legislation is a negation of the possibility of an Islamic way of life, not its realization [because] such efforts are doomed to failure at horrendous human and material costs and counter productive."[102]

There is no doubting the fact that Islamic societies have a right to self-determination in terms of asserting their identity, reclaiming and sustaining cherished cultural values and traditions. However, I agree with An-Na'im,[103] that to achieve this, "Islamic societies must categori-

100. Ibid., 32.
101. Political *Sharia* and the Obasanjo Regime. November 2, 2001 TV Interview, NTA 2001.
102. Abdullahi Ahmed An-Na'im, *Sharia and Positive Legislation*, 30.
103. Ibid., 36.

cally renounce any commitment to a romantic ideal of an Islamic state that never was, and expressly abandon expectations of the enforcement of *sharia* as such by the state." Muslims, like any other people, have the right to (political and cultural) self-determination; they are guaranteed the right to organize the lives (both private and public) in accordance with the guidance of their faith. However, self-determination is not an absolute right since the way in which one group exercises their rights portent consequences or implication for the rights of others.[104] An-Na'im described the situation correctly, when he asserts:

> An Islamic state as a political institution is conceptually impossible, historically inaccurate, and practically not viable today . . . the lack of historical precedent is more significant, I would add, in view of the total transformation of the local and global context in which the state has to operate today . . . A state constituted according to the theory of *sharia* is simply unworkable in the present national and international context. Difficulties facing this model include the profound ambivalence of the founding jurists of *sharia* to political authority. They neither sought to control nor knew how to make those who hold it accountable to the *sharia* itself. Economic activities will be crippled by the formal enforcement of prohibition of fixed rate of interest on loans (*riba*), and of insurance as based on speculative contracts (*gharar*). The enforcement of corporal punishments for certain specified offences (*hudud*) faces serious unresolved procedural and evidently objections, let alone human rights concerns about cruel, inhuman or degrading treatment or punishment. Another type of problem is that of the denial of basic citizenship rights for women and non-Muslims will face serious challenges by these groups internally, and by the international community at large.[105]

The pursuance of self-determination as freedom to change ones values, which will definitely adversely affect and infringe on another persons' rights, say the right of Christians living in the twelve *sharia* compliant states to sell and consume liquor in public, should not involve state legislation. Furthermore, legislation is not needed for enforcement of *sharia* law, which is a private affair to be observed at the discretion of the individual mind. For instance, that *riba* and *gharar* contracts are not illegal in a given country does not mean that

104. Ibid., 38.
105. Ibid., 37–38.

Muslims have to engage in these practices. Any person can choose to abstain from such commercial transactions or personal behavior in accordance with his/her religious convictions. Any enforcement of *shari'a* law by the state is undesirable, but individuals can privately choose to conform with the dictates of their religious beliefs.[106]

Some may argue that the concept of civil society is a Western, and therefore a foreign stereotype; individual liberty and/or freedom is the bogey of the twentieth-century colonial and neo-colonial enterprise—which ensures that the only news that is disseminated about Africa in the Western media is squalor, poverty and HIV/AIDS, while their mineral resources are still being harnessed; democracy is the latest instrument of imperialism for the sake of unequal free market—IMF and the destruction of the Nigerian economy; education is still defined from the Western paradigm, self-first, skills first, gain first, consumerist culture.[107]

The Islamic religion and Muslims worldwide have the capacity to develop a viable civil society, democracy, educational system, a sense of patriotism and a consumer culture that are culturally and religiously attuned and not in opposition to their way of life, without necessarily having to return to *shari'a* re-implementation. Attempts to recapture or re-enact historical events of the past (generally referred to as fundamentalism) have never been successfully pursued with desired successes by any human society. Moreover, the societies in which we live today are far more complex than earlier societies.

All states of Islamic societies signed and ratified all such international treaties as the UN Charter and are thus customarily bound by these internationally-acclaimed humanitarian laws. These sources set clear limits concerning what these Islamic states may or may not do, within and outside, and in their interrelationships with other states and their citizens. Other states practically act on these internally standardized principles while dealing with the Islamic states, economically, politically, socially, security etc.

---

106. Ibid., 38.
107. Bewaji, "Culture, Poverty and Civil society," 54ff.

Bibliography

Ahmad, Ali. "In Defence of Islamic Sharia." *Viewpoint Manawatu Evening* Standard, Palmerton North, New Zealand, Friday, October 25, 2002.

Ambali, M. A. *The Practice of Muslim Family Law in Nigeria*. Zaria: Tamaza, 1998.

An-Na'im, Abdullahi Ahmed. "Introduction: Competing Claims to Religious Freedom and Communal Self-Determination in Africa." In *Proselytization and Communal Self-Determination in Africa*. Edited by Abdullahi Ahmed An-Na'im, 1–28. Religion and Human Rights Series. Maryknoll, NY: Orbis, 1999.

———. "Islam and Human Rights in Sahelian Africa." In *African Islam and Islam in Africa: Encounters Between Sufis Islamists*, edited by David Westerlund and Eva-Evers Rosander, 79–192. London: Hurst, 1997.

———. *Islamic Family Law in a Changing World: A Global Resource Book*. London: Zed, 2002.

———. "The Islamic Law of Apostasy and its Modern Applicability: A Case from the Sudan." *Religion* 16 (1986) 197–224.

———. *Shari'a and Positive Legislation: Is an Islamic State Possible or Viable?* Kluwer Law International, 2000.

———. "Sudanese Identities." In *The Search for Peace and Unity in the Sudan*, edited by Francis Mading Deng and Paul Gifford. Washington: The Wilson Centre, 1987.

———. *Toward an Islamic Reformation: Civil Liberties, Human Rights and International Law*. Syracuse, NY: Syracuse University Press, 1990.

Anderson, J. N. "Law and Customs in Muslim Areas of Africa: Recent Developments in Nigeria." *Studia Islamica* 6 (1956).

Ayubi, Nuzih. *Political Islam: Religion and Politics in the Arab World*. London: Routledge, 1993.

Bambale, Yahaya Yunusa. *Crimes and Punishments under Islamic Law*. Kaduna, Nigeria: Infoprint, 1998.

Bello, Ahmadu. *My Life: An Autobiography*. London: Cambridge University Press, 1962.

Bello, Mohammad (Honourable Justice, Former Chief Justice of the Supreme Court). "Obstacles before the Shari'a." Keynote Address at the National Seminar on Shari'a in Kaduna held February 10–12, 2000. Friday, March 10. Forward by Mobolajie Aluko: *Idilinet*.

Bewaji, John A.I. "Culture, Poverty and Civil Society: A Critical Analysis of aspects of Leadership in Africa and its Diaspora." In *The Humanities, Nationalism and Democracy*, edited by Sola Akinrinade, Dipo Fashina and David O. Ogunbile, 54–86. Ile-Ife, Nigeria: Obafemi Awolowo University Press, 2006.

Bouslimani, Chabha. "Islamism in Algeria: The Risks and Prospects of Inter-Islamic Proselytization." In *Proselytization and Communal Self-Determination in Africa*, edited by Abdullahi Ahmed An-Na'im, 291–302. Religion and Human Rights Series. Maryknoll, NY: Orbis, 1999.

Byang, Danjuma. *Sharia in Nigeria: A Christian Perspective*. Jos, Nigeria: Challenge, 1986.

Clarke, Peter B. *West Africa and Islam: A Study of Religious Development from the 8th to the 20th Century*. London: Edward Arnold, 1982.

Danfulani, Umar H. D. *Expansion of Sharia Criminal Law and Human Rights in Northern Nigeria*. Forthcoming.

———. "Responses of TAMANI and Other Christian Groups to Shari'ah Implementation in Northern Nigeria." *MANDYENG: Journal of Central Nigerian Studies* (2002) 183–92.

———. "The Sharia Issue and Christian-Muslim Relations in Contemporary Nigeria." Studies on Inter-Religious Relations 15. Stockholm: Universitestryckeriet, 2005.

———. *The Talakawa Masses under Shari'ah in Northern Nigeria: Who Will Emancipate Them?* Forthcoming.

Deng, Francis Mading. "Scramble for Souls: Religious Intervention among the Dinka in Sudan." In *Proselytization and Communal Self-Determination in Africa*, edited by Abdullahi Ahmed An-Na'im, 191–227. Religion and Human Rights Series. Maryknoll, NY: Orbis, 1999.

Doi, Abdur-Rahman I. *Shariah: The Islamic Law*. Ibadan: Iksan Islamic, 1990.

Elias, T. Olawale, editor. *Law in a Developing Society*. Ethiope Law Series. Benin City, Nigeria:Ethiope, 1973.

———. *The Nigerian Legal System*. London: Routledge, 1954.

FOS. Federal Office of Statistics, Abuja, Nigeria. "Demographic and Health Survey, 1990."

FRN. Federal Republic of Nigeria, *Report of the Presidential Committee on the Review of the 1999 Constitution*, Section 13, Volume 1, Main Report, February, 2001.

Hanafi, Hassan. *Al-Turath wa al-tajdid (Heritage and Renewal)*. Cairo, Egypt: Al-Markaz al-Arabi, 1980.

Hallencreutz, Carl F., and David Westerlund. "Introduction: Anti-Secularist Policies of Religion." In *Questioning the Secular State: The Worldwide Resurgence of Religion in Politics*, edited by David Westerlund. London: Hurst, 1996.

Hermet, Guy. "Introduction: The age of Democracy." *International Social Science Journal* (May 1991) 249–55.

Holm, Nils, G., editor. "Introduction." In *Teaching Islam in Finland*. Religionsvetenskapliga Skrifter nr. 26. Abo: Abor Akademi, 1993.

Hunwick, John. "Sub-Saharan Africa and the Wider World of Islam: Historical and Contemporary Perspectives." In *African Islam and Islam in Africa: Encounters Between Sufis Islamists*, edited by David Westerlund and Eva-Evers Rosander, 28–54. London: Hurst, 1997.

Illesanmi, Simeon O. *Religious Pluralism and the Nigerian State*. International Studies African Series no. 66.Athens, Ohio: Ohio Center for International Studies Monographs, 1997.

Isma'il, Mustapha Hussain. "Shari'ah Sources and the Defence of Women's Rights." In *Shari'a Penal and Family Laws in Nigeria and in the Muslim World: Rights Based Approach*, edited by Jibrin Ibrahim, 139–71. Samaru, Zaria–Nigeria: Global Rights, 2004.

Keay, E. A., and S. S. Richardson. *The Native and Customary Courts of Nigeria*. London: Sweet and Maxwell, 1966.

Kukah, Matthew Hassan. *Democracy and Civil Society in Nigeria*. Ibadan, Owerri, Kaduna and Lagos: Spectrum, 1999.

———. *Religion, Politics and Power*. Ibadan, Owerri, Kaduna and Lagos: Spectrum, 1993.

Kumo, Suleiman. "The Organisation and Procedure of Shari'a Courts in Northern Nigeria." PhD Diss, SOAS, London, 1972.

Ladan, Mohammed Tawfiq. "Women's Rights and Access to Justice under the Shari'a in Northern Nigeria." In *Shari'a & Women's Human Rights in Nigeria: Strategies for Action*. Edited by Joy Ngozi Ezeilo and Abiola Akiyode Afolabi, 37–88. Somolu, Lagos: Frankad, 2003.

———. *Women's Rights under Shari'a in Northern Nigeria: A Case Study of Safiya" in Protection of Women's Rights Under Shari'a Law: Safiya Tugartudu Huseini–A Case Study*. Somolu, Lagos: Frankad, 2002.

Lewis, Peter M., Pearl Robinson, and Barnett R. Rubin. *Stabilizing Nigeria: Sanctions, Incentives and Support for Civil Society*. Center for Preventive Action. New York: Century Foundation, 1998.

Lubeck, Paul, Ronnie Lipschutz, and Erik Weeks. "The Globality of Islam: Shari'ah as a 'Self-Determination' Movement." Working Paper Number 106, Center for Global, International and Regional Studies, University of California, Santa Cruz, CA, 95064. Presented at the Conference on Globalisation and Self-Determination, London, Friday April 4, 2003.

Maududi, Sayyid A. A. *Islamic Law and Constitution*. New Delhi: Taj Company, 1986.

Moghadam, Val. "Women, Work and Ideology in the Islamic Republic." *International Journal of Middle East Studies* 20:2 (1988).

Mohammed, Abubakar Siddique, Sa'idu Hassan Adamu, and Alkasun Abba. *The Living Conditions of the Talakawa and the Shari'ah in Contemporary Nigeria*. Centre for Democratic Development, Research and Training. Occasional Publication, 2. Hanwa–Zaria, Nigeria, 2000.

Nash, R. F. *The Right of Nature, A History of Environmental Ethics*. Madison, WI: University of Wisconsin Press, 1989.

Nasir, J. M. "Cedaw and the Women Under Sharia." *Current Jos Law Journal* 5:5 (1999) 20–33.

Nnoli, Okwudiba. "Ethnicity and Democracy in Africa: Intervening Variables." CASS Occasional Monographs Number 4. Oxford, UK: Malthouse, 1994.

Nwokedi, Emeka. "Democratic Transition and Democratization in Francophone Africa." Paper Presented at the Conference of CORDESIA/Rockefeller Foundation Reflections on Development Fellows held in Bellagiog, Italy, September, 1992.

Obasanjo, Olusegun. Political Shari'a and the Obasanjo Regime. November 2, 2001 TV Interview, NTA 2001.

Ostien, Philip. *A Study of the Court Systems of Northern Nigeria with: A Proposal for the Creation of Lower Sharia Courts in Some Northern States*. University of Jos: Centre for Development Studies, Research Report n.1/99, June 1999.

———. "Ten Good Things About Shari'a." Lagos: *Newswatch*. July, 9, 2001.

Paden, John N. *Religion and Politics in Kano*. Berkeley: University of California Press, 1973.

Rosander, Eva-Evers. "Introduction: the Islamization of 'Tradition' and 'Modernity.'" In *African Islam and Islam in Africa: Encounters Between Sufis Islamists*. Edited by David Westerlund and Eva-Evers Rosander, 1–27. London: Hurst & Company, in Co-operation with the Nordic African Institute, Uppsala, Sweden, 1997.

Schacht, Joseph. *An Introduction to Islamic Law*. Oxford: Clarendon,1964.
Stamer, P. Josef. *Islam in Sub-Saharan Africa*. Königstein, Allemagne: Aide à l'Eglise en Détresse, 1996.
ter Haar, Gerrie. *Rats, Cockroaches and People Like Us: Views of Humanity and Human Rights*. The Hague, The Netherlands: Institute of Social Studies, 2000.
Tergel, Alf. *Human Rights in Cultural and Religious Traditions*. Uppsala Studies in Faith and Ideologies, 8. Uppsala: Acta Universitatis Uppsaliensis, 1998.
Turaki, Yusuf. "Socio-Political Role and Status of non-Muslim Groups of Northern Nigeria: Analysis of a Colonial Legacy." PhD diss, Boston University, 1982.
UNDP. "Nigeria: Selected Health Indicators by Region." *Nigerian Human Development Report*, 1996, Lagos, 1997.
USAID. The *USAID Integrated Baseline Health Survey* of 1995.
Usman, Yusufu Balo, editor. *Studies in the History of the Sokoto Caliphate*. Zaria: Nigeria: Ahmadu Bello University Press. 1979.
———. *The Manipulation of Religion in Nigeria, 1977–1987*. Kaduna: Vanguard, 1987.
———. "Rural and Agricultural Sample Survey, 1984/85 and 85/86." Federal Office of Statistics. *Katsina State in Nigerian Federation: The Basic Realities*. Kaduna, 1994.
Yazid, Imrana. "The Role of Agriculture in the Development of Nigeria." In *Nigeria: The State of the Nation and the Way Forward*. Adamu Mahadi, et al. Arewa House: Kaduna, 1994.
Yusuf, (Hon. Justice) Sanusi C. "An Overview of Shari'a Law and Practice in Nigeria."In *Shari'a Penal and Family Laws in Nigeria and in the Muslim World: Rights Based Approach*. Edited by Jibrin Ibrahim, 129–38. Samaru, Zaria-Nigeria: Global Rights, 2004.
Wakili, T. K. *The Sharia and OIC in Nigeria: Their Effects on Non-Muslims*. Seleja, Abuja: NOMAX, 2000.
Weiss, Bernard. The Spirit of Islamic Law, Athens, GA: University of Georgia Press, 1998.
Steed, Christopher and David Westerlund. "Nigeria." In *Islam Outside the Arab World*. Edited by David Westerlund and Ingvar Svanberg. Richmond, Surrey UK: Curzon, 1999.
Westerlund, David, "Reaction and Action: Accounting for the Rise of Islamism." In *African Islam and Islam in Africa: Encounters Between Sufis Islamists*. Edited by David Westerlund and Eva-Evers Rosander, 308–33. London: Hurst & Co, 1997.
Whitaker, C. Sylvester. *The Politics of Tradition: Continuity and Change in Northern Nigeria, 1946–66*. Princeton: Princeton University Press, 1970.
Williams, Pat and Toyin Falola. *Religious Impact in the Nation State: The Nigerian Predicament. The Making of Modern Africa Series*. Aldershot: Avebury, 1995.

# 12

Nigerian Civil Government and the Application of Islamic Law

Can Conflict Lead to Accommodation?

Yushau Sodiq

Texas Christian University, Fort Worth, Texas

> The Shariah issue in Nigeria raises both moral and legal questions. The moral questions we should be asking ourselves, as Nigerians, are twofold:
>
> 1) Why can Nigerian Muslim (or at least some of them) not leave the Shariah issue to rest in peace? 2) Why are Nigerian non-Muslims (or at least some of them) ever on alert to oppose every Shariah initiative? An objective dialogue on these moral questions would provide the mutual understanding essential to what I call a justical approach to the main question about the legality of the application of Shariah in Nigeria. When issues about rights and duties are in controversy, morality and reciprocity are essential factors that aid legality.
>
> —Mashood A. Baderin.[1]

Introduction

My attempt in this paper is to discuss the controversy about the constitutionality of the application of Sharia law in Northern Nigeria. Does the application of Sharia amount to Islam becoming the religion of the

1. Baderin, "Shariah Alteration."

state? Does applying severe punishment on Muslims through Islamic laws discriminate against them? I will bring forth the evidences for and against Sharia and analyze the causes of tension between the advocates of Sharia and its protagonists. While the supporters for and opponents against Sharia law hardly agree on what should be done to solve the problem of Sharia, we strongly believe that both parties can amicably work together and resolve this issue through a genuine dialogue and commitment to tolerance toward one another for the sake of peace. It is morally wrong for Muslims to impose their laws on those that do not adhere to their religious beliefs. Also, under democratic rule, citizens should be free to choose their legal systems even if these systems are informed by religious beliefs. Therefore, if Muslims opt to be ruled by Islamic laws, the Constitution should protect their interest and enable them to achieve their goals.

Nigeria and Its History of the Application of *Sharia* (Islamic law)

Nigeria, the most populated country in Africa, is beautiful and rich in culture and natural resources. Its inhabitants are from diverse ethnic groups and backgrounds. They speak different languages and subscribe to three different legal systems. Before the colonial occupation, Southern and Eastern Nigerians governed themselves through their kings and religious leaders. They followed Native laws, which were established and executed by the council of elders and their appointees. The Fulanis and Hausas in the North were governed by their Muslim leaders known as Emirs.They subscribed to Islamic law as far back as the 15th century. Of course, the full application of Islamic law in all aspects of life was not effective until the Jihad of Uthman Dan Fodio, who founded the Sokoto Caliphate in the early 19th century. Islamic law became the law of the land during his reign and the reign of his descendants. When Luggard conquered Sokoto in 1903, he found an elaborated system of law in operation in the North. He admired the system and retained it with minor modifications except the Islamic criminal law (*Hudud*), which he abolished. Since then, the Islamic law has remained in operation in Northern Nigeria until today. While Islamic law is applied in family matters in all Northern States, from the year 2000, twelve states from the North have opted for a full application of Islamic law in all aspects of life, including criminal laws (*hudud*). This application caused a lot of controversy between Muslims and non-Muslims, between Northern and Southern Nigerians.

What is Islamic Law?

Islamic law is the manifestation of the divine will, which finds its expression in the Qur'an, the Muslim scripture, and in the Hadith, the sayings, deeds, and approvals of the Prophet Muhammad. These two sources—Qur'an and Hadith—contain the revealed laws, which regulated the daily lives of the Muslims. These laws are technically known as Sharia, the path to the source of life that Muslims believe they have to follow. They believe that it would lead them to a peaceful and harmonious life. Sharia law is said to be comprehensive in that it includes belief laws (*aqa'id*), rituals (*ibadat*), civil and transactional laws (*mu'amalat*), and ethics (*Akhlaq*).[2] This inclusive nature distinguishes Islamic law from Common law, which regulates only the transactional laws. Common law deals not with how people should behave or practice their religions. It separates between the church and the state; it deals not with religious issues. On the contrary, Islam separates not between church and state[3] and hence the Islamic laws regulate all aspects of human lives. Muslims believe that the religious life is not divorced from the mundane life.

In addition, the laws of God as expressed in the Qur'an and Hadith require proper understanding in order to be applied. Therefore Muslim jurists developed the science of (*Fiqh*) as a tool to understand the Qur'an and Hadith. The scholars who specialize in employing this method are called (*Fuquha*) the jurists. They are in charge of interpreting the law, applying, and expanding it to areas, which are not covered by the primary texts, the Qur'an and Hadith. To facilitate such a process, they explore *Itjihad*, a method by which the jurists exert their efforts to address and apply the law to novel issues not addressed by the Qur'an or the Hadith. This process is known as the "process of crack-

---

2. Hasan, *Principles of Islamic Jurisprudence*, 1.

3. Islam does not specify any particular system of governance to be followed by the Muslims. They are at liberty to choose any system which serves their interest as long as the law of God is observed. Hence they can choose democratic system. Democracy is not against Islam as some have alleged.

ing the nuts."[4] The nut metaphorically represents the basic law revealed by God. But in order for the nut to be useful for humans, it has to be cracked properly and diligently. There are many tools available today to crack any nut. However, in the past, the nut was cracked by stone, then by steel—hammer, then by machines, and today by pressing a button in major factories. Certainly, the law of God has been interpreted, understood, and applied in the past in different ways. Today, the jurists must employ all the tools at their disposal to interpret, understand and apply it to meet the needs of the Muslims with consideration to the environment and community in which they dwell. The law of Islam, many Muslims believe, is dynamic, flexible and can be applied to all cases in any generation and in any country as long as the objectives of the law are kept in mind.

The Status of *Sharia* Law in Northern Nigeria before 1999

Sharia law was in application in the pre-colonial era, both in civil and criminal matters. When the British came, they found an organized and efficient judicial system in the North and retained it. The British did not interfere with the civil law but made adjustment to the criminal law. It substituted the following:

a. Death by hanging for the offences of homicide instead of beheading by sword.

b. Imprisonment for adultery instead of stoning to death.

c. Imprisonment for theft instead of amputation of hand

d. Abolition of payment of (*Diya*) restitutes in lieu of capital punishment.

Justice Bello, the former Chief Justice of Nigeria, pointed out that Sharia Courts adjudicated both civil and criminal cases. The only change made by the British was the right to appeal against the decisions of an Alkali (judge) of an Area court. Such appeal goes to the Sharia Court of Appeal on all personal laws and to the High Court of the state on all other matters. He added that when an Area Court decided a case based on Sharia law, all the courts exercising appellate jurisdiction over

---

4. For more information on the theory of *Ijtihad,* see Sodiq, "Ijtihad," 1–61.

the case, including the Supreme Court, are bound by the law to apply the Sharia law. This is one of the reasons why the Constitution, under Section 288 requires that the judges in the Supreme Court of Appeal must include judges who are learned in the Sharia law,[5] so that they can render an Islamic point of view on the cases presented to them.

He added that in order for any person to be convicted of any offense and be punished under any law in Nigeria, there must be a provision for such an offense in a written form and the punishment must be clearly stated. The offence must be enacted by the National Assembly or by the State House of Assembly under Section 36 (12) of the 1999 Constitution.

> Subject as otherwise provided by this Constitution, a person shall not be convicted of a criminal offence unless that offence is defined and the penalty therefore is prescribed in a written law, and in this subsection, a written law refers to an Act of the National Assembly or a Law of a State, any subsidiary legislation or instrument under the provisions of a law. (Section 36 (12)[6]

In the past, the Northerners formed a panel to recommend a code of law for them because many laws in the Qur'an and Hadith are not coded. Members of this panel were the Chief Justice of Sudan, Justice of the Pakistan Supreme court, Professor J. D. N. Anderson of SOAS, Sir Kassem Ibrahim, Alkali Musa Bidda, and Perter Chingu.[7] The panel recommended the following.

The enactment of a criminal law, which would apply uniformly to all persons living within Northern Nigeria and which will not discriminate against any section of the community; that since the majority of the people in Northern Nigeria are Muslims, the criminal law should not be in conflict with the injunctions of the Holy Qur'an and Sunnah.[8]

---

5. Bello, "Obstacles Before the Sharia," This article is a lecture delivered by Justice Bello on Seminar on Sharia.

6. This section is Section 33 (12) of the 1979 Constitution which also was an adaptation of the old Constitution of 1999.

7. This group was the committee appointed by the then Northern Nigeria government to look into the Sharia and suggest how it can be improved and applied in the North. It is said that this committee traveled to some Arab countries and Pakistan to observe how Islamic law is practiced in those countries.

8. Ibid.

As a result, a penal code was written, adopted and enforced as of October 1, 1960 by the Federal government. The new Constitution of 1999 adopts the old Penal Code.

Does Any State Have the Legitimate Power to Enact New Laws?

Section 7 of the 1999 Constitution answers this question.

The House of Assembly of a State shall have the power to make laws for the peace, order and good government of the State or any part thereof with respect to the following matters, that is to say:

a. any matter not included in the Exclusive Legislative List set out in Part 1 of the Second Schedule to this Constitution.

b. any matter included in the Concurrent Legislative List set out in the first column of Part 11 of the Second Schedule to this Constitution to the extent prescribed in the second column opposite thereto; and

c. any other matter with respect to which it is empowered to make laws in accordance with the provisions of this Constitution.

From the above, if the State House of Assembly enacts any laws relating to Sharia, their application is constitutional; the Constitution gives the State the power to do so. Hence, the application of Islamic law to Muslims would not be against the Constitution of Nigeria. The only exemption to this provision is the law of apostasy in Sharia, which carries capital punishment. The law of apostasy (*Ridda*) is unconstitutional because it is inconsistent with Section 38 (1) that ensures for every person in Nigeria the right of the freedom of thought, conscience, and religion. This includes freedom to change one's religion or belief to another religion or faith. And he who does so should not be subjected to any punishment.

Sharia and the New Civilian Government

Nigeria since 1966 has been ruled by successive military regimes until 1979 and from 1984 until May 1999. In 1999 a new civilian president was elected. He vowed to bring the country back to democracy. He adopted a new Constitution, which recognizes three legal systems: English Common law, Customary law, and Islamic law. Since 1903, these systems were in operation except that the Native law was not charged with adjudicating criminal, homicide, or murder cases. However, the new Constitution allows each State the freedom to apply whatever law it endorses. In 2000, the Governor of Zamfara State, Ahmad Sani Yerima, went to the State's House of Assembly and sought that Sharia be the law of the State and be extended to all aspects of life. His request was approved and the Zamfara Penal Code was adopted on January 18, 2000. Zamfara's adoption of Sharia and its expansion to adjudicate criminal cases raised a lot of tension. Many Christians and a few Muslims objected to the full application of Sharia in all aspects of life. They considered it an infringement upon their civil rights and a discrimination against Nigerian citizens.

What Is at Stake About the Application of Sharia?

There are several issues at stake regarding the application of Sharia. Some are religious, some are political and some are moral. Major areas of controversy are questions about the constitutionality of the Sharia itself.

a. Is the application of Sharia constitutional?

b. Is the application of Sharia discriminatory?

c. Does the application of Sharia violate the principle of separation between the state and the church?

d. Is Nigeria a secular or a religious state?

e. Does the application of Sharia promote justice and fairness for all Nigerians as the advocates of Sharia proclaim?

Arguments for the Application of Sharia

The proponents of Sharia argue as follows:

1. The Nigerian Constitution of 1999 guarantees freedom of religion to all her citizens. Nigerian Muslims are Nigerians, thus they are entitled to freedom of religion. And since the application of Sharia and abiding by Sharia law is central to the practicing of Islamic religion, Muslims

should be free to adhere to their religion. Any denial of Sharia is tantamount to the denial of religious freedom for Muslims. Their right to religious practice / freedom is expressed in Section 38 (1) of the 1999 Constitution:

> Every person shall be entitled to freedom of thought, conscience and religion, including freedom to change his religion or belief, and freedom (either alone or in community with others, and in public or private) to manifest and propagate his religion or belief in worship, teaching, practice and observance.[9]

Muslims claim that they would not have any degree of authenticity unless the Sharia law governs them.[10] It is argued therefore that Nigerian Muslims, wherever they live or dwell, whether as minority or majority, claim to have a moral and a legal duty to adhere to their religion and to Sharia, unless they are denied the freedom to do so. They opt for Islamic law due to their conviction in its ultimate goals of substantive justice and betterment of their social and moral lives.[11]

Those who oppose Sharia argue that recognizing Islam as a religion and the freedom to be a Muslim does not imply the demand to be governed by Islamic law (Sharia). If that assumption were to be accepted, every adherent of any religion in Nigeria would be allowed to apply his / her religious laws and that would be tantamount to having several legal systems. Such allowance would not keep Nigeria a unified country.

2. The second argument for Sharia is that the Nigerian Constitution of 1999 provides for the establishment of three legal systems: Common law, Customary law, and Sharia law. Separate courts are established for each legal system. "There shall be a Sharia Court of Appeal of the Federal Capital Territory, Abuja." (Section 260 [1]). Thus, when the Constitution permits the establishment of Sharia courts and Sharia Courts of Appeal, it recognizes and acknowledges as legitimate, a set of laws based on Islamic faith and its tenets. Therefore, the application of Sharia is constitutional. Each State is allowed to establish Sharia court and it is empowered to adjudicate all Islamic personal laws as well as any other jurisdiction which the National Assembly or State Assembly

---

9. Constitution of the Federal Republic of Nigeria, 1999, Section 38 (1).
10. Basri, *Nigeria and Shari`ah*, 43, quoting from the New Nigerian, May 8, 1977.
11. Baderin, Online: www.nigeriaworld.com.

(of any State) confers on it as stated in Section 262 (1) and 277 (1) of the 1999 Constitution.

The Sharia Court of Appeal shall, in addition to such other jurisdiction as may be conferred upon it by an Act of the National Assembly, exercise such appellate and supervisory jurisdiction in civil proceedings involving questions of Islamic personal law. (Section 262 [1]).

In response to this argument, the opponents of Sharia argue that the problem is not the establishment of Sharia Court itself but the expansion of its jurisdiction to cover all aspects of life, especially criminal cases, which will make the Sharia a rival and superior to the Common law.

3. The proponents of Sharia also argue that since the Constitution permits the application of Sharia, it must be implemented fully, because Sharia is an organic whole which allows no partial application. Its partial application would amount to invalidity of the whole Islamic legal system. Thus, in order to avoid this partial implementation, the Sharia Court should be given the power to adjudicate all Islamic laws whether they are criminal law or civil law or business law, as conferred unto it by the State House of Assembly. Sharia can function smoothly and demonstrate its efficacy when it is applied fully.[12]

4. In addition, the proponents also argue that Sharia would only be applied on Muslims in the North. Since the majority are Muslims in Northern Nigeria, it was considered that it is within the premise of justice and fairness that the law, which commands the approval of the majority, has the right to become the law of the State. On the other hand, the non-Muslim minority have the right to take their case to Common law or Customary courts, which are established in each State of the Federation.[13] Non- Muslims are not forced to adjudicate by Sharia. Perhaps, if they opt for it, they would not be denied. However, it would be unfair for Muslims who are the majority (in the North) to be asked by the minority to abandon their rights and practice laws that are against their convictions.

In response to this argument, the opponents of Sharia reject the unsupported claim that Muslims are in majority in Northern Nigeria.

12. Basri, *Nigeria and Shariʿah*, 47–48.
13. Ibid., 48.

They argue this claim has no empirical evidence.[14] On the other hand, they say that the majority has not been asked whether they wanted Sharia to be applied to them. It is a few people, especially those in the authority who want to impose Sharia on their subject, the general public in the States that apply Sharia began to petition the Chief Justice of the Federation, Mr. Godwin Agabi, to stop the application of Sharia. Thus on March 18, 2002, he issued a statement and declared the application of Sharia unconstitutional and discriminatory; he appealed to all States to stop it.[15]

5. The proponents of Sharia further argue that Nigeria before and after the independence has multi-judicial systems: Common law, Sharia, and Customary law. If the Muslims decide to expand the Sharia to include criminal cases, a matter which affects them, they should be free to do so. They wonder why other religious groups should not recognize the expansion of Sharia while the Common law is expanded and modified at any time and no one raises objection to such expansion.

Arguments Against the Application of Sharia (Islamic Law)

Many people who oppose the application of Sharia law in Nigeria have little knowledge about Nigerian judicial system, which recognizes three legal systems. They are unaware that Sharia law was in full operation before the arrival of the colonial regime. Sharia has never disappeared in Nigerian legal system. Of course, its application has always been a cause of tension among the political leaders. At times, some areas of Sharia jurisdiction are curtailed and at times they are retained. Even in the South, among the Yorubas, the demand for the application of

---

14. There is strong evidence that Muslims are the majority in the North. Any almanac one consults will state that Muslims are majority in the North. To deny this is to deny a reality. Likewise, Christians are the majority in Eastern Nigeria. There is a great controversy as to who is the majority in Western Nigeria, the Muslims or the Christians? Each group claims to be the majority. At present there is no conclusive research work to support either claim.

15. The Governors of those states that apply Sharia did not stop the application. They asked the Chief Justice to take the issue to the court. However, one of the governors, the governor of Niger State, Alhaji Kuru, responded and said that the application of Sharia is constitutional and not discriminatory.

Sharia has been recorded as early back as the 1890s.[16] The Kwara State, whose citizens are Yorubas, applies Sharia law since the independence and has a Sharia Court of Appeal.

1. The first argument of the opponents of Sharia is that Nigeria is a secular country. It prohibits adoption of any state religion as espoused in Section 10 of the Nigerian Constitution of 1999. *"The Government of the Federation or of a State shall not adopt any religion as State religion."* The establishment of Islamic courts and implementing of Sharia laws by several states in the North are considered and interpreted as an adoption of Islam as the religion of the State. In other words, allowing Sharia to be implemented negate the "noble" concept of separation of state and religion. The government should maintain its secular status by not approving any religion to be the religion of any State in Nigeria. Also, the taxpayer's money should not be spent on establishing Islamic courts, which directly or indirectly promote Islam over other religions.

The proponents of Sharia responded to this argument by stating that the endorsement of Sharia as a legal system of a State does not constitute adoption of Islam as a State religion which is prohibited in Section 10 of the Constitution. The former Chief Justice of Nigeria, Justice Mohammed Bello, points out that the Constitution stops short of whether a state may adopt established religious laws or enacts laws based on religion. He argues that those twelve states which decided to apply Sharia law have not adopted or declared Islam as a State religion. Those states have adopted Sharia as the governing law in their states just as the Southern States adopt Common or Customary laws as the governing laws in their states. The adoption of any legal system does not violate the rule of separation between state and church or the Constitution in any sense. "The Sharia," Justice Bello adds, "through the deliberate constitutionally pemissible establishment of the Sharia Courts and Sharia Courts of Appeal, is intended to run concurrently with any other laws [in Nigeria].[17] Hence that Nigeria is a secular state does not mean that its citizens cannot choose Sharia as their governing law. They are free to do so.

---

16. Gbadamosi, *Growth of Islam Among the Yoruba*.
17. Bello, "Obstacles Before Sharia."

Further, a secular state should not be conceived as an anti-religious state. It is a state, which cares about the interests of its citizens regardless of their beliefs. The state must treat all its members fairly and also promote their rights and protect their religious freedom. If non-Muslims opt for a law that suits their religion, they should be granted and be entitled to it just like the Muslims. However, they should not enforce their religions on others as the Sharia advocates should not enforce Sharia on non-Muslims.

Therefore, the argument that the application of Sharia is unconstitutional because it violates the principle of separation of the state from the church is weak. The Nigerian Constitution endorses the establishment of different legal systems and since the Sharia court is permitted to be established, the government knows for sure that Sharia court will apply Islamic laws. Sections 260 and 275 in the Constitution give recognition and acknowledgement to Sharia. *"There shall be for any State that requires it a Sharia Court of Appeal for that State."* (Section 275)

In each State that applies Sharia law, there are Area courts,[18] which adjudicate Islamic personal laws. Appeals from Area courts go to the Sharia Court of Appeal in the State, appeals from the Sharia courts of Appeal go to the State High Court, and appeals from the State High Court go to the Supreme / Federal Court of Nigeria in Kaduna or Lagos, which has the finality of determinations as expressed in Section 235 of the 1999 Constitution.

2. The second argument by the opponents of Sharia is that the application of Sharia in full scale and to all aspects of Muslim life will amount to the supremacy of Sharia over the Constitution. While the Constitution is supreme according to Section 1, the Sharia law, unfortunately in theory, does not permit or admit the supremacy of any other laws as pointed out by Justice Bello. In this sense, Sharia is a rival to the Constitution. However, in application, he who does not agree

---

18. Area Court is the new name given to the former Native court. Native court was the name given by the British colonial to the Alkali court after the conquest of Sokoto in 1903. The word "Native" was used then to neutralize the existing courts, which were Islamic from their religious connotations. Alkali court is a lower court headed by a judge learned in Islamic law. Usually, the judge in Alkali court decides the cases by himself. Emir court is composed of the Emir of the city, and a number of learned persons in Islamic law as assessors. For more information on the History of Islamic law in Nigeria, see: Sodiq, "A History of Islamic Law in Nigeria," 85–108.

with the decision of the Sharia court can appeal to a higher court or to the Supreme High Court, which maintains the final decision.

Thus, in practice, the Constitution is supreme; Sharia is inferior and the decisions of the Sharia courts, including the State Sharia Court of Appeal, are subject to change and modification or even nullification by the Supreme High Court. There are a few appeal cases, which go from the Sharia courts to the Supreme Court and the latter reversed the decision of the Sharia Court of Appeal as occurred in the case of Karimatu Yakubu and Alhaji Mahmud Ndatsu vs Alhaji Yakubu Tafida Paiko and Alhaji Umaru Gwagwada.[19]

3. Another strong argument against Sharia has a political overtone. It states that a full application of Sharia is politically motivated to weaken the government of the newly elected President Obasanjo, who is a Christian from the South. And instead of paying attention to the needs of the State, the authority pays great attention to religious matters at the expense of the needs of the State and thus distracting the public from the important things to less important issues. The opponents stressed that the Muslims from the North were in the position of leadership from 1979-1999, yet they failed to implement Sharia on a full scale. Why is it that during the presidency of Olusegun Obansanjo that they wanted a total implementation of Sharia if not for political purposes and to create tension among the political parties?

Nobody doubts the political motivation of Sharia, but Islam does not differentiate between religion and politics. Other political parties utilize politics to advance their interests and fulfill their goals, whether those goals or objectives are religious or not. Political parties often seize an opportune time to advance their own interest and promote their own agenda. President Obasanjo himself acknowledged the political motivation of Sharia. When he was asked to react against the application of Sharia, he refrained and responded that Sharia as projected by the Northerners was a political game and it would soon fade away.[20]

---

19. This case is reported by Shani and Ahangar, "Marriage Guardianship in Islam," 278.

20. Nobody hears anything about Sharia today. Of course, the issue will be raised again during the coming election in April of 2007. At present, little is written or published about Sharia. In fact the problem facing Nigeria is not the problem of Sharia but of poverty, corruption and unfair distribution of wealth.

4. The opponents also argue that Sharia has been used to oppress the poor. They cite a few cases where poor people were convicted of crimes and punished while the elite and the rich who committed similar crimes were not severely persecuted like the poor. For instance, when Peri Partum Bariya was convicted of fornication, she received eighty lashes and the man who fornicated with her was set free for lack of adequate evidence and witnesses to convict him. In addition, the hands of those who stole cows, donkeys, goats and a few Naira (Nigerian currency) were severed, while the government workers and officers, who embezzled millions of Naira were not convicted and punished merely because they have money to hire lawyers to take their cases to trial and plead for them.[21]

5. Further, the opponents argue that Sharia is imposed on non-Muslims despite the promise that it will not be applied on non-Muslims. Mbahi, in his article *"Sharia, Northern Ethnic and Religious Minority and the Federal Government: A Perspective,"* cites the pronouncement of the Governor of Yobe State, who declared that he would start compelling non-Muslim women to put on head cover (*hijab*). Mbahi wonders how an elected governor, who is presumably, charged with the protection of the overall interests of all members of his State, regardless of their religious beliefs, could attempt to enforce the wearing of head cover (*hijab*) on non-Muslims?[22]

It is this sort of approach and the attempt from the higher authorities in the State to impose Islamic laws on non-Muslims that the masses are objecting to. In our view, this is a misuse of power by the Governor of Yobe. The Constitution does not grant any power to a governor or anyone else to tell people what to wear or how to dress. Islam only encourages Muslims, males and females to dress modestly. Muslim leaders should not impose any dress code on anyone. If they do, they should be challenged and brought to justice.

---

21. This is an abuse of law. However, law is often abused in Nigeria be it sharia law or common law. Many Nigerians who were in charge of wealth had and continue to embezzle millions on Naira without being brought to justice. It is during the government of Obansanjo that the government has begun to persecute corrupt civil servants and governors. It is a new beginning of checks and balances that we hope will continue.

22. Mbahi, "Sharia, Northern Ethnic and Religious Minority and the Federal Government." As of present, there is no evidence that the governor has enforced the wearing of head-cover (Hijab) upon his subjects.

6. One of the strongest arguments against Sharia lies in the claim that its application is discriminatory in the sense that Muslims receive a harsher punishment than any other Nigerian who commits the same crime. And since the Constitution prohibits such discrimination, it follows that the application of Sharia law, especially the criminal laws, is unconstitutional as stated below.

> A citizen of Nigeria of a particular community, ethnic group, place of origin, sex, religion or political opinion shall not, by reason only that he is such a person:
>
> a) be subjected either expressly by, or in the practical application of, any law in force in Nigeria or any executive or administrative action of the government, to disabilities or restrictions to which citizens of Nigeria of other communities, ethnic groups, places of origin, sex, religions or political opinions are not made subject. (Section 42) (1A)

Based on the above Section 42 (1)(a), the Chief Justice of the Federation, Mr. Agabi, wrote a letter to the twelve states that apply Sharia law that they should stop administering Islamic law because its application is inconsistent with the Constitution and that it is discriminatory against the Muslims. He requested that both individuals and the States should comply with the provision of the Constitution. In his letter, he stated that:

> The fact that Sharia law applies only to Moslems or to those who elect to be bound by it makes imperative that the rights of such persons to equality with other citizens under the Constitution be not infringed. A Moslem should not be subjected to a punishment more severe than would be imposed on other Nigerians for the same offence. Equality before the law means that Moslems should not be discriminated against. As an elected Governor, I am certain that you would not tolerate such disparity in the allocation of punishment. It is not only against the Constitution but also against equity and good conscience. Individuals and states must comply with the Constitution. A court, which imposes discriminatory punishments, is deliberately flouting the Constitution. The stability, unity and integrity of the nation are threatened by such action. In order to implement policies or programmes inconsistent with the Constitution we must first secure its amendment. Until that is done, we have to abide by it. To proceed on the basis either that the Constitution does not exist or that it is ir-

relevant is to deny the existence of the nation itself. We cannot
deny the rule of law and hope to have peace and stability.²³

His letter implies that the application of Sharia is an arbitrary implementation and amounts to the denial of the "existence of the nation itself."

Many writers consider the above argument the strongest one against the implementation of Sharia because this analysis/refutation came from the Chief Justice and the Attorney General of the Federal Republic of Nigeria. However, under critical examination, it appears to be an unconvincing argument in that the application of Sharia does not amount to discrimination against Muslims. If what the Chief Justice meant by discrimination is to apply different rules to the same offence, one could argue then that the nature of operating three legal systems implies that there would be different punishments for the same offence in these different legal systems. Each legal system differs from one another and functions differently to meet the needs of a certain group of people in Nigeria.²⁴ Would a Yoruba woman whose husband is permitted under Customary law to marry a second wife consider herself to be discriminated against just because the Common law does not allow the husband of her Christian friend in the same city to marry a second wife? Of course not. Is there anything so harmful to a woman than to see her husband marrying a second wife legally and bringing her home? That Sharia prescribes a harsher punishment for certain crimes does not amount to discrimination. An American who lives in Texas would receive the death penalty if he was convicted of homicide; whereas, if he lives in New Jersey, he would receive life imprisonment. Can a Texan inmate argue that he has been discriminated against even though he is an American? Of course not.²⁵ Justice Agabi's

---

23. Agabi, "Prohibition of Discriminatory Punishments," a letter written to all the twelve states that apply Sharia law, on March 18, 2002. See, *Jender: A Journal of Culture and African Women* 1&2 (2002).This letter was widely distributed in Nigeria and around the world. Unfortunately, the states to whom he addressed his letter did not respond except Niger and Zamfara states.

24. A perfect example for applying different rules to the same issue is the case of inheritance in Nigeria. The three legal systems in Nigeria have different rules regarding the distribution of wealth by a diseased person.

25. It should be pointed out that Texas is one of the States that endorse capital punishment. More criminals are executed in Texas than any other state in the United States. Human rights advocates and Amnesty International have objected to capital punishment in Texas but the State legislators always endorse the capital punishment.

argument implies that there is a unified system of law in Nigeria. He knows more than anyone that there are three systems and they are all of equal status. Applying the Sharia on Muslims is not a discrimination at all.

Our understanding of Section 42 (1) (a) is that if any court or judge claims to be applying Common law for instance, then the convicted persons under Common law should receive equal treatment wherever they reside in Nigeria. They should not be discriminated against in any part of Nigeria. Likewise, the Sharia law should be applied justly and equitably to all Muslims who reside in the States that apply Sharia. That a person receives the death penalty in a State, which adopts capital punishment, is not a discrimination against a person who receives a life imprisonment for the same crime/offence at another State which does not adopt capital punishment. Hence, the allegation that the application of Sharia imposes discriminatory punishment upon Muslims, and thus it amounts to "flouting the Constitution," is weak. The Constitution approves the establishment of Sharia courts and Sharia Courts of Appeal and also endorses the application of the Penal Code whose provisions apply only in the North according to Section 315 of 1999 Constitution.

The Governor of Niger State, Alhaji, Abdukadir Kure, responded to Mr. Agabi, arguing:

> The concern expressed by you on the validity of some of our personalization in the light of the provision of section 42 of the Constitution has prompted us to look once more at the said provisions and our respective laws in order to place the fears thus expressed or identify any inconsistency. With respect, we are unable to see any. Those of our laws, especially the penal legislation relating to theft, adultery, homicide, defamation, intoxication, etc. which have been a subject of heated debates in recent times, were informed by some basic principles expressed and entrenched in our Constitution. These principles are contained in Section 4 (7), 5, 6, 38 and the preamble to our Constitution. There is no doubt that the penal legislations are not new and have been tested. Between 1966 and 1999, the Penal Code law (was) applicable in all the Northern States of

---

No one argues that the Texans are discriminated against by the American law. The State in America has the right to adopt any law it wants. The law represents the will of the people.

Nigeria in Section 68 subsection 2 for the infliction of harsh punishment to offenders of the Muslim faith.[26]

It also should be pointed out that the Sharia courts are not the only courts that apply the Penal Code. All the courts in Northern Nigeria: the High Courts, Magistrate Courts, and Area Courts, whether they are presided over by a Muslim (alkali) judge or not, apply the Penal Code. Thus the allegation that Sharia Courts inflict harsh punishment on its members was an unexamined statement. Actually, none of the courts in the North, including the Supreme Court, is allowed by law, to apply the Common criminal law of England. Any appeal from the Sharia and Area courts to the Courts of Appeal and the Supreme courts is adjudicated according to the Penal Code. It should also be understood that where an Area Court decides a case on Sharia, then all the courts exercising appellate jurisdiction over the case, including the Supreme Court, are bound by law to apply Sharia law. This is one of the reasons, argues Justice Mohammed Bello, that under section 288 of the 1999 constitution, it is required to have judges in the Court of Appeal and in the Supreme Court, who are learned in Sharia law.[27]

From the above analysis, we may argue that the application of Sharia is constitutional due to the fact that the 1999 Constitution acknowledges the establishment of Islamic courts including the Federal Sharia Court of Appeal, which receives appeals from the Area Courts and Sharia State Courts. Under the Constitution Section 7, the State has power to make laws, including laws relating to Sharia. Under this power twelve Northern States adopted Sharia and adopted laws and Penal Codes that were endorsed by their State House of Assembly. The Constitution Section 36 (12) states that:

> A person shall not be convicted of a criminal offence unless that offence is defined and the penalty therefore is prescribed in a written law, and in this subsection, a written law refer to an Act of the National Assembly or a Law of a State, any subsidiary legislation or instrument under the provision of a law.

On this ground, the States that apply Sharia law made sure that their Penal Codes were passed and adopted by their State House of Assembly. Hence, they are not operating any illegal laws; their adju-

26. Ihenacho, "Warped World of the Sharia Protagonists."

27. Bello, "Obstacles Before the Sharia," keynote address at the National Seminar on Sharia in Kaduna on February 10–12, 2000.

dication is constitutional. The Zamfara Penal Code was adopted by the State House of Assembly of Zamfara on January 18, 2000. If these States apply any criminal law which has not been codified or adopted by the National Assembly or the State House of Assembly, such an application shall be considered unconstitutional.

It should be pointed out that adopting Sharia as an operating legal system in any state does not constitute an adoption of Islam as the state religion which Section 10 of the Constitution prohibits. The assumption that adopting a criminal code based on a religion carries the same weight as adopting the religion itself is a false assumption. If this assumption were to be true, one would be right in claiming that Common law or American law is a Christian law and therefore Christianity is a state religion in Nigeria or America, even though Common law has its roots in Christianity and it is informed by Christian values and its worldviews.[28]

On close examination, Islam has not become a State religion in Northern Nigeria despite the fact that the majority of the population is Muslim. At the same time, it would be unrealistic to assume that the application of Sharia would not affect Christian minority in the North. Christians would definitely be affected in many areas, socially and politically by the application of Sharia. The mere fact that they are minority would not allow them to have a sufficient voice in deciding issues affecting all the citizens in those states that apply Sharia. Their rights would be curtailed in some areas and the application of Sharia law would definitely affect their businesses especially the selling of alcoholic beverages and gambling.

New Sharia Cases

Since the adoption of Sharia in 2000, a few cases have drawn the attention of the world community to Nigeria. More common among these cases are the convictions of Amina Lawal and Safiyatu Husaini. Both were sentenced to death by stoning for adultery: illegal sex outside the wedlock after one has been married. Fortunately, Safiyatu's case has been dismissed for a legal technicality after her appeal to the Supreme Court and because of the objection by the world community. People around the world objected to the ruling of stoning on both convicted

---

28. Haruna, "Sharia."

women on the ground that the punishment is cruel and that Sharia is an outdated law, which should be abandoned for its repugnance to the civil society.

The Media, both in Nigeria and abroad, has exaggerated these cases without any objectivity by emphasizing the harsh punishment of Islamic laws. These events in Nigeria give the media and the opponents of Sharia an ample chance to "vent" their anger and dissatisfaction to the Islamic legal system, which they know little about. Some call the application *"Talibanization of Nigeria,"* even though Safiyatu had been sentenced to death before September 11. Some Nigerians call for the separation of the North from the South by taking arms as if Sharia was just launched in year 2000 by Zamfara governor. Unfortunately, the world community danced to that tone by condemning Islam, Muslims and Islamic law in Nigeria. Thus, when Safiyatu Husaini's case was dismissed, the thirty-five year old received an invitation from Rome, Italy; she went and was given a warm welcome; she was awarded an honorary award for being freed from the yoke of Sharia. Was she awarded to recognize and promote her illegal practice or to condemn Sharia or both? Should the Vatican promote illegal sexual relationships and embrace those who fornicate? The motives of the opponents of Sharia are yet to be seen.

Why Do the Northerners Resort to the Application of Sharia?

There is no easy answer to this question. However, one may surmise that they are searching for a unified identity. They want to regain some of their alleged old glories of unified North. When the Governor of Zamfara State, Ahmed Sani Yerima announced that he would apply Sharia in 1999, it was expected that people would reject his appeal, especially the people of Kano and Kaduna, who are perceived as liberal due to their dwelling at the center of commerce in the North. However, it appears that the majority of people in these states were dissatisfied with the secularization, globalization, and Westernization that they witnessed from 1960 until 1999, even though Nigerian leaders during that period came from the North and ruled Nigeria for thirty-one years. They did not bring peace or harmony to Nigeria because of their corruption, mismanagement, and lack of vision. Many scholars from the North attribute the corruption to secular education, which paves ways to Westernization that led, they assumed, to moral decadence. They paid little attention to moral values as they degrade the role of religion in building Nigerian society. Therefore, the rallying around Sharia is believed to be an attempt by the Northerners to regroup themselves under a religious umbrella—Islam. If it is successful, it would be a great unified power for them which they can exploit politically against the Southerners to win the future elections. The majority of the Northerners believe that it is through the banner of Islam that they can all be united. Even though many label the Northerners as Hausas, there are many groups in the North which are not Hausas like the Fulanis and the Tivs.

Can the Application of Sharia Law Be Stopped?

The expansion of the application of Sharia to cover all aspects of life has irritated many Nigerians including some Muslims. Therefore, this tension has to be resolved amicably through dialogue between the Muslim leaders and the government. All differences between these two parties can adequately be worked out through sincere and genuine dialogue rather than through the court or by civil war or separation from the Federal government as suggested by a few Christians from the South. Nigeria should never attempt separation along religious line for it would lead to disaster. No one would benefit from it. We should recognize that Muslims and non-Muslims, Hausas, Yorubas and Ibos are neighbors. No ethnic group would leave its locale or place of residence for another. Hence, we are bound to live together peacefully in Nigeria. Separation of each ethnic group will not solve our social, religious and political problems. The core of our social problems is not religious but corruption, unfair distribution of the national wealth and lack of patriotism for the country by many Nigerians.[29] There are many Nigerians abroad in America and Europe with high levels of education but the majority of them prefer to stay abroad than to return home and sacrifice for the country as Indians, Chinese and Israelis do by return-

---

29. Ben Zwinkels in his recent article in "Africa Today" mentions that "the Muslim Sharia law, which has been introduced in the Northern regions some years ago and which was given a lot of international attention, is now not any more an issue and not anymore always used." The issue, he argues, is about corruption and allevation of poverty for many Nigerians. See www.Africa-interactive.net, March 3, 2007.

ing home and building their country after they receive their education in America and Europe.

We believe that one of the areas of discontent is the application of Islamic criminal laws (*hudud*), especially the stoning to death of an adulterer and the amputation of a thief's hand. Both areas are subject to reinterpretation. Both punishments can be modified. We should point out that while the source of Islamic law is divine for being a revealed law, its application is human. Muslim scholars have the duty to determine how Islamic law should be applied in this contemporary age to ensure that justice and fairness are achieved. The primary aim of Sharia in inflicting severe punishment on offenders, who commit adultery, theft, and armed robbery, is to let the punishment be deterrent to potential offenders.[30] Yet this objective can be achieved in various ways. Such an approach to Sharia needs an effort from the legal scholars and leaders to be realistic as did Sardauna of Sokoto, Sir Ahmad Bello, in 1956 when he convinced the Emirs in the Northern Nigeria to accept the provisions of the Penal Code despite that the stoning to death was removed from it. The amputation of a thief's hand is not the objective of the Sharia but the maintainance of security of all members of the society whereby their properties and lives are saved.

We should recognize that Muslims and non-Muslims have to live together in Nigeria. The issue of Sharia will never cease appearing in Nigerian politics as long as there are Muslims dwelling among us, and this necessitates finding amicable solution to the Sharia issue. Condemning its application under any guise of human right's violation or invoking the violation of the Constitution will not solve the problem. On the other hand, we believe that the media can do a better job in bringing people together rather than creating creepy and fallacious images of Sharia. We should recognize our diversity, appreciate our differences, learn how to communicate with one another with civility and live together peacefully.

Finally, since the beginning of the application of Sharia in 2000, we have no empirical evidences to substantiate the claim of the Islamists that the social life of the people has improved due to this

---

30. The opponents of Sharia law have argued strongly that the imposition of harsh punishment hardly deters criminals from committing crimes. The exponents of Sharia argue otherwise and cite the low percentage of crimes in those countries that apply Islamic law like Saudi Arabia and even in the Northern Nigeria itself. Of course, Saudi Arabia has its own social and political problems.

application. Are the people where Sharia is applied better off educationally, economically, and socially? Are the people living where Sharia is applied safer than people living in non-Sharia States? Are their cities and rural areas more developed or less developed? Do these States pay adequate attention to educating their citizens and sanitation of their states? These are areas that need more research to assess the usefulness of Sharia and its accomplishments if any. We believe that a great deal of attention should be paid to empirical researches in these areas if we are to achieve any reliable assessment. If the Sharia is used as a cover-up identity and it does not bring peace and progress to the people, then it should be suspended.

We should realize too that there are millions of Muslim Hausas who dwell among the Yorubas and Ibos in Southern Nigeria where Sharia is not practiced. These Hausas accommodate their neighbors and host and respect their religions and laws. So, the Yorubas and Ibos, who live in the North, should respect the Hausas and their religious traditions and beliefs. Nigerians should stop thinking that Hausas are less civilized and that the Yorubas and Ibos are morally responsible to civilize them through Western ways of life or by bringing to them Christianity. The Northern Muslims should also refrain from the sense of religious superiority by labeling the Southerners as *"Kafirinchi"* non-believers. All Nigerians should long and aspire for industrialization, development and advancement of the whole country. Above all, if the Northerners do not want anyone to force Christianity on them under any guise, they too should not force any law on their Christian neighbors under the pretext of applying Islamic law. Our social, religious, and ethnic diversity should be respected and each group should have the freedom to be left alone to determine and practice its religion. If the majority of the people in the North desire to be governed by Sharia law, as did the twelve states, and they feel satisfied with it, they should be left alone. It is not necessary that all Nigerians subscribe to a unified legal system. Even in America, each state has its own legal system that meets the needs of the citizens of that particular state. If we as Nigerians dislike to see the Islamic law imposed upon us, what right do we have to impose Western Common law on the Muslims in the North if they do not want it? There is no legal system that is value-free. Common law is partially based on Christian and Western values, which have no strong appeal to Muslims in general because of its reliance on materialism and secularization. At the same time, Muslims should not impose their law and will upon others in the name of Islam for there is no compulsion in Islam. Justice and fair play should be the aim of any State in Nigeria for it is through justice and peaceful co-existence that we can attain peace in Nigeria.

Conclusion

The controversy over the application of Sharia in Nigeria is not new. But before anyone, however, begins blaming Islam and Muslims for this application, it should be noted that the Northern States are operating within the Constitution of Nigeria in adopting Sharia as the legal system in their states. The establishment of Sharia does not constitute adoption of Islam as a State religion, which the Constitution of 1999 prohibits. Each state has been allowed by the Constitution to establish Sharia courts to apply Islamic laws to meet the Muslim legal needs. I have argued too that applying Sharia on Muslims constitutes no discrimination against them. Muslims reject the notion that Islamic punishments are hard to bear. Muslims are, without a doubt, the majority in the North, and if they desire to be governed by Sharia law, they should be free to do so as any other citizens in Nigeria may ask for their rights to apply the law they want. Nigeria, being a secular state, and a republic for that matter, does not debar its citizens from practicing their beliefs and exercising their religious rights in applying Islamic law as long as they do not enforce it on others. The tension between Muslims and non-Muslims stems from mistrust and suspicion of one another due to the long age rivalry between Islam and Christianity and there is no sign that this rivalry will end soon.

The application of Sharia should not lead to social problems or civil war in our view. Sharia is a law, and the function of law should be to integrate the society through administration of justice and the legal structure. If Sharia law can bring peace, justice, harmony, fairness and equal treatment of the citizens of the North, then the Muslim North should be free to apply it. Certainly, the Nigerian Constitution endorses three legal systems and this implies that each system differs from one another. No group in Nigeria advocates for the unification of all the legal systems. The diversity of the system is unique and should be perceived as strength for meeting the needs of Nigerian citizens.

Appendix: Sections of the Nigerian Constitution quoted in this article which relate to the issue of Sharia law:

1. (1) This Constitution is supreme and its provisions shall have binding force on the authorities and persons throughout the Federal Republic of Nigeria.

4. In addition and without prejudice to the powers conferred by subsection (2) of this section, the National Assembly shall have power to make laws with respect to the following matters, that is to say:

(a) any matter in the Concurrent Legislative List set out in the first column of Part II of the Second Schedule to this Constitution to the extent prescribed in the second column opposite thereto; and

(b) any other matter with respect to which it is empowered to make laws in accordance with the provisions of this Constitution.

4 (5) If any Law enacted by the House of Assembly of a State is inconsistent with any law validly made by the National Assembly, the law made by the National Assembly shall prevail, and that other Law shall, to the extent of the inconsistency, be void.

4 (6) The legislative powers of a State of the Federation shall be vested in the House of Assembly of the State.

4 (7) The House of Assembly of a State shall have power to make laws for the peace, order and good government of the State or any part thereof with respect to the following matters, that is to say:-

(a) any matter not included in the Exclusive Legislative List set out in Part I of the Second Schedule to this Constitution.

(b) any matter included in the Concurrent Legislative List set out in the first column of Part II of the Second Schedule to this Constitution to the extent prescribed in the second column opposite thereto; and

(c) any other matter with respect to which it is empowered to make laws in accordance with the provisions of this Constitution.

10. The Government of the Federation or of a State shall not adopt any religion as State religion.

36 (12) A person shall not be convicted of a criminal offence unless that offence is defined and the penalty therefore is prescribed in a written law, and in this subsection, a written law refer to an Act of the National Assembly or a Law of a State, any subsidiary legislation or instrument under the provision of a law.

38. (1) Every person shall be entitled to freedom of thought, conscience and religion, including freedom to change his religion or belief, and freedom (either alone or in community with others, and in public or in private) to manifest and propagate his religion or belief in worship, teaching, practice and observance.

42 (1) A citizen of Nigeria of a particular community, ethnic group, place of origin, sex, religion or political opinion shall not, by reason only that he is such a person:

a) be subjected either expressly by, or in the practical application of, any law in force in Nigeria or any executive or administrative action of the government, to disabilities or restrictions to which citizens of Nigeria of other communities, ethnic groups, places of origin, sex, religions or political opinions are not made subject (Section 42) (1A).

68. (2) The President of the Senate or the Speaker of the House of Representatives, as the case may be, shall give effect to the provisions of subsection (1) of this section, so however that the President of the Senate or the Speaker of the House of Representatives or a member shall first present evidence satisfactory to the House concerned that any of the provisions of that subsection has become applicable in respect of that member.

233. (1) The Supreme Court shall have jurisdiction, to the exclusion of any other court of law in Nigeria, to hear and determine appeals from the Court of Appeal.

235. Without prejudice to the powers of the President or of the Governor of a state with respect to prerogative of mercy, no appeal shall lie to any other body or person from any determination of the Supreme Court.

260 (1) There shall be a Sharia Court of Appeal of the Federal Capital Territory, Abuja.

261. (1) The appointment of a person to the office of the Grand Kadi of the Sharia Court of Appeal of the Federal Capital Territory, Abuja shall be made by the President on the recommendation of the National

(2) The appointment of a person to the office of a Kadi of the Sharia Court of Appeal shall be made by the President on the recommendation of the National Judicial Council.

(3) A person shall not be qualified to hold office as Grand Kadi or Kadi of the Sharia Court of Appeal of the Federal Capital Territory, Abuja unless—

(a) he is a legal practitioner in Nigeria and has so qualified for a period of not less than ten years and has obtained a recognised qualification in Islamic law from an institution acceptable to the National Judicial Council; or

(b) he has attended and has obtained a recognized qualification in Islamic law from an institution approved by the National Judicial Council and has held the qualification for a period of not less than twelve years; and

(i) he either has considerable experience in the Practice of Islamic law, or

(ii) he is a distinguished scholar of Islamic law.

262 (1) The Sharia Court of Appeal shall, in addition to such other jurisdiction as may be conferred upon it by an Act of the National Assembly, exercise such appellate and supervisory jurisdiction in civil proceedings involving questions of Islamic personal law.

275. "There shall be for any State that requires it a Sharia Court of Appeal for that State. 277. (1) The Sharia Court of Appeal of a State shall, in addition to such other jurisdiction as may be conferred upon it by the law of the State, exercise such appellate and supervisory jurisdiction in civil proceedings involving questions of Islamic personal

Law which the court is competent to decide in accordance with the provisions of subsection (2) of this section.

(2) For the purposes of subsection (1) of this section, the Sharia Court of Appeal shall be competent to decide—

(a) any question of Islamic personal Law regarding a marriage concluded in accordance with that Law, including a question relating to the validity or dissolution of such a marriage or a question that depends on such a marriage and relating to family relationship or the guardianship of an infant;

(b) where all the parties to the proceedings are muslims, any question of Islamic personal Law regarding a marriage, including the validity or dissolution of that marriage, or regarding family relationship, a founding or the guarding of an infant;

(c) any question of Islamic personal Law regarding a wakf, gift, will or succession where the endower, donor, testator or deceased person is a muslim;

(d) any question of Islamic personal Law regarding an infant, prodigal or person of unsound mind who is a muslim or the maintenance or the guardianship of a muslim who is physically or mentally infirm; or

(e) where all the parties to the proceedings, being muslims, have requested the court that hears the case in the first instance to determine that case in accordance with Islamic personal law, any other question.

287. (1) The decisions of the supreme Court shall be enforced in any part of the Federation by all authorities and persons, and by courts with subordinate jurisdiction to that of the Supreme Court.

(2) The decisions of the Court of Appeal shall be enforced in any part of the Federation by all authorities and persons, and by courts with subordinate jurisdiction to that of the Court of Appeal.

(3) The decisions of the Federal High Court, a High Court and of all other courts established by this Constitution shall be enforced in any part of the Federation by all authorities and persons, and by other

courts of law with subordinate jurisdiction to that of the Federal High Court, a High Court and those other courts, respectively.

288. (1) In exercising his powers under the foregoing provisions of this Chapter in respect of appointments to the offices of Justice of the Supreme Court and Justices of the Courts of Appeal, the president shall have regard to the need to ensure that there are among the holders of such offices persons learned in Islamic personal law and 315.

(1) Subject to the provisions of this Constitution, an existing law shall have effect with such modifications as may be necessary to bring it into conformity with the provisions of this Constitution and shall be deemed to be—

(a) an Act of the National Assembly to the extent that it is a law with respect to any matter on which the National Assembly is empowered by this Constitution to make laws; and

(b) a Law made by a House of Assembly to the extent that it is a law with respect to any matter on which a House of Assembly is empowered by this Constitution to make laws.

2 (a) a person shall be deemed to be learned in Islamic personal law if he is a legal practitioner in Nigeria and has been so qualified for a period of not less than fifteen years in the case of a Justice of the Supreme Court or not less than twelve years in the case of a Justice of the Court of Appeal and has in either case obtained a recognized qualification in Islamic law from an institution acceptable to the national Judicial Council; and

(b) a person shall be deemed to be learned in Customary law if he is a legal practitioner in Nigeria and has been so qualified for a period of not less than fifteen years in the case of a Justice of the Supreme Court or not less than twelve years in the case of a Justice of the Court of Appeal and has in either case and in the opinion of the National Judicial Council considerable knowledge of and experience in the practice of Customary law.

Bibliography

Baderin, Mashood A. "The Shariah Alteration: The Moral and Legal Questions." Online: www.nigeriaworld.com.

Basri, Ghazali. *Nigeria and Shari`ah: Aspirations and Apprehensions*. Leicester: The Islamic Foudation, 1994.

Basr, Ghazali. *Nigeria and Shari`ah*. Leicester: Islamic Foundation, 1994.

Bello, Justice Muhammad. "Obstacles Before the Sharia." Online: www.nigeriaworld.com.

Constitution of the Federal Republic of Nigeria, 1999.

Gbadamosi, T. G. O. *The Growth of Islam Among the Yoruba, 1841–1908*. Ibadan History Series. London: Longman, 1978.

Haruna, Mohammed. "Sharia: Where The Solution Lies." *Today Newspaper*, April 16–22, 2000.

Hasan, Ahamad. *The Principles of Islamic Jurisprudence*. Pakistan, Islamabad: Islamic Research Institute, 1993.

Ihenacho, David Asonye. "The Warped World of the Sharia Protagonists." Online: www.nigeriaworld.com.

Kanu Agabi, Justice Godwin. "Prohibition of Discriminatory Punishments." A letter written to all the twelve states that apply Sharia law, on March 18, 2002. See, *Jender: A Journal of Culture and African Women* 1&2, 2002.

Ma'ji Isa Shani, Alhaji and Mohammad Altaf Hussain Ahangar. "Marriage Guardianship in Islam: Reflections on a Recent Nigeria Judgment." *Islamic and Comparative Law Quarterly* 6:4 (1986) 278.

Mbahi, Muhammad. "Sharia, Northern Ethnic and Religious Minority and the Federal Government: A Perspective." Online: www.nigeriaworld.com.

Sodiq, Yushau. "A History of Islamic Law in Nigeria: Past and Present." *Islamic Studies* 31 (Spring 1992) 85–108.

———. "Ijtihad: the Art of Cracking the Nuts." *The Nigerian Journal of Islamic Political Thought* 1:1 (2004) 1–61.

Zwinkels, Ben. "Africa Today." Online: www.Africa-interactive.net.

www.ingramcontent.com/pod-product-compliance
Lightning Source LLC
Chambersburg PA
CBHW071144300426
44113CB00009B/1079